Transforming Learning for the Workplace of the New Millennium

Students and Workers as Critical Learners

Book 2
Voyager: Direction for Learning & Careers

Secondary Curriculum
The Journey Begins

Eleni Roulis

Minneapolis Regional Chamber of Commerce

ScarecrowEducation
Lanham, Maryland • Toronto • Oxford
2004

Published in the United States of America
by ScarecrowEducation
An imprint of the Rowman & Littlefield Publishing Group, Inc.
4501 Forbes Boulevard, Suite 200, Lanham, Maryland 20706
www.scarecroweducation.com

PO Box 317
Oxford
OX2 9RU, UK

British Library Cataloguing in Publication Information Available

Library of Congress Cataloging-in-Publication Data Available

Roulis, Eleni, 1947–
    Transforming learning for the workplace of the new millennium : students and
workers as critical learners / Eleni Roulis.
        p. cm.
"A ScarecrowEducation book."
"Book 2, Voyager: Direction for Learning and Careers, secondary curriculum."
Includes bibliographical references.

    1.   Voyager: Direction for Learning & Careers (Program) 2. School-to-work
transition—United States—Handbooks, manuals, etc. 3. Career education—United
States—Handbooks, manuals, etc.   I. Voyager: Direction for Learning & Careers
(Program) II. Title.
LC1037.5 .R69 2004
371.11'3'0973—dc21

                                                                        2002012353

    ISBN 1-57886-050-4

Contents

Foreword

As the global economy, e-commerce, and the "information age" spark dramatic changes in the workplace, corporate leaders are sending a clear message about the need to develop education programs that will prepare students to seize the opportunities resulting from these changes.

Over the past six years, the Minneapolis Regional Chamber of Commerce has dedicated an enormous amount of time and energy to addressing this mismatch between educational outcomes and the needs of employers. Voyager: Direction for Learning & Careers is the result.

Voyager is a unique work readiness curriculum model that represents the best of the school-to-work concept. Students are not "tracked" into careers; instead, high standards of achievement are partnered with the fundamentals of effective communication, ethical leadership, and lifelong learning in order to equip students with the tools to achieve in any path they choose.

Curriculum development is not generally the territory of chambers of commerce, but our members saw the opportunity to drive change. From school and work site to the project-planning table, the most qualified and dedicated professionals were in charge of Voyager's destiny, bringing a depth of experience and skills.

The partnership with an urban school district, like Minneapolis public schools, combined with the leadership of corporations with multiple national and international sites, presents a unique opportunity to replicate the Voyager model in other communities. We believe the basic concepts and principles of the program are readily transferable and the content adaptable. We hope that other communities will benefit from the groundbreaking work of this project, drawing on Voyager's experiences to move quickly through the developmental stages, applying energy and resources to implementation.

This book is about Voyager's creation, development, academic foundations, and the many sectors of the community that came together to build the program. Dr. Eleni Roulis has done a wonderful job of organizing and presenting this information in a practical, simple framework that all schools can follow.

Welcome to the Minneapolis Regional Chamber of Commerce's Voyager: Direction for Learning & Careers program and the visions of transforming school-to-career education.

David Jennings
Former President and CEO
Minneapolis Regional Chamber of Commerce

Preface

Book Two: Transforming Learning in the Workplace of the New Millennium: Students and Workers as Critical Learners Series—Secondary Curriculum: The Journey Begins, is a comprehensive two-year high school program and curriculum model that includes weekly career and work-site seminar topics and individual lesson plans with optional activities that teachers can modify for use with diverse learners and settings. The curriculum frames academic and workplace expectations for students and uses authentic collaborative projects and problem-posing situations that give students connecting bridges to work-site orientation. It is a practical hands-on guide to the secondary Voyager curriculum model, to the program's critical pedagogy philosophy, and the culture of "learning to learn" in the classroom and in the workplace. It is a companion to the other three volumes of the Voyager: Direction for Learning & Careers series. This book and companion volumes are steeped in the premise that schools, workplaces, and communities are sites of critical work education, supporting workers and learners to collaborate, learn, and build a more socially just and democratic society. Book four, *Voyager Community Resource Handbook* (Roulis 2003), is the student textbook for use with the secondary curriculum model.

Voyager challenges the theory and pedagogy of traditional school-to-work paradigms. The Voyager model for critical work education reform addresses how students and workers recognize and activate their civic responsibility in the classroom and in the workplace. It requires teaching and learning in ways that encourage a cultural critique of accepted assumptions, an exploration of possibilities for creating democratic, participatory workplaces, and the development of a social vision for education.

Throughout the entire program, Voyager students cocreate the curriculum with the instructor and address issues, ideas, and concepts that are essential to their cohort's learning and to the individual learner's needs. Each seminar includes a variety of optional ideas and activities for teachers and students to choose from and to engage in to continuously build a viable and dynamic learning community. The Voyager curriculum is an integrated approach to learning that is applicable to schools and to workplaces.

Real school-to-career reform and critical work education are grounded in students' lives and lived experiences. Both support and encourage student initiative, provide safe spaces for students to openly question and challenge the status quo, and then support students to take action for change in their multiple worlds. Finally, critical work education builds positive and hopeful visions for the future, not utopian or unreachable visions, but real educational change that reflects possibilities in real people's lives and needs.

This book is divided into five parts: Overview of Voyager Program and Secondary Seminar, Secondary Seminar Years, Junior Year Seminar Units, Senior Year Seminar Units, and Epilogue.

VOYAGER PROGRAM AND OVERVIEW

Chapter 1 introduces program themes, competencies, expectations, work-connected activities, portfolio preparation and assessment, and guidelines for successful achievement in the Voyager program. This section also provides ways for students to examine the Voyager program in terms of options for career choices and preparing for work education. It outlines several areas where students, instructors, and business representatives collaborate to establish expectations and explore opportunities for professional growth and success. There are clear expectations as to how students will become self-sufficient adults who know what is expected of them in school and on the job and how the two are intricately related. The program builds the ability to translate knowledge to application and to recognize how application informs knowledge. As young twenty-first-century students and workers, they must meet, unpack, and solve the challenges and problems of a twenty-first-century economy that is being labeled "the knowledge age."

INTRODUCTION TO SECONDARY CAREER
AND WORK-SITE SEMINAR YEARS

Chapter 2 provides an overview of the secondary career and work-site seminar, its philosophy, and purpose and sets forth the requirements that students must successfully complete during the first level of the Voyager program. It identifies the key features of the program, describes critical pedagogy and participatory learning, connects real-world collaborative projects to students' interests, and organizes themes for study drawn from students' lived experiences. It further describes how students, instructors, and businesspeople collaborate to create a course of study that meets the needs of and resonates with the contexts of the students involved. The progression of learning over the two secondary years is highlighted in the brief overview of each of the secondary units. The secondary career and work-site seminar reinforces the need to connect classroom and workplace learning, to integrate students' workplace topics, to develop lifelong learning skills, to unpack and apply the philosophical roots of John Dewey and Paulo Freire, and to foster the collaboration among all community stakeholders.

JUNIOR YEAR CAREER AND WORK-SITE SEMINAR UNITS

Chapter 3 contains the seven seminar units covering the entire Voyager junior year. All students are required to attend every seminar throughout the year. The initial summer career and work-site seminar sets the stage and frames the expectations, goals, and priorities for the first two years of the Voyager program. Each of the career and work-site seminars undergirds the need to continue preparing students for active membership in a democratic society. There is an enormous amount of information exchange and support as the students navigate this new transition.

The themes of lifelong learning, literacy, effective communication skills, group dynamics, corporate culture, and ethics are woven throughout the junior year units. Students use the case study method to analyze and problem-pose real-world dilemmas as well as cocreate curricula with their instructor to include current topics and themes they are facing in their workplaces. Overall, this is a year to learn to develop greater self-sufficiency and collaborative teamwork, gather and interpret information on career choices, and take responsibility for success.

SENIOR YEAR CAREER AND WORK-SITE SEMINAR UNITS

Chapter 4 contains the nine career and work-site seminar units Voyager students need to complete the program and attain their Level 1 Voyager certificate. Senior year units and lessons include an array of topics that empower students to develop the knowledge, dispositions, and skills for career and life development in a technological world and global economy. The learning of this final year in the secondary program supports the students as they are navigating transitions to career development and entering postsecondary institutions and training programs.

As seniors in the program, they address issues of ethical leadership, global economies, and workplaces and continue to work with each other to build the Voyager company and community. Self-assessment of their work progress as well as assessing their self-concept in regards to values, beliefs, and interest are prominent centers of discussion and thought. Students design and complete their portfolio for review, create multimedia presentations for the community and the new junior year Voyager students, and develop their graduation rituals and performances.

EPILOGUE: WHAT SCHOOLS AND BUSINESSES CAN DO—CRITICAL PEDAGOGY AND THE NEW WORK ORDER

Voyager is a successful model for school-to-career education in the new millennium and a call to action for all who believe that dynamic democracy and critical dialogue are essential elements for real school-to-career reform. The previous divisions between school and workplace learning are now fused, strengthening both environments and providing new growth opportunities for all stakeholders. The economic and geopolitical changes of the first three years of the twenty-first century evidence for us the need to remain flexible so that knowledge and skills can be successfully transported to multiple career pathways or regions of the world. It is clear from the experience with Voyager that when schools and business are partnered, when policy and practice are aligned, and when students cocreate their learning, powerful and compelling change takes place.

CONCLUDING THOUGHTS

Voyager presents an agenda for change and a frame for rethinking the preparation of workers and learners in the new work order. As school districts across the nation and worldwide rush to develop school-to-career programs, questions are being raised about how to reconcile the contradictions that have plagued student success in work education for decades. Schools cannot be mere training sites to serve economic community interests, and yet students need to be educated in the realities of life in the job market and must be prepared for the workplace. Voyager models the relationship between work and school as the practice and application of theory. It embodies multiple perspectives of critical pedagogy that seek to critique and interpret education in its widest sense and then produce new knowledge that deepens commitment and supports action for change in a new generation of workers and learners.

Voyager is not a magical prescription for school-to-career reform, but it is a program that models critical reform elements. It incorporates several important factors that need to be acknowledged and carried out in order to affect real change in school-to-career programs. There is a need for closer collaboration between business and education with a focus on issues of equity and justice, and a balanced blend of educational traditions and employee training. There must also be a "bridge builder," that is, an agency that brings together all of the stakeholders—teachers, parents, administrators, business leaders, and university faculty—to the table in order to build the solid infrastructure and support systems that undergird high-quality school-to-career programs. To grasp the Voyager model's goals and philosophy, it is important to understand the history and traditions that have preceded it. The early and adopted aims of vocational education served narrow interests for both education and business, categorizing and tracking students and creating schisms between academic and vocational worlds in the public schools. There were positive movements in the late twentieth century that started to counter the prior narrow shaping of academic and vocational education. The Voyager program builds on these positive movements and continues to broaden the scope of study. It embodies different assumptions about work and education for the twenty-first century and presents itself as a school-to-career program of equal standing to other academic programs.

Today's high-performance workplaces call for the same kind of person John Dewey (1916) sought to develop. He argued that education for all learners should include engagement and confrontation with values in contexts that give meaning. He advocated for academic and vocational training that helps students and workers develop their intelligence and skills, grasp meaning from their work lives, broaden their worldview, and interrogate ideas. Schools today are communities of young women and men from many backgrounds who want and need to develop academic, technical, and manual abilities. They need real opportunities to choose careers based on skill, talent, and interest rather than being constrained by race, ethnicity, economics, or social background. Voyager is a tested and proven model for providing those real opportunities and the preparation students need to capitalize on them.

Acknowledgments by the Author

I am grateful to have friends and family around me who, throughout the years, have all been responsible in one way or another for the creation of this book. Their passion, hard work, and dedication to social justice have inspired and enriched me.

To all of the Voyager students who I have had the pleasure of working with over the years and who have given their time and energy to offer suggestions for change. They have kept the dream and spirit of the program alive.

To my initial colleagues and collaborators at the Minneapolis Regional Chamber of Commerce, Shelly Regan, Kelly Altmeyer, and the board of directors who originally brought me into the Voyager program, who have walked the road with me all these years, and who had the courage to be leaders in this territory.

To the teachers and students I have worked with over the years in New York City: your faith and courage to maintain the struggle in the midst of such difficult conditions will always remain part of who I am.

To Rosemary Rocco for her constant encouragement, keen insights and sage advice for each draft, deep friendship, and belief in my work over the years; her intelligence and strength are a continual source of inspiration.

To Carrie Clark for the wisdom and original thoughts she has provided throughout the years both on this draft and in our ongoing conversations, the constant joy of her friendship, and the love she creates around her.

To Polly Patrick for her careful reading of the manuscript, her sense of humor that helped me not take myself so seriously, and her outstanding work in preparing teachers and honoring student accomplishments.

To Daisy Pellant for constantly reading, questioning, and dialoguing with me; her constant encouragement and expertise as a psychologist provided many helpful suggestions.

To Christene Sirois, the diva of administration, for her consistent management of this project from methodical and patient editing of the multiple drafts to her generous assistance and support to Voyager students.

To my generous colleagues at the University of St. Thomas who always stopped to listen and were willing to engage in lively conversations that expanded my thinking.

To Louise Sundin, President of Minneapolis Federation of Teachers, who supported and guided this project with such wisdom and vision.

To Mike Mendez, the genius of technology who made my life so less stressful.

To Michelle Filkins, the consummate librarian and researcher extraordinaire, who added so many ideas that helped Voyager students achieve and succeed.

To Bruce Kramer and Margo Lloyd who successfully pioneered the postsecondary seminars.

To Maggy Anderson who read so carefully and stayed constant making comments along the way.

To Bob Brown, Tom Koerner, and Cindy Tursman at ScarecrowEducation who believed in this project and provided clear guidance.

To Lynn Weber for her expert editing, cheerleading, and sense of humor.

To Paulo Freire who has helped me understand that the commitment to critical pedagogy and social justice is a lifetime struggle that requires going against the status quo and opening new worlds of possibilities for all of us to "read the world and become authentic revolutionary leaders."

To Ira Shor, Sonia Nieto, Stephen Brookfield, Marcia Moraes, and Peter McLaren for enlightening me with their work and conversations, and continuously reminding me why the struggle for social justice matters so much.

Acknowledgments by the Minneapolis Regional Chamber of Commerce

This book represents the culmination of six years of hard work. The Minneapolis Regional Chamber of Commerce expresses its thanks and gratefully acknowledges the following organizations and individuals for making Voyager: Direction for Learning & Careers possible.

The following corporate and private foundations believed in the Chamber's school-to-career vision and provided us with the financial support necessary to create Voyager:

The Cargill Foundation
W. K. Kellogg Foundation
Thrivent Financial for Lutherans
3M Foundation
Northwest Area Foundation
The Piper Family Fund of the Minneapolis Foundation
ING
TCF Foundation
Target Foundation
Wells Fargo Foundation on behalf of: Wells Fargo Bank Minnesota, Wells Fargo Brokerage Services, Wells Fargo Institutional Investments, Lowry Hill, and Wells Fargo Private Client Services

The staff, members, and board of directors of the Minneapolis Regional Chamber of Commerce exhibited unwavering commitment, despite numerous challenges, to making an investment in the future of students. The Minneapolis Public School District teachers, staff, and administration, led by Superintendent Carol Johnson, set the school-to-career vision in motion, and R. Craig Vana made it happen. A special thanks to the teachers, staff, and administrators at Edison High School who piloted Voyager. Sandra Scott, Shelly Regan, and Connie Levi laid the framework for the Voyager model—their contributions were invaluable. A dedicated group of community leaders were Voyager's greatest champions: Tyrone Thayer, Teresa Egge, and Louise Thoreson.

Eleni Roulis's extraordinary, innovative curriculum captured the best of the ideas raised by educators and businesspeople.

Kelly Altmeyer's passionate commitment and dedication to the Voyager program was a source of continuous inspiration.

Most of all, many thanks to the pioneering students who seized the opportunity to connect with the world of work and accepted the challenges that Voyager placed in front of them. Their achievements are our greatest success!

General Introduction for All Four Volumes

In 1994, with the leadership of the Minneapolis Regional Chamber of Commerce (MRCC), thirteen businesses, the Minneapolis public schools, and the City of Minneapolis formed a partnership and focused on developing a classroom and work-site curriculum to prepare students for employment in the financial services sector, a critical underpinning of the Minneapolis–St. Paul economy. Looking to the guidelines of the federal School-to-Career Opportunities Act, the partnership began the development of a comprehensive, standards-based, transforming school-to-work model. The result was Voyager: Direction for Learning & Careers, a four-year program that combines secondary and postsecondary instruction, work readiness training, and on-the-job experience.

The publication of this book and its companion volumes marks the successful implementation of the Voyager program and attainment of the partners' desire to drive an overall systems change—resulting in on-target education, increased career options for students from diverse backgrounds, and well-prepared, highly skilled twenty-first-century workers. The partners created a model that serves as a template for educational institutions, businesses, and business organizations in other communities to collaborate and launch innovative school-to-career programs. Reflecting the unique aspects of Voyager, these books blend documentation of the program's development and implementation process, a four-year curriculum, and guides to program involvement for each of the stakeholder groups. They are the distillation of five years of collaborative work, joint evaluation, and shared refinement of the model.

Bringing the worlds of work and classroom learning together is essential so that educators and employers combine efforts to prepare highly skilled twenty-first-century workers. Creating this substantive connection provides students the opportunity to be better prepared for the rapidly changing world—a world that includes a workplace that continuously changes, bringing new challenges and new jobs. The Voyager program seminars integrate academic and career studies where students examine the meaning of work in society, their communities, and their own lives. Students, families, teachers, school district leaders, workplace supervisors, employers, and other stakeholders collaborate to provide the exposure and support needed for students to reach beyond limiting boundaries and incorporate broader career preparation through real-world application. During the Voyager program students begin to define ways of knowing and learning beyond the simple development and acquisition of a basic set of skills or techniques that can be pulled out whenever needed. It is the vital experience of "learning to learn" and moving comfortably in the world of academics and the workplace that contributes to the individual and group development of all students. The Voyager program addresses the limits of either pure classroom learning or only worksite experience, encouraging active integrated learning.

The Voyager program breaks away from a tradition of work education that has a history of being irrelevant and disconnected from the realities of students' lives, goals, dreams, and futures. Such a tradition endorses and perpetuates inequities in schooling and society in the quest to supply workers trained to fit preconfigured molds. It fails to recognize the rich yield that results from growing professionals who are both invested in and passionate about their work. The goal is to develop professionals who are committed to making substantive contributions based on reflection and dialogue with all the people in their work communities. Traditional work education does not prepare students for the work of the twenty-first century, wherein the ability to think, reflect, and adapt is required to respond to complexities that texture the workday, from cube to corner office, from factory floor to boardroom. Voyager is designed to prepare lifelong workers and learners who anticipate and envision alternative possibilities to new situations. Workers who uphold rigor in the workplace participate in vigorous discussions and are also able to critically examine and challenge the assumptions underlying accepted ways of working, knowing, thinking, and doing. Voyager graduates have forged new pathways for redefining democratic classrooms, transforming workplaces, and learning how to value work and see the value of their own work.

During the Voyager program, patterns of thinking and knowing emerge with respect to understanding the self as learner, the self as a participant in an active relationship in a learning community who develops professional relationships with teachers and mentors, and becomes firmly established in a professional community with supervisors and employers. All of the relationships combine with authentic learning experiences to build new knowledge and support professional practices for all students. Voyager is about preparing students for a high-performance future. There is a recognized need for a talent pool broader in its education and deeper in its abilities to think critically and reflectively, communicate effectively, work collaboratively in teams, creatively solve problems, and meet the demands of the workplace. Voyager promotes and encourages policies and systems that welcome and involve young people in the responsibilities, roles, and rewards of a productive future.

In addition to broadening classroom and workplace knowledge, Voyager students apply and share their new knowledge with adults connected to the professional fields they have chosen to explore. Students experience a range of adults who mentor, coach, and evaluate them. They become skillful in making judgments about their own abilities, reflecting on their learning habits, and taking the opportunity to design their own futures. They see themselves as thinking workers and learners empowered to act and who are treated as professionals. The inclusion of students' life experiences and perspectives in the program validates that the students already have knowledge that they bring with them to the classroom and the work site, and reinforces self-confidence and belief in themselves. As they assume responsibility for their own learning and lives, they redefine student roles both in the traditional classroom and workplace.

Voyager is not a "how to" program; rather, it is a model that succeeded because business and education formed an authentic partnership to develop new ways of thinking and acting in the world, a model that believes in and supports possibility and change for all of the learners involved. Voyager builds a frame for learning that can be contextualized for a variety of settings, students, and economic environments. In the Voyager program model, the emphasis is on developing what Joseph Raelin (2000) calls the "meta-competence of learning," or learning to learn. Through this process, students gain the knowledge and ability needed to change and adapt skills from one context to another and to handle variability in both their work and school demands. Learning becomes continuous and connected for them. In constructing the Voyager model, we challenged our whole assumptive framework of students and workers as learners. Throughout the four years of the program we invited and encouraged learners to examine traditional and underlying assumptions that guide their thinking and work, and through reflection and dialogue envision new possibilities, new pathways, and new ways of learning.

Voyager is a tested framework that worked successfully for the group of students whose stories are portrayed in volume 1. The Voyager model challenges status quo thinking, encourages developing curricular materials for school-to-career programs that build critically educated workers for the future, and promotes education and business partnerships. The model is designed to have the specific needs of business and the academic standards of individual communities, both of which may evolve over time, fitted to its frame.

Why these books and how are they different from other program development and curriculum books on the market? This book and its companion volumes speak to a variety of audiences and have multifaceted purposes. Readers will find guides for developing partnerships between business organizations (and their business members), and high schools and higher educational institutions that result in:

- Creating effective school-to-career programs that prepare work-ready and career-bound students;
- Classroom instruction, work-site induction, and cross-discipline coordination for teachers, site supervisors, and business and education mentors; and
- Family involvement in Voyager.

The curriculum and the teaching suggestions emphasize the importance of learning how to work and learn through critical inquiry, engagement, and dialogue. Voyager breaks the stereotype of traditional school/work ideas and transforms the concept into one which embodies the profile of the educated worker of the future: a worker who is in critical engagement with her or his world and who is committed to academics and work; who wants to be a part of a learning community; and who is invested in her or his company's growth and development because it directly involves her or his individual growth and development.

Voyager: Direction for Learning & Careers is a model that establishes its vitality and need as a central component of schooling. It is not an add-on to be used for student tracking. This model is not just an avenue for preparing workers for industry; it prepares students to think about their multiple worlds, to learn to navigate their process and goals for success. Adequate preparation of students for the twenty-first century requires changing what students are taught, how they are taught, and how work and learning are assessed.

Voyager is based on the premise that schools are sites where personal, professional, and social growth are enhanced. It addresses crucial issues in educational and career development, including work-site concepts, and presents a clear and principled practice of learning and career education. Voyager allows students to speak from their own specificity, giving them the opportunity and the space to speak about historical and social practices that have shaped their own lives in particular ways while enhancing hope and possibility in their lives.

Students gain knowledge of the realities of work and the job market, while increasing their effective participation in analyzing the realities of the practices governing their work lives. Voyager transforms the traditional ideas embedded in work education—theory and practice are rooted in self-reflection, critical awareness, and critical engagement, contributing a significant building block for lifelong learning plans. Voyager examines how personal, social, political, cultural, and educational factors relate to the success or failure of student learning and focuses in on factors such as language, culture, and literacy as well as multinational issues for dynamic curriculum building. Questions and suggestions that stimulate dialogue around issues of power, knowledge, and social change develop opportunities for critical professional conversations among all constituents: educators, learners, business partners, mentors.

There are multiple purposes, foci, and audiences built into the Voyager program. Through in-depth discussions of teaching, learning, and actual lessons, Voyager clarifies the tensions between market-oriented and academic career–oriented curricula, as well as emphasizing questions of educational practice. All lessons and teaching suggestions can be adapted and modified to local histories and contexts as well as to local economic realities and needs.

The books are addressed to:

- Secondary teachers in any one of the many types of work education programs;
- Businesses seeking a model to establish high benefit-to-cost ratio partnerships with educational institutions;
- Community agencies involved in adult education and retraining programs or literacy programs;
- Postsecondary programs for career investigation and life skills;
- University and college teacher preparation programs;
- Global cultural workers building communities and workers for the twenty-first century in developing countries;
- School districts nationwide struggling to retain educated workers in their industries; and
- Countries experiencing emerging markets and new waves of immigration that are changing the profile of their school populations.

The leadership of a chamber of commerce and participation of corporations with multiple sites nationally and internationally presented unique opportunities.

Readers are invited to become partners in this endeavor by approaching Voyager as a template rather than a recipe, and to view the books as chronicles of the program's development. We look forward to all feedback and suggestions from readers. Your ideas will keep Voyager dynamic and strengthen the goal of a transformed school-to-career education.

1

Overview of Voyager Program and Secondary Seminar

Welcome to Voyager: Direction for Learning & Careers and the secondary phase of the four-year program. This book is designed to be used by Voyager students, mentors, work-site supervisors, and postsecondary seminar coordinators as they work through the first two years of the Voyager program and Voyager certification process. The book includes materials and information relevant to the cooperative effort of all participants and a detailed guide to the curriculum for the junior and senior seminars. It is recommended that this volume be used in conjunction with *Direction for Learning & Careers Community Handbook,* book four in the series. The handbook is a resource for all members of the Voyager community.

MISSION

To develop self-sufficient adults and high-quality employees utilizing a school-to-career system that combines secondary and postsecondary classroom learning, career exploration, and work experience.

GOALS

Voyager students will:

1. Demonstrate strong academics and applied skills needed to be proactive and productive citizens of diverse communities;
2. Demonstrate applied skills and work-based experience that will be documented with Voyager certificates;
3. Earn a high school diploma that successfully meets the career investigation graduation standard;

4. Enter a two-year or four-year postsecondary program that is integrated with their Voyager postsecondary seminar study and registered with Voyager certificates;
5. Develop and maintain an ongoing personal and professional career portfolio that demonstrates achievement of all program components and levels;
6. Experience choices in multiple educational directions and career investigations; and
7. Have access to job placement and supportive services.

PROGRAM PHILOSOPHY

The underpinning philosophy of Voyager: Direction for Learning & Careers is that students who seek to be work ready and career bound must engage in a supportive reflective process where they develop the abilities to think critically and creatively, thoughtfully engage with their environment, and accurately interpret information for good decision making. Because preparing students to participate in global and cross-cultural arenas is paramount to both education and business, educated workers of the new millennium must be equipped with the knowledge, skills, and abilities that help them communicate effectively and work cooperatively across racial, linguistic, and cultural boundaries.

Voyager provides a comprehensive program that weaves high school and postsecondary educational experiences with on-site work experiences to develop and support workers and lifelong learners for the future. Voyager sees "learning to learn" as a natural way of life both in the classroom and on the job. Both the classroom and the workplace are important locations for varied learning, participation in teamwork, opportunities to reflect with others, and even having fun. The continuation of the Voyager program through two years of postsecondary study emphasizes a comprehensive strategy that supports students from a holistic approach to learning and working throughout their studies. Both the two- and four-year models of Voyager demonstrate a commitment to creating workers who are critical thinkers, lifelong learners, and prepared citizens equipped to succeed in their careers.

VOYAGER THEMES FOR SECONDARY STUDENTS

Voyager embodies four themes that are relevant to successful educational development and professional outcomes. The Voyager themes guide the program's design and are the desired student outcomes of the program. Thus, the Voyager program intends to prepare learners and workers who are effective communicators; ethical, professional career leaders; knowledgeable global citizens; and lifelong learners. The themes are integrated throughout all components of Voyager. What follows is an overview of how Voyager secondary students work toward achievement in each theme area (overviews for post-secondary students follow). Voyager teachers and students are encouraged to contextualize the competencies listed below to fit their individual learning needs and plans.

Effective Communicators—Secondary

Students will demonstrate effective communication (oral and written) through the development of a series of skills, including interpersonal, teamwork, presentational, effective use of technology, intercultural negotiation, and corporate-appropriate communication.

Demonstrated Outcomes and Competencies

1. Deliver information through many powerful communication formats, including public speaking, presentations, conferences, panels, and interviews.
2. Prepare written materials using various writing formats for communications and business: résumés and cover letters for interviews, follow-up letters, memos, responses to inquiries, executive summaries, meeting agendas and minutes.
3. Read and write critically (analyze and synthesize facts for information, dissemination, and decision making).
4. Facilitate and participate in effective group dynamics and teamwork.
5. Use technology to enhance presentations and to do research.
6. Develop an awareness of diverse social factors and identities (e.g., gender, race, regional, ethnic, cultural) to enhance communication competence through the development of various language conventions.
7. Develop conflict resolution and problem-solving communication skills.
8. Demonstrate the actual practice of conflict resolution skills through the development of peer mediation plans and other developed plans.
9. Reflect on development of communication skills; demonstrate growth and record it through ongoing journal writing and portfolio updates.
10. Learn and understand career-specific language.
11. Identify and develop individual communication styles appropriate to various contexts.
12. Explore the use of technology for effective Internet and web-based communication.
13. Understand and effectively use written and spoken professional communication.

14. Develop strategies for intercultural communication.
15. Understand corporate and organizational communication.
16. Determine the appropriate information to be communicated in a given situation.
17. Create documents for job seeking and college entrance.
18. Effectively articulate concerns and develop plans for change regarding unethical situations in the classroom, work site, and community.

Ethical, Professional Career Leaders—Secondary

Students will demonstrate professional and leadership skills that exemplify moral responsibility and credible influence. Their leadership development will demonstrate an intentional sense of personal and professional ethics through responsibilities and actions related to organizational change.

Demonstrated Outcomes and Competencies

1. Define and identify diverse leadership styles.
2. Identify major ethical standards of the businesses in the Voyager partnership.
3. Self-evaluate and develop an individual leadership style.
4. Describe leadership ethics and responsibilities.
5. Clarify and develop professional career plan.
6. Describe and analyze various corporate cultures including their belief and value systems.
7. Understand and demonstrate leadership and communication styles.
8. Develop a leadership guide with assessment procedures.
9. Develop and convey a shared vision for work and for attaining goals.
10. Understand the world and the workplace with a global mindset that thinks beyond restricting boundaries.
11. Demonstrate understanding of forming teams and facilitating teamwork.
12. Understand the importance of ethics and spirituality in the workplace.
13. Develop guides and presentations for Voyager groups.
14. Set up networking opportunities with local business and educational leaders.
15. Develop and sustain a Voyager Company, which exemplifies leadership character and includes creating cutting-edge team projects and developing and maintaining ethical standards.

Knowledgeable Global Citizens—Secondary

Students will demonstrate the abilities to be flexible, comfortable, and responsible in multiple contexts and with diverse populations. They will develop intercultural navigation strategies and knowledge of corporate expectations, practices, and frameworks for working with diverse communities.

Demonstrated Outcomes and Competencies

1. Demonstrate shared knowledge of systems, issues, and challenges when working with diverse groups.
2. Create and use human relation strategies to develop comfort in a variety of classroom and work situations.
3. Prepare for career choices and internship responsibilities.
4. Evaluate career choices in relation to goals and personal attributes.
5. Develop self-assessment inventory for career strengths and interests.
6. Produce an inventory of personal resources including skills, talents, and resource people.
7. Identify skills and resources for success in the workplace.
8. Evaluate college preparation in relation to career choices.
9. Perform in a manner that demonstrates the concept of good citizenship.
10. Identify personal development opportunities.
11. Understand, create, and apply strategies for working with diverse groups and meeting challenges.
12. Demonstrate cultural awareness and competency.
13. Understand and practice equitable and fair treatment for all groups.
14. Examine and describe the diversity that exists within students' neighborhood, school, and community groups.
15. Understand and describe how schools and communities can support each other.
16. Develop community building skills and demonstrate these skills while building the Voyager community.

Lifelong Learners—Secondary

Students will demonstrate the ability to articulate their personal and professional vision and to remain open to and actively pursue new knowledge, skills, and understandings as they develop throughout the program. As part of this process they will demonstrate the ability to critically reflect upon their career positions through a series of self-assessment activities that stretch them toward continuous and professional growth throughout their lives.

Demonstrated Outcomes and Competencies

1. Develop personal plans and visions that demonstrate growth and change.
2. Outline a career plan and strategies for adjusting the plan throughout the program.

3. Develop a variety of decision-making skills that demonstrate intentional thought processes.
4. Identify and implement reflective practice skills.
5. Identify and develop a list of strategies and adaptive skills to deal with future uncertainties and changes.
6. Identify and develop a variety of skills for success in the workplace.
7. Stretch and challenge present use of knowledge and skills by reading and writing a variety of academic and career materials.
8. Develop a set of self-assessment criteria.
9. Articulate clear goals, objectives, and strategies for one-, two-, and three-year plans after graduation.
10. Design effective coping methods that will support change, stress, and uncertain times.
11. Develop a reading list with common and individual choices.
12. Create a professional work plan and understand the specifics of planning.
13. Create and self-assess time management plans that also demonstrate fiscal responsibility.
14. Create fiscal plans to manage finances during and after high school graduation.
15. Enhance technology skills to maintain knowledge base consistent with requirements of higher education and advanced professional development.

VOYAGER THEMES FOR POSTSECONDARY (YEAR ONE) STUDENTS

During their freshman year of college, Voyager students will identify and intentionally handle the transition from high school to college. Members will continue to add communication skills, with special emphasis on technology as a communication and information medium.

Effective Communicators

Demonstrated Outcomes and Competencies

1. Establish academic goals.
2. Refine career goals.
3. Demonstrate advanced skills in business writing protocols, comprehension, and understanding.
4. Revise résumé.
5. Maintain ongoing electronic portfolio development.

Ethical, Professional Career Leaders

Demonstrated Outcomes and Competencies

1. Mentor Voyager high school seniors on transition issues.
2. Organize a transition seminar.
3. Establish career networks and update Voyager web site.
4. Enhance networking skills.
5. Increase understanding of multiple career pathways.
6. Complete a self-assessment of leadership skills.

Knowledgeable Global Citizens

Demonstrated Outcomes and Competencies

1. Make presentations on industry and diversity.
2. Research and analyze dimensions of the global economy.
3. Participate in work-site teleconference (national and international).
4. Develop an action plan for dealing with cultural differences.

Lifelong Learners

Demonstrated Outcomes and Competencies

1. Complete a self-assessment on Voyager themes and standards.
2. Plan individual interventions to strengthen various skills.
3. Investigate special topics (for example, developing personal inventory, problem-solving, and meeting challenges).
4. Discuss common readings and cases for discussion.

VOYAGER THEMES FOR POSTSECONDARY (YEAR TWO) STUDENTS

During their sophomore year of college, Voyager students will identify and continue developing their academic and career goals. Members will continue to refine interpersonal communication skills with special emphasis on ethical leadership practices and activities that support lifelong learning skills.

Effective Communicators

Demonstrated Outcomes and Competencies

1. Refine presentation skills.
2. Continue developing technology skills.

3. Develop skills in conflict resolution in the workplace and in listening for action.
4. Revise résumé.

Ethical, Professional Career Leaders

Demonstrated Outcomes and Competencies

1. Mentor Voyager high school juniors on issues of personal and career planning.
2. Organize and present Voyager oral history seminar.
3. Evaluate and assess: Ethical Leadership in Today's Businesses.
4. Continue networking skills.
5. Define personal ethical standards.

Knowledgeable Global Citizens

Demonstrated Outcomes and Competencies

1. Evaluate and assess: Ethical Issues in Global Business.
2. Evaluate and assess: Ethical Issues in the Workplace.
3. Evaluate and assess: Global Leadership in the Twenty-First Century.
4. Evaluate and assess: Impact of Nation Building on Global Economy.

Lifelong Learners

Demonstrated Outcomes and Competencies

1. Continue self-assessment on Voyager themes and standards.
2. Plan individual interventions to heighten skills.
3. Create and analyze topics—common reading and cases for discussion.
4. Reframe and re-envision career and training plan.

Voyager students are expected to meet specific standards in all areas of their program. The Voyager handbook outlines students' expectations and should be referred to whenever necessary. Knowing what is expected at school and on the job supports success. In addition to the academic requirements and standards that need to be met, the high quality of the work-site experience is based on clearly defined purposes understood and designed by all concerned. Since the work-site experience is part of the total Voyager program, the goals and purposes of the career seminar must be consistent with the intent of the credentialing partners, educational institutions, and business partners.

VOYAGER FOUR-YEAR CURRICULUM MODEL

Secondary Career and Work-Site Seminar: Junior Year

Unit 1. Personal and Professional Growth

- Orientation, icebreakers, and setting expectations
- Creating classroom rituals, codes, and building community
- Developing critical reflection and voice
- Co-creating the curriculum to take action
- Professional goal planning and effective résumé writing

Unit 2. Conflict Resolution

- Defining alternative options to violence in schools
- Applying conflict resolution process
- Developing negotiation and perspective-taking skills

Unit 3. The Voyager Company

- Organizing the Voyager Company—case study method
- Developing company mission, goals, and objectives
- Career investigation and social justice
- Community and business partnerships

Unit 4. Cooperative Learning

- Designing a successful learning community
- Building a cooperative learning community
- Team building and relationships
- Group process procedures

Unit 5. Organizational Development

- Corporate culture
- Building organization and organizational relationships
- Connecting business ethics, ethical decision making, and business practices
- Global business ethics

Unit 6. Intercultural Communication

- Challenges of living in an intercultural world
- Concepts of intercultural competence
- Language and literacy for learning and working

Unit 7. Self-Assessment and Reflection

- Develop a process for self-assessment
- Building future action plans
- Lifelong learning practices

Secondary Career and Work-Site Seminar: Senior Year

Unit 1. Personal and Professional Growth

- Learning tools for reflection and self-assessment
- Revisiting classroom codes and rituals
- Career investigation and professional goals
- Enhancing critical dialogue
- Co-creating the curriculum

Unit 2. College Preparation

- College admission procedures and preparation
- Meeting the university faculty and facing the challenges
- Writing the college autobiography and essay

Unit 3. The Résumé

- Assessing abilities and potential
- Sharpening professional skills and marketing yourself
- Communicating your strengths and ideas

Unit 4. Interviewing

- Interviewing: questions, preparation, guidelines
- Developing a positive profile
- Networking skills
- Multiple career pathways

Unit 5. Letter Writing

- Writing conventions
- Letter writing, presentation, and research skills
- Effective letters of inquiry for work and college

Unit 6. The Voyager Company

- Company reorganization
- Annual team planning, company goals, agendas, and functions
- Highly effective people
- Community and company project

Unit 7. Intercultural Communication Skills

- Diverse cultures and styles in the workplace
- Workplace environments and issues
- Dealing with difference and misunderstandings
- Global challenges to intercultural communication

Unit 8. Leadership and Ethics

- Attributes of effective leadership
- Traditional and emerging concepts in leadership
- Ethics in leadership
- Women in leadership
- Developing leadership identities and personal style

Unit 9. Reflection, Assessment, and Future Work

- Portfolio review
- Self-assessment and reflection
- Personal inventory—getting ready for work and postsecondary education
- Academic growth and future plans

Postsecondary Career and Work-Site Seminar: Freshman Year

Focus: Transition and Communication

Unit 1. Expanding New Vistas of Possibility

- How do we integrate all parts of ourselves?
- Unleash creativity
- Knowledge skills and attitudes necessary for successful lifelong learning and work

Unit 2. Group Dynamics and Communication Skills: Synergistic Interdependence

- Building trust and respect
- Learning to work collectively
- Analysis of situations: interrogating a problem

Unit 3. Workplace Literacy

- Concept of literacies: reading the word and reading the world
- Literacy: cultural forces and practices
- What is critical literacy?

Unit 4. Cybersociety 2000 and Beyond

- Technology, philosophy, and work
- The Information Age: What does this mean? How do we navigate it?
- Media literacy: What are we viewing? How do we assess it?
- Creating powerful presentations

Unit 5. Sociopolitical Differences in the Workplace

- Language, culture, and forging identity
- Case studies: What do we learn from them?
- Literacy and social practices: What are literate behaviors? What is the effect of class, culture, and gender on student learning?
- Non-Western and nonmainstream cultures

Unit 6. Ethical Leadership

- Conversations with powerful women and men—using authentic biographies
- Interrogation and assumptions about leadership and social justice
- Global perspectives

Unit 7. Corporate Culture, Success, and Organizational Theory

- Succeeding on your own terms
- Reflection, action, and transformation: steps for success
- Professional development and networking

Unit 8. Case Studies

- Making the case: interrogating and problem solving
- Document analysis
- Corporate studies

Unit 9. Transition, Learning, and Work

- Learning from our stories, told in our voices

Unit 10. The Future as Social Practice

- Lifelong learning—preparing and thinking for the future
- Creating future plans

Postsecondary Career and Work-Site Seminar: Sophomore Year

Focus: Ethical Leaders for Tomorrow's Businesses

Unit 1. Career Investigation, Knowledge, and Professional Identities

- Networking
- Integrating our realities—workplace, home, family, and culture
- Updated résumé
- Self-assessment
- Work design

Unit 2. Technology and Multimedia: Creating New Metaphors

- Integrate the use of animation, sound, and video into PowerPoint presentations
- Cyber learning: the relation of technology to learning
- How to make technology work for you

Unit 3. Ethical Decision Making

- Case studies
- Corporate culture and expectations

Unit 4. Courage and Risk: Not Shortchanging Ourselves

- Resiliency
- Challenging basic assumptions—breaking the stereotypes of learning and work
- The legacy from which we work—both in school-to-work programs and cultural differences
- Redefining learning to work
- Who are our heroes?
- Consciousness, action, and change
- Perspectives on problem-posing curriculum

Unit 5. Habits of Mind and Effective People

- Defining our principles
- Developing work habits and time management skills

Unit 6. Voices from the Next Generation: Critical Workers and Learners

- What is this next generation like?
- What are the differences—what are the similarities?
- Lessons from within the ranks: narratives from the heart, experiences of learning
- Spirited voices telling our stories

Unit 7. Future Pathways

- Continuing to be a lifelong learner and global citizen

Unit 8. Presentation and Celebration

- Criteria and rubrics for assessment
- Performance review
- Assessment and certification

PROGRAM FRAMEWORK

Secondary Years

The process for entry into the Voyager program begins during spring semester of grade 10. All students in the school who meet the base requirements of a 2.0 grade point average (GPA) and passage of basic math, writing, and reading comprehension tests are invited to apply. Students must also submit a current résumé and a philosophy statement, "Why I Want to Join Voyager," for the interview process. Upon acceptance, students begin registration for the prescribed courses and activities of junior and senior years.

At the start of grade 11, students begin the secondary career and work-site seminar and meet their Voyager secondary coordinator. The curriculum for the seminar is specifically developed to provide the knowledge, dispositions, and skills necessary for success in school and on the job. Students must sign the student contract at this time (see fig. 1.1), which sets the basic standards they must meet throughout their participation in Voyager.

During the secondary years of the program, Voyager students study topics such as cooperative learning skills, communication skills, personal and professional career planning, conflict resolution, corporate culture, team building, decision making, and leadership skills. The first two years of Voyager are steeped in developing keen academic and work-site skills as well as responsibility. At the end of grade 11, students are placed in summer internships with local business institutions and corporations. In grade 12, numerous college tours are built in, complementing the study of topics of the career and work-site seminar that focus on college preparation. More in-depth information about the secondary years is contained later in this book and book four of the series.

Postsecondary College Years

After successful completion of the high school component, Voyager students move on to the college or university of their choice where they progress through years one and two of the college career and work-site seminar. During this time they continue their work-site experience and their mentoring relationships

Figure 1.1.   The Student Contract

Voyager Agreement for Participation

I, _____, agree to the following:

1. I have read the purpose statement of the Voyager secondary seminar and understand the goals of the program.
2. I will attend all meetings of the secondary seminar. I understand that failure to attend seminar meetings will result in my not receiving my Voyager certification.
3. I will arrive on time and remain for the entire seminar.
4. I will attend the official Voyager functions identified to me as essential to participating in Voyager.
5. I will complete all assignments.
6. I will contact the Voyager coordinator in the event I am having difficulties with my studies or my work, or if something happens that will affect my participation in Voyager.
7. I understand that I am a representative of myself, my school, my workplace, and Voyager, and I agree to act appropriately as said representative. I understand that failure to conduct myself with proper decorum may result in my dismissal from Voyager.
8. I understand the above commitment and agree to fulfill my responsibilities.

_____   _____
Signature   Date

while completing course work toward their college degree—either a two-year associate's degree or a four-year bachelor's degree. The postsecondary college years continue to foster the foundational skills developed in the secondary program with concentrated advanced studies. Each of the postsecondary years is tailored to meet the individual and group learning needs. Both the selection of topics and the activities within these topics are carefully co-created by teachers and students. It is important to meet the changing learning needs of each of the student groups.

Much of the work in both years focuses on the review and analysis of real-life business cases based on the Harvard Business School Case Study program. Students will use methodologies and systems discussed in class and addressed in their readings to analyze a case study.

ASSESSING STUDENT PERFORMANCE

Assessment is one of the most comprehensive words used in our vocabulary. In the Voyager program, there is an integrated and collaborative view of assessment. The underlying rationale is to move away from only the mastery of a skill or competency to the actual use and demonstration of it. How students learn to use a competency, as well as broadening the opportunities to demonstrate uses of it, is paramount in this process. The process of assessment involves an entire range of appraisals and procedures that are indications of what is happening with student learning. It provides a series of snapshots and perspectives taking into consideration the whole student and what he or she is accomplishing. In Voyager, students are assessed in a variety of ways and by different people. Students are taught and encouraged early on to personally reflect and self-assess continuously throughout their studies. In this program, a preoccupation with the surface appearance of getting the right answers is replaced by an interest in student growth, learning as demonstrated through the application of knowledge, and authentic hands-on experiences. The goal is to start where the student is and move him or her as far as possible. (See fig. 1.2 for sample rubric and grading guidelines.)

Performance-Based Assessment

For the past ten years, there has been an ongoing dialogue across the nation regarding the types of knowledge that students at all levels should possess

Figure 1.2.   Voyager Grading Guidelines

Voyager Grading Guidelines

Students are encouraged to keep track of their work, their tasks, and their achievements throughout the program. There are a variety of ways that students are guided into keeping track of their work. Co-creating criteria and rubrics provides a good way for all learners to understand what is expected and how they may reach their desired levels of achievement. In order to get credit for the Voyager career and work-site seminar, students must attain the grade B or adept level on all course assignments and activities. The possible grades for this course are A, B, or I. If students do not meet the identified adept level, they will be given opportunities to learn what is needed to reach that level.

To earn a B for the course, students must reach the adept level on all activities and 80 percent on all assessments. To earn an A, students must have 90 percent on all assessments and have met the advanced level on all papers, projects, and presentations. Students have the opportunity to do independent projects in addition to the regular class work. Potential independent projects will be given for each unit. Independent project proposals must be discussed with the instructor ahead of time and certainly before the end of the semester. Criteria for the evaluation will be set during a project proposal conference between the student and the instructor. Projects must be completed by the end of the semester. If students receive a 2 on their activities and tasks, their work is approaching completion but is below standard level.

(continued)

Figure 1.2. Voyager Grading Guidelines *(continued)*

SAMPLE RUBRIC AND CRITERIA STANDARDS FOR A VOYAGER PRESENTATION

Advanced (4 = Excellent)

- Each team member demonstrated obvious careful and extensive preparation and practice of her or his part of the presentation.
- Technology was well integrated as a tool with at least one multimedia enhancement.
- Each team member demonstrated a great deal of variety in her or his communication skills to engage her or his audience. There was variety in voice tone, volume, expression, and eye contact with the audience.
- Each team member demonstrated extensive research skills (traditional and Internet), covered and supported the assignment, and was interesting and highly informative.
- Presentation lasted at least seven to eight minutes.

Adept (3 = Good)

- Each team member demonstrated preparation and practice of her or his part.
- Some technology was integrated in the presentation.
- Each team member demonstrated an attempt of a variety of communication skills.
- Each team member demonstrated basic research skills covering the assignment and presented important information.
- Presentation lasted a minimum of four minutes.

Approaching (2 = Needs Improvement)

- Each team member demonstrated minimal-level preparation and practice of the presentation.
- Technology used was ineffective and only paper handouts were used.
- Communication skills lacked basic levels in at least two areas: clear speech patterns and too much note reading.
- Research demonstrated few resources and poor quality for those chosen.
- Presentation lasted three minutes.

Incomplete (1 = Unacceptable)

- Each team member demonstrated little or no preparation and practice of the presentation.
- A majority of the group members spoke in a monotone, were difficult to hear and to understand, and only read from their notes.
- Materials presented demonstrated insufficient research and were incomplete, simplistic, and unimportant.
- No technology was incorporated into the presentation.
- Presentation lasted less than three minutes.

and how they should be able to demonstrate ability to apply this knowledge. The goal continues to be an effort requiring vision, energy, and commitment on the part of teachers, students, families, and the community.

Performance-based assessments may be used to conduct baseline and ongoing assessment or final evaluation and are a key component of the overall assessment practices for graduation. Assessment is a continuous process that informs student performance and learning through multiple measures. Such assessments can be made with a variety of demonstrations (as adapted from the Minnesota Department of Education's web site at http://education.state.mn.us):

- Authentic—the task or learning activity simulates the way information or practices are handled in the workplace and the greater society.
- Nondiscriminatory—all students have an opportunity to achieve as the task or learning activity does not rely on special or narrow knowledge. It provides for different learning styles and is inclusive with respect to culture, gender, ethnicity, race, and class.
- Developmental—the tasks and learning activities are aligned with the students' intellectual and psychosocial maturity.
- Embedded—the learning activities and tasks are an integral part of the classroom and work-site experience.
- Constructivist—students are active decision makers regarding their learning.

Graduation Standard for Voyager: Career Investigation

The state of Minnesota's profile of learning delineates numerous high standards in which students must demonstrate competency (see the web site at http://cfl.state.mn.us/GRAD/).

Career investigation is one of the graduation standards that needs to be met for successful completion of the Voyager program and reads as follows:

A student shall demonstrate understanding of a variety of career clusters, attributes, and aptitudes needed in particular types of occupations and careers, how attitudes and behaviors affect the climate of a workplace, how systems within a workplace affect or interact with systems in the community, and how systems affect an individual worker by:

- determining personal interest, aptitudes, and abilities;
- establishing explicit career action plan, including selecting a program that meets a career of vocational preparation goals;
- investigating a career through research, internship, mentorship, or community service placement; and
- evaluating career choices in relationship to life goals and personal attributes.

Evaluation is about making a judgment and assessment and evaluation come together to create a grade. The mandated scoring system for the graduation standard requires scoring with a 4, 3, 2, 1, or 0 based on created rubrics and criteria to rate student work on successful mastery of the competencies. Teachers and students co-create criteria and rubrics for each assessment task and then teachers holistically evaluate student performance to assess if the standard for the class has been met. These various procedures and activities are important as they help students become aware of what is important in the process of performance-based assessments early in the Voyager program. Students then work toward this graduation standard each semester, deepening and broadening their success both in the classroom and at the work site. Performance standards describe the kind of mastery students are working to achieve. The standards identify what is to be learned and the performance-based assessments identify how well the students learned. Performance-based assessments can be identified on different levels: basic, proficient, and advanced levels of achievement. Upon meeting the graduation standard, student records will include the rubric score, completion date, title of the standard, and an indication if the student has met the standard. Graduation standards are not meant to constrict but to guide teaching and learning. They are flexible enough to allow teachers the discretion to make alternative decisions to suit particular teaching conditions and particular student needs. Successful completion of the career investigation graduation standard is one of the multiple assessments that is included to determine student achievement of Voyager program objectives.

Fulfilling Program Themes and Competencies

Threaded throughout the program are the many competencies that have been designated as most valuable for classroom and career success, such as interpersonal communication skills, writing and speaking in the English language, effective speaking and listening skills, understanding of people and cultures, time management, and decision making. These competencies are embedded in the four Voyager themes (effective communicators; ethical, professional career leaders; knowledgeable global citizens; lifelong learners), which will be assessed both in the classroom and in the work site.

Use of mass testing and standardized testing instruments to assess basic and higher-order thinking skills by schools, districts, state agencies, and national agencies has increased over the past two decades. Thus, the standardized assessments are part of the overall evaluation process for students. Without debating the merit of testing, it is important to acknowledge that standardized tests prevail and are part of high school graduation requirements nationwide. It is therefore important to delineate strategies that support students in this endeavor. We have added elements to this program that will provide coverage of required test items and that will allow students to benefit from both traditional and nontraditional modes of assessment and evaluation.

In addition to supporting achievement in academic standards, Voyager integrates skills that have been recognized as essential for job performance. In 1990, the secretary of labor and the Secretary's Commission on Achieving Necessary Skills (SCANS) identified workplace know-how and levels of skills proficiency that lead to effective job performance. The Voyager curriculum as created addresses the foundational skills and competencies required for effective classroom and workplace learning and achievement: competence in basic skills, thinking skills, personal qualities, and the ability to productively use resources, interpersonal skills, information, systems, and technology. The competencies as outlined by SCANS are generic and are the types of abilities all students will need in the workplace and as citizens. They are not specific to any particular occupation or to students who have been evaluated as incapable of or disengaged from the challenges of academic learning. They are the abilities needed for both college and workplace success.

In Voyager, assessment is ongoing. It is important to remember that students are continuously assessing themselves as well as responding to others' assessments of them. There are no surprises when it comes to assessment practices in this program. Everyone involved is clear on the criteria developed for assessing all work in the classroom and at the work site. Students are in collaboration with their peers, teachers, and supervisors at all times. They must take part in a continuous series of self-definition and self-description processes so that assessments are not made without student input. Assessments are authentic, involving real-life applications, thus engaging students in the same types of activities they experience while they are learning in the classroom and on the work site; assessments are transparent so they are understandable by students, teachers, parents, and work-site supervisors; assessments are responsive to student growth and in accordance with recognizing and fostering good learning.

PORTFOLIOS AND ASSESSMENT

Portfolio Definitions

There is an extraordinary range of definitions and purposes associated with portfolio development. Although there might have been a clear definition in the original author's conception, today each professional and user adapts the definition for his or her particular purpose or use and unique field of endeavor. Portfolios in the Voyager program are considered to be professional portfolios and are used for a variety of purposes throughout the program. Primarily, they are used as an authentic ongoing documentation and assessment of students' work and learning process. All students receive their portfolio binder during the initial summer workshop prior to the start of grade 11. The portfolio is consistently developed over the duration of the program, becoming a dynamic record of growth and learning.

The portfolio consists of a three-ring binder with multiple sections for organizing student work. The four Voyager themes including the competencies, the graduation standard, a work-in-progress section, a Voyager Company section, a work-site experience section, and a notebook for journaling are compulsory. There are other sections that students create themselves to help organize their work. In addition to being an assessment tool, the portfolio serves as a presentation portfolio at different times throughout the year, as an employment portfolio for prospective job interviews, and a Certification Competency Portfolio at each level of the Voyager program.

Creating the Portfolio

To the student: The portfolio should provide clear artifacts of your knowledge, skills, and abilities that you develop as a young professional. The collection of work is a visual display that illustrates your organizational skills and creativity. The portfolio should not be enormous, nor should it hold all of your work. It should be a selective representation of work and activities that highlight your strengths in a streamlined format. You are encouraged to choose materials that illustrate the range of class projects, work experiences, and program activities. It is a valuable professional development tool that should be maintained and updated throughout your years in Voyager as well as your professional working years. In this way, all of your accomplishments can be shared at different points in your career with all members of the Voyager community. The portfolio will have many looks throughout the year. It will be a working portfolio during each semester so that teachers, peers, parents, and work-site supervisors may review it with you. You will be asked to present and demonstrate your understanding of the course content at various points in the program. You may want to create an interactive portfolio demonstrating particular features you have contributed such as an electronic portfolio, original videos, audiotapes, or web sites as part of your presentations. The portfolio is the result of gathering artifacts and thinking about why they represent you, your skills, your ideas, and your accomplishments. It demonstrates how you have grown and learned over time. Sharing your portfolio with a prospective employer in a thoughtful, intentional manner allows the employer some insight into who you are. The portfolio is a valuable tool to prepare you for your classroom, workplace, and future employment interviews. A complete portfolio of your own creation inspires you to respond confidently during these important experiences.

Organizing the Portfolio

Your secondary career and work-site coordinator will guide you in the organization of your work. During specific times throughout each semester as designated by your seminar, you will collaborate with the coordinator to discuss and review what you should be collecting. You will need to create a preliminary table of contents. Some possible artifacts for your portfolio include: classroom and workplace diagrams; photos; drawings; original work; reflective, creative pieces; specific assignments; materials related to the Voyager Company project; audio- or videotapes from projects; copies of pages from and the URL of your web site; personal and professional career goals; philosophy of education and work; documentation of honors and awards; your reflections on ideas or events; parents', teachers', supervisors', or mentors' reflections; competencies as required by that particular semester; journal work; and graduation standard progress. You are encouraged to include documentation and work entries that reflect your life outside of school as well. Selecting and organizing work can be difficult when there is so much from which to choose. The portfolio should include evidence of your progress in all requirements as you move through the program, as well as become a showcase of your work and reflections.

Voyager portfolios are a combination of many models and purposes. They are:

- a collection of documents and artifacts that include well-defined areas of knowledge (including Voyager themes, assessment criteria for merit, and evidence of critical reflection) and skills in the classroom and in the workplace;
- a method for facilitating and enhancing communication with teachers, parents, families, mentors, work-site supervisors, and prospective employers;
- a measure for students to learn and develop the skills of self-reflection and self-assessment;
- an intentional collection of documents agreed upon and selected by both student and teacher to demonstrate the student's best work; and
- a record of successful achievement in the selected graduation standards and performance-based assessment.

Portfolio Outcomes

Portfolios provide an intentional record of students' progress through a set of experiences and achievement of program goals. Through this process students become more independent, reflective, and self-directed. They learn to advocate for themselves more effectively. The portfolio encourages students to reflect on the many facets of the educational, work-site, and career decision-making experiences while also serving as a repository for their work. Students understand the relationship between educational achievement, current and future career needs, and opportunities. The portfolio is a representation of personal and professional growth and provides a foundation for critical reflection, self-analysis, goal setting, and introspection as the student moves from one semester to another. It is the basis for assessing student learning, progress, and program completion.

During the final review and celebration, it allows students a means to say, "Here is who I have become," through exhibiting a range of their best works in the classroom, at work, at home, and in the community. Students can also use the completed portfolio as part of their dossier to help them in job placement interviews and college admission.

Students have been given the responsibility of assessing and evaluating themselves throughout each semester. They are also encouraged to grade themselves, and during this process it has been found that they do a reasonable and accurate job of assigning their own grade. They have a great deal of choice in what is to be evaluated, choosing the best of their work, usually after consulting with and receiving feedback from peers and teachers. Grading and evaluation become far less threatening when the proper foundation has been laid: criteria for evaluation are clear and concise, multiple assessments and lots of feedback have been given throughout the semester, and there have been many opportunities for self-evaluation and reflective thought.

At the final Voyager celebration, students are encouraged to write and present a metacognitive piece introducing the portfolio, explaining its contents, and discussing the selection of the different pieces that are included. They also speak to the process they experienced in compiling their portfolio. The portfolio is a living and changing document. It is not a test that will be tossed in the trash and forgotten, but a physical, tangible, and ongoing representation. Through this collection of their work and the development of a safe forum in which to discuss it, students get to know themselves better. The portfolio will reinforce lifelong learning and guide them to make decisions about how to represent themselves long after they have completed the program.

Suggestions for Portfolio Review

Portfolio reviews are made several times during the semester, during the entire program, and at the final review for Levels 1 and 2 certification. Level 1 certification is given at the successful completion of the two-year secondary, grades 11 and 12. Specific guidelines for each review will be outlined in the seminars. Below is a suggested outline of areas to be addressed in a final portfolio. Changes and alternative inclusions can be made in collaboration with the program coordinator.

- A one-page reflective opening piece introducing the portfolio
- Table of contents
- The student's personal philosophy of education and work
- A personal reflection on the Voyager experience
- A professional résumé
- Artifacts that demonstrate the student's best ideas (as determined by the student) and work from (1) class work and (2) the business experience
- The student's professional development career plans and goals
- The student's personal development goals
- The student's best (as determined by the student) junior/senior project
- A complete set of journal reflections
- A one-page final reflection stating the student's future goals, dreams, and aspirations

SUCCESSFUL COMPLETION OF THE VOYAGER PROGRAM

After four years in the program, successful Voyager students will gain a high school diploma, college admission, work-ready and career-bound skills, earned income, practical experience and training, and networking and business contacts, and will receive Voyager certification. Employers also benefit from the Voyager program in that Voyager interns and workers prove to be qualified and motivated workers. Throughout the program, schools and businesses are involved cooperatively in raising graduates' qualifications. In some instances, Voyager students are hired to fill open positions in the ongoing workforce of the business.

Voyager Program Certificate

The certificates are endorsed by all Voyager program stakeholders—business organizations (such as the Minneapolis Regional Chamber of Commerce), business partners, and the school district—and convey recognition of an exceptionally prepared student to future educational institutions and prospective employers. Successful Voyager students will receive certificates at two stages in the program.

First-level credentials will be granted upon successful completion of the two-year secondary program. To be eligible for the first-level Voyager certificate, students must achieve the following:

I. Grades 11 and 12: Level 1—Effective Communicator and Lifelong Learner (High School Graduation)
   A. Portfolio development and achievement in compliance with Voyager themes and competencies
   B. Students will provide specific examples of their work for review by their peers, teachers, and work-site supervisors.
   C. Portfolio success will demonstrate satisfactory achievement in:
      1. Voyager themes (effective communicators; ethical, professional career leaders; knowledgeable global citizens; lifelong learners)
      2. Journal writing and reflection
      3. Successful achievement of the graduation standards—career investigation and interpersonal communication skills
   D. Work-site success—job shadowing and summer internship
   E. Academic—GPA of 2.0 or better
   F. Attendance records of 90 percent or better

Second-level credentials will be granted upon successful completion of the two-year college program. To be eligible for the second-level Voyager certificate, students need to complete the following:

I. Grades 13 and 14: Level 2—Ethical Leaders for Tomorrow's Business (Postsecondary)
   A. Portfolio development and achievement in alignment with Voyager themes
   B. Ten monthly seminar meetings, two to three hours in length
   C. Attendance is required for nine out of ten of the seminars for certification
   D. Theme emphasis
      1. Appropriate use of technology in communication and presentation
      2. Interpersonal skills
      3. Secondary-postsecondary developmental and transition issues
   E. Plan and deliver one seminar for Voyager Level 1 students

F. Academic success—maintain GPA of 2.0 or better to remain in good standing in the postsecondary institution

G. Work-site success—continue to work successfully with positive performance reviews from work-site supervisor

II. Postsecondary—Year 2—Ethical Leaders for Tomorrow's Businesses

A. Portfolio development and achievement in alignment with Voyager themes

B. Eight monthly or bimonthly seminar meetings, three to six hours in length

C. Attendance required at eight seminars for certification

D. Plan and deliver one seminar for Voyager Level 1 students

E. Theme emphasis
   1. Communication skills
   2. Ethical and leadership issues in the workplace

F. Academic success—maintain GPA of 2.0 or better to remain in good standing in the postsecondary institution

G. Work-site success—continue to work successfully with positive performance reviews from work-site supervisor

H. Ethnographic Eye on the Classroom (eight submissions)

Figure 1.3. Voyager Program Evaluation

Voyager Program Evaluation

At the end of your Voyager program, you will be asked to supply feedback regarding various points and factors in the program. Below are some points for you to consider. Please go through each point and tell us what you think we need to know to keep Voyager dynamic and meeting the needs of students. We appreciate and value your feedback.

What were your ideas about this program and career work-site seminar when you first began? What did you think it was going to be about?

Now that you have successfully completed the program, how would you describe it to future Voyager students?

The program has been described as an authentic learning and school-to-career program, preparing students to be highly skilled workers in the new global millennium. Do you agree with this statement or should something be added to it? If you do agree, explain what this means to students who are just starting the program.

What did you enjoy most throughout the program?

What did you enjoy the least?

Write any suggestions or comments that you feel would be useful to the instructor and to future Voyager students.

Certificate assessment teams for Levels 1 and 2 are comprised of business partners, community members, work-site supervisors, and faculty who review, finalize, and award achievement of Voyager credentials and certification. These teams are brought together in a workshop for training in evaluating the portfolio.

Closing Celebration and Voyager Certification

At the end of each year, there will be a commemorative dinner and celebration to honor Voyager candidates and to thank all community stakeholders. Students who have successfully achieved all of the required competencies and standards are awarded Voyager certificates for each of the levels described above.

Students are expected to fill out the evaluation at the end of the program (see fig. 1.3).

2

Secondary Seminar Years

The *Voyager Secondary Career and Work-site Seminar Curriculum* provides a comprehensive two-year model of curriculum and work-site connections for the Voyager: Direction for Learning & Careers Program. Transformation of workplace organizations and systems requires identifying a variety of learning and instructional possibilities for change both in schools and in workplaces. The change of coupling on-the-job training with work-based learning experiences that focus on preparation for immediate employment and career development offers the possibility of future workers equipped with new work skills such as creative and critical thinking, problem solving, and leadership development. As global corporations become global alliances and, therefore, multinational in identification and as technology continues to advance rapidly, companies are looking toward employees to assume more responsibility and to continually upgrade their education and skills. Lifelong learning is no longer a luxury of choice but a requirement for future workers who will need to know how to carefully prepare themselves to succeed in this new work regime.

In today's knowledge-value era, power has shifted into the hands of employees who have developed skill sets and continuously improve their knowledge. "Workers are no longer interchangeable, and people can no longer be treated like cogs in an industrial machine. Workers of the new millennium will need to develop additional skills that help them expand on the conventions and understandings of yesterday's workplace practices. Workers who can manage ambiguity and mobility, who engage in lifelong learning, and who are entrepreneurial, will find amazing opportunities" (Thornburg, 2002, p. 31). As a result of these changes, all of the workers involved have to possess central knowledge of the company's goals and direction, and the ability and skills to improvise and make decisions when necessary and as demanded by markets and customers. They must personify social vision, personal agency, and civic responsibility in their work and world views. In many ways, notions of promotion and job success are not assured with a position in the hierarchy, but rather by a mastery of knowledge.

In this two- and four-year Voyager curriculum model, there is a departure from the way work and career/vocational training education has traditionally been replicated without modification to reflect changes in the field. The Voyager model demonstrates a multidisciplinary approach to teaching and learning that enhances current occupational practices by connecting them with reformist and critical perspectives. The lens of critical career education addresses the need for new conversations that provide students and workers with a process to develop their abilities and to recognize and activate their civic responsibilities. Workers today are expected to be active co-learners, to be grounded in democratic work culture, and to be social change agents. In every year of the program, students co-create a dynamic and tailored curriculum to meet their needs, prepare them for the real world, and help them to develop as professionals in their field. Voyager bridges the disparate cultures of school and workplace by providing a tangible way for students to try on various work identities and new ways of learning. It is a model of work education for the twenty-first century. Voyager combines secondary and postsecondary instruction, work readiness training, and on-the-job experience through internships. It was designed under the guidelines of the federal School to Work Opportunities Act by the Minneapolis Regional Chamber of Commerce, the Minneapolis Public Schools, postsecondary educators, and business leaders in the city of Minneapolis. It is a collaboration between employers and educators that will sustain regional competitiveness through a skilled workforce.

Key Features of the Voyager Program (grades 11–14)

This program combines classroom instruction with on-the-job learning and connects high school with postsecondary training.

1. **School-Based Learning (Career and Work-site Seminar)**—The school-to-career program is about restructuring education so that students in this program understand how their learning in school relates to the world of work and to authentic realities in their lives. The secondary seminar is taught once per week and the postsecondary seminar is once per month. In this school-based learning seminar:

- high-quality academic and career preparation is foundational,
- teachers, students, and employers work together to develop broad-based curricula that incorporate knowledge, dispositions, and skills for the new millennium,
- fulfilling graduation standards is required to earn a Voyager certificate
- students fulfill and apply Voyager themes and competencies throughout the curriculum,
- student portfolios are developed and assessed,
- student teams develop real-world projects, explore career opportunities, and develop various skill sets, and
- professionals from diverse disciplines and backgrounds work together to develop an integrated curriculum designed to make classroom projects and other activities relevant to work and to life.

2. **Connecting Activities**—Voyager builds bridges between school and work. Students grasp how intricately these two learning areas are woven together. A range of activities integrating school and work ensures that students will have the support necessary to connect the two worlds. These connecting activities include:
   - mentoring, both face-to-face and online, from educational, business, and community leaders starts at the beginning of their program and continues throughout;
   - career exploration that includes experiences in job shadowing, corporate site tours, attending business conferences, résumé writing and interview preparation, and networking opportunities within and across careers; and,
   - college and other postsecondary training with college/vocational tours, application assistance, scholarship searches, and financial aid planning.

3. **Work-Based Learning**—Voyager students are active learners within multiple work contexts. Work-based learning provides students with opportunities to perform complex tasks and develop vital workplace skills in a hands-on environment. The work-based experiences include:
   - on-the-job training with a work-site supervisor who meets with students throughout their work experience; the training is either a part-time summer or a year-round internship;
   - firsthand career experience by working in multiple teams, problem solving, performance-based career assessments; and,
   - developing Secretary's Commission on Achieving Necessary Skills (SCANS) to productively use resources, interpersonal skills, information, systems, and technology.

The Voyager seminar coordinator matches students with work-site supervisors and mentors who also participate in the Voyager training. Full information on the training and supervisor/mentor roles and responsibilities can be found in the Voyager Community Handbook Set (Roulis, 2003a).

4. **The Voyager Company**—This student-operated company is an Ideas Bank that is created during the first year of the Voyager program and continued through senior year. Students brainstorm ideas on what they want to learn about business and community issues and how they can go about doing it. The goals and the texture of the Voyager Company are developed and redeveloped through the thinking and work of each of the Voyager groups. In this way, the Voyager Company is developed to fit the needs of multiple career fields: health, travel, manufacturing, financial, and the like. Collaborative real-world projects are at the heart of the secondary program and company. Students work with business and community leaders to research, consult, and take action on developing creative solutions. In the company setting, students:
   - develop projects,
   - explore the development of new work cultures,
   - sharpen interpersonal skills, and
   - practice teamwork skills that lead to mutual understandings and collective responsibility.

5. **Personal Development**—Engagement in classroom projects and workplace activity promotes the linking of analysis, critical inquiry, and reflection. Students are supported in their endeavor to research and work with community-based groups and businesses to explore and problem solve current issues in the community. Participatory education is redefined as the "act of doing" at school, in the workplace, and in the community, providing fertile ground for student leadership development. Students also develop time management skills that support a balanced life while exploring activities to feed their minds, bodies, and souls. For many of the students, the program represents new frontiers of learning and working that may conflict with their home life, their family responsibilities, and their cultural orientations. The program provides opportunities to discuss personal and professional management strategies.

Introduction to Voyager Course of Study

At the core of the Voyager program's curriculum model is an educative process involving an interdisciplinary scope of study both in school and at work. Success relies on the extent of authentic and connected learning experiences in the classroom, in the workplace, and in the community. This program focuses on challenging students to meet higher academic standards, giving them a foundation for continuing on to postsecondary education and for developing the tools of lifelong learning. Workplace experiences allow students to take advantage of career opportunities in their area of interest as well as introduce them to other potential career possibilities. Learning how to learn in the context of work is an important feature of this program. The experiences are structured so students become knowledgeable about workplace life and the expectations of workers in the global economy. Work is demystified by understanding the development and process for redefining:

1. Work ethics
2. Social skills
3. Professionalism
4. Work cultures and styles

Visible, ongoing reflective questions create "habits of mind" that are essential to learning, living, and working in this new millennium:

1. What are my personal and professional goals?
2. How am I learning to learn?
3. What are sound learning habits for me?
4. In what ways are my school and work experiences related?
5. What type of work world is suited for me and how am I going to get the skills I need to get there?
6. How will I integrate action for social justice into my work life?

Curriculum Foundations and Philosophical Beliefs

Curriculum increases in value when teachers and students can teach and learn together, and work is both contextual and global. The lessons in these units provide a group-learning experience that fits participants' diverse needs. The curriculum encourages all learners to reflect on what vital questions and issues they are facing and need to explore in depth for successful professional development. The Voyager curriculum reinforces a student-centered curriculum. Students are encouraged and supported to acquire global perspectives that are dynamic and interactive. Students, teachers, businesses, and people in the community are constantly engaged in dialogue with each other to explore and unpack ideas posed in the curriculum. As a student-centered and real-world-based curriculum, the Voyager program supports students in thinking reflectively, questioning, problem solving, and taking action.

Critical Pedagogy and Social Change

Central to the curriculum and to student learning is the understanding of how ideals of social justice and transformative action are necessary and attainable goals of the classroom, workplace, and community. This is not a transmission process or banking model of education with narrow expectations that end up constraining student development. The activities, discussion topics, collaborative projects, workplace experiences, and connecting activities provide a framework for an intense participatory learning and work process.

Brazilian educator and philosopher Paulo Freire believed in critical approaches to learning and democratic models for social change. The Voyager program is founded on such principles. Empowering and liberatory education for all learners is the focus. The entire curriculum is designed to provide opportunities for teachers and students to work cooperatively in an environment of critical pedagogy (the critical inquiry of issues and ideas such as examining power and social arrangements that are connected to social change through praxis), authentic dialogue, and thoughtful reflection coupled with informed action. By designing a problem-posing curriculum, teachers and students investigate issues embedded in social contexts that are relevant to students' lives. Everyone gets to participate as co-learners in this curriculum, blending the richness of their experiences and their knowledge. Through this process, the message to students is a powerful invitation to participate and engage in their learning. Learning in this manner weaves in trust and respect, allows all voices to be heard, entertains different perspectives, and illuminates new understandings of self and others. The environment allows ideas to become the center of the conversations. Through critical dialogue, reflection, and action the classroom environment reflects socially just practices that can be applied in the workplace and the community. The curriculum begins by examining issues through the students' personal histories, through local community issues, and then through critical dialogue with the business and community people who participate in the learning. Students are stretched to make global connections that broaden their perspectives.

Students start to regard themselves as thinkers, interpreters, reflective change agents, and contributors to their multiple worlds and to the greater society. Teachers move beyond lecturing to develop ideas and co-create new knowledge. By examining both the themes that motivate the students and the issues that are a part of their everyday life, the classroom comes alive with energy. Soon the ability to critically examine and interrogate their own and other perspectives becomes part of a natural process of being active co-learners. The teacher provides direct instruction when helpful and also brings in additional information to expand the discussions that take place to produce new knowledge and new understandings. But the overall theory and practice guiding this curriculum is that education is not being done *for* a student or *to* a student but *with* a student. "The goals of this pedagogy are to relate personal growth to public life by developing strong skills, academic knowledge, habits of inquiry, and critical curiosity about society, power, inequality, and change" (Shor, 1993, p. 15).

Participatory Learning

This curriculum presents a sustained study of school-to-career personal and professional development. It combines teaching and learning from academic courses, the career and work-site seminar, and workplace experiences. The content of the academic arena sets high expectations for all students. It is interdisciplinary in that material is brought in from multiple areas such as literature, film, sociology, anthropology, science, business, and psychology just to name a few. The multiple group projects, in-class activities, role-plays, simulations, creative and imaginative writing, and optional activities provide for a differentiated curriculum that will engage a range of learners, abilities, and learning styles. Instead of just hearing about work or community life, power, ethics, or leadership, students encounter and experience all of these concepts firsthand. There are no academic limits to the way teachers, students, and community and business people can learn and work together.

Students' Lives as Texts

Organizing program themes are drawn from students' lived experiences. In essence, their lives and stories become another text for the program. They are urged to critically examine their lives and to see their experiences as part of the curriculum. Students examine and redefine power and power relationships in the classroom, the community, and the workplace. It is the type of curriculum design that opens up passages for more diverse groups of students to speak up and enables them to see acts of learning as worth their time and effort. Since school and work life are crucial in shaping their attitudes and a sense of their own capabilities and cannot be accepted as unquestioned facts of life, but rather ones that require reflective examination. Developing confidence is set in motion through a multidimensional classroom where lessons and projects create a foundation of confidence through team effort, perseverance, resilience, and caring. Everyone is considered smart, with something to offer, and differences are a rich source of new perspectives.

Real-World Collaborative Projects

In this program, school and work are associated and connected with the real productive life of a community and real-world activities. Students are asked to participate in collaborative projects that are career based and connected to their interests. They are expected to translate their academic studies and workplace experiences into performance projects that require multimedia and other advanced technology applications. The curriculum guides students to make connections with other school-to-career programs, workers, and professionals, both nationally and internationally. Assessment strategies are used for improving teaching and learning, and students become adept at employing a variety of appropriate procedures throughout their program, making assessment a vital learning tool. There are a variety of authentic assessments, including panels of outside experts who assess students' exhibitions (portfolios, research projects, technology presentations) at different intervals in the program. It is a goal of this program that students are not threatened or labeled by assessment, but rather use it as a tool to guide what they learn throughout their seminars and workplaces. They continuously participate in critical dialogues and feedback sessions regarding their work in an established safe classroom environment with their peers and other professionals from the field. A sense of activism is awakened in the students while they work on community and class projects. They then transfer decision-making skills outside the classroom to shape their lives. Learning and participating in change become an exciting and passionate process.

Secondary Career and Work-site Seminar Unit Descriptions

Each of the units includes lessons with formats that cover a range of ideas and components to help the instructor and students work together to develop a richer environment for learning that can be contextualized from a template to meet their goals and needs. The lessons include teaching notes which set the stage, summarize the learning objectives, describe past classroom experiences, and suggest critical perspectives from which to develop the lesson. They also include the required academic standards for graduation, learning objectives, small- and large-group activities, performance-based assessments, outside assignments, and optional suggestions for either further developing the lesson themes or for substitution.

Beginning with the introductory seminar in Chapter 3, the junior year curriculum, Unit 1: Personal and Professional Development, students are immediately introduced to:

1. The four organizing themes of the program
2. A discussion of expectations (both teacher and student)
3. Understanding and practicing the processes of critical pedagogy

From the beginning, knowledge is dynamic and is co-produced by teachers, students, business partners, and all other community members collectively through critical dialogue and informed action. Guided by these precepts, substantial time is focused on creating a democratic Voyager learning community.

Unit 2, Conflict Resolution, opens up in-depth discussions examining personal and societal perspectives on violence and conflict. A main question that is explored is: how have students' lives been impacted by violence? The discussions and analysis of data allow for a more comprehensive look at the topic. Although there are multiple goals in this unit, the umbrella goal is to see how students will change the way they respond to violence and conflict both personally and professionally. In Unit 3, The Voyager Company, the focus is on students creating and developing their own company and a project that the company will undertake throughout the secondary program. In setting up the company, students probe larger frameworks of work education; they define goals, strategies, timelines, outcomes, and assessments for all of their work and tasks; and they focus on developing specific skills (e.g., writing up meeting minutes, creating agendas, inviting and preparing for guest speakers). They also work directly with business leaders in the community and engage in ongoing conversations for new perspectives on organizational culture, job possibilities, and education requirements, and they engage in discussing and finding solutions for current issues in the companies they are exploring and in their communities.

In Unit 4, Cooperative Learning, there is a focus on building a caring and mutually supportive environment where learning is honored and nurtured. Students participate in shared learning that includes cooperative research projects, cooperative assessment activities, cooperative presentations and group work, peer tutoring, peer editing, and even cooperative writing. Additionally, all of these activities are steeped in real events and issues supporting authentic learning experiences that connect the classroom and the workplace.

In Unit 5, Organization Behavior and Development, students become active researchers and ethnographers of the actual workplace cultures that they are experiencing. They look at the workings of organizations firsthand in terms of organizational relationships, customs, and rituals, and by studying business ethics, exploring ethical decision making, and analyzing business practices locally, nationally, and internationally.

In Unit 6, Intercultural Communication, many of the challenges of living and working in an intercultural world are addressed. Specifically, students will cover the various components and concepts of intercultural competence and understanding they need to develop a repertoire of professional communication skills as they work with diverse groups in classrooms and workplaces.

In Unit 7, Self-Assessment and Reflection, the final unit for junior year, students have the opportunity to present authentic profiles of themselves after their first year in the program. They highlight their strengths and outline their future paths and possibilities. Working individually and in their base groups, they respond to each other's work and begin to prepare their portfolio for final assessment, demonstrating how they have become responsible for their own learning and growth.

In Chapter 4, the senior year curriculum, Unit 1, Personal and Professional Growth, students continue to self-assess their academic and internship success and to forecast their needs for senior year and beyond. It sets the stage for successful completion of the Voyager secondary program, which includes high school graduation and Voyager certification. Students edit, rewrite, and re-envision their goals for the year as well as address new areas for growth.

Unit 2, Postsecondary Preparation, helps students to develop a plan for some type of postsecondary study and training. All students read, review, and analyze postsecondary admission requirements and materials for admission to schools of advanced training, make site visits, and invite postsecondary faculty to class.

Unit 3, The Résumé, begins the important process for students to organize and present themselves in the best possible light to prospective educational institutions and business employers. The discussions and exchanges among the students provide opportunities for them to explore assumptions and information they have about themselves and effective ways to convey that information. Editing for success and clarity as well as assessing one's own abilities becomes predominant. Unit 4, Interviewing, prepares students for actual formal interviews for educational institutions and/or for work. A series of mock interviews both in the classroom and at arranged business sites is part of the process. The legal and ethical aspects of interviewing are discussed with the goal of making the interview process an empowering experience in students' lives. Communication skills are stressed and reviewed both from the videotape of the interview and from the perspectives of all of the class members.

Unit 5, Letter Writing, provides an opportunity for students to engage in the art of letter writing from a variety of perspectives: inquiry, job response, follow-up, and thank you. Students actually respond to real jobs. In Unit 6, The Voyager Company, students continue their collaborative projects. Although there are lessons with this unit, much of the work is completed by students outside of class and through email and discussion board communication. Students have choices to expand on their previous year's project or to develop new ones and work with different business and community groups.

Unit 7, Intercultural Communication Skills, addresses the need for a highly skilled workforce to understand and navigate in a global and multinational society. Students continue to build and develop strategies that deal directly with diversity issues and discrimination. Unit 8, Leadership and Ethics, reviews and critically analyzes the research on leadership and how students see themselves as leaders. It calls into question the corporate scandals and the ethics and ways of doing business in today's world.

Unit 9, Reflection, Assessment, and Future Work, is the final seminar unit that brings the first two years to a successful completion. Students focus on finalizing their work, archiving their experiences, and forging new ways for the Voyager program to grow. They prepare for closure to one segment of the program and for the start of the postsecondary program, continuing the momentum from one year to another.

Always Tinkering with a "Work in Progress"

Development of this curriculum from 1997 to 2002 was always a collaborative effort. Much energy and time were generously donated by a variety of stakeholders—many of whom would never have sat down at the same table together before this time. Teachers, college faculty and administrators, business and community people were willing to dialogue and review what was working and what needed change in the program. The Voyager students also were willing to write and discuss what needed to be changed—their thoughts and ideas are represented throughout this program. The ever-improving Voyager curriculum could have continued to be a work in progress, so at some point, we had to stop and say, "This is it for now." Please accept what we have learned and are offering, not as an official recipe but as curriculum that is a work in progress for you to change now! As Paulo Freire stated about his work, "Take my ideas and reinvent them" (Freire, 1997) to suit your contexts and needs. Schools and workplaces need to play a major part in reinforcing hope and enthusiasm for the future.

This curriculum builds on the sharing of students' lived experiences, that is, those events that have shaped and continue to shape the students who are present in the classroom. It is the first two years of a living and practical four-year curriculum model based on uniting theory and practice, co-created with teachers, students, and business and community leaders. It is dynamic in nature because of the inclusion of the ongoing voices and feedback from all Voyager stakeholders. Although there are specific units with lesson plans, the hope is that each school site and all teaching personnel will take the curriculum as a model that can and should be contextualized for their specific needs and students. It is crafted to be flexible for multiple communities and programs. This is not a picture of a 100 percent classroom success story—but it is a picture of success. Schools and workplaces can inspire and support social justice and remind us that everyone can make a difference. And when we start from this premise, students respond.

3

Junior Year Seminar Units

Unit 1A

Personal and Professional Growth

LESSON TOPIC:
WELCOME TO VOYAGER—ORIENTATION SEMINAR

Teaching Note

The summer workshop day is vital. It serves as an in-depth orientation to the Voyager program. It is also a workshop that models the outstanding and signature components of the program that will be maintained throughout the curriculum. From this first meeting, students experience educators and businesspeople working together to provide leadership for the type of authentic learning, work experience, and community building that will take place throughout the program. Together, teachers and students begin to plan the procedures required for success in the program. The workshop offers teaching and learning approaches that are different from those found in traditional classrooms. In this program, educators value guiding over telling, freedom of choice rather than control, and supporting students' growth so they can learn with confidence. The workshop must model the various components of the program and introduce students to participatory education—it sets the tone and standards. As a result of full participation and engagement in this program, students will come to find their voice, know that when they are speaking they will be heard, and know that their ideas will be given thoughtful consideration. They need to believe that their opinions count as they create new understandings about the realities of their lives—in society, at school, and in the workplace.

It is paramount that the foundational components of the curriculum such as reflective practice, collaborative project-based learning, critical inquiry, and community building are emphasized and experienced from the initial class meeting. Additionally, the workshop allows time for students to become acquainted with each other and with program expectations: portfolio development, journal writing, graduation standards, and the participatory process of learning, which is not only a process of the acquisition of skills and knowledge but also one producing additional knowledge. The workshop also serves as a preparation period for students to explore and begin the process of their personal and professional goal planning. Students can begin to connect the program's authentic learning and workplace realities with their individual plans for the future. They are invited from the first day to be active learners and interpreters of their worlds in a participatory class and a learning experience that bridges the gap between classroom learning and the workplace.

There is a lot of material to cover and the workshop coordinator needs to make ongoing assessments and decisions as to the day's pace and monitor the amount of material that will be covered successfully. As Ira Shor argues in *Empowering Education* (1992), this experience by students is a social interaction inviting thought and feeling. The Voyager classroom is a site where social justice and transformative action are central to the curriculum and to learning. The orientation is also the first day of the students' actual community building and immersion in a different learning environment. Students and business and other people will have dinner together at the end of the workshop.

Objectives

To orient students to the Voyager program

To understand and build portfolios to meet Voyager expectations, credentials, and graduation standards

To create and practice the concepts of self-reflection and self-assessment

To begin introducing members of the Voyager Business Community as integral partners to the learning process throughout the program

Domains

Cognitive: Understand and apply Voyager themes, competencies, and standards

Affective: Learn appropriate strategies and set appropriate boundaries to build a community of learners

Skills: Develop speaking and listening skills

Academic Standard:
Write and Speak in the English Language

Interpersonal Communication Skills
Effective speaking and listening skills
Create self-assessment and skills for appropriately giving and receiving feedback

Materials

Large posters with Voyager themes and graduation standards (Interpersonal Communication Skills and Career Investigation)
Sample portfolios with journal notebooks included
Collages from past classes and students (if available)
Portfolio binders for each student that include indices for certification categories, notebooks for journals, and rubrics and assessment criteria
Sample Level 1 and Level 2 Voyager certificates

Figure 3.1. Welcome Letter

Dear Voyager Students and Families (use actual names):

Welcome to the Voyager: Direction for Learning & Careers program and community. Congratulations! You have been selected to participate in a new and innovative program that supports students in their academic and career work. We will work together as a learning community for the next two years, exploring the world of work and various career pathways for your future professional development. We have planned many new and unique learning events for you throughout the years.

We look forward to seeing you and your family at our Voyager celebrations of Learning and Achievement throughout each year. These events include student presentations, mentors sharing feedback, and business partners reflecting on their roles. The celebrations are also important opportunities for all Voyager community members to share in the benefits of participating in the program and to communicate suggestions for future projects.

Parents become new members of our Voyager learning community and we invite you to our first parent/school/business partners board meeting dinner. The specifics of place and time will be provided in the invitation you will be receiving soon. Prior to the dinner, the program's advisory board will deliver its first report to you about the program.

Thank you for participating in our Voyager program. Your support, as parents and as students, is vital to our continued success. We look forward to our collaboration as the Voyager learning community continues to grow.

Please feel free to contact us with any suggestions, questions, or comments.

Sincerely

History of Work Education articles for homework assignment

Snippets of videos that serve as a preview of what they will see throughout the program

Voyager community resource handbook (*Transforming Learning for the Workplace of the New Millennium, Book 4*, Roulis, 2003a)

Welcome letter (fig. 3.1)

Pre-Instructional

At least two weeks prior to the first workshop, send Voyager program materials to each student. Include a welcome letter for parents and students to the program (see fig. 3.1), Voyager highlights and events for the year, and a seminar syllabus. Students and business and community leaders are invited to dinner at the end of the workshop to celebrate the beginning of their new program.

Introductory Framework

This program is special because of the unique components that connect school- and work-based learning. This program is built on real learning models that can be used in students' academics and in their workplaces. Successful achievement in the program is based on creating both community and individual goals that need to be fulfilled and identifying challenges that need to be addressed in order to achieve those goals. This program is also special because of the unique design and people involved with it. It is the only program of its kind in the nation that has a four-year curriculum model and also that supports students in achieving their academic and work goals throughout the entire time. Introduce self as coordinator and introduce other members who are present: teachers, parents, alumni, mentors, business members, and Voyager board members. Ask each member to speak about her or his experience in the program.

Continue with an overview of the program, including:

1. Program philosophy
2. Four-year course of study
3. Expectations
4. Competencies
5. Certification process

Stress that students will receive full support from the educational and business communities throughout the program. This includes mentors, job placement, academic guidance, networking, and career counseling. There are no surprises in this program, as students work with their teachers and supervisors continually as a team that supports them for achievement of goals and for success.

Motivation

We don't have many chances to sit back and take a look at who we are, where we have come from, and where we want to go. Most of the time our lives are so filled with "doing things"—school, work, family responsibilities—that we hardly have time "to think about" who we are and what we want to do. What does time for reflection mean to you? How do you practice it? What does it look like? What do you learn from it? (Brainstorm by saying anything that comes to mind, by understanding that there are no right or wrong answers, by not judging or making comments on any of the responses, and by understanding that quantity is most important—the idea is to list as many responses as possible; say things even if you think they are crazy—many crazy ideas lead to great ideas. Then list all student responses on the board.)

There are many ways we can engage in self-reflection as a lifelong learning process as demonstrated by this list. Sometimes we will reflect and dialogue individually, other times in a small group, or as a whole class, or with a partner. Other times we journal, write to colleagues and friends, read, or sit quietly by ourselves and think. Everyone has his or her unique ways of reflecting.

During our first few seminars we will engage in some preliminary activities to begin this process of self-reflection. It is the goal of systematic reflective practice that all of us—teachers and students—will gain new perspectives on ourselves; examine and question assumptions we have about ourselves, others, or ideas; start to think more deliberately about decisions; and confront any dilemmas or contradictions of living that we are experiencing. The reflective journey produces a deepening sense of self and new perspectives on assumptions of how we teach and learn that have been accepted without question up to this point. Through the development of the reflective process, each of us is then prepared to take intentional and transformational action.

INSTRUCTIONAL IMPLEMENTATION

Icebreaker: My Dictionary Definition (fig. 3.2)

Have the teacher:

1. Ask for volunteers to go to the board, write their definitions, and talk about their entries. Many times it is helpful to break the ice by having the teacher write his or her definition on the board as well.

2. Class members should provide feedback on definitions. (One suggested direction for this exercise is to ask students to look at what characteristic they listed first; how/why they prioritized their definitions; what conclusions they can draw from how they prioritized their definitions; why they listed themselves as a verb, adjective, or noun, and so on; how they think other students would define them.)

3. Ask for feedback from other class members. Do they perceive the student in the same way as he or she defined himself or herself? How differently? Why? Be sure to reinforce that answers are merely suggestions and different perspectives; they are not meant to be taken as criticisms or shortcomings.)

4. How has this activity changed or sharpened your self-image and focus? What new thoughts do you have on this process?

Figure 3.2. Icebreaker—My Dictionary Definition

This exercise is called "My Dictionary Definition" and will be the first item placed in your Voyager portfolio, which will become part of your personal development throughout this course.

1. Think about what a dictionary definition looks like. What are the different parts you would find in a dictionary definition?
2. Please take the next ten minutes to write a definition of yourself as you would want to find in a dictionary. Your definition should include a word pattern, phonetic pronunciation, part of speech, and the actual definition.
3. Which characteristic did you list first in your definition?
4. Why and how did you prioritize the characteristics of your definition?
5. How do you think your classmates would define you?

After going over the definitions, what we see are glimpses of ourselves, images of who we are at this moment, what we are about in terms of our own self-perceptions, and what we think is important to us. It will be interesting to see differences in our definitions next year—how we will define ourselves differently and identify with different parts of ourselves.

Small Group Activity: Self-Reflection and Assessment (fig. 3.3)

Let's return to the students' original lists generated on self-reflection and exchange further ideas on self-reflection and self-assessment.

1. Have students move into groups of four or five for fifteen minutes.
2. Choose a student recorder and discuss why this is or is not a process they will learn from. (Students will exchange ideas on what they have

found out about themselves based on the brainstorming model on re-flection from the first large group discussion.)

3. Have each group record and then report its ideas to the entire class.

The culminating activity for this topic will be an original collage done in any medium, print or electronic, that the student creates representing the different aspects of his or her personal and professional life. (Demonstrate past examples of students' collage work.) Some students have used a picture collage with a frame, some have used a paper bag (using artifacts for both the outside and the inside), and some have created a diorama. The goal is for the students to be cre-ative and represent themselves from their reflection and perspective.

We will continue to use this process of self-reflection through a variety of activities during each seminar. (Who are you now—in this moment?) Please make sure you save all work that is relevant for your portfolios.

Figure 3.3. Self-Reflection and Assessment (Sample)

Recall the lists you generated earlier, the lists of what time to reflect means to you, how you practice reflection, and what you learn from reflection. In groups of four or five, discuss why or why not reflection is a process you will learn from. Your group will re-port on its ideas to the larger group.

1. Why reflection is a process we will learn from.
2. Why reflection is not a process we will learn from.

Small Group Activity: More about Each of Us—Why Voyager?

Have students pair up and take thirty minutes to meet. Distribute crayons and cards to each.

1. They will interview each other for ten minutes, asking each of the Stu-dent Interview Questions that follow, and then draw significant sym-bols (i.e., sketches of stamps for someone who is a stamp collector or a big heart for a person who does volunteer work) of what they think represents the other person.
2. Here are some potential student interview questions:
   • Why did you join this program?
   • What do you hope to gain from this program?
   • What are your career and college goals?
   • What is one unique thing you would like us to know about you?
   • What is one question you want answered by the program this year?
3. At the end of the thirty minutes, have students introduce their partner to the class and hold up the drawing they have created.

Large Group Activity: Overview and Highlights of Some of the Unique Components of Voyager

Distribute the *Voyager Community Resource Handbook, Transforming Learning in the Workplace of the New Millennium: Students and Workers as Critical Learners, Book 4* (Roulis, 2003), to each student.

This is one of your textbooks for the program. Please refer to it often. It was written to give you an overview of the program and to guide you along as you complete each phase. The coordinator will go over the different parts of the book with the class and locate what information is included. It will be impossible to go over the entire book at this time. Let students know that the text will be used constantly throughout the program.

Why is this program unique? This is a great opportunity to discuss the many questions and answers students have as they go through the book. Figure 3.4 provides some ideas for a guided discussion.

Figure 3.4. Voyager Community Resource Handbook Investigation (Sample)

1. Have several Voyager alumni return with their e-portfolios demonstrating their job placements and have them talk about what their experiences are like. Allow time for current students to ask questions and have the alumni answer.
2. Show PowerPoint presentations of what other students have accomplished, giving them an idea of what they can and will learn from these events.
3. Show that the program is both in-depth and interactive—hands-on project-based learning.
4. Describe the Voyager Company—how students have created company goals and worked with businesspeople.
5. Describe sample products—student-created web sites, slide shows, CDs, multimedia presentations.
6. Discuss the role of student leaders—students given opportunities for leadership.
7. Demonstrate examples of how students will take the lead in different areas and what they are responsible for (e.g., interviewing people, planning panel presentations, field trips).
8. Describe developing personal and professional growth action plans. This is ongoing—plans are written and rewritten to ascertain and meet students' changing needs each semester.
9. Describe authentic and ongoing assessment—all assessments are relative to student learning and have real-world contexts.
10. Explain college admission procedures—working and visiting with actual college admissions teams to begin the process for successful application and admission to two- and four-year colleges.
11. Describe job shadowing, job placements, and internships—give an overall review of these activities and the responsibilities connected to them.
12. Ask students to think about why the Voyager student narratives have been included in the handbook. Have each student read one student narrative and have them write down their impressions of what they learned from the student's life.

Large Group Activity: Introduce the Concept of Critical Pedagogy

Paulo Freire, Brazilian educator and philosopher, believed that education needed to change. He saw that education in his own country was in trouble because so many of the people, especially peasants, could not read and were not active citizens standing up for themselves in their own behalf. Their literacy development was nonexistent. He felt it was time to ask new questions and seek new answers for education so that schools and communities would not become stagnant sites where little was learned or unlearned. (There are many books available for students and teachers to read about Freire's development of critical pedagogy as well as other critical pedagogues. See references for further works.)

In his work for change, Freire wanted to create a new understanding of teaching and learning, and he challenged himself to develop the capacity for human beings to know. Freire's initial work was in reading and writing—attending to the literacy problems in his country. From the beginning he did not view literacy training as the application of techniques but rather he was concerned with the process of reading and writing. In his words, "for me from the beginning, it was not ever possible to separate reading words from reading the world . . . and it is not possible to separate reading the world from writing the world" (Freire, 1997, p. 304). In essence, a critical reading of the world also implies a connection to the historical and cultural reading of the world. Meaning and reading were connected to the learner and his or her world, history, and culture; they were not separate acts of knowing.

Freire began one of the first literacy programs in Brazil during the 1960s using students' language as the starting point for learning, and he also believed it was important not to overemphasize the beginning of their studies and move them to acquiring and developing multiple literacies and discourses. Language helps us understand what matters to us, and, like Vyogotsky, Freire believed that one of the most important connections was to create new knowledge through understanding the relationship between thought and language. Juxtaposed and very much connected to the relationship of language, meaning, and thought is the ability for teachers and learners to look at fundamental issues of power and social arrangements and to examine how these concepts affect schools and other civil institutions. Paulo was eventually jailed for his national literacy campaign, because he not only taught the peasants to read, but he also taught them to look at and observe their oppressed conditions and to critically read the world. Once the peasants began to read, they developed a powerful literacy based on their lived experiences, which helped them to think and speak differently.

Critical pedagogy is about putting on a pair of glasses with new lenses that provide a new perspective on ourselves, on our lived experiences, on our relationship with others, on our long-held and unexamined assumptions, and allow us to find new meanings for our lives and for the society we live in. Freire believed in and used the term "conscientization," which is the power to take action once we have reflected and come to know what we believe in. In essence it is the ability to come to our voice, the ability to turn our beliefs into lived behaviors. Coming to voice is not a gift someone bestows on someone else; it is a human and democratic right for everyone. Freire believed that his literacy campaign and work with the peasants helped to break what was termed the "culture of silence." In working with the peasants, Paulo saw that they were able to observe and to articulate how they were once silenced by others. His work greatly influences this curriculum and the Voyager program as it supports the possibilities of critical work education and the worker of the new millennium. The Voyager program is also steeped in the belief that schools are sites for critical teaching and learning that challenge existing practices and beliefs (Shor, 1980).

Large Group Activity: Introduce Portfolios

What is a portfolio? What purposes does it serve? How will it be used? Have you ever used a portfolio? Usually portfolios have been used in the arts. Artist portfolios are used to display an artist's finest work throughout the years, especially when she or he is looking for a job. In academic portfolios students compile their best work through multiple samples as evidence of their learning and development over a period of time. Display the overhead of an artist carrying a portfolio or some similar picture demonstrating the use of portfolios. Display sample portfolios from past students. Distribute portfolio binders for each student. Distribute sample portfolios to the students and ask them to investigate them with a partner (fig. 3.5).

Introduction and Guidelines: Portfolios are an authentic way for teachers and students to pursue teaching and learning that is crafted to a particular classroom or project. What does that statement mean to you? There are no set rules for selecting the materials you will place in your portfolios. Material selection is your choice with guidance from your classmates and your teacher. You can revise and re-edit materials until you are satisfied that they belong in the portfolio and that they meet the competency achievement that is being assessed. We have found that each student will add her or his individuality to her or his portfolio. For both teacher and student, this will be a new way to keep track of what learning is taking place throughout the year, to revamp processes in the classroom, examine and assess the way in which we teach, and explore new avenues of possibilities. There are specific guidelines for the final portfolio

Figure 3.5.   Portfolio Introduction (Sample)

You and a partner are to examine the sample portfolio you have been given. Portfolios are an authentic way for teachers and students to pursue teaching and learning that is crafted to a particular classroom or project. What does this statement mean to you?

Portfolio Guidelines

Document Selection	Reason for Selecting This Document	Document Revision	Document Peer Assessment	Document Final Presentation	Document Demonstrates Competency

reviews, which occur at the end of each semester and also for high school graduation. Connected with your development of portfolios are the criteria and rubrics that have been created to guide assessment procedures. Rubrics and assessment procedures will be part of future lessons. All of the guidelines for review will be covered in depth by your coordinator. It is important to remember that your portfolios need to be well organized and support your knowledge, capabilities, and experience with concrete examples. The portfolio is an organized documentation of your professional growth, competence in your field, and ability to meet goals and standards. The portfolio can certainly be a mixed-media creation.

You will be involved with two types of portfolios:

1. The Working Portfolio, which contains almost all of your working documents and artifacts that demonstrate your professional growth in both the classroom and work site; many of your documents might be stored on computer disks and files, others stored in boxes, or in your notebooks; there are a variety of artifacts that you will develop over the course of the program that reflect your achievements and knowledge.

2. The Presentation Portfolio, which is an organized, selective, and compact demonstration of your skills and professional growth. In this portfolio, you will have multiple audiences (teachers, mentors, business and community people) who will be assessing your growth and achievement of goals. A presentation portfolio is also a valuable tool for prospective employers. Please look in the Voyager handbook for further information on your portfolios and also know that we will do further work during many of our seminars on the portfolios.

Large Group Activity: Designing Journals—Reflecting, Creating, and Unleashing

Journals are used for your reflections and your creativity. In this program there are some constructed journal entries and some open-ended ones (fig. 3.6). Journal reflections will cover classroom, workplace, home, and community thoughts and ideas. You will also have the opportunity to use your journals at any time for other ideas you might want to pursue. How have you used journals before either in school, work, or in your personal life? We have provided a bound notebook for your journal reflections. You may want to divide your journal into sections to establish different areas you wish to write about. If you want to include information that you hold as private, you can put this in a section that you mark as private.

Figure 3.6. Journal Reflections

Personal Goals

What are your personal goals for the year? List two things you want to take action on this semester. Why and how will you accomplish your goals? Name two or three role models who you feel are good examples of what you would like to become, and tell why you chose them. You may wish to set a time to speak with them about your goals.

Professional Career Plan and Goals

What future career interests you? What are the skills needed for this position? What do you need to do to become successful in this skill? What are the ways you can set up your own networking? What are two things you can take action on right away to get started on your career plan?

Open Writing Topic

Write freely on any topic or issue that is on your mind. Topics may include work situations, educational issues, or future ideas. Unleash your creativity: write an original piece—poem, song, short story, or comic strip—design a web site, or create any artwork.

Conversational Styles

During the next week become a keen observer of people having conversations. This observation can take place anywhere: a restaurant, a classroom, the schoolyard, your place of work, at home, on the street, on the bus, and so on. Describe a conversation you observed. Why was it interesting to you? Describe where it took place, who was involved, how many people were involved, what the people were like, the conversation's main topic, what you heard, and how you would analyze the conversation.

Resolving Conflict

During the week, take notice of any conflict that has taken place either at school, at work, at home, at a game, in a department store, or the like. What was the argument about, who was involved, what was the outcome? Would you have done anything differently than the people involved in the conflict?

Open Writing Topic

Write freely on any topic or issue that is on your mind. Topics may include work situations, educational issues, or future ideas. Unleash your creativity: write an original piece—poem, song, short story, or comic strip—design a web site, or create any artwork.

Voyager Company Goals and Roles

What is the purpose of a Voyager Company? What do you think are significant goals for the Voyager Company to set up and successfully attain this year? Why? What do you see as your role with the Voyager Company? What are your thoughts about being a member of the Voyager Company?

Senior Presentation

After the senior presentation, where do you see yourself in the program? What ideas were important to you? What are some ideas the seniors brought up that were new to you? Do you have more questions? How would you evaluate this presentation? How would you assess yourself so far in this program? What would you like to say to them about their presentations?

(continued)

Figure 3.6.   Journal Reflections *(continued)*

Personal and Professional Self-Assessment and Reflection
The junior year is finished. As you look back, describe your experience this semester.
What adjectives would you use to describe this semester? Do you see yourself as successful? Why or why not? How would you rate the program so far? What will you do
differently next year to make the program work better for you?

Large Group Activity: Voyager Program Themes and Demonstrated Competencies

What are the themes of the Voyager program? Use posters for theme display and use reflective sheets (fig. 3.7). Why are they valid? Review each
theme with students and ask them to explain in their own words how they
understand the four themes and their importance. How will teachers and
students know they have successfully completed the themes? There are
competencies associated with each of the themes and ways in which students can demonstrate their accomplishment. These competencies are by
no means an exhaustive list. They were written for students with a range
of abilities and talents. The curriculum approaches teaching a differentiated classroom so that learning is adjusted to meet the needs of all students. Refer to themes and the demonstrated competencies listed in their
portfolios and in the handbook. Students are also invited to create their
own performance-based activities as there are multiple forms of assessment that can be co-created between students and teachers as they
progress in the program.

Have students take the "My Dictionary Definition" exercise and place it
in the proper area of their portfolio. This is the first assignment for self-reflection and self-assessment.

Large Group Activity: Graduation Standards

1. Discuss the graduation standards with the students.
2. Distribute the graduation standards, Career Investigation and Interpersonal Communication Skills, which will frame their studies in the program.
3. Ask students to reflect and brainstorm on how achievement of the
   standards will be demonstrated in the portfolios they will be compiling.
4. Encourage the students to analyze and interpret the pros and cons of
   "standards" in education in a follow-up discussion. How do these stan-

Figure 3.7. Voyager Program Themes

---

1. Look at each of the displayed posters that list a theme of the Voyager program. Below, make a note about the meaning of each theme:

   - Theme:
   - Meaning:

   - Theme:
   - Meaning:

   - Theme:
   - Meaning:

   - Theme:
   - Meaning:

2. For each theme, list some ways we can measure whether we've successfully achieved each theme:

---

dards influence their lives? What are their concerns? How are they interpreting these standards? How relevant are they to their lives and to their learning? What concerns do they have about fulfilling these standards? What type of support will they need (this is an ongoing question)?

Graduation/Academic Standard: Decision Making—
Career Investigation

Students demonstrate understanding of a variety of career clusters, attributes, and aptitudes needed in particular types of occupations and careers; how attitudes and behaviors affect the climate of a workplace; how systems within a workplace affect or interact with systems in the community; and how systems affect an individual worker by:

- Determining personal interest, aptitudes, and abilities
- Establishing an explicit career action plan, including selecting a program that meets a career or vocational preparation goal
- Investigating a career through research, internship, mentorship, or community service
- Evaluating career choices in relationship to life goals and personal attributes

Graduation/Academic Standard: Write and Speak—
Interpersonal Communication

Students demonstrate understanding of interpersonal communication strategies, the components of the interpersonal communication process, and how various patterns affect patterns of communication, interaction, and problem solving in group settings by:

- Using appropriate English language conventions and communication skills in varied interpersonal situations
- Demonstrating effective speaking skills, effective listening skills, appropriate feedback, problem-solving techniques, effective group skills, and communication strategies in a variety of simulated or authentic situations; and using skills of conciliation, mediation, or negotiation to improve communication

Voyager Certificates Introduction

The successful mastery of the Voyager program themes and the graduation standards and completion of connected workplace internships and activities will result in the awarding of Voyager certification (fig. 3.8). These certificates are endorsed by the Chamber of Commerce and the school district. Assessment teams composed of all Voyager community stakeholders will review and finalize achievement of credentials. These certificates are held in high esteem by the education and business communities as they symbolize the successful completion of a rigorous and substantial program. Voyager certification enables students to obtain an edge over other applicants for future jobs because of the value placed on this preparation program.

1. Show the Voyager program credentials (from the Voyager student handbook, Book Four) and explain what expectations—including work and academic—need to be met. Why do you think credentials are necessary?
2. Ask students to think about what it will take to fulfill the requirements for the credentials.
3. Show a sample of the certificate. Explain different levels of Voyager certification (use overhead). Level 1 is awarded to secondary students; Level 2 is awarded to postsecondary students.
4. Ask if they have questions regarding any of the above.

Voyager Community Events

These events are directly connected to the various program aspects and provide the additional support for Voyager students. The events could include parent and family Celebration of Achievement dinners; advisory board meet-

Figure 3.8.   Voyager Certificate

VOYAGER: DIRECTION FOR LEARNING & CAREERS®
Minneapolis Regional Chamber *of* Commerce

THE MINNEAPOLIS REGIONAL CHAMBER OF COMMERCE
AND THE MINNEAPOLIS PUBLIC SCHOOLS

CERTIFY THAT

Student Name

has successfully completed the
Voyager Program

DATE

President/CEO, Minneapolis Regional Chamber of Commerce   Superintendent of Minneapolis Public Schools

ings with parents, teachers, and business partners; career-oriented meetings with parents; meetings with other teachers; networking meetings with business partners; and the Annual Chamber of Commerce Quality of Life dinner, which highlights the Voyager program and ways for Voyager students to network with business leaders. (Facilitator can show PowerPoint pictures from previous Voyager events.) Ask students to think about a timeline for these events. How do you begin to plan your year to include all these events? What are some other events you might want to include in this program? What are some of the challenges you will have to meet this commitment? What help do you need?

Large Group Activity: Managing Time Effectively

Begin a discussion of developing time management and what importance it plays in everyone's lives. Time management is not an illusive and difficult practice to understand, nor is it a difficult set of skills to develop. The challenge is doing it! What is necessary in time management is to establish and then prioritize what you need to do in a day. How do you manage your day and make plans?

1. Have the students brainstorm general routines and procedures—both positive and negative—that they currently engage in.
2. Introduce planner and start out with blank calendars for the next semester.

Managing your time in the Voyager program will be paramount. You will need to be prepared at all times and effectively integrate your home and personal life. When we are out of balance with our time management, conflicts occur because we are overbooked and cannot follow through on our commitments, our stress level increases to unmanageable levels, and we can even feel bad about who we are because our goals are not completed.

1. Distribute a blank day calendar (fig. 3.9).
2. Time Management Practice: Ask students to write down their entire day beginning at 7:00 A.M. going through until 10:00 P.M. (not just their

Figure 3.9.　Your Date Timer: What Do You Do Each Day?

Take the time to write down what you do each part of the next three days. After three days, decide where you could have done things differently. According to this sheet, how do you spend your time? How can you manage your time better? What one time management goal will you now set? On the back of this sheet, brainstorm some ideas you have for how you could change how you manage your time.

Time of Day	Day One	Day Two	Day Three
7:00–8:00 A.M.			
8:00–9:00 A.M.			
9:00–10:00 A.M.			
11:00 A.M.–12:00 P.M.			
12:00–1:00 P.M.			
1:00–2:00 P.M.			
2:00–3:00 P.M.			
3:00–4:00 P.M.			
4:00–5:00 P.M.			
5:00–6:00 P.M.			
6:00–7:00 P.M.			
7:00–8:00 P.M.			
8:00–9:00 P.M.			
9:00–10:00 P.M.			

school day) and to explain how they will manage to meet all of their responsibilities for that day. How do you spend your time? How do you manage your time? What are the challenges you face in meeting different commitments? Are there some other ways that will help you better manage your time? How do you find time to do your schoolwork? How do you set goals for what you want to accomplish? Who are some of the people who can help you with your time management? Brainstorm ways that provide strategies for change.

Large Group Activity: Meet Business Leaders—Team Collaboration and Meeting Project Goals

Each year, businesspeople come in and work on current ideas and issues facing the business community. Students have the opportunity to see how businesses work and to experience team-based learning and problem solving from the start of the program. During this part of the workshop day, students will have a chance to meet and work with business representatives for several hours both on an individual level and in teams. They get a close look at authentic business practices and begin to ask important questions as to how things are run in certain companies—questions that look at ethical decision making, social justice, and democratic communities. It is also at this time that students learn to connect both the head and the hand and bridge the gap between academic and work-site education as they work on projects. There is a real benefit to this component when they can see the practical application of knowledge and ideas, apply their skills to real-world problems, and communicate their thoughts to each other. Working on projects brought in by the business representatives actively engages them and models the collaborative teamwork that is now so prominent in the workplace.

This is the initial immersion of the Voyager students to work with business in a formal setting. This is also another component that engenders learning by doing and learning to learn. Students usually characterize this segment as more interesting and demanding than they previously envisioned. They are treated as developing professionals who will be supported with ongoing assistance as they make decisions for their future careers and who have optimal expectations placed before them.

Plan these activities for the students:

1. Have a business leader come in to the class with an actual miniproject to get students working together to solve problems on issues presented. Business leaders set the stage regarding the issue to be solved, give directions for outcome, and have the class work in teams to come up with a solution. Each team must develop a plan that identifies the team's

goals, tasks to be accomplished to achieve the goals, who is responsible for achieving the tasks, and a timeline to monitor progress.

Suggestions for team projects that have proven successful:

- Analyze company data to solve a current problem on which the company must make a decision.
- Use case studies from personnel issues where teams must determine how they would work out these disputes.
- Make plans for a new community-based project with the business. The teams have to organize a timeline and plan of action that would work.
- Decide on charitable disbursement of $250,000 in company contributions. The team will identify and choose recipients, decide how much each recipient receives, and explain why each recipient was awarded funds.
- Write and produce the company newsletter. The team must determine topics and deadlines, who writes which story and why, and how proofing and editing will be accomplished.
- Coordinate a volunteer program for all company employees. The team will coordinate and schedule activities as well as promote employee participation.
- Create a new product or production plan.
- Create a new company image based on market research.

2. As an alternative activity, have a technology assessment survey and demonstration. Have a technology assistant and computer lab (or sufficient laptops) available. This is an opportune time to survey the students for their technology abilities and skills. What levels of understanding and capabilities exist so that future lessons are built on the skills of the current group? It also provides an opportunity to demonstrate what past Voyager students have accomplished and possibilities for future projects. Student demonstrations include: use of PowerPoint for future classroom presentations, use of e-portfolio software, email distribution lists, and bulletin board discussions. This technology training needs to continue throughout the program, especially as student groups become more sophisticated with the different uses of technology and have access to a variety of programs for research gathering.

Usually this lesson component suggests alternative or additional activities for students who are working at various learning levels and who demonstrate various interests. In this workshop, we have found that students will need more time to understand the different areas of the Voyager program.

1. Let the students choose which of the following areas they want to work in. This provides one of the first activities for self-assessment and choice. Many will need more information on some of the different components presented to them today.
2. As the students are working, walk around and work with each of the groups as the students work collaboratively in small groups and learn to help each other.
   - Students continue work on portfolio development. They can brainstorm other materials that will be useful; they can develop questions for further examination of portfolio usage by reading from the Voyager community handbook where ideas regarding assessment, evaluation, and demonstrated competencies are clearly laid out.
   - Students can begin writing their personal philosophy on lifelong learning, including "formal" education, and work on their first portfolio document.
   - Students can begin sketching out ideas for final collage.
   - Students can write a journal entry reflecting on the day's events as well as include what questions and/or concerns they have for the program.

Performance-Based Assessments

- Self-reflection skills and values
- Initial portfolio document
- Students begin working in groups to build interview skills

CONCLUSION

Recap major points from the lesson. What important points throughout the day resonated for you? What lingering concerns do you have?

Small groups will choose one area to discuss and describe categories of expectations that must be fulfilled in order to be a successful Voyager community member and to answer the above questions. Groups then report to the entire class.

ASSIGNMENT

1. Distribute articles on the history of work education. Groups of students (assigned by random numbering) will be responsible for one of the six articles and will teach the class what they have learned—through cooperative learning and the jigsaw strategy—from the article. Each group will pose two questions that it wants discussed by the rest of the class. Articles are researched by both coordinator and students. Some

examples are excerpts from *How Do We Tell the Workers?* (Kincheloe, 1999); "Vocational Education as Symbolic Action: Connecting School with the Workplace" (Kliebard, 1990); *History of Industrial Education in the United States* (Barlow, 1967); and "Sociocultural Perspectives on Work and Schooling in Urban America" (Edson, 1979). Teachers are encouraged to find other articles that are a better fit for their context.

The jigsaw strategy (Aronson, 1978) is a procedure where each person in the group is given a different section of an article to read and learn. Students will take different sections of the article and then depend on each other to develop a successful presentation and to teach the rest of the class about their section. Each group will receive one of the six articles regarding the history of work education. The students will take time to meet with the other students in their group and decide what sections each member will take and how each will present the information at the first class meeting. One of the most important ways we learn is from each other—cooperative learning. By having different groups read and present the material, everyone in class gets the benefit of learning more information through a variety of teaching methods that go beyond reading and lecturing. Each group member is responsible for learning the information so that he or she can participate in the group to organize the presentation to the rest of the class. Each group is responsible for learning and presenting the materials in a clear and understandable manner. They are also encouraged to critique the material and to pose questions regarding the topics. This is the first time they will work together to unpack and analyze information regarding historical and cultural trends. Although the students will be given time to meet together before they have to present, please have them make arrangements to meet outside of class as well. Have them exchange telephone numbers or email addresses in order to have discussions. Each member must write out one question that he or she wants answered as a result of the reading. Then the group will decide which questions will be posed to the class.

2. Have students complete the first journal reflection: Personal and Professional Goals. Please refer to the list of journal entries in figure 3.6 for a full description of this writing assignment. Distribute the list of journal entries that need to be included in the students' portfolios. Students are urged to write as many entries as they wish as long as they fulfill the journal entry.

3. Distribute the Personal Growth Action Plan handout (fig. 3.10). Now that we are beginning to see ourselves from different perspectives, it is

Figure 3.10.   Personal Growth Action Plan

---

1. List and describe three things you want to change about yourself this year. You can include anything you want. What I want to change and why I want to change it:
   -
   -
   -
2. How will I accomplish these changes? What do I need to do to accomplish them?
3. Who will I ask for help? How will I make decisions for change? Who are my role models and mentors? What have they contributed to my growth?
4. What is my timeline? Create a chart with your changes and timeline.

---

time to plan to take action for change. Write a Personal Growth Action Plan for yourself. List and describe three personal changes that you will make for yourself this year. These can be any type of changes, such as quitting smoking, reading two novels per month, riding your bike each day until you reach seven miles per day, joining a club, learning how to drive, and so on. These should be real goals that you have always wanted to fulfill and now have the chance to accomplish. Write out how you will accomplish your goals, who you will ask for help, and what your timeline for achieving these goals will be. This assignment will be due at our next meeting. Remember Personal Growth Plans are created as temporary outlooks to our future. They will need to be edited and adjusted from time to time.

Unit 1B

Personal and Professional Growth

LESSON TOPIC: PERSPECTIVES ON THE HISTORY OF WORK AND VOCATIONAL EDUCATION

Teaching Note

Setting the stage for program success and career development begins by taking a critical perspective of academic and work education over the last one hundred years. Students will explore the social, political, and historical influences that have shaped work education. They will investigate their legacy—what has been part of the history of school-to-career development. In this way they will begin to develop a critical inquiry and critical consciousness of various school reforms and attitudes toward work education, and they will be able to create a vision for the future. The readings and classroom dialogues set the stage for dealing with contradictory information and evidence that they will need to analyze and reinterpret in their own lives. This lesson will begin to introduce and alert students to the complexities of the contentious history of academic and vocational education, the realities of the work world they are currently experiencing, and the opportunities for producing new meanings of justice and democracy for their future worlds.

This topic is not usually covered from a critical lens in the curriculum, and as students are urged to do a more in-depth study, teachers will have to develop some new strategies for dealing with opposing perspectives and differing social experiences voiced in the classroom discussions. By employing new strategies of critical inquiry and reflection, both students and teachers can begin an in-depth examination of workplace realities and develop an understanding of shared problems across various career pathways steeped in respectful classroom discussions. They will also be asked to create new possibilities for themselves and their career aspirations.

Objectives

To understand the historical, social, and political forces that shaped the current state of work education
To identify workforce changes and future needs

Domains

Cognitive: Develop analytic and critical interpretation of historical vocational education
Affective: Demonstrate cooperative learning behavior and language
Skills: Use evaluation and analysis skills

Academic Standard: Write and Speak in the English Language

Interpersonal Communication Skills
Effective speaking and listening skills
Effective group skills

Materials

Articles describing the history of work education (coordinator will select a variety of articles that represent different aspects of the history of work education describing how schools and business have functioned in the past)
Workers and Working at the Turn of the Century handout (fig. 3.11)
Working by Studs Terkel (excerpts of worker profiles)
Pictures/slides/postcards/posters from the different decades throughout the industrial revolution to the 1990s depicting different worlds of work and learning. Most are available from various state historical societies.
The Life and Times of Rosie the Riveter video

Pre-Instructional

Students will complete a Personal Growth Action Plan (fig. 3.10). They will read from a variety of articles and chapters on the history of work education (for example: Studs Terkel, *Working*; Joe Kincheloe, *Toil and Trouble*; Richard Lakes, *Critical Pedagogy for Vocational-Technical Educators*; Eleni Roulis, *Perspectives on Work Education*; Herbert Kliebard, *Schooled to Work*).

Also, students will have attended a summer workshop for an entire day that includes:

- Teamwork development as demonstrated by actually working on a miniproject
- Portfolio development and ways to meet program expectations

Introductory Framework

At our first meeting, we focused on personal growth and self-reflection. Our focus was taking time for self-reflection and understanding more about different aspects of who we are. We will continue to explore this area of self-discovery for further development. We will then focus on how current academic and work education opportunities have been shaped by the past century:

1. What impact will there be on future work opportunities?
2. What does it mean to be a smart worker?
3. What is good work?
4. How can schools reform academic studies so that they will foster good work and produce smart workers?

Motivation

Have the students think about this question: Who am I today?

Allow students around fifteen minutes to complete the Examining and Challenging My Values, Goals, and Assumptions activity; it is the second in the series that started with My Dictionary Definition. Please note that you will have to determine how much time to spend on each strategy and on the discussion that follows a strategy. We prefer to leave this decision to your discretion as you know the needs of your own group better than we possibly could. Needless to say, you should plan the exercise beforehand and estimate roughly how much time it will take. When using these strategies and activities, please encourage a classroom atmosphere of openness, honesty, acceptance, good listening skills, respect, and thoughtful reflection. If students do not want to respond, they are given the right to pass without question or comment from the group.

1. Have the students list in their notebook twenty things they like to do in life (adapted from Simon, Howe, and Kirschenbaum, 1972). Only they will see the list, so have them write down as much as they want. They don't need to use complete sentences—have them brainstorm with themselves. They can list big things that they like to do, or little things. They can think in terms of seasons, occupation, hobbies, sports, or any other category.

The teacher can also engage in creating his or her own list. This exercise can be developed into a spreadsheet and used throughout the year so that students can start to compare their lists over a period of time. Teachers can add other categories to this list (R = actions that are risky; C = items that are conventional; UC = items that are unconventional; E = items that need further education. But adding more than five or six categories at one sitting can result in an overload for students). Lists can be shorter or longer than twenty items.

2. When everyone is finished, go over the following instructions and complete them together. Place:

   A—next to everything you do only alone,

   P—next to everything you only do with other people,

   A/P—next to everything you do equally alone and with other people,

   $—next to all the things that cost $10 or more to do (money amount varies depending on your group), and

   N5—next to all the things you would not have done five years ago.

   Each class member will look at her or his list and make an analysis. For example, how many people listed twenty items that they do alone or with other people? Fewer than fifteen? Fewer than ten? Fewer than five? What are some categories that appear to emerge for the students? (For example, artistic, sports, physical, and so on.) How can we draw conclusions? Remind students that conclusions are not criticisms—they are observations that may not have value attached to them.

3. Next, based on the conclusions from the above activity, have students write a paragraph that begins with any of the following:

   • I was happy to find out that I . . .

   • I was surprised to find out that I . . .

   • I was disappointed to find out that I . . .

   • I learned that I . . .

   • I realized that I . . .

   Ask students to volunteer to share some of their new insights and conclusions. Advise students to keep lists and to think how they might add some information toward the creation of their final collage of Who Am I Today?

INSTRUCTIONAL IMPLEMENTATION

Large Group Activity: Workers and Working at the Turn of the Century (Fig. 3.11)

The history of work education has taken many turns throughout the last one hundred years. Basically, there has always been a contention between what

Figure 3.11.   Workers and Working at the Turn of the Century

---

1. What is the difference between academic and vocational education?

2. What did you see in the slides that you:
   - knew?
   - were surprised by?
   - liked?
   - didn't like?

3. What type of world is being portrayed in these pictures?

4. How would you interpret this idea: "Working with your hands versus working with your mind"?

5. How does this view play out in today's world?
   - Economically?
   - Politically?
   - Professionally?
   - Educationally?

---

was called academic and vocational education. Show slides of turn-of-the-century workers in action (some videos are also available in these areas). As slides are shown, have students interpret and comment on what they see, answering the following questions:

1. What is the difference between academic and vocational education?
2. What did you see in the slides that you knew about already?
3. What did you see in the slides that you were surprised by?
4. What did you see in the slides that you liked?
5. What did you see in the slides that you didn't like?
6. What type of world is being portrayed in these pictures?
7. How would you interpret the phrase "working with your hands versus working with your mind"?
8. How does this view play out in today's world—economically, politically, professionally, educationally? Are these work scenes still viable in today's world?

Small Group Activity: The Poetry of Real People—The Hardness of Real Lives

Student triads will work together on this segment. Each triad will choose and read excerpts from *Working* by Studs Terkel, a book of portraits of workers and their lives, to each other. After each excerpt, each student will comment on what he or she has learned regarding this particular profile and his or her response to the reading. Following are some suggestions for small group discussion:

1. Why do you think other writers and critics have described this book as being about "violence to the mind and to the spirit"?
2. Would you consider the people in this book heroes and heroines?
3. What qualities and spirit do they bring to their stories and to their work that goes beyond a salary?
4. How do these stories make us look at our own lives and work?
5. What are some conclusions about work and workers that can be made from Terkel's book?

Each triad will report to the entire class and student leaders will record answers on large poster boards. Then all of the lists will be typed up and stored in the career center for future reference. Extra copies will be made for any student who wishes to keep them in his or her own portfolio.

Large Group Activity: A Legacy and a Search for the Mystique of Work

1. What is meant by work education? What are some of the strategies that have been used to promote a particular kind of work education?
2. From what we have just viewed in slides and video excerpts, how has this idea been defined in terms of social, political, and economic concerns?
3. How would you redefine work education using a critical pedagogy lens?
4. How does having power involve learning to act in one's own behalf? Do you think that corporations and other political groups want to see work education redefined and to question the decisions that are being made to shape their and their fellow workers' futures?
5. How have working-class families been stereotyped in terms of their abilities and their career choices?
6. How have past educational and work practices discriminated against and separated women, people of color, immigrants, and the poor by tracking them into certain programs?
7. How are professionals being defined differently?
8. Where do you see yourself in this history and how has it affected you and your family? What do you want to have as your legacy of work?

Small Group Activity: Perspectives on Work and Education

Each group will gather and meet for twenty minutes to rehearse their presentation based on their response to the article they have read for homework.

The students will determine the procedure for presentation, as well as encourage class discussion when the presentation is completed. Each group will have fifteen minutes to present their viewpoints. During this time, students must synthesize the information they gleaned from the article and then pose questions for discussion to the class. Each group will select a facilitator for the whole class discussion.

Large Group Activity: An Analysis of the Video *The Life and Times of Rosie the Riveter* (or Any Video of Teacher's Choice)

How does this video accurately portray the women and work at these times? What conflicting issues do you find? Do they still hold true today? What has changed? What needs to change? Introduce the following guidelines for watching and responding to the video:

1. Have students free write on what they expect to see in the video—what are their ideas regarding this historical period?
2. Have students take notes on what resonates for them. What are they particularly struck by? (Class notes can be collected, collated, and shared by all.)
3. What questions do students have about the video? Keep a list of questions, about the author, about the character, about the historical events, the time and place.
4. What perspective is being shown—is this a fair or biased presentation of the situation?
5. What is some of the historical background that is presented?
6. How far removed are the time and place from students' current lives?
7. Ask students to consider the differences between the world they live in and the world portrayed in the film. How are women viewed in this world? How are they viewed today?

How to Use the Voyager Classroom Critical Event Survey (Adapted from Brookfield, 1995) (fig. 3.12)

Please take a few minutes to respond to each of the Voyager Classroom Critical Event Survey questions about this week's seminar. This survey helps teachers and students understand how and what is being learned in the seminar. Please respond openly and honestly to the following questions. All of the responses will be collected anonymously and then summarized for all to read at the next seminar. Please leave one copy of the survey form on the teacher's desk as you leave the room.

In this way, the teacher will be able to be more responsive to the students' concerns, and students will be able to describe moments that are significant

Figure 3.12.   Voyager Classroom Critical Event Survey

1. What was the most exciting and interesting moment you had during class today?
2. What moments or events caused you to lose interest during class today?
3. Did anything surprise you in class today? For example, something that was said, an action that someone took, your reaction to something.
4. What new piece of information did you learn today?
5. What would you like to see added to this class lesson the next time it is taught?
6. What else would you like to add that you would want all of us to know about?

Adapted from Brookfield, 1995.

to them. In order to best understand what has been learned or not learned in class, it is important for the coordinator to know how students understood and felt about the lesson. Pass out the survey and then go over the directions. At the end of every other seminar, the students will take five minutes before the end of class to reflect about the day and give feedback regarding the class. All responses will remain anonymous, and students will receive the summarized responses during the next class. Each of the surveys is printed on carbonless paper so that both the coordinator and the students each have a copy of the remarks that they keep for the entire semester.

Optional Plans

1. Students can interview family members and/or friends on how they experienced choosing careers, working, and learning when they were in school. What were their career choices based on? Did they feel they had choices? What were any restrictions they encountered? How did they find a way around the restrictions or were they unable to choose from options? Were they able to achieve economic security? Did they have access to career advancement and financial mobility?
2. Show other videos and clips from television of working-class issues—either documentaries or sitcoms. Have students explain what they see and what is presented as reality to them. What do they agree/disagree with?
3. Show clips from movies that highlight and signify success in certain professions (e.g., *Trading Places, 9-5, Wall Street, Working Girl, The Associates, The Firm,* and so on). How does the film industry shape our worlds of work—what are the myths that are perpetrated on young people, especially those from working-class or immigrant families?
4. Create a survey, with demographics of gender, age, and job description (using both closed and open-ended questions), that asks

workers what they think was missing in their education that would have helped them in career choices and in planning their futures. Students should clear this with their work supervisors before employing the survey.

5. Have students re-create in video a type of atmosphere like the one presented in *Working* by Studs Terkel; have them take video cameras around town and interview different people working in different careers. They will need to create a set of questions before interviewing the workers. They will also need to have a signed video release from each of the persons being taped.

6. Show the video *The Women of Summer: The Bryn Mawr School for Women Workers* and work with students to create an analysis of the film. What was most surprising in this video? Have them research other videos along the same themes, such as *Union Maids* and *Babies and Banners*.

7. Have students create a Work Education Center with historical information, current/local information, and a career networking and people section that they will continuously develop throughout the program. This center will serve as an authentic, practical research and investigation resource that students will utilize and operate throughout their two years of study.

8. Have students create a common folder for collecting current shared experiences and issues they have encountered at work that will be examined and analyzed by the class. They can use these experiences to create a class project, to present to new Voyager students, or to create a discussion forum on their web site that will assist and support students in clarifying their professional goals.

9. Have students engage in The Organic Goodie Simulation found in *The Power in Our Hands,* by William Bigelow and Norman Diamond (1988). This simulation has students experience the pressures workers face in organizing themselves and asks the question "Can people work together to accomplish needed changes?"

10. Bring in speakers to talk about aspects of the work and academic worlds captured in the videos the students viewed (e.g., historians, workers in that time, etc.).

11. Have students research the Smith-Hughes Act or the Perkins Act and analyze its impact on work education and similar school-to-career programs such as theirs around the nation.

12. Have students research local companies and their work practices. What has happened to these companies as a result of economic changes, demographic changes, and decisions to recruit employees

outside the area to save money? What about at their stories? For example, in Minnesota, the LTV steel mill, the taconite industry, and the logging industry have all had to deal with uncertainty, downsizing, and extinction.

13. Have students interview and invite labor organizers in their city to come in and participate in a panel discussion. Ask organizers to bring in union materials. Students need to research the unions and their work before the representatives come to class so that they will have informed questions for the discussion.

14. Students can choose to create a timeline covering the last century based on the complex historical events globally and demonstrating how different economies and workers were affected. This timeline can remain fixed on the wall throughout the year as students add information to it. Using this information, they are able to create an understanding of critical pedagogy for work education to use in future projects.

15. Have students research and debate the inconsistencies of vocational work education. Why is it that the training that students often get in these programs falls short of a good education and certainly does not prepare them for the social mobility that they seek and believe in? Good work and a democratic workplace will not automatically appear as proselytized by many political groups. It is imperative that students reshape the concept of work in relation to their lives as democratic participants. Have them review, analyze, and suggest alternatives to the following myths:

    • You have been born into a situation with bad odds, but play the game and try to get ahead. You are bound to succeed because look at all of the others who have gone against the odds even when they have started from the bottom rung of the ladder.

    • Just accept the fate of your family and your parents—work hard at a dead-end job. You can always get consolation and address the pain of such work through other means (like alcohol, gambling, drugs).

    • When you don't know what to do—join the military. There you will have access to so many privileges and adventures, including obtaining a good education.

    • Become a dropout. Take the big risk—leave school and join up with a gang or with other scam runners who break the law and find the big payoff. That is the essence of entrepreneurial spirit.

16. Compare and contrast Michael Moore's documentary *Flint, Michigan* and *Babies and Banners* by Lorraine Gray.

Performance-Based Assessments

- Student presentations on work education
- Student responses to slide show and videos

CONCLUSION

Take five minutes to do freewriting, reflecting on what you have become aware of today. What are the outstanding forces that have shaped education and working in the last one hundred years? What changes are necessary for the twenty-first century? What do you expect to fulfill in your work education? What type of education do we need to prepare students for an alternative vision of work?

Figure 3.13.   Professional Career Action Plan

Think about your life goals. Set four major goals in your life at this time. In essence, you are creating your life map; you are setting a direction for your life. What are your long-term goals? What do you not want to do?

Using a chart with the headings Goals, Steps to Take, Time, Challenges, and People to Contact for Help, write down your one- and two-year goals. Set timelines for each. What challenges do you have to take into consideration? Write down your goals for this week and for this month. List any challenges you would have to attaining these goals.

Announce your goals out loud. Have your friends serve as consultants and give you feedback on your goals.

Are there any assumptions or beliefs you would have to give up in order to attain your goals?

ASSIGNMENT

1. Complete the Professional Career Action Plan (fig. 3.13).
2. Choose an artifact to present to the class that you believe symbolizes who you are.

Unit 1C

Personal and Professional Growth

LESSON TOPIC: CREATING CLASSROOM RITUALS AND CODES AND BUILDING A DEMOCRATIC LEARNING COMMUNITY

Teaching Note

Understanding, defining, and establishing a democratic learning community involves incorporating multiple learning perspectives that build trust so that students can learn to work together. Students are not often asked to design or to define a democratic learning community in which they will learn and work together. Often they have been in places that use a listing of things "not to do" in school. Here they are asked to define and interpret the concept of democracy, how it plays into their lives and in the classroom, what challenges and contradictions they find in a democracy, and how to change democracy for themselves. Dewey's idea, "to conceive and construct the school as a social institution, having social life and value within itself" (1916, p. 417), is the organizing principle for a unified and participatory curriculum based on students' interpersonal and academic activities. It is key in fostering values of cooperation and moral reasoning for common good.

Voyager students will stay together as a group for two years. They are called upon to decide what beliefs and strategies they need to implement in order to work together successfully. They will determine what rituals and traditions need to be created and developed that will support their growth, both individually and socially. They will also determine classroom operations and will be responsible for becoming citizens of the classroom, the school, and society. This learning community will provide a positive forum for the expression of opposing and multiple views and will be developed as the students move through the program. Students will produce a revitalized democracy as they learn to respect each other's perspectives and work together employing alternative classroom practices. In creating such a classroom, the responsibility falls on all Voyager community members to participate and engage—both individually and as a group. The Voyager classroom is an intentionally created environment of support and trust where students of all abilities will achieve. This is not about a quick fix to control student behavior or to make everyone sit down, listen to each other, and be nice. Forging a real community results from struggling with issues, developing an ethic of care, and respecting others while discussing opposing viewpoints. Students connect with each other through sharing their stories, perspectives, passions, and power. The learning environment provides opportunities for students to talk to each other about joyful and painful matters, to learn through developing caring and respectful relationships. The support comes from a curriculum that teaches them about genuine empathy. The caring relationships offer radical ways of changing classroom culture, dynamics, and experiences among students, as well as between students and teachers. How do we make cooperation/collaboration a reality? How can we learn to work well together? How can we find ways to problem solve, negotiate, engage with, and be kind to each other? How can we build a positive climate together? They are then encouraged to see how this type of learning environment can be utilized in the workplace as well.

Objectives

To create a democratic classroom code that will build authentic community learning and affirm positive interaction and learning relationships among Voyager students

To develop healthy habits of mind so that students will model good citizenry in their action in school, at work, and in the community

Domains

Cognitive: Understand and learn to choose from alternatives
Affective: Demonstrate cooperative learning and caring behavior
Skills: Develop good citizenship skills

Academic Standard: Write and Speak in the English Language

Interpersonal Communication Skills
Effective speaking and listening skills

Effective group skills
Résumé writing

Materials

Colored sticker dots, any size
Large poster boards or flipcharts
Overhead with Voyager social contract statement for each to individually
sign; it is then framed and hung up (this social contract can have various
names: Class Constitution, Class Bill of Rights, Voyager Social Justice
Agreement, etc.)
Voyager contract also needs to be individually signed
Individual Learning Contract

Pre-Instructional

Students are to have completed the Professional Career Action Plan from the
last seminar meeting.

Students bring personal artifacts with them. They will research and share
the history of their name (i.e., from what language is their name derived?).
What does their name mean? Who were they named for? Where do other
names in class originate? What do you like or dislike about your name?

Introductory Framework

At our last meeting, we focused on personal growth, reflecting upon our current life situations and developing goals for the future. Our focus was taking
time for self-reflection and understanding about different aspects of who we
are—examining our assumptions and asking what we know about ourselves,
how we came to know it, and who we want to become. We will continue this
process and then move our focus to how we will work and learn together
over the next two years. How do we establish a caring classroom? How will
we define what a caring classroom will look and feel like?

Motivation

Students were asked to bring in one illustrative symbol/artifact and also to tell
the class about the history of their names. Ask each student to come to the
front of the room and show his or her artifact and explain how it represents
him or her. Have them talk about their name and the history of it. (Students
can choose to do this either in a large group or in a small group depending
upon how much time will be allotted for this activity.) Students will talk about
how the symbol/artifact represents who they are, their culture, and their

beliefs. For example, one student displayed a teapot she received from her grandmother and explained that for her it represents a quiet time, gratitude, and a way of inviting someone into her space to share conversation. Another student displayed a braid of sweetgrass and explained that it is symbolic of his tribe's purification rituals. He volunteered to perform the ceremony with the class at the end of the seminar. With this activity, students begin to share their stories and cultural histories. It is a time when they can begin to get inside each other's lives and become real people to each other. This is the foundation for the empathy we spoke of earlier. This is the beginning of bringing students' lives from the margins and placing them in the center of the curriculum. Much new and rich information is exchanged. This experience will lead to creating a learning and empathetic community. Other students in the class are invited to respond to the artifact—without judgment—as well as ask questions. Whether in a small or large group, students need to keep a list of the artifacts and an explanation of them for the Voyager archives (fig. 3.14). Students can also combine artifacts for expression of a group identity.

An alternative to bringing in artifacts (or an additional activity for students) emerged from one group of Voyager students that decided to tell how they were named and where their names originated. The class had a mix of names from twelve different countries and many students had tried to adopt nicknames to make their names more accommodating to American pronunciation. When students are willing to conduct a history of their naming, their stories create an opportunity to learn more about each other's stories, cultural backgrounds, families, and experiences. This activity also placed students and their lives squarely into the heart of the curriculum and prompted them to get to know each other's names from the beginning. (They discovered how naming is connected to familial obligations, religious beliefs, cultural traditions, national affiliations, and political and historical events that stripped many families of their names and identity.)

This activity provided another opportunity to develop a foundation for a respectful learning community. Students connected with the diverse cultural heritages represented in the classroom and the school, and they could understand each other in terms of their varying social and cultural contexts. They began to know each other on more personal, intimate, and real levels.

INSTRUCTIONAL IMPLEMENTATION

Large Group Activity: Communities and Democracy (fig. 3.15)

Ask students to take a few minutes to write down their understanding of the words "building community." *Community* comes from the Latin word *communitas* and is defined as people who live in the same place or who share something in common. There are many types of community—neighborhoods,

Figure 3.14. Artifacts: Story of a Life

Student	Voyager Class	Artifact	Story

sports, religious, school, work. What are some indicators of community? What does creating community require? Take time to respond to the questions on your reflection sheet: Communities and Democracy.

Large Group Activity: Creating a Democratic Community (fig. 3.16)

Give students a framework. You will be together as a group for the next two years. You will build the Voyager community together. Each Voyager group is distinctive and has its own unique characteristics and needs. The Voyager community, or cohort (a group of people who are studying or

Figure 3.15.   Reflection: Communities and Democracy

1. What are your first thoughts when you read the words *building community*? "Community" comes from the Latin word *communitas* and is defined as people who live in the same place or who share something in common. There are many types of community—neighborhood, sports, religious, school, work. What are some indicators of community? What does creating community require?
2. What communities do you belong to?
3. Describe what it means to you to belong to these communities. How have you experienced being part of a community in other areas (e.g., club, place of work, team, theatrical production, etc.)?
4. List what has been positive and what has been not so positive about your experience in building community.
5. Why should we value community as part of our societal norm?
6. What is an ideal community for you?

working on a project together), structure will offer a variety of opportunities for everyone to work, grow, and learn together. Just as we are concerned with transforming workplace priorities, we are concerned with educational and learning priorities. This is the chance to change and to create ways to learn. We need to create ways of building community that will be beneficial for everyone. How will we build an effective Voyager community that allows for individual growth, the formation of a connected cohort group, mutual respect, and positive interaction among group members as some of our primary goals? How is this connected to a caring classroom?

In a democratic classroom students are engaged in the cooperative, reflective, and dynamic processes of developing and evaluating concepts and procedures. They must be permitted to critique classroom routines and activities. They must be able to identify and discuss underlying issues (such as social, political, and power issues) within situations when conflict arises as a result of multiple perspectives being demonstrated in the class. They must produce their own "social contract."

Figure 3.16.   Reflection: Creating a Democratic Community

1. How can we help each other to build individual competencies as well as group successes?
2. How can we create shared decision making?
3. What are the risks you are taking to be involved in this type of classroom?
4. What happens if people start establishing power?
5. What are the advantages to a democratic classroom?
6. What would a caring classroom look like?
7. How is a caring classroom different from a teacher "taking care of" you?
8. What happens in a democratic classroom if someone wants to be "in control"?

Move into a discussion format. The following are some questions to guide a discussion:

- What is a social contract and what responsibilities does it have for individuals?
- What does this statement mean to you?
- How does working collectively (not meant in terms of happy harmony) promote acknowledging and incorporating differences?
- What are different ways we can use these differences?
- What does it require of us as learners in the class? Example: Analyze the following school rule: No talking in the hallways.
- What are the underlying issues of this rule?
- Why do you think it was written?
- Discuss systems (such as schools) and how they operate, the existence of power relations, the pressing social issues, students' individual connection to the "No talking in the hallways" rule, societal demands, the pressures to conform, and so on.
- What other rules are there in school with underlying meanings?
- Years ago, the school system was created by and built on the success and efficiency of the factory model. What does this mean to you? What connections are being made between education and the factory model? Are they legitimate connections?

We need to create classroom rituals and codes on which we can agree. For some people, such rituals and codes have been defined as "habits of mind." What are the mental habits of mind that deal with differences appropriately and that make for good citizens—for school, work, and society? The following questions guide a student free write and class discussion:

- How can we help each other to build individual competencies as well as group successes?
- How can we create shared decision making?
- What do powerful relationships look like? What are the risks you are taking to be involved in this type of classroom? What are the benefits?
- How can we learn effectively together?
- What does a caring classroom mean or suggest? What beliefs does it constitute? Caring suggests that we come to know and be receptive to the needs of others. How can we devote attention to what others need and be open to this knowledge?
- How is caring different than taking care of someone (as in a hospital)? A caring relationship is one in which two people are involved in an equal relationship and are willing to extend time, effort, and understanding to each other.

- What does it mean to be compassionate?
- How does this type of classroom and learning bring our ethics and attitudes into question?
- What is a community steeped in management and control? What are the beliefs inherent in this type of community?

Students free write each time the above questions are asked so that they have started to develop their thoughts before multiple answers and responses are volunteered. Student leaders will write all brainstormed answers on flipcharts.

- As a follow-up to these ideas, consider these questions: How can the classroom and schools become a "sacred space"? Define what that means for you. Where else do you experience sacred space? Have some students research this concept on the web. Is this belief and value something we would like to incorporate into our work and classroom life? How can we define it for ourselves? What will this concept mean to others who enter our sacred space? What rituals and beliefs are connected to creating and maintaining a sacred space?

Small Group Follow-Up Activity: Defining Democracy

Have students break into small groups and consider the following questions:

- Define democracy—what does it look like in action?
- How can it be employed in this class? How would the roles and responsibilities of students and teachers change?
- What advantages are there in developing a democratic classroom?
- What does democracy have to do with power?
- What is challenging about democracy?
- What do you think the following statement means? "There is no right way to teach democracy unless we also practice it."
- Describe a time when you have participated in a democratic situation. The situation does not need to have taken place in a school setting.
- Be ready to report your findings to the whole class.

Have groups share their findings and discuss values with the whole group. Define values and then concretely apply them to students, teachers, and the Voyager program. It is important that no one is excluded. What are some highly regarded beliefs and behaviors that we have? Give concrete examples. (Some examples may be "all voices count," "diversity is a resource," "doing one's part," or "bringing clarity to injustice and unjust practices.") How do these beliefs become a natural part of our classroom life?

Have students return to their small groups and create a class motto. In small groups students are asked to write a class motto that will guide teaching, learning, and behavior for the next two years in this seminar. Be sure to give a clear and simple definition of what a motto is and provide examples.

Each group reports back to the entire class and a vote is taken. The class motto will be printed and posted in the classroom.

Small Group Follow-Up Activity: How Do We Develop Democratic Capacities?

Each group discusses ways in which all students can engage as healthy and active citizens. Here are some ideas:

1. How do you take responsibility for your education?
2. How can we be actively involved with each other, with learning, and with projects? In what ways should we be accountable to each other?
3. What is participatory education?
4. What does a safe classroom look and feel like? How is that connected to appropriate behavior? What does an unsafe classroom look and feel like?
5. What does an antiracist, democratic, multicultural classroom look like?

Large Group Activity: Redefining Power

Have students write down what *power* means to them. Then lead a class discussion using the following questions:

- Who do you consider powerful?
- What are powerful relationships?
- What is authentic power? Think of Rosa Parks, Mahatma Gandhi, or Mother Teresa—not Donald Trump. What is sustained in the face of almost all? What is the power of a Donald Trump? What is the power of a Bill Gates? What is the power of an Oprah Winfrey?
- Individually, students will share their definition and then they will write a group definition. Again, print the group definition and post it in class.

Next, have students discuss the following:

- What structures can be built to ensure equality and care in a classroom?
- How can this classroom be developed differently from others you have experienced? How do we include ideas on power and inequalities, power over another, privilege and rights?

- Does this lead to a richer conception of democracy?
- In this case, democracy is about individuals in relations who recipro-cally acknowledge each other, share some ends, and take themselves to be members of a community. They intentionally share common inter-ests. What do we also mean by a community of practice?

Bring closure by having students record "A community of practice is a group of people who come and work together around a mutual idea, goal, or project." What would you add to this statement?

Large Group Activity: Making Sure Things Go Better—A Class Bill of Rights or a Class Constitution or Social Contract

Lead a discussion using these questions:

1. What is a code? (Have students brainstorm synonyms for "code" as used in family and friend groups.)
2. Why do we have codes?
3. What do they help us with?
4. What are some codes you use?
5. Are there negative aspects to codes?
6. What is a ritual?
7. When have we experienced rituals? (Possible answers may include "in church," "at restaurants," "at meetings.")
8. Why do we have rituals?
9. What rituals or codes exist in your communities and cultures?
10. How do rituals and codes help develop community?
11. What is the distinction between a code and a ritual?
12. From your experiences, what kinds of codes or rituals exist in a busi-nesslike atmosphere?
13. Do you think having rituals serves an appropriate purpose? For ex-ample, while working together for the next two, possibly four, years, what are some of the artifacts you would like to create and have as memorabilia for graduation and after?
14. What artifacts might demonstrate our rituals and traditions and act as a history of how your group worked together?

Small Group Activity: Developing Classroom Codes

This is a great time to remind students about respectful process. A good dis-cussion would be to explore the process of consensus (a collective opinion or agreement). What is it? What does it look like? Making decisions as a group requires practice and understanding. There are steps in the consensus process but the designs will vary with each group and decision: (1) everyone gets to talk, brainstorm ideas, and prioritize items; (2) there is a discussion where everyone can make a pitch for his or her ideas; and (3) a final ranking and vote are made for each of the ideas. Consensus means that we can all live with the decision and publicly and privately support it.

Following is a process the students can follow to devise classroom codes:

1. Students break up into small groups of between four and five members and develop the top five classroom codes they feel will build a respectful and innovative Voyager community. Have each group select a recorder and facilitator for the activity.
2. Allow students approximately twenty minutes for this exercise.
3. Ask them to keep in mind the expectations they have of themselves and each other, and issues such as leadership and power sharing and building relationships.
4. They must brainstorm, discuss, and then come to consensus for the top five. Note: It is important that this exercise begins to engage students as change agents who have a responsibility to discuss their concerns and take action. Additionally, the goals are to tap into the concepts that all questioning is healthy and that it is acceptable to disagree, and to examine how to form opinions and make decisions with an inherent concern to treat each other fairly.
5. Bring the groups together and discuss as a class.
6. Once all of the groups have reported, give each student ten stick-on dots for them to use to vote for their top ten classroom codes. The ten responses that receive the most votes will be the Voyager guidelines for this group.
7. Vote.
8. After the vote has been completed, make a clean copy of the classroom guidelines and post them in the classroom for all to see.
9. Tell the students that the guidelines can be revisited and changed with participants' consent as the year develops. The class motto and class definitions (of power, success) also keep changing as the class matures together.

The following are some classroom codes suggested by past Voyager students:

- Everyone must do his or her part.
- Respect human dignity for all.
- Treat each other as intelligent students.
- Have integrity in all that we do and say.
- Take the other person's perspective and become a caring person.
- Seek peaceful resolution.

- Students' lives and stories are important.
- Actively pursue social and individual responsibility—what do we want to change in class, at home, and at work?
- Use moral and just behavior in treatment of others.

The teacher should also list classroom operations students will be responsible for (such as attendance, bulletin board, collecting assignments) as examples of active democracy, and create and maintain an atmosphere and ground rules so that students engage in conversations that are respectful, inclusive, and democratic.

Now have the students create the foundations for class rituals. Voyager students develop these rituals throughout the program. Some are related to in-class activities. For example, once per month students bring in food/cultural items of their choice to share with each other. (This ritual replaced the usual pizza and soda that was brought in to ensure that students would have an established time to eat together.) Or have them start each class with a check-in by students to make announcements or share ideas and information. Another ritual might be having a parent or other significant adult in their lives visit the class as a guest speaker once a month. Some rituals demonstrate working toward long-range goals (e.g., collaborating on local community projects, cultural events, or fund-raisers). Others might include creating the class motto and logo, creating a bulletin board for networking and/or messages, and creating time for a town meeting—class members set aside specific time to discuss class and Voyager issues that they will make a decision on. One group decided to create a Voyager Council, which met with the coordinator to discuss seminar development and suggestions for change.

Optional Plans

1. Continue work on classroom codes that involves a question/problem-posing approach (e.g., the code that appropriate behavior is required at all times requires the students to discuss and redefine the meaning of *appropriate*) that allows for a dialogue forum where students probe more deeply into the ideas of codes and rituals and how they want them enacted in the classroom. Do their codes represent how they value learning? What influence has the creation of classroom codes had on their learning environment? They must understand and agree to their understanding of the deep (not superficial) meaning of the code.
2. Invite Voyager alumni to talk about challenges or sticking points in the development of "group" identity. Ask them to share what it was

like to be part of a learning community for four years. How did they begin to share common concerns with each other and what were the common concerns they shared? How did they learn to reconsider their views at a deeper level? What would they do differently?

3. Have students begin to write a list of questions that they have and would like to work on for the year to help them more fully develop democratic ideas.

4. Brainstorm and create a decision-making process in class. Does the process vary during different activities and projects? As a community of learners, how do we raise questions and what expectations do we have of ourselves and each other? In what ways do these processes shape the culture of the classroom?

5. Develop artifacts for the Voyager community.

6. Have students brainstorm outside community projects where they can connect with tangible ideas and actions that they might commit to as community activists.

7. Have students design all the environments of their classroom, ones that are most appropriate for the teaching and learning that will take place throughout the year (circle of desks, various sections for reading and small group and base group work, learning centers, ways to communicate outside of school for classroom assignments and for other class projects, etc.). Have students self-assign responsibilities for the boards, desks, and so on.

8. Begin to brainstorm what ideas, issues, concepts, and skills they would like to see included in the curriculum for the year.

9. Organize a telephone and email tree so that students have easy access to each other and can work together.

10. Create a system for collecting a Voyager file with materials for future use. Students' original works (interviews, polls/surveys they have taken, current events, original poetry, songs) can be compiled in a large looseleaf or artwork binder that also weaves ideas from other content areas such as math, English, social studies, mass media, and so on.

11. Form Voyager student action committees that will work on continuing creation of class rituals and then report back to the entire class for feedback. The goal is to put meat on the bones of abstract terms such as *respect* and *trust* that are real and that address students' perceptions of these issues and how they want to see the ideals demonstrated in class. There can be a variety of standing student action committees that are different from small group work activities. The action committees have specific charges and functions and meet until the goals have been ac-

complished. Examples include: a multimedia committee, which will work to make a variety of productions (tape interviews with guest speakers, create PowerPoint presentations, create a media collage of projects and year's events, make presentations at the end-of-the-year celebrations), and a community cultural events committee, which develops and connects the Voyager program with the community.

12. Use excerpts (either read aloud to entire class or printed out and read in small groups) from fiction to address issues of social equity and justice that allow students to see their own lives and ideas reflected back to them, a contact point between themselves and literature. Some examples are *A Hero Ain't Nothin' but a Sandwich* (Alice Childress), *The Outsiders* (S.E. Hinton), *The Pigman* (Paul Zindel), and *Dinky Hocker Shoots Smack* (M.E. Kerr).

13. Analyze a sample of codes of conduct from either current school documents or school documents from previous decades. In some cases, you may want to search out artifacts from other school communities and other geographic locations.

14. Begin to define and to demonstrate key concepts of programs, such as student leadership, cooperative learning, interdisciplinary learning, jigsaw, dyads and triads, fishbowl, and so on.

15. Debate the idea of commonalities of the traditional classroom and factory assembly lines. Who is considered a dutiful worker in smooth-running factories? Who is considered a dutiful learner in a smooth-running classroom? How are concepts of discipline and control valued over choice in both of these sites? (See video from WNET Films, *The Factory Model*.) What is striking about how schools were conceived and what students have to say about them today? Compare this excerpt with schools in the video *All Our Children* by Bill Moyers. What is the difference in the philosophy of these different educational settings— both from the perspective of the teacher and the students? What parts of these schools would you like to incorporate in Voyager? What parts would you not like to see incorporated into your program?

16. Have students define the 9/11 generation. What new teaching and learning skills must teachers and students utilize for this 9/11 generation? How are today's young people different as a result of 9/11? Identify new skills that you believe the 9/11 generation needs in order to find success in school and in careers. Find or create songs, poetry, articles, and children's stories that help us all to understand war and violence. How might teachers change their classrooms to teach this new generation? What changes do schools need to make in order to better serve today's young people?

17. Work with a seminar coordinator to create a Parents' Advisory Council for Voyager. List responsibilities and tasks for this board, meeting times, and length of membership. Clearly define their charge and mission. A letter inviting parents to join the board needs to be written and sent to all parents.

18. Have students reflect and write on the following: When you were growing up, did you have opportunities to interact with children and adults with individual differences? How are persons with disabilities and those from cultural and linguistic backgrounds different from your own pictured in books, on television, in movies, and in cartoons? How do these portrayals affect your understanding and acceptance of individual differences?

Performance-Based Assessments

- Authentic social contract, codes, and rituals
- Class social contract and rituals
- Definitions, response sheets, and identifying class social contract and rituals

CONCLUSION

Students will provide and present an edited copy of the Code of Classroom Civility for final review and acceptance by the group. (How was this arrived at through consensus—what is consensus?) For classroom discussion, ask students to reflect and write on the following questions: As a result of our work together, how are you looking at your classroom differently? How will things go better this year? How can you accept responsibility for your own learning? How do you want the rest of the community to help you? How are you becoming a community of learners—a community of practice?

ASSIGNMENT

1. Complete your collage for presentation to the group.
2. List your top three professional goals for the year. How will you accomplish these goals? Who will you contact to ask for help in accomplishing your goals? What is your timeline for accomplishing your goals?
3. In your current workplace position, what are the written and unwritten rituals, codes, and rules? Do you have the power to change any of them?

Unit 1D

Personal and Professional Growth

LESSON TOPIC:
PROFESSIONAL GOALS AND EFFECTIVE RÉSUMÉ WRITING

Teaching Note

Résumé writing provides more opportunities for students to:

1. Reflect on goal development
2. Discover themselves
3. Know each other
4. Grow throughout the program as they apply for jobs and college admission

Students are asked to engage empathetically with peers by listening, asking questions, and offering suggestions to help each other put their best profile together. They begin to formulate direct connections with what they hope to achieve and the skills and experience they currently possess. They need to challenge themselves on how to achieve their goals. Many are surprised at all they have accomplished as they identify the range of skills they already possess. Writing résumés early on provides a strong foundation for students to build the résumés they will need to write long before graduation, for their job interviews and for postsecondary education admission processes. It also provides students with ways to reflect on and represent themselves. They begin to see themselves as unique individuals with a future filled with far more possibilities than they initially imagined. They also begin to reflect on their actual career interests, learn how to create a structure to explore, and learn the steps of career planning.

Objectives

To develop résumé writing skills and professional goal plans
To develop the knowledge and skills needed to present oneself in future job
   interviews and postsecondary education admission processes

Domains

Cognitive: Describe and create a professional action plan
Affective: Develop empathy behaviors and group skills
Skills: Demonstrate effective communication skills

Academic Standard: Write and Speak in the English Language

Interpersonal Communication Skills
Effective speaking and listening skills
Effective group skills
Résumé writing

Materials

Professional Growth Plan
Outline for résumé writing
Sample résumés (fig. 3.17)

Pre-Instructional

Students are to bring to class lists of their top three professional goals and
career choices from the previous lesson's journal reflection assignment. In
this assignment, they are to reflect and write about their individual strengths
and abilities, their preferred work style, their ability to handle stress, how
they plan to grow and develop, and skills they want to learn. This process is
an investment in students' future careers and their ability to cope with
change.

Introductory Framework

We have focused on personal growth and reflection. Our focus was taking
time to understand more about different aspects of who we are. Our next focus was building our Voyager community. Now, we will look at our professional growth action plans. How can we begin to plan for and take action on
our future goals, college admission, and work-site success?

Figure 3.17. Sample Résumés

K. Hannah Yamada
2403 N. 57th Street
New York, NY 10016
(212) 871-5380

Objective
Seeking a professional career opportunity that requires a combination of analytical, interpersonal, and leadership skills. Prefer position with challenge and opportunity for professional advancement.

Education
State University of New York, Buffalo
Bachelor of Arts in Business Administration and Quantitative Methods in Computer Science
Anticipated Graduation Date: May 2000

College
State University of New York Academic Scholarship
Helen and Hans Reiss Scholarship

Employment
Administrative Assistant, May 1997–Present
Department of Educational Leadership, State University of New York—Buffalo
—*Provide technical and administrative support to the chair and members of the department*

Data Entry, July 1996–April 1997
Green Financial Corporation—Buffalo, NY
–*Enter credit applications*
–*Assist vendors over the phone*

Student Assistant Supervisor, February 1995–May 1997
Education Outreach Programs
State University of New York—Buffalo
–*Create information flyers and coordinate large mailings*
–*Create and maintain databases*
–*Supervise student assistants*

Qualifications
Knowledge of Microsoft Excel, Word, and PowerPoint, FileMaker Pro, Adobe PageMaker, Netscape Navigator, Microsoft Outlook
Experience with both Mac and PC platforms

References available upon request.

(continued)

Figure 3.17. Sample Résumés *(continued)*

Christene Sirois
257 Saratoga St S
St. Paul MN 55105
651.952.1124

PROFESSIONAL EXPERIENCE

6.98–Present **University of St. Thomas, School of Education • Minneapolis, Minnesota**
Department Assistant, Curriculum and Instruction
Coordinate services for department chair, full-time and adjunct faculty members, and graduate students; responsibilities include event planning and coordinating, assisting with new degree program research and development, enrollment tracking and management, new student admissions, program and course scheduling, course staffing, budget management, inventory/supply management, honorarium processing and tracking, supervision of student assistants, liaison with dean's office, coordinate publication of School of Education manual

5.03–Present University Staff Council, Elected Member
6.99–Present School of Education Leadership Council, Elected Member, Staff Representative
6.98–6.99 School of Education Leadership Council, Elected Alternate Member

1.96–6.98 **University of St. Thomas, School of Education • St. Paul, Minnesota**
Department Assistant, Gifted and Special Education
Department Assistant, Organization Learning and Development
Provided direct support to two department chairs, nine full-time faculty members, and 10+ adjunct faculty members; responsibilities included event planning and coordinating, program and course scheduling, course staffing, budget maintenance, honorarium processing and tracking, supervision of student assistants

11.95–11.96 **Travelways, Inc. (Formerly First World Travel) • Wayzata, Minnesota**
Administrative Assistant
Responsibilities included creating travel-related written and electronic communications to corporate and private clients, managing communications with vendors, maintaining client databases, processing airline tickets

1.95–11.95 **Capitol Travel and Incentives • St. Paul, Minnesota**
Administrative Assistant
Assisted account managers on incentive travel program promotions and implementation; responsibilities included processing airline and cruise tickets, assembling travel packets, tracking delivery of travel documents

(continued)

Figure 3.17. Sample Résumés *(continued)*

1.94–1.95   **Dr. Deborah A. Lehnus • St. Paul, Minnesota**
Office Manager
Responsibilities included creating and tracking written communications with insurance and supply companies and patients, insurance claim processing, client file maintenance, data entry and calendar management

5.91–1.94   **Dr. David T. Kubes • St. Paul, Minnesota**
Office Manager
Responsibilities included creating and tracking written communications with insurance and supply companies and patients, insurance claim processing, client file maintenance, data entry and calendar management

EDUCATION

University of St. Thomas • St. Paul, Minnesota
Master of Arts Degree in Education • December 2002
Courses included Gender, Power and Pedagogy, Principles of Educational Research, Theories of Cognition, Women, Writing and Film, Issues in Criticism, African-American Literature, Issues: American Literature & Culture, The Politics of Film: Technologies of Representation

Macalester College • St. Paul, Minnesota
Bachelor of Arts Degree in English (Creative Writing Emphasis) •
May 1992
Courses included Introduction to Creative Writing, Literature from a Critical Perspective, Intermediate Creative Writing: Fiction, Twentieth Century American Literature, Writing III: Poetry Workshop, Native American Literature, American Literature of the Gilded Age

TECHNICAL SKILLS

Microsoft Office Suite
PowerPoint
PageMaker
Photoshop
FileMaker Pro
Microsoft Outlook
Internet Browsers
APA Reference Style
MLA Reference Style
Typing Speed: 95+WPM

References available upon request

Motivation

You have been asked to assemble a collage that represents different aspects of who you are—both personally and professionally. This collage will also include parts of your personality that are unknown to others that you are willing to reveal at this time. (Students will volunteer to present their collages to the rest of the class.) This is another foundational opportunity for students to connect with and learn more about each other. During this time of sharing, more information regarding dreams, aspirations, family culture and heritage, and pride in oneself are demonstrated in creative and different ways. Fellow class members are invited to share their impressions of their colleagues as well.

INSTRUCTIONAL IMPLEMENTATION

Large Group Activity: Setting the Framework

Lead the class in setting the framework. Use the following initial brainstorming questions:

- What are some of the careers that interest you and why?
- What is your definition of a good career/not-so-good career? (Student leaders list ideas on the board and then the class discusses them.)

Have the class discuss the following:

- How have you assessed and come to a conclusion about these different careers?
- How do career choices connect with work values?
- How will you balance what's important in your life with work?
- What are some challenges you might have to overcome in order to succeed in these careers? For example, would you need more training in a specific area or more job experience? Would you need to polish up your communication skills, technology skills, and so on? How will you do this? Will you take night classes, attend seminars, get an apprenticeship, use networking or mentoring? (Go over these terms and ideas with the class.)

Divide the students' lists into categories: career goals, work-site success, and college admissions. Ask students to describe their ideal job by writing a job description for that job.

Small Group Activity: Where Do I Want to Go?

Have students break up into small groups of three and ask them to take out their list of professional goals. Each student will have two minutes to present her or his top goal and the ways she or he needs to accomplish this goal. Students will give feedback and ask questions after each person speaks.

Small groups will make a master list of their members' goals and present them to the larger group. During the small group reports to the entire class, student leaders will write responses on the flipcharts. Once all the groups have reported, talk about students' concerns about jobs and success in the job market.

Large Group Activity: Résumés for Work and College

One way to help achieve job success is to make sure you have an exemplary résumé—one that makes you stand out and go after the job you would like to attain, or the college you would like to attend.

Have the students carry out the following activities:

1. Describe what a résumé is used for.
2. Explain why they should prepare a résumé (and list their responses on the board). Use the following questions to guide discussion:
   - What categories should a résumé include?
   - What do you want your résumé to say?
   - What do you think prospective employers are looking for?
   - What are you interested in telling a prospective employer?
   - How does the type of information vary from job to job?
   - What are the different formats available for résumé writing?
   - As we progress in developing our résumés, what are some other formats we might include to highlight our experiences and abilities?
   - Clearly, we all want to put our best foot forward. What are some ethical considerations we must keep in mind when highlighting, but not exaggerating, our experience? What do we want our prospective employers to know about us?
   - How will this information be used?
   - What are some steps to follow in creating a résumé?

Remember that a résumé is a summary of who we are at the moment. It changes continuously as we grow and have new experiences.

Now we are going to start building a résumé that we can add to each year, if not more often.

1. Have the students gather in small groups of three to work on the outline you will give them—this is a working résumé. The class will work on the résumé at different times and keep refining it. We can never remember all that we want to write down at one time. It is always better to have a résumé on file so that we can update it and add information

as it comes up. Also, résumés should change to suit the job position you are going after.

2. Go through one entire résumé application and sample résumé (use the overhead for this project), explaining each section. Ask students what their perceptions are of the person who wrote the résumé. What do they think they know about this person? How did they know? Why do they think this person would/would not be hired? What feedback would they give this person?

Small Group Activity: Résumé Writing

Hand out the Basic Résumé Worksheet (fig. 3.18)—this is the working résumé where students gather and write information about themselves. Have students sit and work together to complete the outline, then exchange ideas out loud within their groups and give each other verbal feedback. Each person in the group receives equal time for feedback. Remind students that feedback requires *active listening:*

• Pay attention to the person speaking.
• Maintain eye contact as evidence that you are paying attention.
• Interpret and draw conclusions from what the speaker is saying.
• Check for understanding or further explanation by asking questions.

The second part of résumé writing requires that you take the working sheet and format the résumé on your computer into the résumé format you have chosen from the models given to you in class.

Figure 3.18. Basic Résumé Worksheet

There is no perfect formula. Fill in the following categories and design your résumé materials to present the type of job you are seeking.

Name
Address
Telephone
Education
Experience
Experience related to career
Other pertinent experience
Honors and recognition
Activities
Special skills and interests
Travel
Memberships
References

Optional Plans

1. Have students continue working in small groups on their résumé sheets.
2. Have a human resources representative come to class and discuss how résumés are assessed when they are received in companies. Ask the representative to bring samples of what are considered model résumés.
3. Have a college admissions counselor talk about résumés that are received with college applications and how they are assessed.
4. Have students find five people and collect their advice and experiences on résumé writing and career ideas. They will write out their findings in the first person as they are asked to be the researchers in this project, presenting findings and drawing some conclusions they want to share with the rest of the class.
5. Have student groups create a survey regarding types of résumés and career connections used in securing employment. Have them collect and analyze data and present findings.
6. Have students search web sites such as monster.com for résumés posted for specific jobs.
7. Have students collect résumés from their families, friends, mentors, workplace, and colleagues and get permission to present them in class.

Performance-Based Assessments

- A profile collage
- Identifying professional goals and challenges
- Résumé writing procedures

CONCLUSION

Recap why a résumé is an important tool. Ask the students: How are you taking control of shaping your future through this process? Think about how this new information about yourself affects your goals for the future and what you plan to do to sustain your own growth. It is also important to take time to realize what is stopping you from reaching your goal, making a dream come true, or changing a situation you want to improve. As you reflect upon your work, experiences, accomplishments, skills, and personal qualities, what are some new things you have learned about yourself?

ASSIGNMENT

1. Write the first draft of your résumé based on all the information you know about yourself. Be sure your résumé accurately reflects who will walk in the door for the interview. Otherwise, your résumé can be seen as padded. Be sure to save this information on a computer disk, hard drive, CD-ROM, or server for future use.

Unit 2A

Conflict Resolution

LESSON TOPIC:
DECREASING VIOLENCE THROUGH ALTERNATIVE OPTIONS

Teaching Note

As members of a working and learning community, Voyager students must be prepared to confront and develop ways to resolve the conflicts, the culture clashes, and the disagreements they will inevitably encounter within the group over the next two years. Intentionally teaching and learning the procedures for conflict resolution have been ignored in many schools and workplaces. Societal messages that conflict is destructive are strong, yet much can be learned from constructive conflict management. It is important for students to have an understanding of conflict and its consequences and to learn positive alternatives to violent responses. Such responses may be different from those they experience in their homes, community, and the media. Violence has shaped and will continue to shape their lives unless they learn alternatives. One young woman in a Voyager class said, "I am surprised and saddened to know that everyone here has experienced some type of violence. I thought it was just me and my people in the ghetto who know violence." This is an effective quote to use in this lesson and in your classroom.

One of the prime goals of the program is to deal with differences of all kinds in an appropriate manner that provides new learning for everyone. Threaded throughout the program's curriculum is the goal of integrating a Freirean problem-posing orientation. Therefore, dialogue with students on issues of violence that are most relevant to them is critical. They need to be encouraged to set and keep positive ground rules for dialogue and problem solving. Guidelines that will inspire trust, openness, and cooperation are appropriate and necessary. Fundamental to creating options for dealing with conflict is the need to develop clear communication skills and the skill of perspective taking. Although this unit does not go into more detail, communication skills are a priority within this program and many times lessons were reconfigured to include more work in communication skills. Interestingly, when the concept of violence was discussed, it was not in the abstract. When the concept was integrated into students' lives, their stories were told in their own voices and students felt they had become an integral part of the curriculum. They were able to take risks, to engage more fully, and to create safe spaces for each other to listen and to talk. Ultimately, this dialogue compelled them to unpack strongly held assumptions about the topic of violence and about each other. Given this opportunity, they learned to safely tangle with discord, knowing that they wouldn't always agree with each other, and struggled through their fights, arguments, and tears to build a community steeped in empathy and caring. They learned to believe that they could actually find solutions to their conflicts. They could confront the violence that was erupting all around them, share their fears, and then begin the process of critiquing violence rather than just sharing war stories. The classroom developed into a space where the students made each other feel cared for and significant.

As Bill Bigelow states (Bigelow, Christenson, Karp, Miner, and Peterson, 2000, p. 1), schools and classrooms should be laboratories for democracy. Creating caring and democratic learning communities is a struggle, one that does not happen overnight. Ira Shor also states in his 1992 book, *Empowering Education: Critical Teaching for Social Change*, students possess empowering knowledge and resources that are ever-present and that need to be recognized and supported by teachers and their peers. Students need to learn to delete the voices of past teachers, parents, and peers who made them feel stupid and unworthy, and to accept that the knowledge they possess is valuable and real. When acknowledging these strengths, new power relations can be constructed in class so that students will feel safe to talk more openly and so that issues such as racism, homophobia, sexism, and classism do not fester and end up destroying a classroom. Rather, what takes place is the creation, by students, of a new vision for their future based on the critical skills and ideas they have experienced in class.

Objectives

To identify and define the concept of violence in today's schools, communities, and society

To develop solutions to violence and conflict at home, in school, and in the community

Domains

Cognitive: Understand the concept of violence
Affective: Value appropriate feedback and an understanding of experience
Skills: Listen and communicate ideas

Academic Standard: Write and Speak in the English Language

Interpersonal Communication Skills
Effective speaking and listening skills
Create self-assessment and appropriate feedback

Materials

School Violence Statistics and Commentaries (fig. 3.19) and definitions overheads
Flipcharts for small group work
Conflict Resolution Survey

Pre-Instructional

1. Have the students write a description of an incident, a conflict they feel they positively/negatively handled, and why they feel the way they do about how they handled it. Ask them to include the steps they followed, a description of how it turned out, and what they would have done differently.
2. Have the students share their stories with one other person in the class.

Introductory Framework

Violence in today's world is prevalent in all that we see, hear, and do. We hear and see violent acts of war, inhumanity, and desperation every night on the news. Although they seem to exist only in faraway places, we know that acts of violence also occur in our everyday lives.

As violence increases among young people, there is a concern and a pressure to create more safe and orderly schools. Schools are struggling with what to do, as is society in general. Examining violence in schools, homes, and communities, and the influences that support violence, helps us understand why we need to learn how to do things differently, how to respond differently in all situations. Refer students to the Statistics on Violence sheet (fig. 3.19). The way that we will learn to manage conflict is critical to our collective future. What do you think are some influences of change?

Figure 3.19. School Violence Statistics and Commentaries

- Twenty-five percent of eighth- and ninth-grade students have witnessed threats to teachers.

- In a 2001 survey of high school students, 17.4% had carried a weapon to school during the thirty days preceding the survey.

- Thirty-seven percent of eighth- and ninth-grade students were afraid of attacks at school.

- Seventy percent of all high school students say "unruly students distract them and undermine classes."

- Forty-one percent of teachers feel that "violence in and around school" is "a serious problem" or a "somewhat serious problem."

- Every school day 13,076 public school students are suspended.

- Four percent of middle and high school students report that they "never feel safe" around school.

- Over a two-year period, 105 school-associated violent deaths occurred. Seventy-seven percent of these deaths involved firearms.

- Twelve percent of sixth- through twelfth-grade students reported they were victims of physical attack, robbery, or bullying in school.

- Teachers in 1996, for the first time, said that discipline is the main reason teachers leave the profession.

- When combined into a category labeled "control," "lack of discipline," and "fighting, violence, and gangs" were cited by the public as the "biggest problem[s] facing local schools."

- The National Crime Victimization Survey data show that an estimated 2.7 million violent crimes take place annually either at school or near schools.

- According to a survey of educators at the National Association of Secondary School Principals Convention, 61 percent have had to confiscate at least one firearm in the past two years; 50 percent require police intervention daily, weekly, or monthly, for violent acts occurring in their schools.

- Every school day more than 150,000 students stay home because they are "sick of violence and afraid they might be stabbed, shot, or beaten."

- Fifty-two percent of secondary school principals who participated in a survey taken by the National Association of Secondary School Principals said that they are facing serious gang problems. Intimidation is the most serious gang problem, said 32 percent, actual violence incidents by gangs were reported occurring at 25 percent of the schools, and 23 percent have students who wear gang colors or clothing.

- Just over 26 percent of high school seniors used an illicit drug once a month or more often during the past school year.

(continued)

Figure 3.19. School Violence Statistics and Commentaries *(continued)*

- Among the graduating class of 1995, 48 percent of students had used an illicit drug by the time they reached their senior year of high school, continuing an upward trend from 40 percent in 1992.

- More students than teachers perceive that increased violence is occurring in schools.

- Forty percent of secondary school teachers think that "physical conflicts among students" are "a problem."

- A National Institute of Justice study found that one in five inner-city school students (one in three males) had been shot at, stabbed, or otherwise injured with a weapon at or in transit to or from school in the past few years.

- In 1995, 14 percent of "violent crimes" occurred "at school."

- The percentages of public secondary school teachers reporting weapons possessions as "a moderate" or "serious problem" in their schools nearly doubled from 1990–1991 to 1993–1994.

- A study from the University of Michigan estimates that students carry 270,000 guns to school each day.

- According to a Senate committee, if drug abuse by children stays the same, the increasing numbers of children in our nation will mean that in fifteen years, more than 200,000 high school seniors will smoke marijuana every day—a 21 percent increase over the 1995 figure of 165,000.

- Approximately 10 percent of children in kindergarten through high school are attacked by schoolmates on a regular basis. These attacks include verbal aggression (e.g., name calling, threats of physical harm) and physical aggression (e.g., hitting, slapping, extortion, robbery, threats with guns and knives).

- While shootings in schools have elevated concerns about firearms on school campuses, knives and razors are the weapons most likely to be carried by students.

- About 26 percent of students nationally report having "very serious problems" in their school with gangs.

- While 42 percent of students nationally say they rarely see violence in or around their school, 41 percent report seeing violence sometimes. Nine percent say they see violence very often in or around their school.

- In 1999, 12 percent of twelve- through eighteen-year-old students reported experiencing "any" form of victimization at school.

- In 1999, twelve- through eighteen-year-old students living in urban and suburban locales were equally vulnerable to serious violent crime at school.

- In 1999, one in six teachers report having been the victim of violence in or around school. This compares to one in nine teachers in 1994.

- Nationwide, 15 percent of high school students had participated in a physical fight in 1998.

(continued)

Figure 3.19. School Violence Statistics and Commentaries

- Fifty-seven percent of expulsions for bringing firearms to school involved high school students, 33 percent involved junior high/middle-school students, and 10 percent involved elementary school students.

- Studies show that child abuse occurs in 30-60 percent of family violence cases that involve families with children.

- Approximately four million adolescents have been victims of a serious physical assault, and nine million have witnessed serious violence during their lifetimes.

- Every year, three to ten million children witness domestic violence.

- One in twelve high schoolers is threatened or injured with a weapon each year.

- In New Haven, Conn., 39 percent of sixth-, eighth-, and tenth-grade students had seen someone shot at in the preceding year.

- In Miami, Fla., more than 90 percent of the high school students witnessed community violence and 44 percent had been a victim of a violent crime.

- In Richmond, Va., 88 percent of the children in one neighborhood heard gunfire near home, and 25 percent saw someone killed.

Adapted from www.nccev.org/resources/statistics/statistics-school.html-12k. Accessed February 11, 2003.

Motivation

1. How many of you have been affected by an act of violence against either you personally or a family member?
2. How did this make you feel?
3. What were the repercussions of the violent act?
4. Why do you think violence is taking place in your neighborhoods and in the school?
5. Why do people want to dominate each other?
6. What do people gain from dominating someone else?
7. Why do people want to control someone?
8. Describe how you feel emotionally and physically when you get angry or are included in a heated conflict. What changes do you go through?
9. What does the expression "When I get angry I see red" mean?
10. How do you feel physically when you get angry?
11. What is the difference between how you feel if you prevail in the conflict and how you feel if you lose? List words, phrases, or sentences, or draw pictures that describe how you feel in both of these instances. Describe any visceral or physical reactions.

INSTRUCTIONAL IMPLEMENTATION

Large Group Activity: Approaching the Causes of Conflict

Conflict is a daily part of adult and student lives. Conflict takes many forms. If you ask someone, "When was the last time you had a conflict?" he or she might say, "this morning."—Now, when was the last time you had a conflict? Why do you think conflict is so prevalent?

Hand out sheets listing examples of the causes of conflict and violence (fig. 3.20) to each of the groups. Ask students to discuss among themselves the ways in which each item on the list may contribute to the creation of conflict and violence. Bring the group together and listen to their feedback. Does conflict have any positive value? What is the potential value of conflict?

Large Group Activity: Defining New Terms

Have the students write a synonym or a phrase that comes to their mind as they listen to you read the following words. They can also use a specific example to explain the word or idea more fully: violence, conflict, peace, options, negotiate, mediate, win/lose. Students will volunteer to place their responses on flipcharts. Discuss how everyone sees and interprets these words differently and what the commonalities are among the ideas.

Figure 3.20. Causes of Conflict and Violence

- Changing patterns of family and community life—what does this mean on a variety of levels? Family violence—domestic abuse, child neglect, less time with parents
- Adolescence and teen years are fraught with raging emotions and ideas
- Economic and social injustice—a number of people earning below the poverty level
- Unequal power and resources among certain communities
- Institutionalized classism, racism, and sexism
- Media portrayals of pretend danger
- Redefining violence as normal and acceptable
- Government policies that disenfranchise many Americans
- Easy access to guns
- Drug abuse
- Accepted modes of social behavior in gender roles
- Neglect and indifference by society
- Discrimination/bias/racism
- Me versus we attitude
- Feeling the need to express power over others
- Gangs
- Global violence

- How are new definitions being formed as we work together to identify and lend more meaning to these words?
- What are some activities that we can undertake to promote peaceful and equitable resolutions to disagreements and opposing viewpoints?
- How do we get to learn from each other?
- What are some basic self-management skills?
- Should we develop a peer mediation group?

Large Group Activity: The Bully Syndrome and Other Unacceptable Subcultures

Hand out the Reflection: Conflict—Bullies and the Bully Syndrome sheet (fig. 3.21). What is a bully? Have you ever been a bully or have you ever been bullied? How does a bully feel? Why do people enjoy having power over other people? What is the outcome of this type of behavior from each perspective? What can schools, teachers, and parents do to help resolve this syndrome? Bring the group together to share their stories and to discuss the principles of bullying and power.

A recent study in the *Journal of the American Medical Association* demonstrated the epidemic proportions of bullying in American schools. This study involved 15,686 students in the United States (grades 6–10), where 29.9 percent of them reported frequent involvement in bullying at school; 13 percent reported acting as a bully, 10.9 percent as a victim, and 6 percent as both (Nansel et al., 2001). With aggression and violence during childhood and adolescence being the focus of much research over the last twenty years, it has been found that serious forms of aggression remain stable from childhood to adulthood while mild forms of aggression (such as bullying) may not begin until adolescence. More information is coming to light in terms of the role that adolescent peers play in promoting bullying and victimization by: reinforcing the aggressor, failing to intervene to stop the victimization, affiliating with the bully, and the code of silence accepted by students and teachers to cover up these behaviors.

Figure 3.21.   Reflection: Conflict—Bullies and the Bully Syndrome

1. Each person in your group is to share her/his best "bully" story. This can be an incident they were involved in, or one that they saw or heard about.
2. After everyone has shared her/his story, the group is to choose one to share with the larger group.
3. After you've heard the stories in the larger group, think about them. What do all of the stories have in common?
4. What is your best advice to teachers or parents trying to stop the bully syndrome?

How do you see these behaviors playing out in your school? In your classroom? How have you participated? What different roles can you play not to intervene in this process? Think about the following questions:

1. Create a study where you interview students in the school to discover how they perceive and describe the problems they witness or experience in school. Do boys and girls experience bullying in the same way?
2. Because a significant number of students are targets of bullying in schools today, what do you think are the short- and long-range effects on young adults both physically and emotionally?
3. What strategies can we identify that will discourage bullying?

Small Group Activity: What Are the Walls in Our Lives? (Jigsaw Activity)

Break the class into small groups of equal numbers. Each small group reads a different literature piece, for example, "Mending Wall" by Robert Frost or the lyrics to "Eleanor Rigby" by the Beatles or songs by Alanis Morissette. (See resources for more titles and videos.)

Each group thinks about and critically analyzes what they have read and how they can start to take down the walls in their lives (fig. 3.22). What risks will they take to create and maintain different connections? How can we intervene during class and use teachable moments when incidents erupt? What type of contingency plan can we develop as a group, remain committed to it, and resolve conflict in productive ways?

Have one member from each group form a new group and all members of the new group present their piece of literature to one another.

Bring the class together to discuss common threads and themes. What suggestions can we make that bring the walls down and allow others to get to know us?

Figure 3.22. Conflict: What Are the Walls in Our Lives?

---

1. Working in small groups, you will read a piece of literature provided by the teacher.
2. As a group, critically analyze the piece you have just read. As you analyze this work, ask yourself and each other how you can take down the "walls" in your own lives.
3. What risks will each of you take to create and maintain different connections in your lives, connections that will help you take down the "walls"?
4. How can we all intervene in class and use teachable moments when an incident erupts?
5. What type of contingency plan can we develop for incidents, a plan that we can all remain committed to?

Large Group Activity: Conflict of Interests

Conflict exists when incompatible activities, goals, and ideas occur. One activity may interfere with the effectiveness of another activity, making them incompatible. Sometimes our interests are congruent and sometimes they conflict. In schools there are conflicts of interest among administrators, teachers, and students. A conflict of interest may occur when the actions of one person's interests or goals are prevented by the actions of another person's interests or goals. There are various ways that conflicts occur in our everyday lives. Have there ever been any constructive conflicts? What were the outcomes of these conflicts? Some historical examples of constructive conflict could be the Revolutionary War, establishing the Bill of Rights, slave uprisings/revolts, the Indian Wars, the Civil Rights Movement, and union strikes. (Students can add their own examples from their experience and from their native homelands and communities.)

Conflict is a natural part of people trying to coexist. Think about and then describe a recent conflict you have had with someone. Then identify the following:

1. All of the people involved in this conflict: classmate or friend; parent, guardian, or other family member; teacher or boss
2. When the conflict started and how long it had been going on (or is it still going on?)
3. The cause of the conflict
4. How this conflict made you feel/how you think it made the other person feel
5. How you have tried to resolve this conflict (is it resolved or still going on?)
6. What you can see now that you could have done differently to resolve the conflict

Have students brainstorm: What does conflict resolution have to offer students and teachers and classroom environments? Answers that have been suggested by students and teachers include these:

- It promotes responsible student behavior.
- It supports violence prevention.
- It helps students see relationships among and across various communities and the law.
- It helps build personal and professional relationships.
- It helps students accept the consequences of their behavior.
- It helps develop anger-management skills.

- It helps to develop skills so that all students act responsibly in the school and work community.
- It helps us all to work together in a pluralistic and diverse society.
- It improves confidence in skills—both academic and personal.
- It helps all learn to solve problems, which helps the entire community.

Voyager Community

What types of conflict do you think might occur in this class over the next two years? (List students' responses on flipcharts.) What are possible strategies to use when these conflicts occur?

Individual Activity: Self-Assessment Questionnaire

Distribute the Conflict Resolution Survey (fig. 3.23). Direct the students to answer each question as truthfully as possible. When they are finished, ask students to rate themselves. Have students reflect on the results and write some interpretations.

Ask students to share their results with one another. What are they surprised about? What are they concerned about? (Refer to the Pre-Instructional and discuss the incidents students have written about.)

Large Group Discussion: Dealing with Conflict Head-On

According to the National Center for Children Exposed to Violence (www .nccev.org) in their 2001 survey of high school students, the following was reported: 17.4 percent had carried a weapon to school, 12 percent of twelve–eighteen-year-old students reported experiencing any form of victimization at school, twelve–eighteen-year-olds living in urban and suburban locales were equally vulnerable to serious crime, one in six teachers reported being the victim of a crime, 15 percent of students reported being in a fight, and 57 percent of school expulsions were for bringing guns to school. What does all of this tell us?

Here are some different ways for all of us to deal with conflict. When honestly engaging in a peaceful resolution process, the following has been recommended (adapted from Sadalla et al., 1987):

1. Look ahead, plan for the meeting, analyze how you are going into this meeting. What are your concerns about this situation and conflict? How am I being continuously affected? Is this important to me—why? What assumptions, biases, or suspicions do I have about this other person? What would make the situation better for me?

Figure 3.23.   Conflict Resolution Survey: How Do You Deal with Conflict?

Respond to the statements below by using the following scale. (The instructor can decide whether or not to use all of the questions listed on this survey.)

1 = Almost never
2 = Occasionally
3 = Half the time
4 = Usually
5 = Almost always

❐ I feel that conflict is a negative experience.
❐ I feel that conflict is a positive experience.
❐ When I resolve a conflict, it improves my relationship.
❐ I am afraid to enter into confrontations.
❐ I feel that in conflicts someone will get hurt.
❐ When I prepare to meet to discuss a conflict, I try to arrange for a mutually acceptable time and setting.
❐ I feel that where a conflict takes place is important.
❐ I try to make people feel comfortable when meeting with them about a conflict.
❐ When I start to discuss a conflict with the other party, I choose my opening statement carefully to establish positive, realistic expectations.
❐ I state my true feelings when dealing with conflict.
❐ During a conflict, I ask questions to clarify a statement that I'm not sure of.
❐ I try to be aware of how my negative and positive self-perceptions influence the way I deal with a conflict.
❐ In conflict, my reactions are based on how I think the other party perceives me.
❐ I feel that only my needs are important.
❐ I feel for a relationship to last, the needs of both parties must be considered.
❐ In a conflict, I strive to distinguish between real needs and desires.
❐ In order to not harm the relationship, I may temporarily put aside some of my own less important personal wants.
❐ I share my positive attitude, hoping they will do the same.
❐ I find it necessary to overpower others to get my own way.
❐ I am aware the other person may need to feel in control of the conflict.
❐ In a conflict, I believe there should be no upper hand.
❐ I find it easy to forgive.
❐ I bring up old issues from the past during a new conflict.
❐ When dealing with a conflict, I consider the future of the long-term relationship.
❐ In a conflict, I try to dominate the other party.
❐ I listen with an open mind to alternative options.
❐ I feel there is just one way to solve a problem.
❐ When dealing with a conflict, I have preconceived notions about the other party that I am unwilling to let go of.
❐ I can accept criticism from others.
❐ I feel that winning the war is more important than winning the battle.
❐ I strive for a complete and genuine resolution of a conflict rather than settling for a temporary agreement.
❐ When dealing with a conflict, I have a predetermined solution to the outcome.

(continued)

Figure 3.23.   Conflict Resolution Survey: How Do You Deal with Conflict? *(continued)*

❐ I feel the need to control an argument.
❐ If I had my own way, I win—you lose.
❐ When in a conflict with someone, I ask him or her to explain his or her position.
❐ At the end of a conflict, it matters to me that the other person's needs have been met as well as my own.
❐ I bargain to resolve conflict.
❐ I express anger constructively.
❐ In difficult conflicts, I would consider requesting a third-party facilitator.
❐ I overlook my partner's anger in order to focus on the real issues to conflict.
❐ I feel that it is okay to disagree on specific issues in a conflict.

Scoring
What do your 1s have in common?
What do your 5s have in common?
If you have mostly 3s, what do you believe that indicates?

Adapted from Values Clarification.

2. How can I set the tone? What are some of my positive intentions and can I say them out loud—this relationship is important to me, I want this to last, I want us to interact differently, and so on? What are ways in which I can validate the other person?

3. How can we discuss and define the problem? Everyone involved must state his or her reasons, issues, and feelings. What are effective listening techniques? What are effective speaking techniques? Can we identify our interests and needs here? Discuss out loud the assumptions, values, and suspicions we all bring to the table.

4. Stop and summarize the situation and the new understandings until this point. Make sure everyone agrees as to what has been summarized.

5. Begin to brainstorm alternative solutions. For each course of action, determine the advantages and disadvantages. What are the consequences? Do a reality check—how can we choose solutions that are mutually satisfactory to all parties?

6. What type of follow-up plan and check-in do we have in the future?

You are encouraged to use the above process and translate it into words that help you when resolving conflicts.

Large Group Activity: Debating Conflict

Should conflict be kept out of education or should we build conflict into education? Distribute the Strategies for Negotiating Resolution handout (fig. 3.24).

Figure 3.24.   Strategies for Negotiating Resolution

Which of these strategies do you practice the most? Why? Which are you willing to try? Give examples of how you would engage in each of these strategies.

Create an effective atmosphere—begin on a positive note.
Clarify perception—what is the problem?
Focus on individual and shared needs—what do you have in common?
Build mutual positive power—power with, not over.
Look to the future—what can be changed?
Develop viable options—what will work?
What are effective steps to action—what are some better ideas?
Develop agreements together and clarify what is expected of each person.

Allow students to debate both sides of this issue with specific ideas illustrating the consequences of each.

Small Group Activity: Dealing with In-Class Conflicts and Disagreements

Each small group will discuss and create appropriate ways to resolve disagreements in class. They are to prioritize their list and be ready to discuss their top three management strategies with the whole class. They are encouraged to research other schools and programs for ideas. Each group will present their findings and the class will pick and choose what are appropriate steps for them. Their final list will be posted in the classroom.

Large Group Activity: Consensus Building

A good discussion would be to explore the process of consensus (a collective opinion or agreement). What is it—what does it look like? Making decisions as a group requires practice and understanding. Have students describe one time since the class has been together when a decision was reached by consensus. Discuss common themes from the stories. (1) Everyone gets to talk, brainstorm ideas, and prioritize items; (2) then there is a discussion where each student can make a pitch for his or her ideas; and (3) there is a final ranking and vote for each of the ideas.

Optional Plans

1. Use headlines from current newspapers depicting violence in communities and schools. Using flipcharts, have students generate a list of words in response to each headline. Have students generate multiple synonyms for each of the words on the flipcharts. Everyone will have many perspectives on these words. How can you explain

some of the violence that is taking place? Are there solutions for these conflicts?

2. Have students answer the following: What do we know about violence in schools? What are some current topics and issues related to violence in schools? What have we learned from the tragic events at Columbine High School and in schools in Nebraska and Kentucky? What impact have the events of September 11, 2001, had on communities, schools, and particular ethnic groups? Why do you think this violence is occurring? What action has usually taken place in schools in response to violence? What other actions must be taken? (Show clips from Michael Moore's film *Bowling for Columbine*.)

3. Have students respond to the following: What types of conflict are inevitable in countries, in societies, or in schools? We know that conflicts can be as small as a disagreement about pencils or lunch, or they can be as huge as a world war. Is there such a thing as a positive conflict? How would you define conflict? What is the start of the continuum — behaviors that start in elementary school with name calling that continue to build and escalate into adulthood. (Brainstorm ideas on the board.)

4. Continue assessment and reflection of the Conflict Resolution Survey.

5. Have students interview community speakers — or invite speakers to the class — on issues related to violence and programs developed in the community to prevent and resolve violence.

6. Have students create their own survey on violence that they will implement either in the school, their community, or their workplace.

7. Explore the idea of violence in the workplace. What does this type of violence look like?

8. Have students interview other students, friends, and family members for their perspectives on violence and experiences of it in their own lives.

9. Have students gather and bring in materials from other classes they are taking at the moment that provide another perspective on the subject and/or support some of the ideas engaged with in this class.

Performance-Based Assessments

- Student results from Conflict Resolution Survey
- Student feedback and strategies relating to violence

CONCLUSION

What do we know about violence today? What do we know and what do we need to know about conflict resolution? What do we need to know about altering educational and work structures in order to change our environment?

ASSIGNMENT

1. Now that we are starting to look at options for the answer to violence, please describe three incidents that allowed you to make a positive change to a situation that potentially could have become violent or ended in a negative outcome. The incidents can be from any of your life experiences—home, work, traveling, or community.

Unit 2B

Conflict Resolution

LESSON TOPIC: THE PROCESS OF
CONFLICT RESOLUTION AND PEACEFUL NEGOTIATION

Teaching Note

Conflicts and disagreements are part of what happens daily to all of us in the classroom, at work, at home, and in the community. In the classroom, chaos results when students deal with conflict by relying on ineffective tactics they have used in the past (e.g., physical dominance, threats, name calling, silent treatment, verbal attacks, etc.) or when they perceive conflict only in negative terms. John Dewey describes the ability of conflict to result in reflection and ingenuity and to provide an opportunity to create new ideas and new learning. In this way, conflict can be viewed as energizing. Conflict often indicates that we're being honest about having different perspectives. Students are encouraged to look at what makes them angry, what frightens them, what pre-existing ideas are still provoking them to act and perceive others in certain ways. They will be asked to put their problem-solving skills to work and to decide what is important to them and how to attain it. They are guided in making this transition and to feel ownership in their learning environment, challenging themselves and each other. Equally important is for teachers to be able to make a transition from the perception that classrooms are smooth-running factories where coercion and efficiency are valued over forging consensus and engaging in healthy conflict. In addition, it is important for teachers to deal with their own conflict issues because, as Einstein put it, "modeling is the only way to teach."

Objective

To learn and apply the conflict resolution process

Domains

Cognitive: Understand positive conflict
Affective: Value others' feelings and perspectives
Skills: Listen and communicate ideas

Academic Standard: Write and Speak in the English Language

Interpersonal Communication Skills
Effective speaking and listening skills
Create self-assessment and appropriate feedback

Materials

Strategies for Negotiating Resolution handout (fig. 3.24)
Flipcharts for small group work
Management Strategies for Conflict sheet (fig. 3.25)
Vignettes for Problem Solving (fig. 3.26)

Pre-Instructional

Have students write a reflective paragraph describing their reactions to the Conflict Resolution Survey they completed at the last meeting. Students are to describe and bring to class conflict incidents and the resolution of these incidents.

Introductory Framework

As we have seen, the causes of violence in society are complex and deep. The figures on children and violence are especially appalling. What are some ideas of prevention programs in schools that you know of? What we know is that traditional models of dealing with violence will not equip any of us to make our schools, our neighborhoods, our society safer. What are some of the traditional ways of managing conflict in schools? (List responses on the board.) Why do you think these ways are ineffective now? We know that the types of violent crimes have changed, not only in numbers but also in type. What were some of the reflections, conclusions, and innovative models you came up with as a result of completing the Conflict Resolution Survey?

Motivation

When have you been excluded in school, in class, and at work? Why were you rejected? How did you feel? How did that change how you approached the next year? How did you interact with your peers? What does full and equal participation mean?

"Too often, some children are rejected year after year. The burden of being rejected falls on a few children. They are made to feel like strangers" (Vivian Paley, 1992, p. 22). In Canada, a new school rule starting in kindergarten is "You can't say you can't play." When the teacher announces this new rule, she also states that with this new rule is the beginning of a new social order. What do you think she means by this? What do you think is the goal of this rule? What is your reaction to this rule? How do you think the kindergartners responded to this new rule? How will students work together differently? What happens when someone hurts or takes advantage of someone else?

INSTRUCTIONAL IMPLEMENTATION

Large Group Activity

Have students read the following quotes aloud and respond to them:

"I hold it to be proof of great prudence for men to abstain from threats and insulting words toward anyone, for neither . . . diminishes the strength of the enemy; but the one makes him more cautious, and the other increases his hatred of you and makes him more persevering in his efforts to injure you." (Machiavelli, *The Discourses*, New York: The Modern Library, p. 373)

"Never doubt that a small group of thoughtful, committed citizens can change the world; indeed, it is the only thing that ever has." (Margaret Mead)

What is the difference in what these two people have had to say? Which do you prefer and why? List all responses to these quotes on the board.

Large Group Discussion: Cultural Practices for Peace and Resolution

In addition to any violence prevention programs, we need to understand that people have been resolving conflicts positively for a long time. From what we have studied about ancient civilizations, we know that many societies used a variety of methods to solve problems and conflicts. In ancient China, people relied on the Confucian method of telling persuasive and moral anecdotes; in Japan, the village leader used mediation and conciliation to settle disputes; in Africa, a neighborhood meeting with a respected village member was held to hear a disagreement; and in many American Indian tribes, the tribal chief or wise man held court to mediate all disagreements. In religious communities priests, rabbis, and ministers have been community mediators. What are some cultural practices for conflict resolution from your own background? What has worked for you?

Figure 3.25.   Management Strategies for Conflict

Decide which of the following strategies suits your situation. How important is your goal and how important is the relationship? Answering these questions will help you decide which of the five strategies listed below will be helpful. It is important to become competent in all of the strategies and know when to engage each one.

Problem-Solving Negotiations
You seek solutions when the goal and the relationship are both important to you. It is necessary to take some risks, such as revealing your interests, in order to resolve the situation satisfactorily for both members.

Smoothing
When the relationship outweighs the goal, you may have to give up your goal to maintain the relationship at the highest quality possible. This strategy is useful when a colleague feels strongly about a goal and you do not.

Forcing Win/Lose Situations
When the goal is highly important and the relationship is not, you persuade or force the other person to yield. Forceful tactics are used, such as imposing a deadline, refusing to give up a position, or setting high demands.

Compromising
Here, both the goal and the relationship is moderately important. Both parties "meet in the middle" to give up some part of their position, especially when neither party has much time for negotiation.

Withdrawing
When neither the goal nor the relationship is important, you may wish to withdraw and give up both. Sometimes parties withdraw in order to have time to calm down.

Feasibility
Choose a strategy from above that you think will work best, based on the problem, the time, and the parties involved.

Figure 3.26.   Vignettes for Problem Solving

In your small groups discuss what strategies you would use in the following cases.

Case 1—Prima Donna
Manager: I can count on most of my staff to cooperate when I give out assignments. I can count on Ralph to give me a hard time. Every time I ask him to head a project, develop a new idea, work late, or give extra time, he has lots of excuses. He gets excited—visibly red and angry when I speak to him in the staff meetings. I do not want to start a scene at the meetings. My strategy has been to give in to his temperamental antics and to try to smooth over the conflicts. This situation is driving me crazy because I feel I am not treating the entire staff equally. He is also wearing down my resistance.

(continued)

Figure 3.26. **Vignettes for Problem Solving** *(continued)*

Ralph: I have over twenty-five years in this company. I have given enough extra time and energy. I will not take on any extra work whether we are busy or not. Let the new underlings take over. It is time for everyone to put in his or her dues just as I have. I also know that not only do I have seniority, but also the boss does not want to antagonize me. I am in a comfortable and protected position.

Case 2—Botchy

Manager: Manny skirts the rules and is just getting by with his work. Although he used to be one of the best workers in the department, now he is late with work, does not show up on time, and misses meetings. Many times his late or missing work affects the rest of the team as his segment is needed to complete the project. I wonder if he thinks he is untouchable in terms of consequences or does he think everyone loves him so much that they will forgive him all the time? How can I get Manny to start working up to his potential?

Manny: Why should I continue to try to work harder or longer? Here you are not rewarded for knocking yourself out. No one really cares or knows if I am working really hard or not at all—it seems to be all the same. They do not really care about me or what I think. No one appreciates my position or all that I have gone through. I receive the same recognition acknowledgment as those workers who do little or nothing.

Case 3—Superworker

Manager: Lela spends a lot of time developing elaborate designs and charts that we do not really need. I have been too subtle with her since she started the job and need to talk with her about priorities. For someone that is new to the job, she certainly presumes to know all the answers. She is determined to call a lot of attention to herself before gaining any experience in the job and wants to make presentations describing our services and how they can be improved. Later, she learns that her suggestions are unworkable for the company. She is making the job larger and more important than it is and causes embarrassment for all of us.

Lela: I want them all to know that this new kid on the block is going to make a difference in their company. I have made elaborate color-coded charts that describe our system. The manager will understand why I have not had time to do what he asked me to do. He will be surprised to see what a grand job I have done. I bring many strengths to this company, especially filling in areas that have been missing. I am a good idea person with lots of vision. They will soon recognize the heights I want to take this company to. Nobody is going to get in my way.

Case 4—Inflators

Manager: How am I always taken in by Julia's pompous and pretentious way of knowing it all? She is an instant expert on everything. At the meeting today, she clearly articulated how the new law will work in our company. Yes, I have experienced how she can be articulate while at the same time she is exaggerating and telling another grand tall tale. I have been caught on matters before as a result of her exaggeration. I do not think she is lying—she has convinced herself she has all the answers. She believes what she is saying at least while she is saying it. I must find a way to stop her from misleading me. She always seems to patch together a position that seems reasonable and yet is not totally true, and when this is proven we will realize how much time she has cost us. She does not take any responsibility for her actions. She always needs her time in the spotlight.

(continued)

Figure 3.26.   Vignettes for Problem Solving *(continued)*

Julia: I really want the boss to know how much I know. From what I heard at the last conference regarding this new law, I am convinced it will apply in certain cases. I do not have time to read the entire law, but I do believe I am right. I have had experience in other areas where the same ideas held true so this feels right to me. Anyway, if he does not believe in me, I can always go to the unit supervisor and tell her.

Case 5—Empire Builders
Manager: Ryan is charming, enthusiastic, and very convincing when it comes to serve his purpose. In public and at our staff meetings, he is quick to volunteer for many activities and is full of many ideas and suggestions. What usually results is a lot of complaining from the staff especially when it is time to work on a team project and to get it in on time—he usually disappears and passes his work off to someone else. At other times, he stays and takes control of the group, especially if he can receive a lot of personal attention and recognition. His insensitivity and lack of cooperative spirit is affecting the outcome of many projects and is demoralizing the staff. He is using his position as a stepping-stone for personal glory, recognition, and promotion.

Ryan: I want the boss to assign me to this new planning division. The planning team has an assignment that is in line with all the major points outlined by the CEO in our recent newsletter. I would like to expand the work to include lots of different divisions. This way I could get to work with lots of key people and win attention from the real higher ups. I know what I am doing and it is time for others to acknowledge and reward me for all that I know.

Large Group Activity: The World According to Melissa

Let us try resolving one conflict together: Melissa is always talking—she is full of enthusiasm and life and has lots of stories to tell. Jasmine is a member of a cooperative group with Melissa and she is frustrated and irritated. Melissa has become the bossiest student in the group, telling everyone what to do. She does not allow anyone else to take a leadership role. Some of the other students are also irritated and frustrated, yet no one is willing to say anything.

Have students volunteer to role-play the above scenario in a fish bowl setting while the rest of the class listens and observes. Allow both fish bowl participants and the rest of the class to discuss what they saw, felt, and heard during the role-playing exercise. Using fig. 3.25 as a guide, what resolutions have we come to?

Small Group Activity: Conflict Resolution—Confronting the Opposition

Have students form small groups and distribute the Vignettes for Problem Solving handout (fig. 3.26). Present each group with a vignette to read, discuss, and role-play. Have each group present its role-playing to the rest of the class.

Small Group Activity: Finding Options

Have students remain in their small groups and work out options and ideas on a second set of scenarios. Two groups can take turns being on the inside and being on the outside, reviewing or acting the conflict. Students are urged to write out and role-play scenarios from their own lives, again using figs. 3.24 and 3.25 as their guides.

Optional Plans

1. Have students describe and then brainstorm a school conflict that has taken place recently. Decide if another resolution could have been reached. What was the conflict about? What were the beliefs or attitudes of the persons involved? How did each person respond? What was the consequence to each of the people? What could have been done differently? How did the administration respond? What is the cultural atmosphere (overt or covert) for resolving conflict in the school?
2. Invite to class students who have been trained in a school's conflict resolution program (classroom mediators); have the guests demonstrate their training to the class. Ask them to relate how they have successfully or unsuccessfully used their mediation processes.
3. Invite community representatives and parents in for a forum on community efforts for peaceful conflicts to reduce crime and violence.
4. Use excerpts from literature or videos that outline conflict (e.g., S. E. Hinton books like *The Outsiders*, with accompanying video).
5. Have students read and unpack the conversations in *Death Games* by Scott Russell Sanders, *Chocolate War* by Robert Cormier, *I Am the Cheese* by Robert Cormier, or *Blubber* by Judy Blume.

Performance-Based Assessments

- Role-playing and interpretation of vignettes
- Creating conflict resolution strategies

CONCLUSION

What are some different management strategies for conflict that you will use in the future? Refer back to the strategies for negotiating resolution (fig. 3.24). Add steps or ideas of your own to this process. What would you like to ask of your classmates to help you establish the strategies?

ASSIGNMENT

1. Choose a real conflict with which you are involved. Describe who the conflict is with, what the differences are in the conflict, how you felt

during the conflict, what you wanted in the conflict, and what the other person wanted. Describe your stake in the conflict—what outcome were you looking for and why did you want that outcome?

2. Describe what strategies you will use to resolve the conflict you have described.

3. What agreements will resolve this conflict? If you actually used the conflict resolution process, what was the outcome? How did it feel to go through this process?

4. If this same situation ever occurs again, what alternatives will you try? What else might you want to tell the other person involved in this conflict?

Unit 2C

Conflict Resolution

LESSON TOPIC: PERSPECTIVE TAKING

Teaching Note

Negotiation and perspective taking have been connected together in this lesson as part of a process of empowerment through building communication skills. Improving their communication skills can help students deal with multiple and, at times, conflicting interests and ideas in the class. This can be a powerful lesson in terms of practicing essential team-building skills that need to be transferred to all of the other classroom projects and to the students' work environments. Knowing how to interact with many cultures, perspectives, and settings builds student confidence. As a result, class members participate more cooperatively and in a more engaged manner with the teacher and with each other. They become better able to deal with stress and adversity through shared experiences that build trust. Classrooms can then be, as Antonia Darder describes, "apprenticeships in democracy" (Darder, 1991, p. 62). Using this metaphor, students begin to realize how to build on their own powerful resources. Through the acknowledgment and validation of these student strengths, teachers and students together can deconstruct traditional classrooms and construct and reconstruct democratic classrooms. The classroom offers a powerful environment for changing perspectives and attitudes, a new way of seeing the world. Learning to get along without violence, and dealing with others who don't practice conflict resolution, is a critical lesson that needs constant practice for students from all walks of life.

Objectives

To understand the concept of perspective taking
To negotiate conflict resolution through perspective taking

Domains

Cognitive: Understand and apply concept of perspective taking and negotiation
Affective: Value others' perspectives
Skills: Listen carefully and communicate ideas effectively

Academic Standard: Write and Speak in the English Language

Interpersonal Communication Skills
Effective speaking and listening skills
Create self-assessment and appropriate feedback

Materials

Flipcharts for small group work
Management Strategies for Conflict sheet (fig. 3.25)

Introductory Framework

For the past two seminars, we have studied the history, background, and current concepts of violence, and the application of conflict resolution in the United States. Today, we will look at how to expand the concept through the process of negotiation and perspective taking.

Motivation

We will do a three-minute stream of consciousness writing exercise based on your interpretation of the following quote: "The test of a first rate intelligence is the ability to hold two opposing ideas in the mind at the same time, and still retain the ability to function" (F. Scott Fitzgerald, 1936). What do you think this means?

Have student leaders list brainstorming ideas that come out of the writing exercise on the board. What led you to your interpretations? This is called perspective taking—the ability to understand our own perspective, as well as the perspective of others. To be quiet, listen, and consider others' ideas are the first steps toward mutual respect and cooperation. This is a skill that needs constant practice.

INSTRUCTIONAL IMPLEMENTATION

Individual Activity: Perspective Taking

Tell students to think about a person they know well. Then ask them to recall an incident in which this person was trying to convey a certain meaning or stance to them that was different from their own. This incident could be, for example, trying to get them to vote in a certain way, trying to get them to like the other person, trying to get them to participate in a certain activity, trying to get them to do a favor.

Then students are to list the specific behaviors and strategies that person used to convey these meanings. Bring students together to debrief, using these questions:

- How were you able to understand, interpret, or infer these meanings?
- What evidence did you use to make your judgments? (Students will then share their examples with the class.)
- What happened when you were able to take another's perspective and understand his or her point of view?
- Why is it so difficult to take another's perspective?

Volunteers will make a presentation about their experience with perspective taking and then get feedback from the class members.

Perspective taking is the ability to understand someone else's position or stance. We all come to situations with various understandings and perspectives. For example, at work managers and employees have different perspectives. In order to better understand each other, many times more information is needed so all participants can have a broader view—we all need to see and understand the bigger picture. Can you recall a time at your work site when you and your supervisor had different perceptions of a situation or even of you and your work style or an incident with a work colleague? Free write about the situation. What was the situation? What were the varying perspectives? How was the situation resolved? Ask for students to volunteer to share their recollections and interpretations.

Large Group Activity: Negotiation—The Next Step

Understanding one's own perspective as well as the other person's is part of the process to resolve disagreements and misunderstandings. Ask students how they would define *negotiation,* and write their definitions on the board.

Students should then give examples of how they have negotiated in the past—both successfully and unsuccessfully—and make a presentation on a situation involving negotiation to the rest of the class. Class members will give their feedback.

We negotiate every day of our lives, in one form or another. When any conflicts or disagreements occur, we try to find resolutions and learn to live with the results of negotiations. Negotiating with skill and grace is difficult, but it is an important tool worth learning to use. This is a process that is used by persons who have shared opposing interests and goals and who want to work out an agreement. The problem-solving process can be used with strangers to resolve temporary conflict or with colleagues, friends, and family to resolve ongoing conflicts.

Negotiation is only successful when you are able to take the other person's perspective and understand how the conflict may appear differently to that person and how she or he is reacting both cognitively and emotionally.

For example, Keosha and Kathy are students in the same class. Keosha's family is middle class, while Kathy's family struggles with finances. Both of the young women have won a $150 award in the school writing contest. Keosha says, "Look at that, a $150 prize." Then she returns to her softball game with her friends. When Kathy finds out she begins to shout and jump up and down yelling, "I won, I won, I won $150!" She hugs her friends and begins laughing and crying in her excitement. Why do you think each young woman had such a different reaction to winning?

No two people see an issue in the same way. We are all influenced in our perspectives by the experiences we have in life and by what we want to see. We can have different perspectives at different times. Misunderstandings occur when we make the assumption that everyone sees everything in the same way—or should see everything the same way. (Have students demonstrate the above concepts with examples of their own.) What connections do you see between diversity and conflict?

In order to help understand each other and apply new strategies, let us look at a defined process of negotiation and perspective taking. (Use overhead, fig. 3.24.) Now, let us try one session of negotiation together.

Large Group Activity: Scenario—How Would You Handle This Situation?

You are a newly appointed employee for a fast-food chain. Your supervisor is a highly emotional and organized manager. All of the employees have a formal relationship with him and call him "Mr. Anderson," while he calls everyone by their last name. When he gets angry, he yells at you and your coworkers and becomes abusive. His outbursts occur about once a week. The strategy you and your coworkers have used is to remain silent. You know that a position will be hard to find elsewhere and you are in the process of saving money for college. Yet you are getting angrier as you feel you are a doormat and do not like or agree with Mr. Anderson's behavior. You are becoming more irritable and are taking your feelings out on your family, friends, and coworkers. The situation at work is becoming more intense each week. When he starts in with you today, you have about had it. What will your course of action be? Remember there could be more than one course of action. Be realistic in your approach.

Provide students with the following guide questions as they work out this scenario:

- What were the strategies used to manage in the Mr. Anderson conflict?
- Brainstorm effective and ineffective ways of reacting in this conflict.
- What interpersonal skills were used?
- What skills could have been used?
- What changes in the strategy would you use if you actually were in the situation?

As you read and role-play the scenarios, use these questions as guides for your discussions.

Small Group Activity: Conflict Resolution—Confronting the Opposition

Students will create a scenario similar to Mr. Anderson's from their workplace or community. Allow ten minutes for this activity. Then each group will present their situation and report conflict management options (fig. 3.25) to the class—or have each group present their situation and ask the class for suggestions. See if the class' suggestions match the groups' suggestions.

Performance-Based Assessments

- Students' ability to role-play and strategize for resolutions

Optional Plans

1. Have students continue to practice their negotiating strategies using vignettes they have written from their work experiences.
2. Have students present examples from television and film regarding their interpretation of violence and conflict resolution.
3. Show ten-minute snippets from popular films such as *Boyz in the Hood, Dangerous Minds, Crisis at Central High*, or *Lean on Me*. Have students analyze what is going on in the films. Encourage them to observe and analyze the film from different perspectives.
4. Research and choose materials and guest speakers who address the issues of adolescence and violence, suicide, drugs, and/or gangs.
5. Have students organize panels, with invited guests, centered on the theme of teen life and violence or the theme of "the war on teenagers,"

including perspectives on increased teen unemployment and teens navigating this portion of life. How do gangs contribute to violence in teen life?

6. Discuss initiation into the cacophony of adolescence—making the bridge between youth and adulthood. How have you been initiated into young adulthood? How was this experience different for your parents, other family members, friends? What recommendations would you make to help youth make the transition in our culture? (This proved to be an invigorating topic as many of the students described what it is to be initiated into adulthood in their culture, and how they felt more connected to their community and were able to demonstrate their worth as a result of the initiation.)

7. Have students write to organizations for young people who want to get involved in changing the world around them.

8. Read aloud from children's books to enrich and expand ideas on the peaceable classroom. Using this strategy can help deflect potentially volatile situations and help raise difficult issues in a manner that makes them seem less threatening. Many times, children's books trigger and suggest new ways of thinking about or solving conflicts. For example, check out *Some of My Best Friends Are Polka-Dot Pigs* by Sarah Anderson and *Tales from the Dragon's Cave* by Arlene Williams.

9. Have a variety of articles on various conflicts on hand for small group work. Each group will critically review the articles and share information with the large group. A good resource is the *Journal of Conflict Resolution*.

10. Invite parents and community leaders to become partners in creating a "peaceable classroom" and building bridges among school, community, and home.

CONCLUSION

What impact does perspective taking have on conflict resolution?

ASSIGNMENT

1. Look in the Metro section in one of the local newspapers and find an article that discusses a conflict. Summarize the article and then create your own resolution for the situation.

2. Choose five of the following ideas and write your thoughts on how each could work effectively in one's personal and professional life:

- Ethics of care
- Making better choices
- Changing classroom culture
- Communication and relationships
- The excitement of violence
- Communities are built on knowing yourself, knowing each other, and interacting in positive, supportive ways
- Increased responsibility for your learning. How is being responsible different from being obedient?

Unit 3A

The Voyager Company

LESSON TOPIC: ORGANIZING THE VOYAGER COMPANY

Teaching Note

Building and creating the Voyager Company is a highlight of this program. This project, developed and implemented throughout the next two years, gives students the opportunity to gain a sense of how all the elements of their academic learning come together and to apply their knowledge to projects beyond school. They research and actively work on real organizational problems that are all established in real time frames by real people and organizations. How they go about composing the Voyager identity is an important part of the process. In this unit's lessons and those of Unit 6 of the senior year, students are formally asked to develop and use multiple abilities, to practice working collaboratively, to analyze business structures, and to raise their awareness of the social, political, and economic factors related to the careers they are investigating, and to research local companies that influence their communities. They meet and continue their work on the Voyager Company throughout the year in a variety of activities such as attending community meetings, interviewing business partners, creating materials via the web, doing research, and analyzing data.

The broad goal of the Voyager Company units and lessons is to engender and support the ability of Voyager students to apply the sum of the learning they gain from the seminars, job shadowing experiences, and internships to the generation of ideas for problem solving or new product development. Students are encouraged to reflect on the kinds of practices that support the development of democratic work environments in which high levels of productivity and work satisfaction are the norm. Critical inquiry and critical consciousness begin to develop as students start to understand their human capacity and potential to transform their environments. The classroom is the "lab site" for such a reform to begin. Teaching and learning both in the classroom and at work engender the philosophy to unpack the assumptions that have been perpetuated by an advanced technological society. The domination of media and popular culture has left aspects of our lives underdeveloped and most citizens marginally aware of necessary work changes. We are led to believe that changes can be made in the corporate world but little has changed to invite employees to be agents of change. In the Voyager Company, students will create an "Ideas Bank" that offers solutions and strategies to real-world companies as well as examining the philosophical foundations undergirding traditional approaches. They build a company from the ground up. They develop goals, mission statements, logs, mottoes, job descriptions, and an organizational plan. They identify and assign tasks and activities, carry out a needs assessment, and ultimately provide a company analysis.

In this unit's lessons, the case study method is employed as a framework for examining a range of businesses. These businesses will be used as reference points as the students build the Voyager Company's Ideas Bank. The case study method will also act as a guide for students in investigating companies in order to discern and understand their internal processes and procedures, and as a method of analysis for generating ideas and strategies for problem solving or product/project/service development. This company can function on multiple levels: local, state, regional, national, or global. It is a decision made by the Voyager community members.

Throughout the units, both teachers and students are active, critical researchers of their worlds. As you teach the lessons in this unit, think about yourself in the role and responsibilities of a corporate consultant and/or portfolio manager. Keeping this perspective foremost in your approach will facilitate students' active engagement in building the Voyager Company. These hands-on projects connect students with actual workplace dilemmas and new challenges for companies in the twenty-first century.

Objectives

To establish the organizational structure of the Voyager Company, and identify the members of the four company divisions

To develop a mission statement of the Voyager Company

To begin the written record and the history of the Voyager Company and to archive all evidence of research and study that has taken place to pass on to the next class of Voyager students. (Much of this work will be done with the integration technology and the development of multimedia materials.)

Domains

Cognitive: Develop an understanding of business structures and organizations
Affective: Value the process of building a company
Skills: Define the different components of a company

Graduation/Academic Standard: Decision Making

Career Investigation
Determine personal interests, aptitudes, and abilities
Investigate a career through research

Materials

Large banner with the Voyager Company name (teacher or students can create)
Voyager Company "stock certificates"
Sample Company Mission Statements and Marketing Slogans
Numbers (six sets of one through four) for drawing team assignments
Small group handouts
Personal Attributes Inventory

Pre-Instructional

Students will complete Personal Attributes Inventories and bring them to the session. Students will also find and bring to class a newspaper or magazine article that describes in depth the corporate structure or organization of a financial business service. The story can be current or historical. Some students will choose to identify a business in their own community that they would like to research and some will identify businesses outside their community.

Introductory Framework

For the lessons in this unit, the teacher is the students' business consultant and portfolio manager. The main asset of the Voyager Company is a bank of ideas for businesses. The students have purchased the company because it is a perfect environment to practice the skills and learning they are going to gain over the next two years in the Voyager program. Please keep in mind that in this company, the student is considered quite valuable because of his or her knowledge and creativity. The teacher will pass out the certificates that represent each student's one equal share in the company (fig. 3.27). Students

Figure 3.27.   Stock Certificate

The Bearer of this certificate shall be entitled to one (1) Equal Share of Ownership in the Voyager Company. Upon completion of Voyager Secondary Seminars, bearer agrees to transfer this certificate of ownership to an incoming junior Voyager student. Bearer further agrees as an owner manager of the Voyager Company to participate fully in efforts to increase the resources of the Voyager Company.

This Certificate has no monetary value and is for use only in Voyager: Direction for Learning & Careers.

will own and run the company, as well as work in it over the next two years. The Voyager Company is theirs to create and define, with support and guidance from business partners.

Twenty-first-century businesses need to respond to the rapidly changing economy of the United States, and twenty-first-century workers need to be both problem solvers and creative thinkers—in essence, knowledge is the greatest skill of workers today. The Voyager Company seeks to meet businesses' needs for effective and efficient problem solving, their need for creative ideas for marketing their products and services, and their need for development of new products and services that expand their market share. As the owners and workers of the Voyager Company, the students will need to use critical thinking skills as they set up the company and develop and market a bank of creative problem-posing and problem-solving ideas based on comprehensive investigation of companies. The students' ideas will be developed and delivered using the case study method, which the class will learn about after setting up the company. Since no one knows what will affect business in the coming years, it is up to the students to examine the emerging trends that will change the nature of work and workplace demands as the years progress. In setting up this company, the class is also investigating the "habits of mind" students and workers will need to practice in order to thrive in the years to come.

Motivation

Take five minutes to free write and describe your last job(s). What was it like to work for the company? What were some of the most satisfying features for you as a worker? What were the features that engendered disengagement? Develop a sharp mental image of what you want to present to us. Student leaders will go to the board and record the brainstorming lists. After all of the lists have been compiled, discuss the unique features and commonalities students experienced while working for their companies. Using your Personal Attributes Inventory, what type of future work will suit you better?

INSTRUCTIONAL IMPLEMENTATION

Small Group Activity: Composing Voyager Identity

As workers and students we have the capacity to make a difference in how we live and work together. This classroom is a site for transformation as we have set up teaching and learning in a different way. The same can be applied to workplaces. Take time in your small groups to develop the identity of the Voyager Company. What are some of the ideas and goals you would want to engage in? Each group must develop a list that will be shared with everyone.

Large Group Activity: Framing the Process with a Mission

It's important to know what the company is about—what are the mission, function, beliefs, and values of this company? Deciding what it will create, develop, and distribute (ideas, projects, products, services) is the first step in organizing the company. The next step is deciding for whom you want to work and why they are your market. Taken together and stated descriptively and concisely, what you are selling, who you are selling it to, and why you are selling it becomes your mission statement and the framework for organizing your company and developing a marketing campaign. Here are some examples of mission statements and corresponding advertising. (Show overhead, fig. 3.28.) After considering them, how would you answer these questions:

Figure 3.28.   Minnesota Companies and Their Mission Statements

1. Target: Expect more. Pay less.
2. JC Penney: JC Penney dedicates itself to satisfying the needs and expectations of our targeted customer segments. We will offer fashion and basic apparel, accessories, and home furnishings in a customer-friendly environment in our stores, in our catalog, and on the Internet.
3. Honeywell: Honeywell Inc. has a single focus: controls. It was the basis of the company's founding in 1885 with the invention of the automatic thermostat control for home heating. Today, we are a global leader in control technology that benefits millions of people and organizations. Honeywell employs people in a wide range of occupations: scientists, engineers, administrators, attorneys, factory workers, accountants, sales and marketing people, and many more categories.
4. Sample Voyager Mission Statement from the previous class: The Voyager Company: Ideas and solutions for today's businesses to meet tomorrow's challenges.

- How would you describe what a mission statement is?
- What do you have to think about in developing a mission statement for your company? Why do you think a mission statement is important for a company?
- What is its purpose? (List the statements and reasons on the board.)

These questions should give you some ideas for working on your mission statement in small groups.

Small Group Activity: The First Steps in Organizing

Lead students in beginning to write the company mission statement as we work in teams. Students should break into their cooperative base groups to work on mission statements.

All mission statements will be placed on post paper for everyone to see and then to weave into one final mission statement. Then set up the company teams in the big group and then break into teams for brainstorming the company mission in the context of the responsibilities of each division. This will be your first team meeting devoted to company business. When we come back together in the big group, each team will present its suggested mission statement and then they will work as the company board to develop a mission statement for the company as a whole.

Large Group Activity: Organizational Structure

During the first year, the student will organize the Voyager Company and prepare for increasing the assets of the Ideas Bank and identifying potential customers for the company's services during the next year.

The first step in organizing the company is gaining a thorough understanding of the company's product/service, how it is delivered, and to whom it is delivered. So let's look at the company. Put up the Organizational Overview overhead (fig. 3.29).

Decide if we will have teams of equal numbers or if some teams need more people than others. Every company has divisions or departments that are responsible for specific areas. Currently, the Voyager Company has four divisions. Use your Personal Attributes Inventory (fig. 3.30) to set up the divisions. Important points to consider are:

- Having enough members who have interest and ability for the tasks of the team
- Incorporating enough difference in personal attributes to spark team creativity

Figure 3.29. Organizational Overview

The Research and Development Division is the team that will research the kinds of problems your customers have, the kinds of solutions they are looking for, and how to develop those solutions. They identify company competitors and how Voyager Company's service stacks up against that competition. They will also do research to identify new customers for the sales and marketing teams. Additionally, they will research challenges being faced in the community and compile resources for both business partners and for the Voyager career center.

The Sales and Marketing Division creates a sales approach, develops a marketing plan, and has the most direct contact with customers. This team will also develop ideas for marketing and advertising materials that the shareholders will review and approve.

The Finance Division will keep track of all the money the Voyager Company will earn. The Finance Division is responsible for developing budgets, revenue and expense statements, and financial reports for shareholders.

The Management Division is responsible for setting company policies, keeping the company on track with its objectives, making sure the other teams have the resources they need to accomplish their responsibilities, and reporting and presenting the company reports to the shareholders.

- Giving you experience working with groups of people who have different perspectives and attributes but who are working toward a common goal, and
- Creating active teams with people who work collaboratively to produce results. For instance:
- The Research and Development Division is the team that will examine the kinds of problems your customers have, the kinds of solutions they are looking for, and how to develop those solutions. They identify company competitors and how Voyager Company's service stacks up against that competition. They will also do research to identify new customers for the sales and marketing team. How many people do we need on this team given the tasks involved? (Write number on overhead.)
- The Sales and Marketing Division creates a sales approach, develops a marketing plan, and has the most direct contact with customers. This division will also develop ideas for marketing and advertising materials that the shareholders will review and approve. How many people do we need on this team given the tasks involved? (Write number on overhead.)
- The Finance Division will keep track of all the money the Voyager Company will earn. The Finance Team is responsible for developing budgets, revenue and expense statements, customer contracts and in-

Figure 3.30. Personal Attributes Inventory

Answer the following questions based on what you would actually do in each situation, not on what you would like to do or think you should do.

1. If you were going to organize things in your life, would you organize them by:
   - ❏ Separating them into logical categories
   - ❏ Prioritizing their importance
2. A problem has come up at work. Would you likely:
   - ❏ Let things develop
   - ❏ Take quick action to solve the problem
3. Would your friend be more likely to say that you:
   - ❏ Think with your head
   - ❏ Think with your heart
4. You are in a large room with many people. Do you typically:
   - ❏ Wait for people to come to you
   - ❏ Introduce yourself to people nearest you
5. Which approach to a challenge is more your style?
   - ❏ Devise a solid plan and keep to it
   - ❏ Play a hunch that just might work
6. When coming home from a crowded party, do you typically feel:
   - ❏ Exhausted
   - ❏ Energized
7. What is more stimulating to you?
   - ❏ The present
   - ❏ The possibilities
8. Which person would upset you the most?
   - ❏ A person lacking in sympathy
   - ❏ A person who is unreasonable
9. When introducing yourself at a job interview, would you describe yourself as:
   - ❏ An ideas person
   - ❏ A details person
10. You have an unpleasant situation to deal with. Are you more likely to:
    - ❏ Put off dealing with it for a while
    - ❏ Jump right in and settle it
11. In terms of your friendships, do you typically:
    - ❏ Make new friends wherever you go
    - ❏ Stay loyal to a core group of old friends
12. When it comes to change, do you tend to:
    - ❏ Go with the flow
    - ❏ Stay the course
13. Would you say you deal better with situations that involve:
    - ❏ Abstract matters
    - ❏ Practical matters
14. When it comes to keeping a schedule, does it:
    - ❏ Cramp your style
    - ❏ Suit your style
15. A new idea comes up at work. Are you more likely to:
    - ❏ Know what you like and don't like about it
    - ❏ Take some time to take it in

(continued)

Figure 3.30. Personal Attributes Inventory *(continued)*

16. Would a new work colleague be more likely to say:
    ❐ You are a reserved person
    ❐ You are easy to talk to
17. Which part of a project is more stimulating to you:
    ❐ Making it actually happen
    ❐ Dreaming it up
18. In making a decision, it is better to:
    ❐ Understand what is important
    ❐ Understand the facts
19. Your boss gives you a big assignment that requires working with a team. Would you:
    ❐ Relish the chance to work with a team
    ❐ Rather work on the assignment yourself
20. What kind of situation are you more comfortable with:
    ❐ Clearly defined situations
    ❐ Open-ended situations

voices, and financial reports for shareholders. How many people do we need on this team given the tasks involved? (Write number on overhead.)

- The Management Division is responsible for setting company policies, keeping the company on track with its objectives, making sure the other teams have the resources they need to accomplish their responsibilities, and reporting and presenting the company reports to the shareholders. How many people do we need for this team given the tasks involved? (Write number on overhead.) Are there any other divisions and/or teams we need to organize that you feel are vital to the company's success?

Activity: Establish Division Action Teams

Set out the six sets of numbers, numbered 1–4, and have students draw numbers to determine their initial division/team assignment. Break into your teams and for the next ten minutes go over your Personal Attributes Inventory. One person in each team needs to volunteer to go through each question and keep a tally of how many people respond to each answer.

After you finish all of the questions, review the tally as a group and decide if you have enough diversity of attributes on your team, or if you need to negotiate with the other teams to "transfer" members from one team/division to another. Review all the team tallies and ask if there need to be any changes made. If changes are needed, facilitate negotiations for members to change teams.

In four small groups, brainstorm a mission statement for the company. Choose one member to present your group's idea to the whole class. Once the groups are set, students then work together to set tasks and agenda for the next meeting. These meetings also take place outside the seminar and online.

Performance-Based Assessments

- Students' completion of Personal Attributes Inventory
- Creation of company work teams and development of company mission statement

CONCLUSION

What surprised you the most about the process today? What were some of the insights you gained from this process? What other factors will we have to take into consideration as we continue to work together to build the Voyager Company and begin to generate ideas?

ASSIGNMENT

1. Based on what you know about the Voyager Company from today, and the responsibilities and role of your team, use your Personal Attributes Inventory to identify additional strengths and abilities you will bring to the team and what skills and abilities you need to enhance or develop.
2. Identify two goals you have for your team and what you think you personally need to do (objectives) to support the team reaching the goals. Write your strengths, goals, and objectives on paper. What are you most looking forward to? What are you most anxious about? Bring this to the next class.

Unit 3B

The Voyager Company

LESSON TOPIC: COMPANY GOALS AND OBJECTIVES

Teaching Note

In setting up the company, Voyager students are asked to examine standard rules and procedures of operation. Through critical inquiry and dialogue, they will:

1. Examine the impact of rules and business procedures on their lives
2. Learn to deal with power struggles
3. Understand discrimination in company politics
4. Learn to undertake an in-depth analysis of businesses
5. Ultimately come up with suggestions to take action for change

Students' ability to engage grows with their active participation, not through listening to lectures about participation. Through mutual and open dialogue, they will become co-creators of knowledge rather than passive recipients of information. A student's impressions, opinions, ideas, and even casual utterances are taken seriously by everyone engaged in the dialogue. Through this shared value of dialogue, everyone can find a deeper meaning to a situation and embark upon reflecting and interpreting unknown material found in this unit. Support students as they learn to take themselves and their ideas seriously. This is an essential problem-posing unit as students are asked to examine:

1. Equitable practices, which include a range of thought and discussion
2. How to provide opportunities for the inclusion and participation of all class members

3. Safety issues in the workplace
4. The role of company unions
5. Accident prevention and types of accidents at work
6. Appropriate health insurance
7. Overtime policies
8. Identification and awareness of discrimination

All of these areas challenge how we have all been educated to think about work and our role as workers. Community in this new world is based on shared values and beliefs, rather than right of birth.

Objectives

To review organization of Voyager Company work teams and the mission statement
To set goals and objectives for divisions/teams and company

Domains

Cognitive: Create company goals and objectives
Affective: Understand team building
Skills: Make choices among company's divisions

Graduation/Academic Standard: Decision Making

Career Investigation
Determine personal interests, aptitudes, and abilities
Investigate a career through research

Materials

Organizational Overview
Small group handouts
Annual reports of businesses that will be presented in Lesson 3

Pre-Instructional

Students are to have completed and brought with them to class a written report on their personal strengths and goals and objectives for their team.

Introductory Framework

Last time, we set the teams and the mission statement for the Voyager Company. Let's review that statement. Are there any changes that we want to

make? Is there anything that we want to add? This will be the mission statement for this year and will guide anything you do with the company. Are
there any changes to the teams?

Today we are going to set team and company objectives. We will set up
the teams in the big group and then break into teams for setting team objectives and for brainstorming company objectives. This will be your first team
meeting. When we come back in the big group, each team will present their
team objectives and suggest company goals, and we will finalize goals for
the year.

Motivation

We set objectives, and plans to reach our goals, every day. An example is resolving to get to school on time; the action you need to take to reach this goal
may be setting your alarm clock ten minutes earlier than you usually do. Or
the action could be going to sleep ten minutes earlier so you feel ready to get
up when the alarm goes off. You have to define your goal—what you want
to achieve—and your objective—what you are going to do to reach the
goal—and together they are a plan. *Goal defined + action/objective = plan.*
You can measure this plan in several ways. You can measure how often you
got to school on time by changing your alarm setting versus how often when
you slept longer. In this example, you can also try both plans and measure if
one is more effective for you than the other.

The goals and objectives you set today will be the beginning of your company's business plan. The goals need to concretely state what you want to do
and who you want to do it for. The objectives need to outline the specific actions you are going to take to reach the goal, and how you are going to measure what you have done.

INSTRUCTIONAL IMPLEMENTATION

Large Group Activity: Rules and Codes of Conduct

Distribute copies of rules for employee behavior handbooks that students
have brought in from their work sites. Let's critically analyze these procedures and see if you want to change them in any way. Go over rules and allow students to vote on keeping or deleting each rule. Debrief with the students using the following questions:

- How do these rules affect the way a company runs?
- Are they fair?
- What do they accomplish?
- Do they restrict creativity?

- Are there any rules you think need to be changed or rules you want to add?
- Why do we need or not need rules?

Write suggestions for changes on the board and have students vote on changes and then vote as a group to adopt the employee handbook. Then one class member will rewrite the handbook with approved changes and distribute copies to all class members.

Team Activity: Team Goals—Defining the What and How

Break into teams again and each team will set three goals and two objectives for each goal that you want to propose as a team for the company's annual work plan. These are goals for this year only. You may decide to keep them as goals for next year as well.

Have each team choose a meeting facilitator. In each team's handout packet, there is a guide for facilitating a meeting that the facilitator can read over while the agenda for the meeting is being set (fig. 3.31).

Use the meeting agenda form (fig. 3.32) to set the meeting agenda and decide who will use the meeting minutes form (fig. 3.33) to record the actions that take place in the meeting. Have students review the handout for company goals.

Team Activity: Putting It All Together—Team Objectives and Action

Have each team write its goals and objectives on the board and review them for any common statements. Go over each goal one at a time and have students vote on accepting or rejecting the goal. Give students time to write down each goal.

Return to the objectives, reminding students that the objectives define the *what* and the *how* of actions they are going to take to achieve company and team goals. Have students vote on each objective. Give students time to write the objectives under the proper goal. Review the goals and objectives and have students vote on adopting the plan as a whole. Students will review and work with the handout describing company objectives.

Performance-Based Assessments

- Students' results from team work
- Completion of goals and objectives

Optional Plans

1. Have students research and analyze goals and objectives from local companies. Have students make a chart that compares the goals and

Figure 3.31. Facilitating a Meeting

Facilitation skills are utilized when presentations become interactive meetings. The facilitator sets the agenda, coaches participants, and guides the pacing. Here is an outline for facilitating a meeting.

Opening
Stimulate interest with:
- a noteworthy event
- a personal experience
- a testimonial
- a quotation

Bridge
Tie your opening directly to your key topic. Your energy and attitude set the tone and provide momentum for this meeting.

Key Topic
- Define the topic/problem/opportunity.
- State the reason for importance.
- Invite comments by audience.
- Encourage participation.
- Record and display key comments on key ideas.

Goals and Problems
- Define the goals.
- Define the problems.
- Encourage participants to focus on the issues and assign priorities.

Solutions and Opportunities
- Invite comments and ideas from the audience.
- Record and display their comments regarding action plans and solutions.
- Invite participants to prioritize options.

Action Plan
Describe the following (where additional information is needed assign responsibility to the logical person):
- Action steps
- Materials needed
- Training needed
- Schedules
- Costs

Close
- Ensure understanding.
- Describe first steps.
- Get commitment.

Figure 3.32. Meeting Agenda

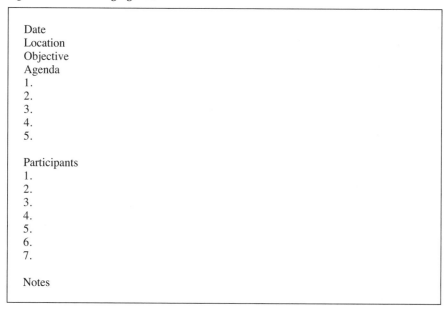

Date
Location
Objective
Agenda
  1.
  2.
  3.
  4.
  5.

Participants
  1.
  2.
  3.
  4.
  5.
  6.
  7.

Notes

objectives of the companies they have researched and then have them discuss what aspects might be incorporated into the Voyager Company.

2. Choose Harvard Business School case studies for analysis and problem solving.
3. Create a needs assessment for working with local companies.
4. Research web sites for additional background on other companies and organizations and how they work.
5. Invite speakers from local businesses to come in and talk about how goals, objectives, and teamwork are set up in their organization.
6. Research how current business events are affecting the community. Bring in speakers when possible. Some examples: Factories closing—who benefits from this decision, how was this decision made? Corporate downsizing—how was this decision made? What impact does it have in the community?
7. Continue to build the Voyager Company web site and include information on the Voyager Company. Create discussion forums, use photos, paste research articles and links in order to assist others who are interested in your work. Include biographies and photos of class members (with their permission, of course).

Figure 3.33.   Meeting Minutes

Date
Location
Objective
Agenda
1.
2.
3.
4.
5.

Participants
1.
2.
3.
4.
5.
6.
7.

Subject
Discussion
Action

CONCLUSION

You have now set up the structure, defined your mission, established teams, and set goals and objectives for the Voyager Company. What are the things that stand out for you from the process of structuring the company? What have you learned that you think will help you as you pursue your career? How do you think the Voyager Company is different from the companies you read about in your articles?

ASSIGNMENT

1. Each student will complete the activity schedule (fig. 3.34) as it relates to his or her division in the Voyager Company and bring it to the next session. After reading one of the company annual reports you have distributed, each student should also develop and write out one brief question related to his or her team responsibilities to be asked of the next meeting's business presenter.

2. Create questions for the business representatives. Students are urged to meet with their team members before the next seminar to discuss and develop questions for the business representatives.

Figure 3.34. Activity Schedule

Today's Date: _____

Division: _____

Division Members: _____

Activity to Be Accomplished: _____

Task	Timeline	Person Responsible	Due Date	Hours Worked

Unit 3C

The Voyager Company

LESSON TOPIC: GATHERING COMPANY DATA

Teaching Note

Inviting business leaders to work with students serves multiple purposes, such as promoting awareness of business practices and trends, and adds authenticity about workplace cultures and thinking. This event requires intentional planning and discussion. Students are responsible for inviting business speakers, planning the event, and framing the discussion. They invite representatives from the businesses that are Voyager partners in your community or representatives from other businesses that they have connections with. Business representatives are asked to send information regarding their company ahead of time and to bring other relevant materials with them. Often, they bring another colleague with them to share an additional perspective on their company and their work. This is not a one-shot day but can and should be repeated throughout the secondary seminar. As students develop their company, business leaders are asked to critique the development and provide professional, constructive feedback to the students. This initial meeting and subsequent meetings can be set up in a variety of ways. For example, because the students have worked on their company mission statement, goals, and objectives, they can ask the business partners for feedback and assessment of their ideas. This results in a thought-provoking session for all parties. Businesspeople get to guide the development of a from-the-ground-up enterprise, and the students get immediate professional feedback for their company. Students can review their needs assessment survey with the business partners for suggestions and edits.

Objectives

To understand the assessment of a company by gathering information on the company structure and product/services and interacting with business representatives

To understand the responsibilities of each of the company divisions

Domains

Cognitive: Understand company structures
Affective: Value all company components
Skills: Listen and give feedback

Graduation/Academic Standard: Decision Making

Career Investigation
Investigate a career through research

Materials

Sample job descriptions from the company presented
Sample annual reports, employee handbooks, policy memos, marketing and advertising materials, and the like from the companies represented

Pre-Instructional

Contact company presenters and ask them to come and present an overview of their company, including the responsibilities of their management, financial, research/development, and marketing divisions. Ask them to send a copy of their most recent public annual report prior to the session. Also ask them to provide you with materials related to the presentation as outlined above for reproduction and distribution to students (e.g., organizational charts, employee performance review forms, code of ethics, safety manuals, etc.). Ask the presenters to pose problems for discussion and analysis in each of the division areas.

Introductory Framework

Introduce the business representative by saying, "Today_____ from_____ will be making a presentation about [her or his] company. The presentation will give you an overview of the company and information about the responsibilities of the Voyager Company Working Teams."

Motivation

The presentation you are about to hear will give you an opportunity to:

1. Get to know one of your potential customers in depth
2. Explore the responsibilities of the career you are looking at
3. See what it might be like to work at a company like Cargill, ING, Target, and the like
4. Gain information and knowledge to enhance the Voyager Company

INSTRUCTIONAL IMPLEMENTATION

Activity: Preparing for a Business Partner Presentation

Before the presenter arrives, break into work teams and review your activity schedules and assign tasks. Review the questions you wrote out as a part of your homework and decide if you need to develop additional questions or if you want to delete some questions.

Activity: Presentation by Business Partner Company and Questions and Answers

Here are some sample questions generated by Voyager students:

1. Why was the organizational plan drawn up like this?
2. How would you describe what your company does?
3. How would you rate your company's success at the moment?
4. What do you see as the future for your company?
5. What skills/abilities and education are you looking for in future and successful workers at various levels in your company?
6. Do you consider your company multinational—what influence does it have on the way you conduct business and make new hires?
7. What ways do you provide for training on the job and training for advancement? What kind of advancement "ladder" does your company use?
8. What are the demographics of your company? How many women, differently abled, and people of color are employed at your company?
9. How does your industry fit into world economics?
10. How does your industry benefit the local communities and the cities?
11. Would you ever think of reorganizing your company into a self-managed company?
12. What do you expect of someone in your position? What kind of education do you expect them to have?
13. Why are people fired from your company?

14. Did you ever have to downsize? How is that type of decision made?
15. Do you think you run a democratic company? Why? How is your company involved in social justice?
16. How would you describe the business ethics that your company is guided by?
17. What do you think a twenty-first-century work education needs to include?
18. How have any changes in demographics affected your company?
19. What is the one problem you would like to pose to the class today regarding your company?

Performance-Based Assessments

Question Sheets
Participation in dialogue with presenters

CONCLUSION

Thank your guest for her or his time, information, and expertise.

ASSIGNMENT

1. Think about the problem posed by one of the presenters and write out two things that are contributing to the problem. Also identify and bring to class a newspaper or magazine article that covers a problem in the sector of business you are exploring. It can be a business in this community or one in another community. Look for stories that relate to the problems posed by the presenters today.
2. Each working team in the Voyager Company will have a problem posed to it that you will use in the next session. Each team will use the case study method to develop a set of creative problem-solving recommendations to the problem posed.

Unit 3D

The Voyager Company

LESSON TOPIC: USING THE CASE STUDY METHOD TO DEVELOP PROBLEM-SOLVING RECOMMENDATIONS

Teaching Note

Everyday life is filled with all kinds and sizes of problems. Creative problem solving supports success in life and will be a key element for twenty-first-century businesses hoping to stay competitive. The case study method is one way to approach problem solving. Remember that, in this program, both teacher and students are critical researchers of their worlds, discovering new approaches to learning and problem solving. Draw on the questions developed for the last seminar to frame the discussion for this session. Highlight and build on the critical thinking skills that the students evidenced during the discussion with business representatives. Remind the students that the ideas they generate will go into the Ideas Bank. They need to identify if the ideas they develop apply only to one situation (proprietary to one company) or if they can be used in many businesses that have similar problems. The case study method provides multiple opportunities for critical dialogue, analysis, and developing on-the-spot decisions.

Objectives

To develop a working understanding of the case study method and apply it to real-life corporate arenas

To develop creative problem-solving recommendations for problems posed and employee performance reports

Domains

Cognitive: Develop problem-solving strategies
Affective: Appreciate a range of recommendations and perspectives
Skills: Listen to all perspectives

Graduation/Academic Standard: Decision Making

Career Investigation
Determine personal interests, aptitudes, and abilities
Investigate a career through research

Materials

Meeting agenda and minutes forms (figs. 3.32 and 3.33)
Case study method overhead (fig. 3.35)
Employee Performance Report handout (fig. 3.36) (double the number of handouts for each group)
"The New Beer," adapted from *Business Ethics: Concepts and Cases,* 4th ed., by Manuel G. Velasquez

Pre-Instructional

Students will find and bring to class a newspaper or magazine article covering a problem in a financial business service. The story can be current or historical. Some classes have chosen to locate a problem in their own community that they would like to research. Have students bring in from the last meeting written problems posed by business representatives. Refer back to previous lessons where ideas regarding local factory closings or business downsizing affected the community.

Figure 3.35.   Case Study Method

Identify the problems.

Examine the contributing causes.

Consider alternative courses of action.

Arrive at a set of recommendations.

Figure 3.36. Employee Performance Report

Section A: Personnel Information
Employee Name:
Department:
Position:
Grade/Level:
Period Covered:

Section B: Type of Report
Annual
Special
Probationary
Probationary (Final)

Section C: Evaluation Factors
Mandatory Factors (Required for all employees)
Adaptability
Attendance
Dependability
Initiative
Employee Relations
Quality of Work
Quantity of Work
Work Habits

Optional Factors (Evaluate if appropriate)
Public Contact
Planning and Organizing
Communication—Verbal
Communication—Written
Supervisory Ability
Management Ability
Other:
Other:

Section D: Performance Levels
Check one for each factor, 1 being the highest
Adaptability
Attendance
Dependability
Initiative
Employee Relations
Quality of Work
Quantity of Work
Work Habits
Public Contact
Planning and Organizing
Communication—Verbal
Communication—Written
Supervisory Ability
Management Ability
Other:
Other:

Introductory Framework

Review and summarize the presentation from the previous session. Highlight information about the responsibilities of positions in each division and the problems posed for the work teams. In addition to developing a set of recommendations for the problems posed, you are going to use the Employee Performance Report in pairs within your work team to evaluate yourselves and one another.

Motivation

Company X will be a potential customer for you next year when you develop marketing materials and contact the Voyager business partners to sell the service of the Idea Bank. It is important that your recommendations be as creative as possible while providing workable solutions to the problems posed. For example, X Company may want to strengthen its ties to the community, becoming more visible in that community by building relationships with community members. What suggestions would you have for Company X?

INSTRUCTIONAL IMPLEMENTATION

Large Group Activity: A Case Study—"The New Beer" (by Manuel G. Velasquez): The Ethics of Consumer Production and Marketing

The case study method (fig. 3.35) begins with identifying the problem to be solved. Here is a story about a company. Read the study of "The New Beer." Break students into groups to discuss the reading and identify the problem with these questions:

- What are the problems the company identified?
- Did you identify problems that the company did not?

Write all suggested problem statements on the overhead or on the board. After identifying the problem, the next step in the case study method is examining the contributing causes. Have the groups discuss what the story says about contributing causes:

- Do you agree or disagree that they are contributing causes of the problem?
- Are there other contributing causes you think are presented, based on the information in the story?
- What other resources can we use for gathering information on the contributing causes?

Write all suggested contributing causes on the overhead or on the board. Encourage "out of the box" thinking. Discuss with the whole class.

The third step in the case study method is considering alternative courses of action that a company can take to solve a problem or improve some area of the company. What alternative courses do you think the company should take? Does the writer of the story suggest any alternative courses? (If "yes," ask the students to analyze whether they think alternatives are suggested in the interest of the company or not. Write all suggested alternative courses on the overhead or on the board.)

Now we have identified the problem, examined the contributing causes, and considered alternative courses for action. The final step in the case study method is arriving at a set of recommendations. Brainstorm recommendations with the whole class. What recommendations do we want to make to this company and why? Write recommendations on the overhead or on the board.

Activity: Unpacking via the Case Study Method

Each work group will receive an individual case (listed below). Each of these cases is taken from *Business Ethics: Concepts and Cases* by Manuel Velasquez. Please apply the case method to the specific case you have been assigned. Be prepared to present to the class:

- "Toy Wars"
- "Dow Corning"
- "Phillip Morris's Troubles"
- "Pepsi's Burma Connection"
- "HB Fuller and the Street Children of Central America"

Have each group present their findings to the class. Summarize the common case study issues. Ask students to discuss whether they think it's possible to have a successful company without ethical problems.

Activity: Suggestions and Solutions

Break into your work teams and use the case study method to develop a set of recommended solutions to the problem in your area of responsibility. Select a meeting facilitator, develop an agenda, and record the minutes of the meeting.

Activity: Recommendations

Bring students back into the big group and have each group write their recommendations on the board. Review the recommendations and engage students in a decision-making process of changing the wording of the recommendations and by adding and deleting recommendations. When completed, ask for volunteers to write up a cover letter and recommendations report to send to the business partner company.

Activity: Employee Performance Report

Break into work teams. In each of your teams, break into pairs. (If there is an uneven number in any team, you may elect to fill in or put students in a group of three.) Teams should approach the performance report in these steps:

1. First take a few minutes to complete the Employee Performance Report (fig. 3.36) for yourself. After completing it, fill out another report for the other person in your pair. Be fair and serious as you complete both reports. Take about ten minutes to fill out the reports. Take another ten minutes to compare the two reports.
2. After completing the reports, discuss them with one another, especially the areas where your responses differ.
3. Use the remaining time to discuss Employee Performance Report outcomes in the big group or use the remaining time to draft the cover letter for the report as a group. Compare this report to the performance report you received during your internship. Do you have suggestions for additions or deletions?

Performance-Based Assessments

- Students' analysis and interpretations of case studies
- Completion of employee performance report

CONCLUSION

As an organizational developer and consultant, what recommendations did you make for each of these corporations? List them on the board.

ASSIGNMENT

Before this assignment, go over how to write a thank-you note and distribute a blank card to each student.

1. Each student is to write a thank-you note to the presenter(s) and bring it to the next meeting.

Unit 4A

Cooperative Learning

LESSON TOPIC:
BUILDING A COOPERATIVE LEARNING COMMUNITY

Teaching Note

In this program, there is an intentional focus and goal to build and nurture the creation of an equitable multiracial and ethnic learning community. Creating a committed learning community among diverse academic and cultural biographies and social standpoints is both necessary and challenging. One of the challenges in creating community is understanding how to sustain an engaged group of adolescents who are invested in the success of this richly diverse group and who are willing to make connections among their differences. What are the conditions that deliberately set the stage for such a community to thrive? Building trust, confidence, and hope are keys to lifting the barriers that may already exist in a school setting. In this community there must be a constant commitment to critically investigate issues of difference, power, and privilege. There must also exist an investment in democratic practice and creating democratic sites of cultural interaction. Democracy in action is not something that happens on its own accord, but is something that requires active participation and practice from all in order to remain dynamic. It is also a messy and often contentious practice.

For most of their educational lives, students are quite direct and open when they describe how they have resisted forming alliances or engaging in participatory practices because they see the educational system as inequitable, denying them participation in curriculum development and in governance practices. In essence, they feel invisible and see no value in their participation. One of the features of this program is that they are treated as young adults and respected for their knowledge and experience and are expected to be active in the democratic process and develop their voice. They also have not been asked in most of their experiences to care for each other. In their view, and from past experiences, caring for each other doesn't further their needs or goals. Therefore, learning to establish and maintain a caring classroom becomes an act of mutual respect and support.

As a committed group of teachers and learners, we must be willing to take on the debates that make us uncomfortable but that will result in sustaining new ways of acknowledging and respecting difference. Initially, students may be reticent to discuss these issues; but when a safe environment of trust and respect has been established, students believe that they have a right to speak and that there will be an audience who will listen to them.

Objectives

To identify and understand the differences between a cooperative and a competitive learning environment and to develop skills for working together
To develop and sustain a community of learners that fosters intellectual and social engagement across racial, ethnic, and gender groups

Domains

Cognitive: Understand the process and goals of cooperative learning
Affective: Appreciate and respect each member's contributions and talents
Skills: Listen and respond to group goals

Academic Standard: Write and Speak in the English Language

Interpersonal Communication Skills
Effective speaking and listening skills
Create self-assessment and appropriate feedback

Materials

Small group activity sheets
Quotations on education
A variety of newspapers and magazines

Pre-Instructional

Students will write what they believe makes a good and trusting friendship. Ask them: How and why are you friendly with some students more than others? Tell whatever you wish to share about this friendship—for example, how did it benefit both people, how did you become friends, what do you do to maintain this friendship, is this friendship still in existence? Then they will identify some positive qualities, strengths, and abilities about themselves.

Introductory Framework

During this seminar, we have looked at ways to promote and support our personal and professional goals, to establish a respectful and businesslike community, and to build a Voyager learning community. Today, we will continue to develop the process of working and learning together.

Motivation

Each classroom has a definite atmosphere and culture to it, based on the individual students, the teacher, the subject matter, and the environment that has been set. What adjectives would you use to describe the classrooms you have experienced? (Have students brainstorm and list all their responses on the board.) What do we mean by classroom culture?

Which did you find the most enjoyable, or not so enjoyable? Explain why you found these classrooms to be this way. For example, did students cheat? Were some students labeled dummies? Did some students express jealousy of other students' success? How were some students discriminated against? Were there different subcultures of students in the classroom with either a positive or a negative value placed on them? Did the teacher play favorites? How do you come to know all of this? How has this discussion been connected to how you described the meaning of friendship and choosing your friends? Are there some similarities? What are the differences? Do you think everyone in this class will be a friend? What were the rules in this particular class that everyone was committed to? Did everyone always know about the rules—were some written out and some not? Were there some hidden rules that only some of the students knew about? Was there an "in crowd" and an "out crowd"? How did the teacher handle these realities?

INSTRUCTIONAL IMPLEMENTATION

There are many different ways to develop a cohort that works well together. What are some of the items you listed in last night's homework regarding your views on friendship and creating alliances? Before we look more closely at these procedures, let us look at the words listed in Large Group Activity: Defining and take a few minutes to define them.

Large Group Activity: Defining

Have students write their responses on a sheet of paper. Please define the following in your own words and use concrete examples for each:

- Competition
- Individualistic
- Social Skills
- Positive Interaction
- Cooperation
- Interdependence
- Team Effort
- Trust
- Synergy

Discuss each of the words and the influence they have on students. Have students find examples of each word in the newspapers or magazines, either positive or negative examples. For example, what happens when competition takes over? How do people treat each other? What happens when people are pitted against each other for rewards? How many people are getting physically sick (heart attack, stomach ailments) due to the number of hours they are putting in as they engage in this structural competition? Discuss the effects of violence when competition becomes so strong. Why do people compete? When is competition good? How do you compete?

Large Group Activity: Learning, Excitement, and Fun

Let's look at this quote together and see what it says to us (display quote on overhead and read it aloud):

> In preschool, achievement is primed with stickers, stars, games, and other symbols of academic success. There is lots of noise and excitement during the day. In elementary school we extend this model to include certificates, badges, and report cards. There continues to be lots of enthusiasm, joking, and laughing. Friendships are a big part of the classroom life. By junior high school, competition is no more fun and games—the pace to succeed and have markers of success has been ramped up. The educational system reaches its apex in senior high when specifications begin to be made for class rank, scholarships, awards, college-board scores, and admission to Ivy League or top ten national colleges. The fun and games of early years have changed into deadly contests. The rewards are limited and more students must walk away losers. (Mary Najeddine, New York City Public School Teacher, Personal communication, June 2001)

What resonates for you in this paragraph? What do you agree or disagree with? Give examples. Now follow the same procedures for analyzing this paragraph and break up into small groups to work on Small Group Activity: The Educational Experience Defined and Redefined.

Small Group Activity: The Educational Experience Defined and Redefined

Distribute activity sheets (fig. 3.37). Each group will be responsible for one of the paragraph descriptions listed on your sheet. What is your understanding of the paragraph you're assigned? Be prepared to present your ideas to the large group and to receive feedback and answer questions.

Large Group Activity: Depending on Each Other

Share responses to activity sheet. Following are some possible discussion questions:

1. What do you see as some roadblocks to cooperation?
2. How do we build strong interdependent teams?
3. How must ideas of power in the classroom be reexamined?
4. How do we link cooperative skills with egalitarian goals?
5. What else would you add from your readings and discussions regarding cooperation?

Optional Plans

1. Students can make posters with charts identifying the strengths and abilities of everyone in class; these can be displayed in the classroom. They can change from month to month as students see themselves changing.
2. Have students (or the teacher can) bring in large puzzles (many of them are historical and can deal with program themes) with over 500 pieces that have to be put together. The puzzle remains out so that each day, groups of students work together on the puzzle. The puzzles can later be glued, shellacked, and framed.
3. Create a bulletin board that generates ideas for behaviors that encourage good listening, responding to speakers, valuing difference, and cooperative learning. This can be in the form of a cartoon, an original poster, a motto, a newspaper clipping. The goal is to see valuing team and collaborative work in all areas of life.
4. Present the slide show of the classic story of *Sadako and the Thousand Paper Cranes* and have students interpret the meaning for themselves.

Figure 3.37. The Educational Experience Defined and Redefined

In your small groups, read each of the following passages. Have a ten-minute discussion on the concept of your passage. How do you interpret it? Read parts of the passage out loud to each other and show how you interpreted and applied what you read. How does this apply in your world and in the experiences you have both in and out of school? Choose someone to be the recorder who will list all members' views and write a master copy demonstrating one cohesive view that everyone agrees upon. Another student will then report your group work to the class.

American Culture
"The state of affairs in American Culture then is that, while paying respectful homage to cooperative ideals, we go right on with our competitive system and justify it on the grounds that 'human nature' is basically and fundamentally competitive and will always be so. In the public school we thus find this curious paradox: the basic structure of the system is competitive, but the ideals of cooperation are emphasized. The set of the school is such that a large portion of daily activities of the pupils is more competitive than cooperative. At the same time all of the human virtues and attitudes that are favorable to cooperation are stressed." How does this paradox hurt our progress? (M. May and L. Doob. 1937. *Competition and Cooperation*. Kagan-Masden Study. New York)

Anglo-Americans
"Anglo-American children took toys away from peers 75% of the time if they couldn't have one. The research shows that many environments for kids are barren of experience that sensitizes them to the possibilities of cooperation. The prevailing attitude is 'what's in it for me' and 'no one is getting a bigger piece of the pie than me.' Anglo-American children fail to realize what they get in a situation is a function of what others do as well as their own efforts. We are not providing enough opportunities for children to develop a team effort, but rather we model the ideal 'I'm number one!'" (Nelson and Kagan)

Collective Responsibility
"What disappears in an individualistic view of things is a ground for community, the felt sense of collective responsibility for the fate of each separate other. What have we learned about community? Are we learning and living in the most constructive way possible? The horror of our present condition is not merely the absence of community or the isolation of self—those have been part of the American tradition for a long time. It is the loss of the ability to remember what is missing, the diminishment of our vision of what is humanely possible or desirable." (Marin 1975)

Cooperation and Sports
"In Montgomery, New York, an elementary school soccer team was cooperatively structured where the team players praised each other, did not tolerate abuse of players and developed group cohesion. After their championship game, all of the children wanted to join the team again; while, in the competitively structured team, children cried and blamed each other for mistakes, with four of the children not wanting to play soccer again. If the aim of sports is to create a constructive, self-rewarding pastime for children, we find that although a cooperative system does not always create a winning team, it does create winning children—boys and girls who have a compassionate understanding of themselves and their friends and who are anxious to continue having fun with people, rather than for people." (J. Lignor, New York, personal communication)

(continued)

Figure 3.37. The Educational Experience Defined and Redefined *(continued)*

Competitive Impulses

"Individualism finds its roots in an attempt to deny the reality and importance of human interdependence. One of the major goals of technology today in America is to free us from the necessity of relating to, submitting to, depending on, or controlling other people. Unfortunately, the more we have succeeded in doing this the more we have disconnected, become bored, lonely, unprotected, unnecessary, and unsafe. No one is ever good enough in a competitive situation. Each success is temporary. Immediately upon achieving success the competition begins for the next prize. Competition encourages separateness." (R. Salo, Preschool Teacher, Minneapolis, personal communication)

---

5. Show and discuss the film *When Women Get to Hurting*, a documentary on the self-managed women's factory.
6. Show and discuss the film *With Babies and Banners*, a documentary on the General Motors strike, Flint, Michigan, 1930.
7. Show and discuss the film *Wrath of Grapes*, a documentary depicting farm workers today and the effects of pesticide spraying.

Performance-Based Assessments

- Student responses and interpretations of quotes
- Student-generated definitions
- Students listening and responding to each other

CONCLUSION

A more formalized definition of cooperative learning is: *A teaching and learning process that helps make classrooms places of increased learning, caring, and cooperation. Students help each other learn together, work cooperatively on a task, and work with each other with more respect and concern. It offers the potential for fulfilling interaction with others, enriching lives in our communities, affirming equity in our nation, and creating peace in the world. Students and teachers work together so everyone succeeds* (Bellanca and Fogarty, 1991, p. 161).

What do you think of this definition? What would you add to or delete from this definition? How is cooperative learning different from working together in a group? How can we link cooperative learning and living to the broader possibilities in our lives, schools, communities, and societies in general? What are disadvantages to cooperation? (For example, it can be time consuming, it's hard work, it requires compromise.)

ASSIGNMENT

1. Describe a project that you are working on (perhaps in another class or outside of school) and plan how it can be accomplished through cooperative planning and working. Be ready to present this to the class next week. We will begin to form cooperative groups for the different projects we will work on.

Unit 4B

Cooperative Learning

LESSON TOPIC: BUILDING COOPERATIVE LEARNING PROCEDURES AND BASE GROUPS

Teaching Note

Learning and working together collaboratively becomes a challenging adventure under the best of circumstances. When there is a diverse group of individuals who have not been supported in working this way, beginning a cooperative adventure can be daunting. Competition, social inequalities, and violent resolutions to interpersonal and international conflicts thwart cooperation. It is apparent from a solid body of literature that students who work together in cooperatively structured classrooms learn to recognize discriminatory practices, become sensitive to cultural stereotypes, and learn to like and accept each other.

This unit is the first attempt in the Voyager program to create a cooperative classroom structure that is unique to our context. We have tried to organize cooperative learning around both academic and work education projects so that students will experience a variety of formats for working together. The base groups are similar to cultural circles as described by Paulo Freire (1970): "A cultural circle is a live and creative dialogue in which everyone knows some things and does not know others, in which all seek together to know more" (p. 87). In working with cultural groups we, as teachers, need to become the coordinator of a cultural circle and learn to grow with the group. Through this method, students also learn to take charge of their learning and an environment that encourages people to rely on each other for learning and for effecting change.

Objectives

To create the nuts and bolts of cooperative learning and to form base groups
To build respect and trust in order to become interdependent on each other
for learning and effecting change

Domains

Cognitive: Identify and apply the process and goals of cooperative learning
Affective: Value individual and group contributions
Skills: Practice collaborative teamwork

Academic Standard: Write and Speak in the English Language

Interpersonal Communication Skills
Effective speaking and listening skills
Create self-assessment and appropriate feedback

Materials

The Function of a Base Group overhead (fig. 3.38)
Cooperative Learning: Elements, Definition of Goals, and Group Evaluation
activity sheets (fig. 3.39)
Box of objects

Pre-Instructional

Homework assignments for cooperative learning.

Figure 3.38. The Functions of a Base Group

1. Gives support and encouragement for understanding and implementing the procedures in cooperative learning, and provides feedback for group development and cohesion.
2. Gives support to teach and develop the social skills required to cooperate effectively.
3. Gives support to teach and develop the academic skills required to cooperate effectively.
4. Serves as a model for cooperative learning.
5. Provides honest feedback for assessment.
6. Provides support so that all members are successful.

Figure 3.39.   Cooperative Learning: Elements, Definition of Goals, and Group Evaluation

ELEMENTS OF COOPERATIVE LEARNING

1. Positive Interdependence: Establish mutual goals and responsibilities; shared resources, assigned roles; agreed timelines and deadlines.
2. Face-to-Face Interaction: Students encourage each other to learn; help with and share resources; take time to explain and discuss what they each know.
3. Individual Accountability: Student's performance is assessed and individual and group know results; everyone stays responsible for his or her assignments.
4. Interpersonal and Small Group Skills: Students need to develop and use collaborative skills; leadership skills; decision-making skills; trust building; communication; conflict resolution.

DEFINITION OF GOALS

Cooperation (We sink or swim together):
• Work together to maximize their own and each other's learning
• Work to achieve shared goals
• Everyone assumes and fulfills his or her responsibility
• Rewards can be unlimited
• One-upmanship is not tolerated
• Diversity in its full meaning is accepted and respected
Competition (If I swim, you sink; I sink, you swim):
• Students work against each other
• Rewards are limited
• Cannot celebrate everyone's success
• Strive to be better than everyone else
• Someone else's failure is celebrated
• Work alone
Individualistic (We are each in this alone):
• Goals are reached individually
• Don't ask for anyone's help
• Your success does not benefit anyone else
• Rewards are viewed as unlimited
• Work alone
• No networking for good support

GROUP EVALUATION

Group Members' Names:
Describe Your Group's Goal:

Everyone contributed ideas and information. (Circle one)
1 Never
2 Sometimes
3 Always

(continued)

Figure 3.39. Cooperative Learning: Elements, Definition of Goals, and Group Evaluation *(continued)*

Everyone helped each other.
1 Never
2 Sometimes
3 Always

The group kept to its timeline.
1 Never
2 Sometimes
3 Always

Everyone was included.
1 Never
2 Sometimes
3 Always

The group reached agreement.
1 Never
2 Sometimes
3 Always

(Adapted from Johnson and Johnson, 1991.)

Introductory Framework

We have a variety of projects that need to be completed during this two-year seminar. Some of these projects will require us to work together toward a common goal; one such large project is the establishment of the Voyager Company. We also need to support each other in our individual goals. In working and learning together we will see that the varied skills of all students are used and respected. Therefore, one of our first activities is to look at the steps, or the nuts and bolts, of implementing cooperative learning.

Motivation

Take out the homework sheet you wrote last week describing an activity/goal/function that you will develop based on cooperative learning. (Have student leaders write ideas on the board. Some examples might be planning a surprise party, planning a banquet, organizing a fund-raiser, planning an auction, doing house repairs, community gardening, etc.). Students will give concrete examples as to the cooperative effort of their events. These experiences all provide opportunities to grow and build together. What were some of the challenges you faced when engaging in these events? How can we transfer these experiences to our learning and to our work environment?

INSTRUCTIONAL IMPLEMENTATION

Large Group Activity: Defining Goals

Here in our class, many of our activities will require more than one person working with another. We will begin by looking at how the goals in different group structures are played out. (Use Definition of Goals handout, fig. 3.39.) The class will add to ideas under each definition.) Now let us try to work together as a group.

Pass out Functions of a Base Group handout (fig. 3.38) to groups and explain how they function. Explain that students will be members of other groups as well. In addition to working together as a group, what other skills are necessary for all of you to work together? (Teacher decides beforehand to construct base groups that will work together for a year on certain projects. There will be other groups formed throughout the year as well when the goals or projects call for students with different affinities and skills to work together.)

Small Group Activity: Describing Unknown Objects

Pass out the Group Evaluation sheet (fig. 3.39). Base groups will be responsible for describing each of the items found in the box for their group (objects can be a seashell, an old coin, an eight-track cassette tape, etc.). At the end of the work group, their description will be read to the class, and the other class members will try to guess the item that was described. Allow twenty minutes for this activity. Each group will fill out an evaluation sheet for itself. This is a beginning evaluation sheet.

Small Group Activity: Group Survival—Synergistic Decision Making (adapted from Human Synergistics International Order #18101)

You and a group of your friends are away for a mid-fall weekend in Maine. Unexpectedly on Saturday morning, you all wake up to a heavy snowfall sticking to the ground. More snow and heavy winds are expected. You and your group are unprepared for this type of weekend and decide to locate a pilot who will take you out of the area in a helicopter. Unfortunately, twenty minutes into the trip, the helicopter crashes. The pilot is dead but the other passengers have survived and no one is hurt. The mountains and blowing winds are an ominous foreboding to your survival.

Here is a list of items you all have: five signal flares, one set of cross-country skis, a large cooking pot, a rechargeable flashlight, fishing line and hooks, disposable lighter, hatchet, a bottle of sedatives, a pair of snowshoes, a ball of rope, a pocket knife, and a loaded rifle. The weather is cold and snowy. There has been communication by radio but you do not know if your call for help will be heard. The group decides it will stick together. How will you spend the night?

Take your list of items and prioritize them by order of importance and why you believe they are important. After you make your individual lists, decide who would like to facilitate the discussion for your small group and come to agreement in the order of importance for each of the items. After all of the groups have made their reports, the student leaders will read the order of importance as established by experts in the field. Average all individual scores, add up team score, subtract the team score from the average individual score; are there any members who scored lower than the team score? Have students examine and interpret the differences between individual scores and the group score.

What are the interpersonal skills you need to develop and to employ? What rational skills? What reflections does your group make about the experience and process of this activity? It is important that all express their experience and observations of the process. What methods are necessary to utilize the full human resources and capacities of groups for synergistic decision making? How can organizations become stronger through individual effectiveness and creative collaboration?

Large Group Activity: Can You Guess What I Am Holding in My Hand?

Each group will select two items to describe to the class; the point is to see how quickly others can guess the items as a result of the group's specific descriptions.

Large Group Activity: Defining Base Groups

During the course of this year, you will work on projects in your base groups consisting of five or six members. As a member of this group you will have certain responsibilities to fulfill—academic, social, personal, and professional.

Have the students work together to provide definitions of the following goals for class members (based on work by Johnson and Johnson, 1991):

1. Cooperation (We sink or swim together):
   * Students work together to maximize their own and each other's learning.
   * Students work to achieve shared goals.
   * Everyone assumes and fulfills his or her responsibility.
   * Rewards can be unlimited.

- One-upmanship is not tolerated.
- Diversity in its full meaning is accepted and respected.

2. Competition (I swim, you sink; I sink, you swim):
   - Students work against each other.
   - Rewards are limited.
   - Cannot celebrate everyone's success.
   - Strive to be better than everyone else.
   - Someone else's failure is celebrated.
   - Work alone.

3. Individualistic (We are each in this alone):
   - Goals are reached individually.
   - Don't ask for anyone's help.
   - Your success does not benefit anyone else.
   - Rewards are viewed as unlimited.
   - Work alone.
   - No networking for good support.

Optional Plans

1. Choose a consensus-building project for this first time. For example, the group must choose three books to take on an extended trip. Which books they will be taking should take everyone's preferences into account.

2. Cooperative Training Exercises. See:
   - **Broken Circles, Broken Squares** (Graves and Graves, 1985). Students have pieces to a puzzle and must put them together in such a way that each student has a complete circle or square; there are specific guidelines listed, such as that the game is played in silence.
   - **Guess My Rule** (Rosenholtz and Rosenholtz, 1977). This exercise illustrates the use of reasoning skills. Students must decide the rule or principle that accounts for all of the different cards and shapes that are placed on a table. One person holds the rule card and announces when each group has made the right deductions regarding the type of category that the cards are in.
   - **Space Ship** (Simon, Howe, and Kirschenbaum, 1972, pp. 292–293). This is a game where seven people, out of the original eleven, are chosen to take a space ship and start a new world. Agreement must be on behalf of the entire group.
   - **Alligator River** (Simon, Howe, and Kirschenbaum, 1972, pp. 292–293). In this exercise, students read a story involving Abigail and some characters she encounters as she helps a friend out. Stu-

dents are asked to rank these characters from bad to worst and give reasons for their decisions.

3. Have each group take an open-ended statement and write out a statement about it. Some examples of open-ended statements are: "Our governor is doing . . ." "Everyone in the United States is . . ." Students must all agree to the statement they write together.

4. Ask cooperative groups to prioritize word lists: list ten overused words, list ten buzz words, and ten new words in the dictionary.

5. Ask cooperative groups to design their ideal school—using poster boards, crayons, magazines, construction paper, and the like, have them describe through words and pictures ideas that present their future vision.

6. Have cooperative groups select a burning issue (current events, election results, corporate incidents, community events, etc.) and have them pose questions, research ideas, and come up with a written narrative as to their discussions and ideas regarding this particular issue.

7. Have cooperative groups research service-learning projects that they could work on in the Voyager program; each base group presents their ideas in class and then the class chooses a project; an alternative to this would be that each group chooses their own service-learning project.

8. Contact Human Synergistics International (info@humansyn.com), which has a variety of decision-making booklets with more exercises.

Performance-Based Assessments

- Student object descriptions
- Base group evaluation sheets

CONCLUSION

Self-assessment—take two minutes to free write about your first experiences with base groups and with the common project. What are some of the common elements of cooperative learning? (Use overhead.) What are some new ways you learned to work together? What obstacles did you find in working together? What did the group members do to make the project goal a success? What will you do differently next time?

ASSIGNMENT

1. Describe the group norms you have set up in one of your outside activities (for example, in a club, on a team, at church, on the job). What role do group norms play? Are they necessary? What do you know about working in a group together successfully?

Unit 4C

Cooperative Learning

LESSON TOPIC: GROUP PROCESS PROCEDURES

Teaching Note

Based on previous discussions, students will negotiate and develop ideas of what they believe are group norms. They must clarify what they envision as acceptable behavior for social interaction and intellectual engagement. It is important to keep processing student progress so students do not see cooperative behavior as something that is an extracurricular activity but one that is a vital part of all learning and working together.

During this time, they will have opportunities to become comfortable with sharing their experiences, engaging in dialogue exchanges, and participating in peer teaching and learning. It is another way of expressing Paulo Freire's concept of reading the word, reading their worlds. They will honor each other's voices and count on each other's input for information. One of the best outcomes of this program has been when the students of one class began to forget that there was a teacher in class and only included her when they needed additional information on pay equity laws in the state. In a democratic classroom, cooperative skills and egalitarian goals become synonymous. Soon strategies and solutions emerge from the students as they analyze their realities and then co-create to come up with new ideas. Students can practice taking action in the classroom and transfer their skills to the workplace. They begin to develop what Ira Shor (1992) calls "action competencies," which are tools for students to develop in a safe environment and then to take out of the classroom into their daily work lives.

Developing and applying group norms among diverse student groups takes a lot of practice and trust building. For many of the students, engaging in a cooperative process may be new, or it has been perceived differently because of their lived cultural experiences. Developing norms through codes allows students to respond to ideas for critical discussion through the use of some physical representation. This can be a written dialogue, a graphic, a story, or a work theme. By using this representation, students are able to discuss their reactions in a focused manner. The issue or problem should be small enough so that there are some possible actions for change. See Auerbach and Wallerstein's *ESL for Action* for numerous examples on using codes in lessons.

Objectives

To develop and apply group norms and procedures for working together
To practice working on real problem-solving dilemmas using codes

Domains

Cognitive: Identify and apply group norms
Affective: Value individual and group contributions
Skills: Practice social skills

Academic Standard: Write and Speak in the English Language

Interpersonal Communication Skills
Effective speaking and listening skills
Create self-assessment and appropriate feedback

Materials

Handbook for Group Work (fig. 3.40)
Connect the Dots handout (fig. 3.41)
Paper clips, rubber bands, rulers, CD cases, etc.

Pre-Instructional

Group norms written description assignment.

Introductory Framework

Today we will continue developing and practicing the procedures for establishing group norms/expectations and cooperative learning. When working in

Figure 3.40.   Handbook for Group Work

GROUP PROJECT PROCEDURES

Session 1

- Introduce yourselves to one another. Exchange telephone numbers (home, work, cell) and email addresses.
- Indicate your list of ideas and why you have an interest in them.
- Identify the person who will write the log and the person who will write the group notes. (Each group meeting will have notes and a log; the log is submitted to the instructor whereas the notes will be placed in a file and used by the group for evaluation after the presentation is given.)
- Each person should indicate what her/his first choice of ideas would be. Each person would also indicate why she/he believes the idea would be a good one to present to the class.
- Make individual assignments if that is appropriate. All group roles rotate.
- Discuss how your group will be run (i.e., how you will avoid having one or two persons dominate the group, what the group members will do to ensure that each person within the group participates in the discussion, what the group will do about people who do not participate, how the group will deal with absenteeism, who will inform the person who is absent about what went on and what needs to be done).
- Identify some of the major issues related to your idea.

Session 2

- Identify the person who will write the log and another person who will write the notes.
- Talk about specifying your idea. What are the goals/interests of the group? Prioritize your list of ideas.
- Report on any outside information you have gathered since last week.
- Make individual assignments if appropriate.
- Discuss the leadership pattern to be followed by your group.
- Select a new leader each session.
- Everyone assumes the position/responsibility for the leader.
- Select one leader for the entire project.
- Person who writes the log is the leader.
- Refine the list of major issues.
- Determine how you will make decisions in your group.
- Make suggestions on how your group should function. In addition to leadership, how will the agenda be handled for the next group meeting? Who is responsible for the agenda? What procedures will you follow for the next meeting?

Session 3

- Identify the person who will write the log and another person who will write the notes today.
- Select the specific topics or issues your group will investigate and then make individual assignments accordingly.
- Develop and begin to refine a tentative idea or ideas.
- Decide the specific areas to be investigated—who will do what and when? How will they all fit together as a complete unit?
- Brainstorm items for each specific area. Do this as a group to help one another—or do this on an individual basis. Do what works!

(continued)

Figure 3.40. Handbook for Group Work *(continued)*

- Remember: decide whether you will investigate one segment of the topic in depth, or if you will consider several facets of the topic in breadth. When planning this way, you will see both the overview of the area to be covered and the important pieces that link together.
- Discuss what you want others to learn about you and this project and what you want them to know about your group.
- What are the norms for your group?
- Have a preliminary discussion about the format of your mural presentation to the class.

Session 4
- Identify the person who will write the log and the person who will write the notes today.
- Report on outside investigation.
- Review the criteria for judging the group presentation. What type of evaluation will your peers use to respond to your group presentation?
- Review the handouts you have developed. Are you satisfied with them? Who will see that the copies are ready for presentation?
- Finalize the format of your ideas. Do you need any props?
- Will you have additional resources to give your class members?
- What parts need to be smoothed out in your presentation? How can you develop and maintain cohesion in your presentation?

GROUP LOG
Recorder/Ethnographer: In this role, each participant gets to observe the group and make notes from an ethnographic/archeology perspective. Be observant and be honest as all of these logs will serve as a learning piece for your next project.

Note the purpose and the content of the meeting.
Note items related to the process of the meeting:
Members present—did anyone's absence have an effect on the meeting?
- **Climate:** Describe the atmosphere at the meeting. Did the climate seem to change at any point? Why do you think this happened?
- **Norms and expectations:** Using the concepts of power, privilege, duties, and disabilities, describe the norms of your group at this point. What are the accepted rules of behavior? Why do you think these rules are developing or developed in your group? Were they imposed or did they just happen?
- **Communication:** Was conversation social in nature or was it focused on task? Was it a combination of both?
- **Verbal Diagram:** Draw the seating arrangement to the best of your memory. Draw lines to show who talked to whom.
- **Nonverbal:** What nonverbals did you observe? How did they affect the group?
- **Decision-Making Procedures:** How were decisions made during the group meeting? What decision-making style(s) was used? How did this affect the group?
- **Leadership:** What leader behaviors did you observe? Were leadership styles democratic, laissez-faire, or autocratic? Were leadership effects eager participation, low commitment, or resisting?
- **Roles/Functions–Task Functions:** Who offers facts, opinions, ideas, suggestions, and information to help group discussions? Who asks for facts, feelings, and infor-

(continued)

Figure 3.40. Handbook for Group Work *(continued)*

mation from others? Who provides plans for how to proceed? Who proposes goals and tasks to initiate action? Who pulls things together and summarizes? Who tries to keep the group on task?

- **Maintenance Functions:** Who encourages others to participate? Who helps iron out differences of opinion and conflicts? Who relieves tensions and makes the meetings fun? Who basically listens? Did anyone exhibit behavior that tended to block or discourage the work of the group? Describe it and its effect on the group.

EVALUATION

How often does your group help each individual express her/his ideas and receive acknowledgment?

1 Never
2
3
4
5 Always

How often are members' feelings expressed and accepted?

1 Never
2
3
4
5 Always

Is each member given the opportunity to be actively involved?

1 Never
2
3
4
5 Always

How well has your group developed effective leadership, either in one person or several?

1 Not at all
2
3
4
5 All the time

E. How well has your group been able to identify and achieve commitment to the group's goals?

1 Not too well
2
3
4
5 Extremely Well

(continued)

Figure 3.40. Handbook for Group Work *(continued)*

F. How satisfied are you with the product of your work so far?
1 Not satisfied
2
3
4
5 Quite satisfied

G. How responsible do you feel for the product of your group?
1 Not at all responsible
2
3
4
5 Quite responsible

GROUP NOTES
Date
Recorder
Group Topic
Group Members
Summary of the reporting/work done
Assignments made (if any)
Decisions made (if any)
What were the items on the agenda today?
Anything that did not happen that should have happened?
Anything that happened that should not have happened?

---

groups, certain procedures and roles must be established for effective group work. Placing people in groups without any goals or tasks does not establish a successful and smooth group process. We all need to be responsible for the success and effective work of our groups.

Motivation

What type of group work have you enjoyed the most—clubs, sports, and so on? Why? What are some of the advantages and some of the disadvantages of working in groups? (Have students brainstorm their ideas and list them on the board.) What have been examples of competition and cooperation during your experiences with these groups? All of these are valid responses. What are the different roles and responsibilities established within these groups? What do we mean by good teamwork? What part does the coach play in all of these activities? What happens when individuals do not hold up their end of the bargain? Now let's see what happens when we try our first activity together.

Figure 3.41.   Connect the Dots

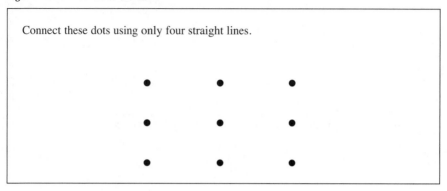

Connect these dots using only four straight lines.

INSTRUCTIONAL IMPLEMENTATION

Small Group Activity: The Multitalented Paper Clip (This activity can be converted to other items as well, such as rubber bands, rulers, CD cases, etc.)

Have students form groups of three to four people and then give everyone several paper clips (or other item of your choice). Each group is directed to come up with as many new ideas as they can for uses of the paper clips. Groups have four minutes to work together. Each group must share their top three ideas with the rest of the class.

Small Group Activity: Connecting the Dots

Pass out the Connect the Dots handout (fig. 3.41). Ask students to try and solve the problem alone (three to four minutes). Then ask them to solve the problem together. How did they feel working alone and then together? (The seminar coordinator can use a variety of these fun activities to get students to work and play together.)

Large Group Activity: So What Is a Code? (adapted from Auerbach and Wallerstein, 1987)

Imagine that you hear the following talk among coworkers:

Michelle: Bonjour Alain. Ca va? Est-ce que tu puis m'aider avec mon fils? Il ne lit pas tres bien en anglais.

Alain: Bien sur mon amie. Peut-tetre pendant ce weekend, s'il est libre.

Harry: There they go again—always yakking, yakking away at work.

Stan:	Yeah, have you noticed that they don't even try to speak English with each other?
Harry:	Don't you wonder what they are talking about?
Stan:	They are probably talking about us—look at how they are looking at us.
Harry:	When will they realize that they are in America now and they better learn to speak English?

Discuss the scenario. Describe the situation. What is going on in this scenario? What languages are represented here? What do the Americans think the French are saying? Clearly identify the problem being presented here. Do you see this problem in your own experiences? How many languages do you speak? When do you speak another language? How do Americans act when you speak your language? How do you feel when you hear coworkers speaking another language? What do you think are the underlying issues here? What do you think the different groups of workers in this scenario should do? What is a loaded issue? Would you consider this scenario a loaded issue? How would they change the situation? What are the perceptions that each group has of the other groups?

As students respond to the questions, list all responses. This activity models the steps and procedures for using codes as starting points for in-depth discussions. First developed by the Brazilian educator Paulo Freire (1973), problem posing starts with students' lives and asks them to believe in themselves. It helps both teachers and students look and listen for critical issues both inside and outside of the classroom that could be threatening and need to be examined and addressed through problem posing, dialogue, and action. Using this method allows students to build self-confidence and believe that they possess the knowledge to discover solutions. This type of activity can be used to illuminate many topics: how to get a job in the United States, how to ask for a raise and a promotion, how to talk to your boss, how to relieve stress, how to understand roles and responsibilities at work, and so on.

Small Group Activity: Planning a Company Picnic

You are the planning committee for the annual company picnic. A memo has just come through that says that if you can have the plans for the picnic to the caterer by 8:00 A.M. tomorrow, the caterer will give a 30 percent discount for the entire event and will take care of all of the details without any additional charge. The one catch is that your plan must be so clear and specific that the caterers will be able to proceed without any phone calls or correspondence with you.

Some of the specific instructions for the picnic need to include: Who and how many will be invited, where and when the picnic will be held, what type of food you want served, how it will be arranged, who will pay for it. In addition, you must set up the social activities, games, prizes, and the like. These are your instructions and the group must now proceed on its own. Use the flipcharts and markers that are available to you. Organize yourselves accordingly. (Students will present their ideas to the class. In doing so, they will be asked to describe the challenges they experienced working as a group.)

Large Group Activity: Handbook for Group Work (fig. 3.40)

Groups need to be organized in one way or another for effectiveness. I am going to assign a project, which you will begin to work on in your base groups. What are the different ways to organize groups? (Go over the group project procedures handbook and answer any questions students may have. Note that each day has a specific topic. All meetings have notes and logs that will be placed in a separate file.)

Small Group Activity: The Voyager Symbol

This project will be building/developing/creating a symbol for your Voyager seminar. This is a two-part project. Each group will decide what they want to develop as part of their legacy to the Voyager seminar. You could decide on projects such as murals, auctions, fund-raisers, a special event, a Voyager book, a T-shirt, a calendar, a video, and so on.

The students should also decide the following:

1. What the mural will look like (at least the piece your group will work on).
2. What each group member's task will be for the next base group presentation.
3. What your presentation to the class will look like.
4. Timelines for presentations to the rest of the class so everyone can come to a decision.

Proceed using the above steps to plan the Voyager event, to develop the Voyager web site, and so on.

CONCLUSION

What do you find the most intriguing about group work? What is the most challenging? What don't you like about group work? Which roles do you like? Which roles do you dislike? What changes will you have to make to work more effectively in the group? How will you deal with inappropriate behaviors by other team members such as power plays, takeovers, and leadership demands?

ASSIGNMENT

1. Prepare tasks, assignments, and information needed for the next base group meeting.

Unit 5A

Organization Behavior and Development

LESSON TOPIC: CORPORATE CULTURE

Teaching Note

This lesson continues to foster the problem-posing process as students develop skills as "social anthropologists" and researchers who study various workplaces. In this lesson, they begin to observe and question the various forces and domains that influence the life of a corporation. Students will be preparing for their first job-shadowing experience during which they will research and report on their work experience. (A job-shadowing guide for taking field notes while observing and questions for interviewing their business leader is presented in the Voyager Community Resource handbook.) For many students, this is the first time they will be seeing a corporate structure as a whole. Their shadowing experience is a unique time to question, analyze, and interpret the reasons for a company's structure or the social and work relations that take place within a company.

Objectives

To understand the different parts of a corporation, how they work and influence each other
To identify ways corporate culture is changing

Domains

Cognitive: Understand the different parts of a corporation
Affective: Appreciate this specific style of writing
Skills: Read and communicate effectively

Graduation/Academic Standard: Decision Making

Career Investigation

Materials

Organization development article from *Harvard Educational Review Series*
Organization development articles "Rethinking the Corporate Workplace:
  Case Managers at Mutual Benefit Life," #9-492-015; and "Saturn: A Different Kind of Car Company," #9-795-010
Domains in an Organization's Environment overhead (fig. 3.42)
Job Shadowing guide in Voyager Community Resource handbook

Figure 3.42. Domains in an Organization's Environment

Domains in an Organization's Environment

Competitors, industry Size and Characteristics, Related Industries

Suppliers, Manufacturers, Real Estate

Labor Market, Employment Agencies, Universities, Training Schools, Employees In Other Companies, Unionization

Age, Values, Beliefs, Education, Religion, Worth Ethics, Urban vs. Rural, Birth Rates

City, State, Federal Laws and Regulations, Taxes, Services, Court System, Political Processes

Stock Markets, Banks, Saving and Loans, Private Investors

Recession, Unemployment Rate, Inflation Rate, Rate of Investment, Economics, Growth

Techniques of Production, Science, Research Centers, Automation, New Materials

Customers, Clients, Potential Users of Products and Services

Industry · Raw Materials · Culture · Human Resources · Government · Organization · Financial Resources · Economic Conditions · Marketing · Technology

Source: Richard L. Daft, *Organization Theory and Design,* **(St. Paul, Minn.: West Publishing, 1983)**

Pre-Instructional

Students are to create a chart and a description of their current or past workplace organization and bring it to class for presentation. Many of the students will use their experience in part-time employment at fast-food chains, department stores, insurance companies, banks, and so on. If any student does not have a workplace to report on, he or she is asked to interview family members or friends who are employed.

Introductory Framework

This unit involves student members working together for two class sessions. The Harvard Business School prepares corporation briefs for study. By reading these briefs, we get a firsthand view of what has transpired in some companies over the course of a year. One such company, Mutual Benefit Life, is featured. We are given a background and an understanding of what changes have been effected in this company through organizational development. Before we look at this large corporation, let us observe some of the environments you have worked in and how you saw the business organized.

Motivation

What exactly is an organization's environment? What does it look like? Who and what are the important components? What are you most surprised at—what do you think is missing? (Students will present the work they have prepared from their previous job experience. They may only have a small view of the company, as in franchises, department stores, and so on, but this activity provides a good entry for the next step in the conversation.)

How would you describe this school's organizational environment? (Use an overhead to discuss the way the school is structured—central administration, clerical staff, teaching staff, support personnel and services; present an organization chart if one is available.) What interpretations can we make about the power relations and the way the school is structured? Who has the most power in the school—how do you know this? What is the culture of this school? What is the culture of this class? How do you think the culture of the school has changed since you first entered?

There is an entire discipline that studies people at work, the actions and attitudes that people exhibit at work. It is called organizational behavior and is studied through designed research studies. The theories and conclusions drawn by organizational consultants come from a variety of other fields: psychology, sociology, social psychology, political science, and anthropology.

Psychology contributes information on individual behaviors and attitudes such as learning, perception, personality, leadership, job satisfaction, and decision making. Sociology studies people in relation to their colleagues and looks at group dynamics, work teams, organizational culture, communication, conflict, and power. Social psychology focuses on the influence of people on one another and investigates implementing change and reducing barriers to change. Anthropology is the study of societies in order to learn about human beings and their activities. Anthropologists study cultures and environments and help us to understand differences in values, attitudes, and behavior between people in different countries and cultures, and within organizations. Much of the knowledge we have about organizations comes through the work of anthropologists and those who use their methods. Political science looks at individual and group behavior related to power and conflict in a political environment. All of these disciplines have concerned themselves with discovering ways in which organizations can become more successful in dealing with dramatic changes such as increasingly diverse workplace populations, globalization, and increasingly empowered workers.

INSTRUCTIONAL IMPLEMENTATION

Large Group Activity: Organization Structure and Development (this activity, and some of the subsequent ones, can be taught with an organizational development specialist visitor)

Although company structures and environments can be classified in many ways, one of the simplest ways is to look at two broad categories of organizational structural emphasis: centralized and decentralized. List on the board or an overhead the major characteristics of organizational types: hierarchy of authority, flexibility, adaptability, problem recognition, implementation, dealing with changes in environmental complexity, rules and procedures, division of labor, use of managerial techniques, coordination and control. What would you add to this list? From your job experience, how has your company fit into the above characteristics? Are they centralized or decentralized? How has this influenced your job satisfaction? What determines job satisfaction? What is cognitive dissonance in a job?

Students bring in ideas from their previous jobs and interviews with friends, family, and relatives. In this way, they can collect a group of experiences and data about organizations and their unique structures. Companies are also affected by the domains in their organization's environment. Look at figure 3.42. What does this generic chart tell us about large organizations? What are you surprised to discover? What would you add to this chart?

Small Group Activity: Organizational Culture

How do you see each of these areas influencing a specific organization? Be specific and use your work experience as a basis for a model:

- Values
- Attitudes and behaviors
- Perceptions and messages
- Work-based learning
- Verbal and nonverbal

How do you think the above list influences and shapes organizational culture? How would you define organizational culture?

Small Group Activity: Teaching Each Other

Distribute Harvard Educational Series of Organizations articles to base groups. Each member of a base group will read one part of the article and tell her or his group members about that part. In this way, each member will have the benefit of reading and teaching the other members of the group. Each group will write an executive summary of the part of the article she or he read, create a list of the major players in the article, and list ideas regarding innovation in the article. Students are urged to use this time to pose questions regarding the materials—further information they might need, challenging the way decisions are made, and so on.

Optional Plans

1. Students will research information on companies that have gone through changes (Gimbels, Sears, Procter and Gamble, etc.).
2. Case Studies—Coca-Cola: The importance of social responsibility, and Heinz: Staying ahead by meeting community needs—free business case studies located on tt100.biz and itdarden.virginia.edu (The Darden Case Collection).
3. Students will research and connect with companies that model democratic communities and that have been linked to school programs, and will present the information to the class. (For example: International Basque Cooperative—Mondragon; West Coast Company—Youth for Environmental Sanity or YES; Athens, Georgia—Rural Entrepreneurship through Action Learning or REAL); Global Education operated by the Institute for International Cooperation and Development, Williamstown, MA; EDTEC—Education Training and Enterprise Center, Camden, NJ; ACEnet—Appalachian Center for Economic Networks, Athens, Ohio.)

4. Students can research other business and career programs being developed in high schools throughout the city and state. (For example: In the state of Minnesota, Robbinsdale School District, Tech High; St. Paul School District, Skills for Tomorrow High School; Business Magnate in St. Paul.) They need to describe the program, its purpose, and its structure. Invite representatives from these local programs to talk about what they have to offer.
5. Invite an organizational development person to speak to the class. What type of career is this and how do they make a difference in their work?
6. Have students interview friends, relatives, and colleagues for their perceptions on workplace environments. Students will write up and present anecdotal data.
7. Review job-shadowing procedures.

CONCLUSION

What new observations did you make today regarding work environments? Do a group environmental check for work readiness on everyone's part. Each group decides how much more work needs to be done with the article. Do they need additional help with the articles or in framing their teaching?

ASSIGNMENT

1. Have students write out questions related to the transactions Mutual Benefit Life and Saturn Car Company made as noted in the articles. Students can address issues such as what the leadership was like, decision-making procedures, and what corporate ethics were used. What does it mean for an organization to have values? Can values and capital gain be compatible?

Unit 5B

Organization Behavior and Development

LESSON TOPIC: BUILDING ORGANIZATIONS, ORGANIZATIONAL RELATIONSHIPS, AND PATHWAYS TO INNOVATION AND CHANGE

Teaching Note

Students are urged to enter and continue the dialogue of corporate/work culture and organization more fully. The stories/anecdotal data they gather from friends, relatives, and colleagues will serve as catalysts for any discrepancies or conflicts they have experienced in their own workplace. Different issues can be discussed based on the different stories they explore as social anthropologists. They can keep working on these ideas in small groups and in their work centers where they will file all of their resource materials. The types of questions that have come up in class discussions have proved valuable across all career choices.

Here are some questions that previous groups generated:

- What does loyalty mean on a job?
- What features of the workplace help new workers show initiative?
- How does one's appearance (looking businesslike versus looking provocative) affect people's response to you?
- How do you begin to look at your work environment differently?
- What happens when you do not agree with how others are being treated?
- Who has the authority to make decisions?

The discussions surrounding these questions provided rich and salient conversations among the students. Solutions to their problems are not as important as the actual discussions and the information they exchange. How can one articulate how he or she is treated on the job? After identifying issues from their initial conversation, they explore and conduct a more in-depth analysis of one company's path to innovation and change.

Objectives

To analyze one company's procedures for organization development and change

To apply concepts of organization theory and culture during students' work-site visits

Domains

Cognitive: Understand and analyze steps in corporate change
Affective: Appreciate this specific style of writing
Skills: Read and communicate effectively

Graduation/Academic Standard: Decision Making

Career Investigation

Materials

Organization development articles "Rethinking the Corporate Workplace: Case Managers at Mutual Benefit Life," #9-492-015; "Saturn: A Different Kind of Car Company," #9-795-010
Domains in an Organization's Environment overhead (fig. 3.42)

Introductory Framework

We will continue our study of this corporation from our own standpoint. As we progress through our internship, our job shadowing, and our future careers, what are some of the questions we will ask ourselves regarding: corporate culture (what is it?), ethical corporate climate (how do you maintain it?), and leadership (what does it look like today?)?

Motivation

What new knowledge and skills will you take with you from your work-site experience? What did you learn that will be helpful? How does your job provide you the opportunity to exercise your knowledge, skills, and abilities, and how does its scope provide for the development of your capacities and extension of your abilities? (Brainstorm ideas on the board. Refer to the handbook for connection with job shadowing and internships.)

INSTRUCTIONAL IMPLEMENTATION

Small Group Activity: Writing Executive Summaries

Have students write an executive summary of the articles from their group: "Rethinking the Corporate Workplace: Case Managers at Mutual Benefit Life" and "Saturn: A Different Kind of Car Company." (See Harvard School of Business publications for other selections.) Have them respond to corporate culture, ethical corporate climate, and leadership as they relate to the article. Then each group will present their summary. Summaries will be collected and then copied for each group to keep. Here are some possible group ideas:

1. Introduction and background
2. The case managers
3. Human Resources
4. Conflict
5. Marketing
6. Resolution

Another alternative would be to have each group develop its own analysis of the company and its response.

Large Group Activity: Bringing the Parts Together for the Whole

Student teams will report on their various parts to the class. As each group is reporting to the class, the others will take notes on the presentation for assessment and feedback.

Optional Plans

1. Students can work with articles from popular periodicals such as *Fortune*, *Business Week*, and local business journals to learn more about the current status and profile of companies like IBM, GE, Saturn, their local telephone company, technology company, and so on; students can then report to each other on what they've discovered.
2. Have students investigate case studies on web sites such as www.itdarden.virginia.edu, which has a collection of case studies called The Darden Case Collection.
3. Research cooperative workplaces around the world, contact them, and then have cultural anthropologists present material to the class.
4. Bring in organization development (OD) professionals and discuss what contradictions, ethical dilemmas, and significant problems they have had to face in their career—either with clients or with situations.
5. Invite in owners and workers from cooperative enterprises within the community (Saturn, Starbucks, etc.). Form a panel of represen-

tatives from different cooperatives. Each representative will give a brief history and background of his or her company. Students hold a critical dialogue throughout the seminar session. Some sample questions are:

- Why did you choose to organize and work in a worker's cooperative?
- How would you describe the success of your organization?
- Do you and your colleagues believe in and develop an idea of democratic work, group consensus, and participatory work styles?
- Are there any learning communities on your shop floor? What are they like and how do they function? If not, how do workers keep learning and participating in the cooperative?
- How is the continuation of education both inside and outside the firm supported and promoted?
- What is a democratic firm?

6. Computer conferencing will effectively extend the learning from this class. Students and coordinator will work together more fully on some of these case studies. Stay brief and focused in each one of your comments. Quality will be defined by the following:
   - Provide supportive evidence for your thoughts when necessary.
   - Write only enough to fill one computer screen.
   - Listen to what others have to say and respond appropriately.
   - Integrate other ideas into your own thoughts as well.
   - Reference clearly what you are responding to.
   - Raise relevant questions and appropriate observations.
   - Participate through a reflection of your own experiences as well as the readings.
   - Learn and have fun in this new medium.

7. Develop a Strengths, Weaknesses, Opportunities, Threats (SWOT) Analysis for your workplace:
   - Internal Analysis: Strengths, Weaknesses
   - External Analysis: Opportunities, Threats

8. Read and unpack other articles in *Harvard Business Review*:
   - Roger Harrison. 1972. "Understanding Your Organization's Character." *Harvard Business Review* (May–June): 119–129.
   - Larry Greiner. 1967. "Patterns of Organization Change." *Harvard Business Review* 45, no. 3 (May–June): 119–130.

CONCLUSION

Now that we have had a closer look at some of the inner workings of several companies, what areas will you look at more closely when you are at the work site? How will you be an ethnographer at your work site?

ASSIGNMENT

1. Each base group must meet and complete the task from the small group activity.
2. Think and respond to the following: Describe a norm that has a negative effect on you or your organization/your family/your friends. How would you like to violate this norm? What are some possible responses to this question?

Unit 6A

Intercultural Communication

LESSON TOPIC: COMMUNICATION ACROSS CULTURES

Teaching Note

Professional communication among people from different groups involves engaging in communication that provides all individuals with an identity and that allows for clarity of understanding. Professional communications covers a broad range of positions in business, government, and education. There are various discourse systems among groups, generations, cultures, genders, professional organizations, and corporations. As professionals, it is important to claim and demonstrate our own complex identities when communicating with others and to cross boundaries to create and interpret other discourse systems in order to work and learn with others more effectively.

We have learned that developing effective communication skills for our learners has been one of the most important areas for growth. As they began to feel comfortable, trusting, and self-confident in their speaking abilities, they demonstrated ease in working with each other patiently. They also realized that the more they learned about each other and their diverse perspectives, the better the interactions became. What becomes apparent to everyone in the group is the need to look at diversity in terms of obvious and not-so-obvious differences and the need to be fully attuned to the various needs, interests, priorities, and communication styles of everyone involved.

Objectives

To introduce concepts of intercultural communication and identify the challenges of living and working in an intercultural world

To practice effective communication to overcome barriers stopping us from connecting with others in our personal and professional lives

Domains

Cognitive: Analyze the changes of living and working in an intercultural world
Affective: Value differences in communication styles
Skills: Listen and communicate effectively

Academic Standard: Write and Speak in the English Language

Interpersonal Communication Skills
Effective speaking and listening skills
Create self-assessment and appropriate feedback

Materials

Census data overhead (fig. 3.43)
Barriers to Communication activity sheet (fig. 3.44)

Figure 3.43.   U.S. Census Data

Between 1990 and 1997, growth in Latino, African American, and Asian American populations accounted for the nation's two-thirds increase.

Current U.S. Population:
European Americans: 72.7%
African Americans: 12.1%
Latinos: 10.9%
Asian Americans: 3.5%
Native Americans: 0.7%

The United States is a multicultural nation. Of the thirty-two million people in the United States, one in eight speaks a language other than English. The population is estimated to increase from 264 million (1997) to 394 million by 2050. By 2005, Latinos will replace African Americans as the second largest cultural group in the United States.

Estimated 2050 U.S. Population:
European Americans: 52.8%
African Americans: 24.5%
Latinos: 13.6%
Asian Americans: 8.2%
Native Americans: 1.0%

Figure 3.44.   Barriers to Communication

Your company has just hired a large number of people from various diverse backgrounds and abilities. The manager is starting to hear employees muttering out loud
that they cannot deal with all these changes and diversity issues. In order to get a better idea of what the issues are, the manager has asked everyone, including you, to fill
out the following survey. After completing the survey, develop strategies for dealing
with each issue you identified.

How do these issues influence your work and your communication with others on the
job (Never, Sometimes, Often)? Record the answer that is the most appropriate. At the
bottom, please list the top three things you see as barriers to communication.

Age
Race
Ethnic origin
Gender
Personality
Inexperience
Inability to perform
Disability
Language issues
Customs
Class differences
Other (specify)

Barrier 1:

Barrier 2:

Barrier 3:

Introductory Framework

We live in remarkable times. All around us, there is an emphasis on global
societies and cultures. What do we mean by the expression "a global village"? What are the things that exist today that support the concept of a
global village that did not exist 50-100 years ago?

Let us consider the enormous changes that have taken place globally, forging alliances and coalitions among vastly different cultural groups. The formation of the European Economic Community (EEC), the negotiation of the
North American Free Trade Agreement (NAFTA), and the expansion of the
Association of Southeast Asian Nations (ASEAN) are just a few of such alliances. The New Russia, new countries in Africa, the end of the cold war,
and the end of the Berlin Wall are also markers in our changing globalization. As we acknowledge these new alliances, we think about the new relationships developing among different peoples. We do not have to travel out

of the United States to experience a myriad of cultures and languages. With all of this change, we need to prepare for the challenges and the possibilities inherent in communication with people in different cultures.

The need to understand the role of culture in interpersonal communications is growing—internationally and domestically, in business, education, health care, and personal lives. The political and economic effectiveness of the United States in the global arena depends on individual and collective abilities to communicate competently with other cultures. (Show fig. 3.43.) What does this chart tell you about changing demographics?

The "browning of America" will be seen in every major cultural and social institution; this phenomenon will have an impact on public schools, higher education, and the workplace. Additionally, more companies will "go global," requiring employees to work abroad for extended periods of time. Success, both personal and professional, will increasingly depend on communicating effectively with diverse cultures.

Motivation

At various times we have experienced miscommunication during or after a conversation with someone. For example, there are two businessmen—one from New York City and one from Hong Kong—enjoying a conversation. As they part, the man from New York says they should get together for lunch. After a few weeks, during which time he has not received an invitation for lunch, the man from Hong Kong feels his New York colleague has been insincere. What is the source of this confusion? What are some examples of miscommunication you have experienced? Why do you think this happened? (List all responses on the board.) Remember miscommunication can result even when people with good intentions are trying their best to understand each other.

INSTRUCTIONAL IMPLEMENTATION

Large Group Activity: Effective Communication

Following are some ideas to consider when working toward effective communication:

1. What is communication? Is it a "symbolic process in which people create shared meaning"? Let's analyze this statement.
2. Symbol—a word, action, or object that represents meaning. Ask the class for examples of a symbol. Show examples from each one of these categories. How are they different in different cultures? For example: What are different ways to demonstrate a stop sign in different countries? What are some of the universal symbols? What are some confusing symbols?

3. People, relationships, activities, objects, and experiences are all part of a dynamic process—what do we mean by a dynamic process? Language is dynamic and has changed over the centuries to reflect the development of each generation and civilization. Present a list of words that were not considered proper for communication but are now standard. With each new edition of Webster's dictionary, new words like cyberspace, exurban, gallactic, frankenfood, dotcommers, headbangers, McJob, micromanaging, and multitasking find themselves listed. These are examples of how language is dynamic and changes to reflect changes in society and culture. Look in the dictionary and see how many new words have been entered as a result of new topics or slang words that have become standard words. Additionally, there are buzz words and hackneyed phrases that have become worn out because of overuse and so now they make little sense. Have students list some. When are you tempted to use any of these phrases? What can you do to avoid them? Ask yourself what it is you really want to say. How you can phrase your ideas differently? How will people perceive what you are saying? What is a fresh and clear way of communicating your ideas?

4. Shared meanings: What is meant by shared meaning? How do we share meanings? How does this promote effective communication?

Many times, the process we just referred to does not work effectively with people we do not know or with people from other cultures. Why do you think this would happen? What have you experienced as barriers when you first came to this country, when you moved to Minnesota, when you moved to another neighborhood, to another state? What barriers have you experienced in general? What about students who have lived abroad and had to learn another language and set of customs?

Communication is probably the most important skill a person needs because of all the aspects of our life that are connected to communication. There are components to communication—two of them are verbal and nonverbal. Research tells us that many times nonverbal communication is more powerful in giving messages and communicating feelings than verbal messages. Nonverbal messages can be ambiguous and difficult to interpret accurately.

Fishbowl Exercise: Understanding Nonverbal Messages

Students will role-play the following:

Sender: Smiles and looks directly at the receiver. "What show did you watch on television last night? Why do you like it?" The sender crosses his or her arms and legs and looks away as the receiver is answering.

Receiver: Responds briefly and only to the question, offering no other information.

Sender: Stands and walks toward the receiver. Asks the receiver two questions, one about school and one about work. As the questions are being asked, the sender moves closer to the receiver, getting in quite close and breaking the comfort zone.
Receiver: Stands up and answers the questions.

Sender: Stands up, smiles at the receiver, and says, "Come into my office with me." Sender begins to walk away, then turns back and repeats the same phrase without a smile and in a harsh and demanding tone.
Receiver: Stands up and follows the sender.

Sender: Walks into the room and says, "Good morning, here is the report you requested."
Receiver: Sits at desk, writing. Does not look up and says in a commanding tone, "Thanks, leave it on the desk." Continues to write.

Sender: Looks at the receiver and simply states, "I really think we should get started on this project."
Receiver: Shakes her or his head to indicate "no" while saying, "Yes, I do too."

Sender: Stands up and walks toward the receiver. Hands the receiver a sheet of paper, looks beyond him or her, and says with a grim face, "This is a terrific idea. Congratulations."
Receiver: Remains sitting, looks at the sender, and says, "Thank you."

After the role-play of each set is completed, discuss reactions and observations.

Large Group Activity: Communication Process

Communication involves more than putting words together. The process involves a sender, a receiver, and an understanding. All of our communications are filled with different aspects of our identities: Gender, age, the region of a country an individual lives in, education, culture, emotional state at the time, beliefs, and experience. Naturally, each of us comes from a different frame of reference. Think about what it is like when you walk into your different classrooms and greet your friends and teachers. What are some of the varying responses? Some smile and say "hi," others may glare and say "what is so good about today," or "why are you so late to class," or "great to see you," or "why are you always so happy," and so on. We usually react unconsciously—our reaction takes place with lightning speed—automatically. There are obvious and not-so-obvious differences at work and at school. What are some not-so-obvious differences (lifestyle, political preferences, class, religion)? What do you think would happen if one day the company you worked for announced a merger with a leading corporation in your industry? How will people perceive things differently?

Let's generate two lists that will begin to guide us in effective and constructive communication: Build Bridges and Hot Buttons. For example, under "Hot Buttons" you could list "you did it wrong." Under "Build Bridges" you could list "you really have a knack for designing marketing materials. Here are some suggestions for improving the layout." This is our first attempt to explore how communication impacts and influences all that we do. It is also the beginning of developing effective communication skills.

Small Group Activity: Oops—I Made a Mistake!

Try to think of a situation where you misperceived another person's nonverbal clues. As you think of the situation, tap into the following three areas and see how they influenced your situation: timing, perspective, and cultural factors. Also consider if there are other factors. Share the situation, the cues used, and then what happened.

Small Group Activity: Customize Your Communication

As you observe your school and work peers, you notice everyone has a unique communication style. One person may dislike small talk and want to get to the bottom line immediately, another might enjoy making small talk and kidding around before starting a serious conversation. What is your communication style like?

Here are some coaching tips for customizing your communication:

1. Watch and learn from professional speakers. Look at television, choosing broadcast journalists who really appeal to you. What qualities do you wish to emulate?
2. Determine what type of profile you exhibit as a speaker: passive (rather submissive and subordinate), aggressive (usually exceeds the bounds of appropriate behavior), or expressive (in the middle, neither brash nor timid).
3. Keep a record of how you interact with different people.
4. List the aspects of your communication style you would like to change.

What else would you add to this list?

Small Group Activity: Barriers to Communication

Distribute the Barriers to Communication activity sheet (fig. 3.44). Have students form base groups. Each student should complete the sheet individually at first, then work together to form one large list to present to the class.

Optional Plans

1. Students create their own scenarios for role-playing based on what they discussed above.
2. Students list their own ways of speaking that are culturally informed and that have caused miscommunication. What suggestions do they offer from their experiences?
3. Have students discuss and come up with solutions to make people realize that their stereotypes of other cultures and co-cultures are probably false and that they need to be changed or eliminated.
4. Have small groups design communication improvement strategies (e.g., be yourself, show concern for the other person who is speaking, be open and friendly, etc.).
5. Discuss the differences between ethnicity and culture and how it affects communication.
6. Have students discuss what it is like to be part of two cultures.
7. Research and present cultural and economic organizational successes (e.g., the Asian Five Dragons and Confucianism).
8. What type of orientation program/manual would you design for new employees in an organization?
9. What type of orientation program/manual would you design for new students in your school? How would you help them and their families become more comfortable in their new situation?
10. Have class members do a study on intercultural communication among students and teachers in their other classes.
11. To what degree do the cultural factors of a society influence its organizational life?

Performance-Based Assessments

- Identifying list of barriers

CONCLUSION

1. What are the challenges to intercultural communication? What is one effective strategy you will use this week?

Unit 6B

Intercultural Communication

LESSON TOPIC: EFFECTIVE COMMUNICATION

Teaching Note

This second lesson on effective communication skills can be developed in a variety of ways depending upon the class. We found that for the first two years of the Voyager program, students were learning about a variety of effective communication strategies so that they could learn about each other. The class chose to look more closely at cultural and language differences. The young women especially wanted to study male and female communication and then make a comparison with their own cultural experiences. They wanted to explore what it meant to communicate as trilinguals: women and women of color in a white standard world. The opportunities for discussion are endless, as illustrated by the additional suggestions. One of the main objectives was to have students reflect upon the realities of their lived experiences, support their ideas and understanding of language and communication, and develop their technical skills as effective communicators. They clearly wanted to know and speak to each other with greater consideration and acceptance.

Objectives

To identify the concepts of intercultural competence
To practice and develop effective communication strategies

Domains

Cognitive: Understand the features of intercultural competence
Affective: Appreciate differences in cultural communication styles
Skills: Listen and communicate effectively

Academic Standard: Write and Speak in the English Language

Interpersonal Communication Skills
Effective speaking and listening skills
Create self-assessment and appropriate feedback

Materials

Concepts of Intercultural Competence overhead (fig. 3.45)
Communication Survey handout (fig. 3.46)
Culture Connections handout (fig. 3.47)

Pre-Instructional

Students should have completed the Barriers to Communication activity sheet from the last meeting.

Introductory Framework

As we saw yesterday, learning to be an effective communicator in an intercultural society poses many challenges. We live in confusing and also remarkable times. What we know is that with the heightened awareness of cultures, there are mixed messages among diverse groups of people. Some seem to encourage understanding and some seem to discourage it. Citizens in the twenty-first century need to cross the barriers, communicate among diverse groups, and maintain understanding. How can we learn from mistakes and directly address areas of misunderstanding?

Figure 3.45.   Concepts of Intercultural Competence

1. **Display of Respect:** The ability to show positive regard and respect for another person.
2. **Display of Listening:** Active listening to another person's speaking.
3. **Orientation to Knowledge:** The terms people use to explain themselves and the world around them. The ability to synthesize their understandings and interpretations.
4. **Empathy:** Capacity to understand the world as others do. Behaviors that initiate ideas related to group work, goals, and relationships.
5. **Relational Behaviors:** Behaviors supporting intergroup harmony through relationship building.
6. **Interaction Management:** Skill in regulating and maintaining conversation.
7. **Tolerance for Ambiguity:** The ability to respond to new and ambiguous situations with comfort. The ability to respond to others in descriptive, nonevaluative, and nonjudgmental ways. The ability to be open to new information and knowledge.

Figure 3.46. Communication Survey

How effective a communicator are you?

Directions: For each of the following statements, select one of the following:
a = rarely
b = sometimes
c = usually

1. Do you knowingly change your speaking style in order to motivate an audience?
2. Do you frame your ideas and presentations so that they will be understandable to your audience?
3. Do you translate messages using the other person's frame of reference?
4. Do you send messages using nonverbals?
5. Do you improve your communication skills by taking classes, taking tips from others, and/or copying techniques used by your role models?
6. Do you plan for communication misunderstandings?
7. Do you blame others when communication breaks down?
8. Do you believe that giving and receiving feedback is necessary for successful communication?
9. Do you feel misunderstood when speaking?
10. Do you get nervous and apprehensive when you have to speak?

Add up the number of times you responded "rarely," the number of times you responded "sometimes," and the number of times you responded "usually."

If you answered "rarely" or "sometimes" to fewer than three of these questions, you're considered a good communicator.

If you answered "rarely" or "sometimes" to between three and six of these questions, you're considered an average communicator.

If you answered "rarely" or "sometimes" to seven or more of these questions, your communication skills need improvement.

Motivation

Read the following quote aloud: "The new mestiza copes by developing a tolerance for contradictions, a tolerance for ambiguity. She learns to be an Indian in Mexican culture, to be Mexican from an Anglo point of view. She learns to juggle cultures. She has a plural personality, she operates in a pluralistic mode—nothing is thrust out, the good, the bad, the ugly, nothing rejected, nothing abandoned. Not only does she sustain contradictions, she turns the ambivalence into something else" (Gloria Anzaldua, 1999). What is this writer saying?

Figure 3.47.   Culture Connections

If the world were a village of 1,000 people, in the village would be:
504 Asians
239 East Indians
116 Africans
76 Latin Americans
45 North Americans
117 Europeans
44 Oceana/Asian Pacific Islanders

There would be:
330 Christians (170 Catholics, 71 Protestants, 89 Others)
196 Muslims
134 Hindus
20 Jews
59 Buddhists
261 Nonreligious, Atheists, or Others

Adapted from U.S. Bureau of the Census, *Statistical Abstract of the United States: 2000*, 117th ed. Washington, DC: U.S. Bureau of the Census, 2000.

INSTRUCTIONAL IMPLEMENTATION

Large Group Activity: Universal Claims

Many times when we frame our statements, we do not realize that we are making universal claims or that our words may be offensive. We make statements based on opinion and state them as if they were facts. We have beliefs based on our knowledge of our own orientation. How could we express the following experiences in a way that is more conducive to intercultural competence?

1. "New Yorkers are a bunch of crazy people living in an impossible city." (One possible answer: "I find New York a difficult place to visit. I do not think I could live there.")
2. "Brits are cold and unemotional people who are not friendly." (One possible answer: "Many of the people I interacted with in England were courteous but not friendly.")
3. "Arranged marriages are barbaric and against human rights." (One possible answer: "I would not want my family to arrange my marriage for me.")

Ask the class if they can give examples from their own lives.

Small Group Activity: Our Experiences in Minnesota

Soon in the middle of the twenty-first century, racial and ethnic groups will outnumber European Americans for the first time. This new American profile will influence and change everything in society—education, politics, workplaces, industry, and culture. The projected increase in U.S. population in 2050 will be from non-European immigrants from Africa, Asia, South and Central America, and the Caribbean. Many of these new immigrants will be highly skilled workers from their own countries and will be valued as new participants in a changing U.S. economy. They will also have to face the experience of encountering a strong sense of culture and ethnic identity, a strong sense of achieving their goals, and not abandoning their culture as a price for their success. How do these students connect with you and your family experiences when you first moved to the United States? Have students share what some of their experiences in Minnesota have been and how they could have avoided miscommunication. Have students create fact sheets about their culture that they feel would help others understand them better. Distribute the Culture Connections handout (fig. 3.47).

Large Group Activity: Diverse Communications

Free write for the next three minutes by finishing this sentence: "When I interact with strangers who are from a different cultural group, speak a different language, I feel . . ." After students reflect, have them brainstorm responses on poster boards.

Let us look at some other ways that allow us to become more comfortable with communication styles involving diverse cultures. Show the Concepts of Intercultural Competence (fig. 3.45) overhead. Have students discuss each concept and then give an example for each of the concepts. Have students stretch and expand each of the concepts and then furnish specific examples of each.

Small Group Activity: Communication Survey (fig. 3.46)

Have base group members complete the survey individually, evaluating their communication skills, and then have them share these with their base group. Each base group will summarize their members' findings and share them with the class. What did you learn about yourself as a communicator? What surprised you? What do you now want to work on for improved communication skills?

Optional Plans

1. Students research ideas in gendered communication—what are communication differences between women and men? Have students create a survey and interview others for opinions on how women and men communicate differently.
2. Have small groups research the history of the English language and examine the connection between language and the transmission of culture and the effect of technology on communication.

3. Plan and have a debate among the students regarding Standard English, slang, dialects, and minority languages.
4. Create a panel of community and private business owners and invite them to the class to talk about intercultural communications within their workplaces.
5. Invite two or three middle-level managers to talk about workplace realities with diverse workforces. Ask them to talk about their business practices and what they think about workplace and global communication needs.
6. Have students review videos demonstrating cultural communication at work and provide alternatives and solutions to the problems the workers are facing in their workplace. For example: *Diversity at Work*, *You Make the Difference*, and *Communicating across Cultures* (all available from Copeland Griggs Productions).

Performance-Based Assessments

- Responses to communication survey
- Responses to all small group activity tasks

CONCLUSION

What are the challenges to intercultural communication? Why is there a pressing need and concern for intercultural competence? Think about the following quote:

> There is no longer a single racial or ethnic group with an overwhelming numerical and political majority. Pluralism is the reality, with no one group a dominant force. This is completely new; we are grappling with a phenomenon that is both puzzling and alarming, fraught with tensions and hostilities, and yet simultaneously brimming with potential and crackling with new energy. Consequently, we swing between hope and concern, optimism and pessimism about the prospects for social life among people from differing racial and cultural groups. (Duster, 1991, p. B2)

What is your understanding of the above quote? How do you respond to the author's statements? What do you offer as alternatives to this scenario of the global village?

ASSIGNMENT (CHOOSE FROM THE FOLLOWING)

1. Interview two people from cultures different from your own. Ask them to describe their communication experiences (at work and in their community) in the United States. Did they experience any difficulties?

How were they perceived by others? What are some challenges they face as people from different cultures?

2. Interview several students who represent several different cultures. Find out how they relate to others and how others relate to them; let them express their difficulties and experiences as multiethnic and multicultural students.

3. Respond to the following quotes. What are the challenges posed by these new domestic imperatives? Be prepared to discuss your responses at the next seminar. Feel free to have others read and react to the quotes as well.

Many Americans are not who they think they are; hundreds of thousands of white people in America are not 'white.' Some know it, others don't. Ten thousand people each year cross the visible and invisible colorline and become 'white.' If a new sociological method of determining race were devised, equal numbers of black people might no longer be black. What happened in my family and many others like it calls into question the concept of color as a means of self-definition. Genes and chromosomes from Africa, Europe, and a pristine American co-mingled and created me. I have been called Egyptian, Italian, Jewish, French, Iranian, Armenian, Syrian, Spanish, Portuguese, and Greek. I have also been called black and nigger and high yellow and bright. I am an American anomaly. I am an American ideal. I am the American nightmare. I am the Martin Luther King dream. I am the new America. (Haizlip, 1994, p. 15)

As a woman with some Cherokee ancestors on my father's side and a blonde blue-eyed daughter, I find it impossible to pin down the meaning of ethnicity. It's an especially delicate business here in the Southwest, where so many of us boil in one pot without melting. We are never allowed to forget we are foreign bodies in the eyes of our neighbors. The annual Winter Holiday Concert at Camille's school features a bright patchwork of languages and rituals, each of which must be learned by a different subset of kids, the others having known it since they could talk. It sounds idyllic, but then spend half an hour on the playground and you're also likely to come away with a whole new vocabulary of racial slurs. On the playground no one's counting the strengths of your character, nor the woman your great-grandfather married unless her genes have dyed your hair and fixed your features. It's the fact on your passport that gets you in. Faces that set us apart, in separate houses. (Kingsolver, 1996, p. 147)

No one prepared Garfield for the great deluge of Southeast Asians, Haitians, and Latinos. And now the folks who have been there a long time blame all the problems on the newcomers. And I want to say to them that the future of Garfield depends upon taking the energy that these new people bring. There's so much fear of brown faces, black faces, languages that they don't understand. Yet that's what we've always been; we've always taken the energy of newcomers and used that to build the country. I think I can articulate that and help people listen to those ideas and think in those terms. Hopefully, my voice will be one of the many around the world that will begin to help people better understand what is happening. This is what it means to think more globally, to hold the knowledge that we are all on this planet together and need to see our diversity as a strength rather than a source of conflict. (Daloz, Keen, Keen, and Park, 1996, p. 84)

By viewing ourselves in a mirror which reflects reality, we can see our past as undistorted and no longer have to peer into our future as through a glass darkly. The face of our cultural future can be found on the western edge of the continent. "California" and especially Los Angeles, a gateway to both Asia and Latin America. Carlos Fuentes posed the question of the coming century: "how do we deal with the Other?" Asked whether California, especially with its multiethnic society, represented the America of the twenty-first century, Alice Walker replied, "If that's not the future reality of the United States, there won't be any United States, because that's who we are." Walker's own ancestry is a combination of Native American, African American, and European American. Paula Gunn Allen also has diverse ethnic roots and says, "that's why I am a multicultural event. . . . It's beautiful, it reflects light and I think that's what a person like me can do." Imagine what a light a multicultural event called America can reflect. (Takaki, 1993, p. 98)

Unit 7A

Self-Assessment and Reflection

LESSON TOPIC:
THE PROCESS OF SELF-ASSESSMENT AND REFLECTION

Teaching Note

The last unit in the junior year provides a more focused picture of how the students see themselves and what possibilities and alternatives they are envisioning. At this point, self-assessment is developing as an organic classroom process. Students have had an entire year to develop self-reflective skills, and student experiences are central to a critical pedagogy of work education. Both the classroom and the work sites offer rich learning potential, places where students have numerous resources to help make sense of the range of their experiences and to connect their learning. The reflective learning experience is a process that moves back and forth from the classroom to the work site and that supplies students with rich opportunities for critical inquiry. It is considered central to this program. Students are encouraged to self-reflect and to also learn from other voices about their work. The end of the year self-evaluation becomes a more engaging process because it has become a core component of the program. Not only are students well-versed in its application, they view it as a real tool from which to learn. They review various aspects of their learning experience: What were the vital goals they set out for themselves? How have they fulfilled these goals? What was the quality of their work? What new areas must they concentrate on? What new goals do they have for themselves?

Teachers can take advantage of both individual and collaborative assessment practices. It is important to enhance the learning potential of this program with the need to develop methods so that students can examine their own experiences and develop an understanding of what these experiences teach. They have a wide range of selection and collection procedures to assess themselves person-ally and professionally, collaborate with others, and re-vision their pathways.

Self-assessment is a way of answering the question "How am I doing?" Students must look further and ask: Am I right for this program? Am I right for this job? Do I really think I am suited for this career? What are my strong characteristics—how do they fit with what I want to do? They are masterful at coming up with their own questions and inquiries. This is also a great time to open up conversations regarding students' and workers' versions of their work reality. They can be challenged to think about alternative versions of work within specific occupational areas.

Objectives

To develop and apply the process of self-assessment
To identify components of success and growth for each individual during the
    first year of the Voyager program

Domains

Cognitive: Understand and apply criteria for developing assessment
Affective: Value one's work
Skills: Listen and provide feedback

Academic Standard: Career Investigation

Effective speaking and listening skills
Create self-assessment and appropriate feedback

Materials

Portfolios/journals
Features of Assessment That Are Respectful for Voyager Students and
    Teachers overhead (fig. 3.48)
Flipcharts for small group work

Pre-Instructional

Students are to work on: reflective paragraph of Voyager portfolio, all Per-sonal and Professional Growth Plans, and work-site reports and materials.

Introductory Framework

This is one of the last units of study for this Voyager year. Throughout the year you have been compiling and finishing many projects. These projects

Figure 3.48. **Features of Assessment That Are Respectful for Voyager Students and Teachers**

- Assessment is based on exactly what the student does throughout the year.
- Assessment addresses the actual classroom learning, connecting activities and work-site experiences the student has completed.
- Assessment clearly describes how the student does over a period of time, over a variety of tasks.
- Assessment involves students as active participants. They choose their artifacts for assessment and create their unique profile for demonstration of their personal and professional growth.
- Assessment is multifaceted and creative, concerning achievement, process, product, and quality.
- Assessment is an interactive and collaborative process including all aspects of teaching and learning (large and small group work, assignments, site visits) and is in line with the program goals. This is not a one-shot deal that demonstrates success or failure.
- Assessment should contribute to the student's knowledge of self.
- Parental, community, and business stakeholders are all part of the assessment process.

have allowed you to read many different materials, write about what you have read, and visit corporate sites and work with employers, community members, and faculty. It is now time to look at your accomplishments for the year and to take time for an in-depth self-assessment.

The complete definition of the academic standard Career Investigation reads as follows: "Career investigation and work experience have been a part of your work this year. Let us look at the performance-based assessment for career investigation and see what aspects of the learning standards you are fulfilling, as well as the components of the portfolio assessment process you are fulfilling. Read and review the following Graduation Standard. Generate ideas for fulfilling this standard."

Academic Standard: Decision Making

A student shall demonstrate understanding of career clusters, attributes, and aptitudes needed in particular types of occupations and careers, how attitudes and behaviors affect the climate of a workplace, how systems within a workplace affect or interact with systems in the community, and how systems affect an individual worker by:

1. Determining personal interest, aptitudes, and abilities.
2. Establishing an explicit career plan, including selecting a program that meets a career or vocational preparation.

3. Investigating a career through research, internship, mentorship, or community service.
4. Evaluating career choices in relationship to life goals and personal attributes

Reread the sheet for expectations of portfolio—remember to follow some of the procedures used in writing class. Have students list all ideas on the board. What are all the materials we need to effectively carry out an assessment procedure? Show the Features of Assessment That Are Respectful for Voyager Students and Teachers overhead (fig. 3.48). The same procedures should be followed for fulfilling the other program requirements, such as Voyager themes, journaling, projects, and so on.

INSTRUCTIONAL IMPLEMENTATION

Small Group Activity

Students will bring their portfolios and a list for compiling their assessment process to their base groups. The teacher will begin one-to-one conferences while the base groups are meeting.

Optional Plans

1. Students will need to work for at least one to two sessions on the assessment process.
2. Bring in Voyager alumni and either business partners or staff to help with the first round of portfolio assessments.

Performance-Based Assessments

• Response and appropriate feedback activities for portfolio assessment

CONCLUSION

What are the different procedures you have developed with your group to develop assessment methods? What other methods to collect data and self-assess will you need?

ASSIGNMENT

1. Complete the newly developed portfolio for the next seminar. Students and teacher make inventory modifications. Students will work with outside assessors (including their mentors and their work supervisors) for feedback on their work.

Unit 7B

Self-Assessment and Reflection

LESSON TOPIC: THE PROCESS OF SELF-ASSESSMENT AND FUTURE ACTION PLANS

Teaching Note

Some of the most important factors influencing this particular seminar are for students to take the time to represent themselves in original and creative ways, listen to feedback from their peers, and take the time to appreciate and relish their successes.

This is an important time to honor them and have them honor themselves and each other. For many, engagement in this process will be experienced for the first time. It will be important to question notions of success and failure. For many students, successful personal and professional growth is purely an individual act based on individual qualities—the John Wayne type of thinking: "pick yourself up by your bootstrap and move on." It is an important moment to capture and critically explore how the ideology of self-reliance conceals the many social factors that influence success and failure. Ira Shor (1992) captures this idea in his phrase "three roads to critical thought," which talks about how important it is to ask different questions of students so that they see their futures as affected by socio-political forces as well as unequal power arrangements. It is not about making certain populations victims. By asking how inequalities in school, work, economic systems, and corporate domination affect personal growth, students are asked to engage in divergent thinking. Such thinking provides ways for them to see links between their personal growth and issues of economic policy, or rising taxes and political corruption, or sexism and cheap labor force practices. As students are encouraged to look beyond their initial ideas, some will become interested in the new perspectives, while others will defend the right of big business and government. This is not an easy debate to have in class, but is certainly an activity in democratic education where multiple themes can be explored and critically examined. Students will reflect and self-assess providing an empowering session where students continue to share the responsibility and authority for their learning. It also serves as a problem-posing strategy for future projects.

Objectives

To develop and address the issues of the self-assessment process in order to write future growth plans
To create closure for the year's academic and workplace studies

Domains

Cognitive: Understand and modify assessment practices
Affective: Appreciate the work for the academic year
Skills: Listen and provide feedback

Academic Standard: Decision Making

Career Investigation
Determining personal and professional interests, aptitudes, and abilities

Materials

Flipcharts for small group work
Small group feedback sheet; peer review sheet for portfolio
Self-Assessment Inventory Sheet (fig. 3.49)
Student-Teacher Conference Inventory sheet (fig. 3.50)
Outside Reviewer Sheet for Portfolio (fig. 3.51)
Peer Reviewer Sheet for Portfolio (fig. 3.52)

Pre-Instructional

What are the top three things you will change for the coming semester? This is based on the pre-assessment procedures completed by you and your peers.

Introductory Framework

You have had time to reflect, assess, and gather feedback from your peers regarding your work. Many times the high level and volume of accomplishments we have made surprise us. Many times we do not see our own suc-

Figure 3.49. Self-Assessment Inventory Sheet

From the list of Voyager program themes below, choose two items to focus on for your self-assessment using the prompts below.

- Work-site success (internships, mentorships, job shadowing)
- Academic success—work that is related to the program in other areas (if connected and aligned with Voyager)
- Outside activities and work (relevant to the program and course of study)
- Personal and professional growth plans
- Reflective writing
- Journal completions
- In-class assignments and activities
- Career investigation standard
- Other

On the next page, write the themes you chose to focus on for your self-assessment in the space provided ("Choice 1" and "Choice 2"). Then answer the questions below each theme you list.

Choice 1:
- Why I chose this particular theme:
- What I learned:
- What my strengths are in this area:
- What my future goals and needs are in this area:

Choice 2
- Why I chose this particular theme:
- What I learned:
- What my strengths are in this area:
- What my future goals and needs are in this area:

cesses immediately. Yet after several months, as we look back we can find many changes in ourselves and in our work.

Motivation

Read the following quote aloud: "Those are a success who have lived well, laughed often and loved much; who have gained the respect of intelligent people and the love of children; who have filled their niche and accomplished their task; who leave the world better than they found it, whether by a perfect poem or a rescued soul; who never lacked the appreciation of the earth's beauty or failed to express it; who looked for the best in others and gave the best they had" (Anderson, 1990). How do you interpret this quote? What is your idea of success? How has your conception of success been influenced by media portrayals of success?

Figure 3.50.   Student-Teacher Conference Inventory

> Portfolio conferences are created so that students and teachers can have an authentic conversation regarding student achievement, future goals, and further teaching instruction. The goals are to benefit both parties.
>
> **Student**
> Present and select pieces that you would like to talk about.
> Why did you choose these pieces? What have you learned?
>
> **Teacher**
> Ask about the student's strengths and future needs.
> Make notes about the uniqueness of each portfolio.

Have students brainstorm all their ideas for success. Have student leaders list responses on flipcharts.

INSTRUCTIONAL IMPLEMENTATION

The seminar coordinator will set up one-to-one conferences with students as they work in small groups. At the conference, students will present their portfolio to the teacher. The student retains control of the portfolio; the teacher

Figure 3.51.   Outside Reviewer Sheet for Portfolio

> Date:
> Name of Student:
> Name of Outside Reviewer:
> Position of Outside Reviewer:
>
> Browse the portfolio. Choose three entries that stand out for you and identify the best or the unique features of each entry. Explain how these features enhance the student's work. Make general comments about the portfolio and how the assessment guide is set up. As you review the portfolio keep in mind the following guidelines:
>
> 1. What is the purpose of this project?
> 2. What outcomes were successfully attained?
> 3. How did the work/projects promote social justice, include a component of activism, and/or develop democratic ideals?
> 4. What was the overall writing quality like?
> 5. What levels of self-reflection and self-assessment of the individual projects and the overall portfolio are demonstrated?
>
> Entry 1
> Entry 2
> Entry 3
> General comments and suggestions:

Figure 3.52. Peer Reviewer Sheet for Portfolio

Date:
Name of Student:
Name of Peer Reviewer:

Browse the portfolio. Choose three entries and identify the best or the unique features of each entry. Explain how these features enhance the student's work. Make general comments about the portfolio and how the assessment guide is set up.

Entry 1
Entry 2
Entry 3
General comments and suggestions:

---

tailors the conference to the individual student, using the Student-Teacher Conference Inventory (fig. 3.50).

Small Group Activity

Have students join their base groups and review their successes for this year. Each student will present her or his success to her or his group and get feedback from each member. A recorder will compile a master sheet of successes for presenting to the class. The teacher will begin one-to-one conferences while the base groups are meeting.

Individual Activity

Distribute the Self-Assessment Inventory Sheet (fig. 3.49) to students and have them work on it while you meet with other students. Review Outside Reviewer Sheet (fig. 3.51) so that students know what to expect. Review Peer Reviewer Sheet (fig. 3.52) and instruct students on how to review and assess their peers' portfolios.

Optional Plans

1. Have students continue working on changing and/or modifying their personal and professional growth plans for the coming semester.
2. During the summer take time to research the best jobs for the twenty-first century. Create categories such as salary, fastest growth, nature of the job, working conditions, training, job outlook, disappearing jobs, and so on.
3. What are some of the skills you want to work on this summer? Who do you want to network with?

4. List and set up a schedule for what you want to accomplish as you prepare for your senior year and for postsecondary education and training. A dream can become a reality but only if you take action to make it so.

Performance-Based Assessments

- Feedback from small group activity sheet
- Presentations

CONCLUSION

What are the different methods you have developed with your group to develop assessment methods?

ASSIGNMENT

A final copy of your personal and professional growth plan with timeline is due at the next class meeting. These plans need to be included in your portfolio for future reference and as a barometer for next year's events. Each group may also want to set goals.

4

Senior Year Seminar Units

Unit 1A

Personal and Professional Growth

LESSON TOPIC: VOYAGER KICKOFF—INTERNSHIP EXPERIENCES, COMMUNITY INPUT, SUMMER WORKSHOP #2

Teaching Note

This summer workshop once again sets the stage for senior year and the robust activity that needs to take place for all Voyager students to successfully complete the program. There are many successful outcomes from meeting during the summer. First, the Voyager community is sustained and supported by all community members. Additionally, students are able to address many housekeeping procedures, exchange information, and reunite and motivate each other to continue and complete the program. They also appreciate getting a head start reviewing and revising their annual goals, thinking about new strategies to achieve their goals, and balancing their workload, both in school and at the workplace. This is also a great time for them to debrief and examine their internship experiences as they share their reflections. Many of them will have very different experiences. Some of the students gain new insights about themselves and wish to change direction. Even with a positive internship experience, they may find "that this just isn't the job for me." Others are thrilled to know the business they've interned at is a career that excites them. They say, "I never knew there were so many different careers to pick from!" Meeting during the summer also supports the authenticity and continuity of this program. Real work and real time are spent on their projects without the challenges and demands of an academic year. It is also a good time for the community and business partners to come in and guide directions for their new projects at the Voyager Company.

Objectives

To assess and develop new Voyager goals and events for the year
To further develop portfolios, refine procedures, and discuss journal entries
To review internship experiences
To meet and work with business and community people who in turn connect
  with classroom learning

Domains

Cognitive: Examine the internship experiences
Affective: Listen and give effective feedback to students about the different
  internship experiences
Skills: Create or adjust strategies and goals for attainment of Voyager certificate

Materials

Portfolio binders
Journal entry sheets
Internship journals
Large poster sheets

Pre-Instructional

1. Send out agendas for the day. This agenda should include objectives for
   the day, business leaders, and other community speakers.
2. Ask students to bring in their internship journals and other documents
   (organizational charts, brochures, job descriptions, etc.) from their
   work experiences. Students need to bring in the items they wish to add
   to the agenda.

Motivation

A range of questions is posed to have students pause, reflect, and understand
their reactions to their own internship experiences. Students need to see how
their vision of the job matched with the actual experience. They get to compare the micro and macro aspects of their work lives.

  As current and future workers of the world, reflect upon the following
questions as you self-assess:

1. What have you learned about yourself?
2. What have you learned about the job?
3. Was this the job for you?

4. What are your concerns about this job? Were there any surprises for you? Have your goals changed in any way?

Now reflect upon a different vision of the job:

1. What would another version or take on this job look like?
2. What job changes would you make that would be more desirable for you?
3. Did you encounter any consequences?
4. Are there other options open to you?
5. Did your internship match up with your preconceived ideas?

Now reflect upon your personal experience:

1. How has this internship experience helped you to see yourself as a changing, developing person? How have you changed during your internship experience?
2. What opportunities, experiences, people, ideas did you encounter that changed the way you looked at certain ideas or issues? How can we also make connections between negative experiences and new learning?
3. Students can describe a negative experience and then reflect on how this was a learning experience for them. Students will volunteer reflections for discussion and receive feedback from the rest of the class.

Introductory Framework

Welcome back to the second annual Voyager Kickoff Workshop! We have several objectives on the agenda today that will make the coming year successful and that will support your goals for graduation, achieving Voyager certification, and attending some type of postsecondary training. We will:

1. Assess the internship experience.
2. Assess the Voyager Company and where we want to go with it.
3. Work with some of our business and community partners to see new directions for projects.
4. Begin our work for the seminar and graduation.

Take time now to add items to the agenda you would like discussed today.

INSTRUCTIONAL IMPLEMENTATION

Small Group Activity: The Internship Experience— Clarifying Our Thoughts

Hand out five to ten Post-its to each student. Each student will have five minutes to list adjectives or images that describe his or her experience in the internship. Students are encouraged to use drawings, symbols, poetry, songs, and the like to describe their ideas. Then have students meet in small groups to share their ideas and mount their images or words on poster board for a group presentation. Small groups then report their findings to the large group; students may choose to read entries from their internship journals and share their job-performance interviews as well; they may also choose to present their internship experiences to the community representatives and business partners.

Voyager Events for the Year

Students will join the action committees in order to accomplish specific tasks to host the Voyager Events for the year. Following are some committees the students can form:

- Voyager Company Presentations (web site, newsletter)
- Parents Achievement and Celebration Dinner
- Board of Directors/Advisory Board Annual Meeting
- Minneapolis Regional Chamber of Commerce Quality of Life Dinner and Networking Event
- Other

Voyager Graduation and Certificate—How Will the Requirements Be Successfully Fulfilled?

Have students review the goals they must achieve to graduate from the Voyager program and attain their certificate. Have them set up a timeline to achieve each goal. They can also review their portfolio, deciding what needs to be deleted and what added. Finally, graduation standards should be reviewed, to be sure that each skill set and competency has been achieved.

Voyager: Co-create the Curriculum

Students will review the syllabus for the year (see the Voyager Community Resource Handbook) and begin to make suggestions for additional topics of study.

Large Group Activity: Panel—The Right Fit and Other Helpful Hints

Assemble a panel of guest speakers from business and the community. The panel provides opportunity for students to work with others' experiences and to explore their own understandings of work and workplace issues with immediate feedback from people in the field. Depending on the needs and desires of the group, this panel can discuss and respond to a variety of themes.

An alternative activity, or in conjunction with the panel, would be to have students interview their work supervisor or other business and community leaders for an hour and bring back the information to share with the class. Following are some sample questions/topics for discussion:

1. What are the next steps in this job and how does it lead to a career pathway?
2. Have them listen to how students' attitudes and interests have changed.
3. Have them probe the question, "Is this job right for you?"
4. Pay/Wage potential—what does that look like in this field?
5. What is fair pay in a labor market?
6. What is a fair exchange for their labor?
7. What do students see as unfair in pay structures?
8. How are "professionals" and "workers" defined and distinguished, especially in terms of pay and income?
9. Share tips for the job search—for those students who want to look for a job during their senior year—what should they focus on?
10. Help them understand how to negotiate with prospective employers (e.g., wages/labor).
11. Students should create and collect charts with data that illustrates differences in workers' pay scales in various industries based on postsecondary education and training. Included in this data should be the cost of an average college education and students could weigh out the pros and cons of wages and postsecondary training.

Large Group Activity: Technology Update and Tutorial

This is a good opportunity to have a discussion regarding the creation of a supportive learning environment for students. Technology becomes another tool that provides opportunities to create classroom environments that respect and promote students' abilities to make good choices about their learning and to see the varied possibilities that learning holds for them. Students are in a computer lab setting so that they can also practice some of the essential tools they will be using this year. Included in this tutorial is the sampling of the uses and applications of various software programs and a review of the applications used in the previous year such as bulletin board/email communication and multimedia and database software. The technology person and the coordinator will help students individually after the class discussion concludes in order to meet one or more of the following objectives.

During this time Voyager students will:

1. Receive coaching and suggestions for editing and developing their e-portfolios

2. Review their individual technology learning plan and make changes
3. Work with the Voyager web site and list possible future web projects as well as develop their individual web pages
4. Work with community and/or business leaders on creating projects with webquest (an inquiry oriented, web-based activity) (see http//:webquest.sdsu.edu for suggestions)
5. Review and receive tutorials for presentational and other software
6. Review procedures and requirements for email and online discussions

ASSIGNMENT

1. Bring in list of ideas/topics of interest for study this year.

Unit 1B

Personal and Professional Growth

LESSON TOPIC: WELCOME AND OVERVIEW—SENIOR GROWTH, GOALS, AND EXPECTATIONS

Teaching Note

The senior year is pivotal for the program as it encompasses a whole new range of areas to be addressed, developed, and completed. Continuing the art of reflective practice and self-assessment is foundational to this year as well. Students begin the processes of preparing for graduation, applying for admission to two- and four-year postsecondary schools, and completing their portfolios for Voyager certification. Many are continuing to work either in their internships or in other positions with business partners. They have much to manage and plan and will need close guidance and support as they move along in their chosen paths for work and school. Emphasize that engaging in activities and completing projects is only part of the learning process. Using reflection and processing thoughts help students "to learn how to learn" and to evaluate what has been learned. Students then see what further work needs to take place. It is also a time to help students see and appreciate themselves as changing and developing young adults. One student remarked "I have changed so much I hardly recognize myself in the mirror." Everyone agrees they have changed as part of their new experiences. It is also an important time to ask the question, "Think back on who you were last year, who you are now, and who you plan to be. How are you different, how are you the same, how do you want to continue to grow?" Combining experience and learning how to learn is key. Students collectively develop their own capabilities and see it as an empowering and natural process. Engaging in reflection and self-assessment accelerates both their learning about themselves and their view about previous assumptions of how things operate. These two learning tools are vital components to develop during the entire program.

Senior year is filled with high excitement and equally high anxiety. There are many important life decisions that will be made regarding both personal pathways and professional development. What is so valuable to know about the Voyager senior year is that "senioritis," or disengagement, is not a major problem. Certainly, the salient component that mitigates this is that students are engaged with real people, real businesses, and real communities. Students and teachers are working and learning in tandem—the room is alive with excitement as all of the participants are engaged in rich and authentic experiences. The learning experiences also extend and support the idea that student learning is both fun and focused.

Objectives

To build learning tools for reflection and self-assessment in order to meet
    Voyager seminar expectations and standards for graduation
To develop new personal growth action plans

Domains

Cognitive: Develop and apply informed decision making
Affective: Respond with appropriate and thoughtful feedback
Skills: Evaluate self-reflective skills

Academic Standard: Write and Speak in the English Language

Interpersonal Communication Skills
Effective speaking and listening skills
Create self-assessment and appropriate feedback

Materials

Class Trip Vignette handout (fig. 4.1)
Decision-Making Vignettes handout (fig. 4.2)
Portfolio binders
Journal entry sheets
Personal Growth Action Plan

Pre-Instructional

1. Send out Voyager Welcome Letter and Career and Work-site Seminar Syllabus.
2. Students will list areas that they wish to address in terms of Voyager themes and graduation standards.

Figure 4.1. Class Trip Vignette

You are on a class trip with your media class. Your teacher wanted to take both of her media classes to the television studios and broadcasting museum so there are a lot of students. This is a special day, as all of you have worked hard during the year on media projects and your teacher has had to make special arrangements to have the television studio people take time to meet with you and discuss your projects. This is an unusual activity for the museum, but they are impressed with your class projects. Everyone is excited. As you are walking toward the studio, you happen to turn around and see two of your classmates dodging into a liquor store. The teacher is in the front of the group and has not seen the students. What would you do?

Introductory Framework

Welcome back to the Voyager seminar. Last year we began building our portfolios for academic and workplace accomplishments. We also developed our individual personal and professional growth action plans. In the senior year, we will continue this process, as all of our work is the constant development of lifelong learning. It will be both interesting and important to see how we all have changed as a result of our life experiences. We need to examine how the experiences of the past year, including summer internships, have had an impact on and changed our goals and future directions. Additionally, there is much to do for admission to either college or other postsecondary schools, completing the career investigation standards, and fulfilling competencies for the Voyager certification.

Motivation

Ask the students to describe one thing they want everyone to know about them after they have successfully completed the first year of the Voyager program. Some possible questions to start them thinking are:

1. What are you proud of?
2. What will you continue to work on?
3. What people or events have been associated with changes that have made you who you are today?

Have students free write responses to one of these questions in their journals for five minutes before responding. Elicit responses and place on board.

INSTRUCTIONAL IMPLEMENTATION

Large Group Activity: Beliefs about Self-Assessment and Self-Reflection

Last year we started off with the question "Who am I today?" Take out some of the work you did during this unit (unit 1A) and read it over. The experiences

Figure 4.2. Decision-Making Vignettes: "What Would You Do?"

In your small groups read each vignette and then decide individually and as a group what you propose as solutions. Recorders will keep track of the solutions to report back to the class.

1. You are on a vacation trip, driving to the beach with your parents. You would like to go to the amusement park, but you are concerned because you have already spent most of the money you had saved for your vacation. Your father stops for fuel and you get out and walk around. A woman is walking back to her car and you see her purse fall open and her wallet fall out. You walk over, and pick up the wallet just as the woman gets into her car to drive away. The edges of several ten-dollar bills are sticking out of the wallet. No one saw you pick the wallet up. What would you do?

2. You have forgotten your last two dentist appointments. The dentist was furious the last time. She is also a friend of your father's from college. You have an appointment today. You look up and see that it is exactly 2:00 P.M., which is when you're supposed to be there. It is a twenty-minute walk to the dentist's office and there are no buses. What would you do?

3. While shopping with a friend, you see a kid three or four years younger than you shoplifting at the local discount store. Although you do not know him, you saw him trying out for junior varsity basketball at school. He has already taken some items in the sports department and now he is looking around for other items. You yourself are unable to afford new sneakers or sports equipment. The kid sees you staring at him and you recognize each other. You're concerned that he'll get into serious trouble if the store detective catches him. What would you do?

4. You are driving on a two-lane road behind another car. You notice that one of the wheels on the car in front of you is wobbling more and more. It looks as if the bolts are coming off, one by one. The driver and passenger carrying on an animated conversation and are oblivious to anything being wrong with their car. There's no way to pass, because cars are coming in the other direction in a steady stream. What would you do?

5. You're taking a really lousy course at the university. The professor is boring and, once when he called on you and you didn't know the answer, he embarrassed you in front of the class. You're not doing well in the course and have little opportunity to improve your grade beyond the final exam. On the day of the final exam, someone offers to sell you a copy of what he claims is the final for only $25.00. What would you do?

6. You've raised your twelve-year-old son not to play with guns. You and your spouse have spent long hours with your son, discussing the dangers of guns. Your rich uncle comes for a long-awaited visit and, without asking you if it would be okay, he brings your son a .22 rifle with lots of ammunition as a gift. You see your son's eyes pop open with delight, despite all of your talks. What would you do?

7. Your parents have been giving you a lot of flack about how much TV you watch. You always finish your homework and complete your tasks before you watch TV. One day you come home from school and the TV set isn't working. You try everything you can to find out what is wrong with it. You suspect your father has done something to the television set. What would you do?

8. Your family is having a discussion about women's rights and contraception and you notice that your twelve-year-old sister becomes extremely anxious. As the conversation continues regarding abortion and the law, your sister jumps up and runs, crying, from the room. What would you do?

we participated in last year helped us to get to know ourselves better and understand what goals we wanted to achieve. They also helped us understand and think through the process of self-reflection. We aren't the same today, are we? What is one difference you see about yourself?

This year we will apply the same question based on other activities that help us continue to examine values and develop goals.

1. What does reflection mean to you? Student leaders will use flipcharts and list all responses.
2. Why is it important to do some self-assessment and self-reflection? What does reflection provide for all of us? Are there different ways to reflect?
3. What is a reality check? Why would you want to do a reality check? Who do you go to, to check this out?

Let us continue some of our work in self-reflection. Frequently, we are faced with making choices among alternatives. Sometimes there are many alternatives that we find appealing, yet we must make a decision. How, and on what basis, do we make our decision? At other times, we find ourselves acting one way in a situation and then later regretting it and wishing we had acted differently. Sometimes, we just change and outgrow our former preferences. All of us may have these experiences at different times and we are able to learn from these experiences and decisions so that we make future choices differently. Ask students for examples of a time in their lives when they took some action—made a choice or decision—that they later regretted, leaving them to wish they had done something differently. What were the consequences for them?

Large Group Activity: Posing Problems and Clarifying Decisions

The clearer we become in our beliefs, the more congruent our actions will be. One way to clarify our beliefs is to consider alternatives for taking action in different situations.

1. Read the Class Trip Vignette (fig. 4.1) to the entire class. Vignette Reflection: Have students explore the following in their discussions.
2. What would you do in this situation? Remember, there are no wrong or right answers so feel free to voice your true thoughts and feelings about the situation.
3. Students will jot down their ideas on the story. They will explore the following in their discussions:
   - What would you do and why? What factors do you take into consideration?
   - What are the consequences of telling or not telling the teacher?

- What codes of behavior were discussed prior to the trip?
- What goes into making responsible decisions?
- How do the decisions we make influence and affect others?
- What are the consequences of the students' decision to enter the liquor store?

4. Proceed with open discussion as to why students made this decision.

The discussion of the problem posed in this vignette provides a model for dialogue and for exploring solutions as students later work together in their small groups. Teacher and students can set the stage with specific rules for discussion before participating in this exercise. Make sure:

1. All voices and ideas are given equal time
2. No judgments are made
3. Students listen carefully to each other
4. All responses are respectful
5. You model how to actively listen and reflect on other's experiences

Small Group Activity: Decision-Making Vignette Sheet—What Would You Do? (Adapted from *Values Clarification*, Simon, Howe, & Kirschenbaum, 1972) (Fig. 4.2)

1. Distribute the vignette sheet.
2. Have students read and respond to the vignettes individually (about ten minutes).
3. Students will present their responses to their small group.
4. Ask the small groups to see how they arrived/did not arrive at a consensus of what to do.
5. Then each small group will choose a student leader who will present their group's response to the large group.

Large Group Activity: Competing Alternatives—Should I or Shouldn't I? (Fig. 4.3)

Each day we make choices between competing alternatives. Some of them are minor choices: "Should I go to the movies tonight, or shall I stay home and watch television?" Others are major decisions we must make: "Should I go to school this summer or should I work?" "Can I accomplish both?" "Should I go directly to college or should I get a job?" Many issues require thought and planning. How and why we are making choices is an important strategy and dynamic to understand and learn.

For this activity, distribute the copy of the Competing Alternatives questionnaire. Have students look at the list and rank order the choices listed after

Figure 4.3.   Competing Alternatives: Should I or Shouldn't I?

Students are to rank order their preferences.

1. **Whom would you prefer to marry? A person with:**
   Intelligence
   Personality
   Sex appeal
   Other (write in your own answer)

2. **Which type of teacher do you most prefer?**
   Strict in the classroom but little homework
   Strict in the classroom and much homework
   Easygoing in the classroom but much homework
   Other (write in your own answer)

3. **Which do you think more government money should be spent on?**
   Space travel
   Neighborhood renovations
   Finding a cure for chronic diseases
   Other (write in your own answer)

4. **Which would you least like to do?**
   Listen to a Beethoven symphony
   Watch a debate
   Watch a play
   Other (write in your own answer)

5. **When you worry about your mark on an exam, do you think about**
   Yourself?
   Your parents?
   Pleasing the teacher?
   Getting into college?
   Other (write in your own answer)?

6. **Which would you most like to improve?**
   Your looks
   The way you use your time
   Your social life
   Your school habits
   Other (write in your own answer)

7. **How do you have the most fun?**
   Alone
   With a large group
   With a few friends
   Other (write in your own answer)

(continued)

Figure 4.3. Competing Alternatives: Should I or Shouldn't I? *(continued)*

8. **If you had $500 to spend on decorating a room, would you spend**
   $200 for artwork and the rest on furniture?
   $400 on furniture and $100 for artwork?
   The entire sum on furniture?
   The entire sum on a computer and music sound system?
   Other (write in your own answer)?

9. **Pretend that you are married and have your own family. Your mother has died and your father is old. What would you do?**
   Invite him to live in your home
   Place him in a home for the aged
   Get him an apartment for himself
   Other (write in your own answer)

10. **If your parents were in constant conflict, which would you rather have them do?**
    Get divorced and your father/mother leaves home
    Stay together and hide their feelings for the sake of the children
    Separate for a while and you live with your father/mother
    Other (write in your own answer)

11. **What would you do for your parents' anniversary?**
    Buy them a nice present, throw them a big party
    Take them out to dinner and a show
    Other (write in your own answer)

12. **If you had two hours to spend with a friend, which would you do?**
    Stand on a corner
    Go to a movie
    Go for a walk
    Go bowling
    Other (write in your own answer)

13. **You've spent a great deal of time picking a gift for a friend. You give it to him or her personally. What would you rather have him or her do if he or she doesn't like the gift?**
    Keep the gift and thank you politely
    Tell you he or she doesn't like it
    Return the gift to the store without telling you
    Other (write in your own answer)

14. **If you were a peace supporter and you found out your friend supports certain wars, would you:**
    Discontinue the relationship?
    Overlook the discrepancy in views?
    Try to change his or her viewpoint?
    Other (write in your own answer)?

each question. Do one example together as a group: "Where would you rather be on a Saturday afternoon in spring?" Rank order your choices:

- At the beach
- In the woods
- At the mall
- Other

After each student has rank ordered his or her choices, the group as a whole will discuss their reasons for ranking. Lead a reflective discussion by asking, "What have you discovered about the decision-making process you just experienced? How did you construct your decision? What have you discovered about yourself?"

Triad Group Activity—Continuing the Decision Making in Competing Alternatives

Students will work in triads to complete the rest of the alternatives sheet. Triads will report their decisions to the entire class.

Large Group Activity: Making Choices and Seeing Outcomes

Everyone has the right to pass and not speak in this activity. Many times making choices is not easy and can have a variety of consequences. Based on the above activity:

1. What were some of the important ideas that came up for you when making alternative choices and decisions?
2. Were there any surprises for you?
3. What is one idea you will keep in mind when making a decision next time?

Student leaders write all class brainstorming responses on the board. The class will choose (vote or consensus) the top five ideas to remember when making decisions and keep them posted in class and in their portfolios.

Large Group Activity: Challenges of the Year Ahead

Now that we have had time to reflect and learn some new things about ourselves and our beliefs, we will look at the challenges and expectations of the Voyager program and how we can make the most of it during this year. One by one, review each aspect of the program:

1. Portfolios: Distribute portfolios for each student. What was your experience with the portfolio last year? What would you like to do

differently? How would you like to be assessed differently? What help would you like with this process?

2. Assessment: Review last year's assessment procedures, and list the process on a flipchart. What components were most beneficial? What changes would you suggest? Student leaders keep record of discussion items.

3. Journals: How can we connect the journal to the portfolio? Distribute journal entry sheets. Discuss different ways students can use their journals for maximum effect.

4. Portfolio assessment: Review the portfolio assessment process. What are the requirements for the Voyager certificate? How will connecting the journal to the portfolios help you complete the requirements?

5. Other goals: What are the other Voyager seminar expectations? Discuss academic GPA, attendance, work-site success, classroom preparedness, and cooperative teamwork.

6. Themes: Let's look at the Voyager themes. What do they mean to us? Have they taken on new meaning for you this year?

7. Graduation standards: How will we work with the graduation standards of career investigation assessment and interpersonal communication skills?

8. New goals: What are some areas you might want to branch out into this year and gather more information on career choices, other internships, and effective communication skills?

9. Interpersonal Communication Standard and Content Standard: Pass out these standards to students, and brainstorm ideas on the board for each of them. Have students enter them in their portfolios as references for the year. What are some of the ways we can help each other accomplish our individual and our class goals?

10. Extra help: On the board, list some examples of things students are asking for help with (for example, having a particular time to examine difficult topics during the seminar, more one-on-one with the coordinator, etc.).

Large Group Activity: Learning Contracts

For many students and adult learners, learning contracts provide a valuable process for defining what and how an individual wants to learn. Review what they are and how they are used by self-directed learners.

Students will:

1. Diagnose their learning needs (where do you want to be in relation to a particular competency or skill?)

2. Start to write and specify their own learning objectives by stating what they will learn
3. Specify how they will fulfill and accomplish each of their objectives
4. Specify what will be evidence that they have accomplished their learning objectives
5. Consult with their coordinator as to how their work will be assessed and validated (what criteria will be used)

Small Group Activity: Model of a Learning Contract (Adapted from Malcolm S. Knowles, 1986)

Discuss the idea of an individual learning plan and contract. Show students what it might look like. What are the benefits of such a plan? Take time to individually start to craft your plan. Students move into groups of four and help each other write their individual learning contracts. Coordinator circulates and helps each group. Here is a sample using one of the Voyager themes—lifelong learning:

The objective of this learning contract is to develop an understanding of the theme of a lifelong learner. In order to do this, students should do the following:

1. Find research, articles, and other materials on this idea
2. Write about their personal reflections on the topic and create a strategy for themselves such as a list of books they will continue to read during their career pathway development
3. Review competencies listed in their handbook for other demonstrations of fulfilling this theme (book four)
4. Present their ideas to peers for written feedback

After a model has been discussed, students write the first draft on their own and then have their peer groups read and review their ideas. Students are encouraged to work with their mentors and work supervisors depending on the type of learning contracts they have created. The coordinator will read, review, and negotiate what is needed so that the contract meets agreed-upon standards. This is an excellent process for students to plan out how they will fulfill all of their competencies for each of the four years.

Small Group Activity: Personal Growth Action Plan (Chapter 3, fig. 3.10) and Professional Career Action Plan (Chapter 3, fig. 3.13)

Every year we look at how we want to change and grow both personally and professionally. Setting goals will guide what you want to accomplish during the year and set the basis for defining what you need to do to reach each goal. Use your last year's plan as a starting point and for comparison. Remember, it is important to share your plan with at least one other person who can support your progress and success.

1. Distribute the Personal Growth Action Plan (Chapter 3, fig. 3.10), which will be filled out in the base groups.
2. Remember you must list exactly what you will take action on.
3. After you have worked individually, divide the remaining time so that every member in your group discusses his or her plan with the group. Members, make sure you ask each other questions regarding your plans and offer any suggestions you have.
4. Follow the same procedures for the Professional Career Action Plan (Chapter 3, fig. 3.13) with your small group.

Small Group Activity: Voyager Classroom Critical Event Survey

This reflection process should take place after each seminar meeting. Take a few minutes to respond to the each of the Voyager ClassroomCritical Event Survey questions (fig. 3.12) about this week's seminar. This survey helps teachers and students understand how and what is being learned in the seminar. Please respond openly and honestly. All of the responses are collected anonymously, and then the coordinator will summarize them for all to read at the next seminar.

Optional Plans

1. Students generate innovative ideas to co-create the seminar this year. (such as creating a new list of speakers, arranging college visits, and participating in community service projects). What suggestions, topics, and questions do they want to include for the coming year?
2. Students begin writing out their time management plan for the next week.
3. Have students interview friends, family, and work colleagues about their time management techniques. Bring results back to class and discuss.
4. Have students create a time management survey and have them use it with people in different occupations. Bring results and analysis back to class.
5. From your interviews and survey, what are some time management strategies you can try to help you more effectively manage your time?
6. "The life which is unexamined is not worth living," Plato tells us. When you reflect on the life you are living is it "congruent or incongruent" with who you really are? How do you know this? Is the makeup and composition of your life and the choices you are making

for your life congruent with who you are and what you want to become? Are you doing things that you do not have a passion for or are really the ideas and dreams of other people in your life—people you want to please? Describe the kind of life that you want and the things that you need to change in order to have this life. As Dr. Phil McGraw (2001) asks, "How do you take control of your life? How do you begin to connect with your authentic self?" Start asking yourself what is important to you. What are some things you have given up on or missed out on or wish were a bigger part of your life? It is time to look at the unvarnished truth about yourself.

Performance-Based Assessments

- Student feedback on large and small group activities
- Students work on the Personal Growth Action Plan
- Students work on professional career plan
- Students work on individual learning contract

CONCLUSION

What are some important decision-making ideas to remember when planning for a successful senior year? What do you need to do to maintain effective management of your time?

ASSIGNMENT

1. Begin keeping your management plan using Your Date Timer form (fig. 4.4).
2. For the next meeting, bring in a reflection on how the Voyager community has helped you grow. What have you liked about being a member of this learning community? List some of the concepts, classroom rituals, and codes that you believe worked well. What are some additional areas for the class to consider adopting?

Figure 4.4. Your Date Timer: What Do You Do Each Day?

Take the time to write down what you do each part of the next three days. After three days, decide where you could have done things differently. According to this sheet, how do you spend your time? How can you manage your time better? What one-time management goal will you now set? On the back of this sheet, brainstorm some ideas you have for how you could change how you manage your time.

Time of Day	Day One	Day Two	Day Three
7:00–8:00 A.M.			
8:00–9:00 A.M.			
9:00–10:00 A.M.			
11:00 A.M.–12:00 P.M.			
12:00–1:00 P.M.			
1:00–2:00 P.M.			
2:00–3:00 P.M.			
3:00–4:00 P.M.			
4:00–5:00 P.M.			
5:00–6:00 P.M.			
6:00–7:00 P.M.			
7:00–8:00 P.M.			
8:00–9:00 P.M.			
9:00–10:00 P.M.			

Unit 1C

Personal and Professional Growth

LESSON TOPIC:
THE DEMOCRATIC CLASSROOM—CODES AND RITUALS

Teaching Note

During this class, students are expected to reflect upon and assess last year's successes in the program in light of their individual growth and as a Voyager community overall. How did the first year work for them? What do the students want to change for this year? In essence, they are asked to "read their world" in a more profound manner. Some significant questions that can be posed include:

1. How have they succeeded as change agents? How have the ideas of a respect for other cultures played out authentically in the classroom?
2. How has a "culture of silence" been broken? Have all voices been heard, acknowledged, and appreciated?
3. What is their definition of classroom culture?
4. What do they need to augment or change for the continuing personal and professional growth in the community?
5. How will they continue to develop as citizens of this democratic learning community and take responsibility for classroom operations and projects?
6. How will their work influence others?
7. How will they take action for change?
8. How are the democratic skills they developed needed not only in class, but also at home, at work, and in the community at large?

Developing a safe, positive environment that is steeped in mutual respect and democratic process is time consuming and requires a new pattern of interactions. No more can we say, "This is everyone's classroom, but only the teacher makes the decisions" or "We live and need to participate in a democracy, but school is not democratic." The management of schools is not about command and control—new paradigms of educational democracy are needed. What assumptions is the class willing to let go of because they are not working well? What do they believe will provide human growth and learning? As active participants in their community, students need to be given more opportunity to develop a sense of self-worth, to enhance and practice civic responsibilities—developing ways to optimize learning conditions, using a caring and collaborative process. As one student told us, "Democracy in action is not the TV version; here in this class you must work hard and listen to each other. Problems are not solved in one class. You must always remain open-minded. Lots of problems don't have just one solution."

Objectives

To review and re-vision the classroom rituals and codes from last year
To continue to develop a democratic learning community
To review any remaining problems that need to be addressed among the Voyager members

Domains

Cognitive: Learn to develop classroom practices
Affective: Value cooperative and respectful working habits
Skills: Develop analysis and organizational skills

Graduation Standard: Write and Speak in the English Language

Interpersonal Communication Skills
Effective speaking and listening skills
Create self-assessment and appropriate feedback

Materials

Classroom rituals and codes from last year
Color sticker dots for voting
Flipcharts/markers

Pre-Instructional

Students will list the highlights (an event, a person they worked with, a project, a new learning tool, a new experience, and so on) for themselves and the Voyager program from the previous year; then they need to explain why they felt this way, and what new directions they would like to see themselves and the class take during this coming year.

Introductory Framework

We know that building an authentic democratic learning community takes effort. Your Voyager community is now beginning its second year. We have experienced working, learning, and interacting with each other in a variety of activities.

Now that we have had time to reflect and learn some things about ourselves and one another, we will look at the challenges and expectations of the program and make decisions for enhancing the development of our classroom environment. Let us build on our successes. We will reflect upon what type of environment is needed in order to meet individual growth needs, to meet the group needs, and to work cooperatively. John Dewey tells us that "Every experience lives on in further experiences. Hence the central problem of . . . education . . . is to select the kind of present experiences that live fruitfully and creatively in subsequent experiences" (Dewey, 1916, pp. 27–28). In the creation of our classroom environment, we are looking at our current situation but also seeking to enrich our dispositions toward future learning. We do this by generating habits of mind that promote rich experiences and continued learning and growth. What are some habits of mind that promote rich experiences for all of us to live and work together? Brainstorm and save the list of ideas generated for later reference in the lesson.

Motivation

What were the biggest challenges (see Challenges Reflection Sheet, fig. 4.5) during last year's classroom practices? Brainstorm and have student leaders list on the flipchart what worked well and what did not work well. Students will list responses on their own tracker sheets as well.

INSTRUCTIONAL IMPLEMENTATION

Larger Group Discussion

How do we sustain a caring democratic community? Students can draw a classroom poster and create symbols that reflect this question.

What are examples of some of the collaborative democratic skills we will need to develop? Following are some examples:

1. Learn to listen attentively to each other. This is different from just waiting your turn to talk. It means you are actually listening to your peers and then connecting to what has just been said.

Figure 4.5.   Challenges Reflection Sheet

---

1. What must happen in this class for you to call it a success?
2. How has membership in this group changed for you since last year?
3. How has the idea of community changed for you?
4. What are concrete markers of community in a school context?
5. What would an outside observer see, hear, and feel in a place that truly deserved to be called a community?
6. What are effective ways to develop a caring learning community? Do you feel that you are a real or a pseudo community?
7. What expectations, norms, and structures have been established in this community to deal with specific incidents?
8. Are students in this community helping each other to develop responsibility?
9. What is a caring community and what invitation does it offer to all of its members?
10. How do we sustain a caring, democratic community?

---

2. Express ideas creatively and develop an individual voice. What is it that I want to say in my own words and my own style? How can I communicate most effectively and respectfully?
3. Become a problem solver, not a side taker. What is the situation, and how can I look at it from different perspectives?
4. Be familiar with conflict resolution. When the heat gets too high, learn to take a different position so that all involved can come to "yes."
5. Come to the table as an informed discussant. Do whatever research needs to be done to unpack a situation and then concentrate on an analysis that includes critical dialogue.

Let us look at some well-intentioned ideas and then develop them more:

- A safe and positive environment. When we say we want to work and learn in such an environment, what does that look like? How does one participate in creating and sustaining such an environment?
- Working respectfully with peers. What does that mean? What are some of the ways we do that? How can we improve?
- Active participation in a democracy with everyone meeting their commitments. What is expected of us in such a process?

Small Group Activity: Reviewing and Changing Last Year's Codes

Give each group a copy of last year's codes. Each group, led by student leaders, must decide which items worked well and which did not. Decide what concerns they have about the codes. Have student group leaders list these ideas for posting. The small groups will then consider the following:

1. What concerns about the class are most important to participants? (Example: One Voyager group voted to have one afternoon per week de-

voted to Voyager class meetings instead of taking time from their weekly seminar time. They met and discussed their concerns, ideas, and suggestions, which they presented to the seminar coordinator.)

2. What actions for change do we want to take?
3. What additions or deletions will we make to the classroom rituals and codes?

When all groups are finished, students will post their suggestions in the room for all to review. Ask students for ideas on how to move beyond a quick fix. Ask them to consider—and discuss—the outcomes they want to see for themselves and the codes that support those outcomes.

Large Group Activity: Voting for Changes

Student leaders read aloud and clarify all of the finished postings from each group. Distribute ten of the colored sticker dots to each student for voting. Ask them to place their dots next to the ten suggested codes they would like to support. The suggestions receiving the most votes (dots) will become a class code.

The class needs to agree that this activity is a majority vote. In order to add anything else to the top ten items, we will need a consensus vote. *Consensus* means that all of the class members agree to this action. Here are some guidelines for reaching consensus:

• Listen carefully while considering opinions expressed by others in the class.
• Try to be open-minded to all that is being said.
• Make sure that all class members express their opinion on each issue.
• Do not change your mind just to avoid conflict.
• Support solutions that you agree with (be sure you agree with them because you believe in them, not because you want others to like you).
• View and value differences of opinion as positive conflict. Explore why and how differences are positive in working groups. Perhaps these discussions will examine areas otherwise overlooked.

Are there other suggestions you have for reaching consensus?

Optional Plans

1. Ask students to discuss how values among group members can conflict. Remind them that value conflict (prioritizing values and ambivalence about values) can often occur in many terrains and venues. Ask students where they have had conflict in values. What happens during "positive conflict"?

2. Ask students to bring in newspaper articles discussing values and to share their reactions with the class.

3. Ask students to look at cartoons in either the newspaper or magazines that highlight values and to share their analysis of them. Remember the cartoons or articles can be about any values.

4. Students will create a bulletin board that reflects current issues, locally and nationally, involving conflicts of interest and values.

5. Show a clip about a conflict from television. Debrief the students on how the characters responded and solved/did not solve the conflict.

6. Organize and schedule a debate in a democratic forum on some current topics of interest. Students will present issues and critically dialogue as informed discussants.

7. How would you define "sacred space" in schools and in your Voyager classroom? This was one of the concepts we established about our class from junior year—how has this experience and concept developed over the program for you and your colleagues? How would you define sacred space? How has defining sacred space changed your learning and comfort level with each other?

8. Research concepts of learning communities online. Describe them and how they function.

9. A stimulating space devoted to creative work is also part of the new work trends. Companies are asking their employees to design spaces dedicated to creative work. They believe that the collective wisdom within a company knows what they need. Have students research "creative space" in local companies. They should interview employees and ask how the space was designed, how it is set up, what its physical properties are, how it is used, what it contributes to the organization, what types of gathering take place in the space, what types of collaborations take place, and what type of work is done in the space. How can Voyager students design such a creative space?

Performance-Based Assessments

- Cooperatively working together in small groups
- Results of the codes and rituals for the senior class

CONCLUSION

Students will make a copy of the completed codes and post them on the wall. Everyone agrees to the codes and rituals. It is also agreed that the class can and should revisit the codes and rituals from time to time during the year as they monitor their community growth. Tomorrow everyone will receive a typed copy for his or her portfolio. Students will volunteer to see that this task is completed as part of their commitment to participating in classroom operations.

ASSIGNMENT

1. Begin rewriting and editing your résumé using the work you started last year and please add all the new information about your professional growth for both prospective employers and for college/secondary institution admission boards. See examples of types of résumés.
2. With all of the topics explored today in democracy, how does your new knowledge on democracy and learning communities extend the meaning of what you have learned? What meaning does it have to the rest of your beliefs and to actions you will take?

Unit 1D

Personal and Professional Growth

LESSON TOPIC:
CAREER, PROFESSIONAL GOALS, AND RÉSUMÉ WRITING

Teaching Note

Although there is another unit in senior year that is totally focused on writing résumés and cover letters and preparing for interviews, it became clear when speaking to former Voyager students that work on updating and expanding their résumé needed to begin early in the term each year. Writing their résumé at this point provides more time for students to review and reflect upon what they have accomplished and to connect their results with their personal and professional development plans. Taking time to review and forecast their needs for senior year is an important aspect of their growth and development process. These activities also provide more in-depth conversations regarding their organizational skills, abilities, interests, and future goals. This process also guides their choices for taking certain classes, updating technology skills, applying for jobs, and preparing for college admission or searching for other postsecondary training options. Students constantly collaborate during this process, helping each other to develop a more comprehensive résumé and cover letter. They also are pleased to learn more about each other and more about themselves. All accomplishments are acknowledged and honored.

Objective

To write a résumé that highlights essential characteristics and connects to career pathways and college admission

Domains

Cognitive: Develop and write a good résumé that is steeped in a positive self-concept

Affective: Respond appropriately to colleagues' ideas and feedback

Skills: Develop effective writing and organizational skills

Graduation Standard: Write and Speak in the English Language

Interpersonal Communication Skills

Effective speaking and listening skills

Create self-assessment and appropriate feedback

Materials

Résumé writing ideas overhead

Different sample résumés handouts

Pre-Instructional

Students have started to rewrite and update their résumés.

Introductory Framework

For college admission, career training, and work application, everyone will need a résumé that effectively presents their work, accomplishments, and aspirations to potential employers and admissions committees. Some people describe résumés as a capsule version of who we are. Résumés also take on different formats and versions depending on the way we need to use them. We write our résumés tailored to the position or agency that we are applying to. Many times, changing the format will change the way résumés are read by prospective employers and will provide the entrée we need to enter a particular organization. There is also a difference between a résumé and a curriculum vitae (CV) for some professions. Coordinators provide a sample of what a CV includes and why it is used in certain professions.

Motivation

What is a résumé? Give the derivation of the word. What do résumés do—in essence, what is the work of résumés? How are they a resource for both the employee and employer? How do they help with wage negotiation? Why is it so difficult to write a résumé about ourselves—in essence, an executive summary of ourselves? All ideas are listed on the board. The seminar coordinator shares her or his personal experiences as well.

Why is it so difficult to represent ourselves to others? Discuss and have students interpret their reasons out loud for feeling threatened, tentative, shy, and so on about résumé writing. We usually have lots to say about ourselves and what we have accomplished when we talk to each other. The challenge will be to find the appropriate presentation of ourselves in each context and through effective writing and presentation skills (see Résumé Components sheet, fig. 4.6). Review the components with the class and expand on meanings.

INSTRUCTIONAL IMPLEMENTATION

Large Group Activity: A Self-Portrait—Editing the Résumé

Our first project will be editing and updating the résumés the students wrote in the junior year program. Each year we change and grow depending on our experiences. It is important to keep a running copy of our résumé to give a more

Figure 4.6.   Résumé Components

1. **Objective**
   To secure an interview by conveying information that will stimulate employer interest
2. **Function**
   To accompany letter
   To serve as a calling card
   To serve as an interview outline
3. **Content**
   Education background; certificates; professional experience and training; related experience including volunteer work, activities, and awards; additional information
4. **Preparation**
   Collect and organize your materials
   Complete a preliminary worksheet
   Select categories
   Write rough draft
   Evaluate and revise
   Get second opinion
   Type final copy on computer
   Select a résumé-duplicating service for high-quality copying or word processing
5. **Appearance**
   Attractive layout with ample margins and suitable spacing
   Free of grammatical and typographical errors
   Visual effects and optional graphics must be discreet and business-like
6. **Production**
   Standard-sized paper (8 1/2" x 11")
   Best available production
   Paper stock of good quality, perhaps with a slight texture; off-white, cream, tan, pale blue, or light grey color

current snapshot of who we are. It becomes a foundational piece demonstrating our professional lives and one that we keep expanding as we grow and develop. We will examine some sample résumés and analyze what each is telling us—both directly and indirectly. Present sample résumés either through PowerPoint or hard copies (Chapter 3, fig. 3.17). It is helpful when the coordinator uses his or her own résumé. It is also helpful if the coordinator talks about his or her personal challenges in writing a résumé and the resources he or she used to complete the résumé. Over the years, business partners have sent résumés where the names and other pertinent data were changed. Show samples from business partners if available. As you read each of these, what do you think employers are looking for? If you were in a managerial position, would you hire these prospective employees? What jumps out for you from these résumés?

Let's review the goals and purposes of the résumé. Students generate lists on poster paper.

1. How were your résumés received last year?
2. What comments and feedback did you receive?
3. What changes do you want to make to them this year?
4. Who will read your résumés this year—college and other postsecondary training programs admissions officers and prospective employers?

Remind students that each résumé that they write may look different; after all they will be responding to different organizations and for different initiatives.

We will work on the employer résumé first (fig. 4.7); therefore, we need to highlight areas that employers would be interested in. Brainstorm ideas on the board (e.g., competency in software programs, all types of technology experience, service areas, volunteer activities, foreign language proficiency, etc.). What categories of information can we generate? Tell students that this is their first draft; they will keep exchanging résumés and editing within their small groups as they go along.

Hand out the Basic Résumé Worksheet (fig. 4.8). Review differences between a functional and chronological résumé (fig. 4.9) (see web addresses and software programs for resource materials).

Large Group Activity: Generating More Ideas for Résumés through Constructive Feedback

Use a fishbowl technique to demonstrate what students will be doing in this activity. Two students will sit in the center of the class to review and ask questions of a student on his or her résumé ideas and then they will make further suggestions for changes and development. The suggestions will be in the form of either questions or statements that will help the student to further

Figure 4.7.   Employer Résumé

Essential items to include on your résumé:
- **Identification**—your name, address(es), phone number(s), and email address(es) for easy contact.
- **Education**—name of institution, location, dates attended, and degree(s) obtained, presented in reverse chronological order (with the most recent degree listed first), and grade point average if 3.5 or above.
- **Relevant Experience**—presented in reverse chronological order (with most recent experience listed first), related employment, volunteer work.

Optional items to include on your résumé:
- Objective (you may describe a particular focus but should avoid "flowery" language)
- Work experiences other than those related to your field
- Areas of knowledge
- Community involvements
- Activities, special skills, interests, and hobbies
- Travel
- Memberships, school activities
- Publications
- List of names of references

Not to be included on your résumé:
- Personal details of age, family life, and other items unrelated to the position requirements
- Salary requirements or expectations
- Limitations on date of employment; geographical preferences; "willing to relocate"
- "Available immediately"
- "References available upon request"

Figure 4.8.   Basic Résumé Worksheet

Note: There is no perfect formula for creating a résumé. Provide information for each of the categories listed below and design your résumé materials to present yourself in the best possible way for the type of job you are seeking.

Name
Address
Telephone
Email
Education
Work Experience
Professional Experience
Experience Related to Career
Other Pertinent Experience
Honors and Recognitions
Activities
Special Skills and Interests
Travel
Memberships
References

Figure 4.9. Functional or Chronological Résumé?

Résumés may be organized to emphasize a chronological record of experience and events or they may be organized around functional skills and abilities. The chronological résumé is appropriate for the person of limited experience with an easily described record of training leading to a specific professional field. The functional résumé is useful for the person with broad experiences who wishes to emphasize specialized skills and to identify details that have applicability to a variety of positions. Skills such as writing, managing, consulting, or training are considered important in the job market. Both the functional and the chronological résumé require the writer to proceed through the three stages—research, organization, and production—and to follow the rules of résumé writing given below:

1. **Economy**—Keep the résumé brief, although people with wide experience and many qualifications may require more than one page.
2. **Supportiveness**—Be positive in your word choice. State firmly and frankly your qualifications. Use action words. Convey enthusiasm.
3. **Completeness/Selectivity**—This may appear to be a contradiction but it isn't. Don't overlook important details in your qualifications. Be selective, focusing on items related to the type of job sought.
4. **Accuracy**—Keep in mind that anything you put in a résumé may be checked by an employer or be the subject of questioning in an interview.
5. **Acceptability**—Select paper stock and color to give the best first impression. Choose a font and duplication method that will read easily. Organize content so that the reader can quickly scan the résumé to find the essential elements.
6. **Chronology**—Reverse chronological order is listing the current or most recent education and employment position first and then moving backward in time. This is the preferred pattern. Employers generally place the greatest emphasis on current or most recent experience.
7. **Creativity**—Your finished résumé should distinguish you from the other applicants. To do this and still follow generally accepted rules of résumé writing is a challenge. Here is your chance to give the essential qualifications and still present something of yourself.

develop his or her résumé. As we listen to the students, we will use the following as criteria for the feedback we offer: Is the feedback Descriptive, Specific, Appropriate, Usable, Clear, Accurate?

Then the entire class will have an opportunity to relate their observations—what did the rest of the class observe in terms of constructive feedback? List all ideas on the board. The teacher can use these lists to further frame criteria to help with this activity. We want to know, what did the two participants experience as they received their feedback? Summary: What suggestions can be made to improve this technique and use it to help each other most effectively? Review ideas for constructive feedback.

Communicating constructive feedback to your group members is a valuable skill that can be learned and practiced. With practice, groups can move to a mature, deeper level of feedback, providing a more effective outcome.

Figure 4.10.   Résumés, Career Ideas, and Planning

Present to your group one career idea—that is, an idea for a career you'd like to pursue.

What skills do you need to develop to participate in that career?
What plans do you need to make to develop those skills?
Who do you need to contact to seek assistance in making your plans?

Small Group Activity: Résumés, Career Ideas, and Planning (Fig. 4.10)

Students will use this time to practice what has been modeled using career ideas and plans for feedback instead of their actual résumés.

Break the class into groups of three. The student triads will have thirty-five minutes to offer each other suggestions for this activity. Students will offer comments and ask questions in order to clarify and make helpful suggestions. Each group chooses a facilitator to take notes for the student who is receiving the feedback. Each group member will start off with five minutes to talk about his or her career plans and then brainstorm about themselves with the group. How do we handle negative feedback?

Small Group Activity: Peer Editing

Model peer editing in a fishbowl technique. Choose a résumé from a former Voyager student and have two students talk to each other about it as the rest of the class watches. Students then work in small groups to edit each other's work. They are to ask clarifying questions, write comments, and offer suggestions. In addition to the oral feedback and discussion, each résumé needs to have two peer editors with their comments and names listed on the review sheet. Peer editing is about putting on an employer's hat and making clarifying comments that will help the writer develop his or her ideas more fully in order to present an accurate account of who he or she is.

Optional Plans

1. Students will work together to create a career exploration map (choose a specific career and get specifics about it, such as: annual income, education or training needed, responsibilities, type of work environment, positives and negatives about this career, related occupations, how do my abilities match up to particular career interests, career outlook, how does this career fit with my picture of the future?).
2. Students will create a networking map: Who do they know (friends, family, relatives, acquaintances, work colleagues, past employers, web

sites, extended networking such as friends of friends or recommendations), how do they start to make connections, what type of notes do they keep, how will they organize their information, how will they constantly update it?

3. Students will create a list of their best assets, strengths, and qualifications, including the challenges and realities they will face in making changes in their lives.

4. Students will describe, in writing, their ideal job.

5. Students invite a panel of speakers, including human resource representatives, business representatives, and school officials, to class to talk about what they are looking for in a good résumé.

6. Students invite a group of local small-business owners or managers to speak directly to questions of hiring practices.

7. Students choose three occupations they are interested in, they find interesting, or they see as major fields in the next decade and then research them for the skills and training needed.

8. Research and discuss the advantages of an electronic résumé. A web-based résumé allows literally thousands of employers worldwide to access your materials, and you can change your résumé at any time; portfolios with accessible graphics and sound showcase your work on the Internet. What are the drawbacks of posting your résumé online? Find a variety of web sites that can help you with this question (for instance, www.monster.com, www.flipdog.com, www.hotDispatch.com, and www.guru.com).

Performance-Based Assessments

- Students' role and feedback in fishbowl activity
- Students' completed work in small groups

CONCLUSION

Résumés serve a variety of purposes. We will be using our résumé both for postsecondary admissions applications and for career investigations. What are some of the suggestions you find most useful? What are the questions you still have regarding this type of writing? Keep in mind that there are always two stages to developing résumés— gathering information and then formatting this information. Each of these stages has multiple tasks associated with it. Writing a résumé is not a linear process, but a circular one that requires revisiting different aspects and components at different times. No matter how many times you write a résumé, it helps to follow these stages.

ASSIGNMENT

1. Completed résumés are due in class in three weeks. Make sure you have at least two other readers sign your résumé, indicating that they have helped you to proofread and edit it. The readers may be from in class or an outside network contact of yours.

Unit 2A

Postsecondary Preparation

LESSON TOPIC:
DEVELOP A PLAN FOR COLLEGE ADMISSION PROCEDURES

Teaching Note

Preparing for two- or four-year college admission or other postsecondary training is uncharted terrain for a majority of the students. They are both excited and frightened at the prospect. The insights and ideas from the different students and families are varied. For many, they are the first in their families to apply for college admission and they are filled with the dreams and aspirations of a brighter future — college, therefore, becomes an oasis of possibility but without role models to aid in the process. For many, attending college means/symbolizes moving beyond the boundaries of their neighborhoods, to perhaps an even stranger cultural climate than relocating to the United States. Many students stated quite clearly that colleges were only to be gazed at from afar — as they would drive by the campuses. They saw college campuses as simultaneously ominous and beautiful, evoking images of unknown worlds, making them feel as if they were stepping out of their league when they entertained the idea of applying to college. The challenge here is to provide a guided format for college information gathering and inquiry. The selected college campus visits provide a whole new way of looking at attending college and take some of the mystique away. The Mike Rose video provides an excellent introduction to this new area of opportunity for them. What are lives on the boundary? What have been the subtle, and not so subtle, signs from adults that students' lives were not worthy of continuing studies or of making a contribution to society? As one young man said, "I don't belong on a college campus—at least, I don't think I do. Well, maybe I could listen to what is being said and then make up my mind." Many of the students talked openly about lack for support from their families and friends, a few even about sabotage. They also talked about how thoughts of college were such a huge cultural shift that meant "switching sides of the tracks" and this was uncomfortable. This class session also provides practice for video observation and review.

Objective

To develop a plan for college admission procedures, postsecondary training, and goals for success

Domains

Cognitive: Identify college and postsecondary training institution admissions requirements and professional goals
Affective: Value and appreciate individual interests for career and college
Skills: Practice critical thinking and analytic skills

Academic Standard: Career Investigation

Materials

Excerpt (preface) from Mike Rose's *Lives on the Boundary* (fig. 4.11)
Mike Rose video: *A World of Ideas: Interview with Bill Moyers*
List of concerns and plans for college
College and Career Activity sheet (fig. 4.12)
Getting Ready with College Resources (fig. 4.13)

Pre-Instructional

Students are to write a reflective/stream of consciousness piece responding to the questions: "Why are you going to college? Why do you want to do postsecondary education?" Included in this piece will be their tentative plans and concerns.

Introductory Framework

Today we will examine why you are going to college or to some other type of postsecondary training and what you need to prepare for admission, and then start your working plan on how to complete these requirements. During this year you will have many opportunities to return to the elements of the

Figure 4.11.   Mike Rose: *Lives on the Boundary* (pp. xi–xii)

This is a hopeful book about those who fail. *Lives on the Boundary* concerns language and human connection, literacy and culture, and it focuses on those who have trouble reading and writing in the schools and the workplace. It is a book about the abilities hidden by class and cultural barriers. And it is a book about movement: about what happens as people who have failed begin to participate in the educational system that has seemed so harsh and distant to them. We are a nation obsessed with evaluating our children, with calibrating their exact distance from some ideal benchmark. In the name of excellence, we test and measure them—as individuals, as a group—and we rejoice or despair over the results. The sad thing is that though we strain to see, we miss so much. All students cringe under the scrutiny, but those most harshly affected, least successful in the competition, possess some of our greatest unperceived riches.

I've worked for twenty years with children and adults deemed slow or remedial or underprepared. And at one time in my own educational life, I was so labeled. But I was lucky. I managed to get redefined. The people I've tutored and taught and the people whose lives I've studied—working-class children, poorly educated Vietnam veterans, underprepared college students, adults in a literacy program—they, for the most part, hadn't been so fortunate. They lived for many of their years in an educational underclass. In trying to present the cognitive and social reality of such a life—the brains as well as the heart of it—I have written a personal book. The stories of my work with literacy interweave with the story of my own engagement with language. *Lives on the Boundary* is both vignette and commentary, reflection and analysis. I didn't know how else to get it right.

admissions process and refine your application items. This planning will include what steps must be taken in your personal lives.

Motivation

College admissions counselors tell us that two words are most important for college success and aspirations: **Plan Ahead**. Let's investigate what this means. What does this mean in terms of action steps you can take? This is not about luck—good or bad—but planning and work.

Figure 4.12.   College and Career Activity

What have I accomplished, and what skills do I need?

Activity
Skills
Competency
Possible Job Match

Figure 4.13. Getting Ready with College Resources

The Yahoo! search engine provides links to Internet sites with a lot of information relating to college admissions and applications.

1. The Minority Online Information Service (MOLIS) provides information on minority institutions, including African American, Latino, and Native American colleges and universities. The URL is: http://web.fie.com/web/mol.
2. The U.S. Department of Education site's URL is: http://www.ed.gov/thinkcollege/index.html.
3. College Edge offers services for applicants. The URL is: http://www.CollegeEdge.com.
4. ACT offers help for the exam at: http://www.act.org.
5. SAT sponsors information at: http://www.collegeboard.org.
6. For more information on jobs look at: http://www.monster.com.

Networking is the key to successful plans. Network with:

- Other students
- Teachers
- Friends
- Mentors
- Supervisors

To work with an organization of senior business executives devoted to improving education and students' futures, go to the Business Roundtable: http://www.brtable.org. For software information to help share ideas and files and work together more collaboratively, go to: http://www.Groove.net.

Senior Year—Postsecondary Admission Requirements and Action Plans

1. Take classes that will shine on your transcript (Voyager is one of these programs).
2. Find materials that will help you prepare for the PSAT exams and for the Math and Reading Tests (form study groups to help you with your preparation).
3. Think about and assess your work experiences and successes in different career pathways.
4. Think about the activities and clubs to which you belong.
5. List other aspects of your work, community, and school experience that add to your repertoire of knowledge.
6. Develop senior year requirements and action plans.
7. Find materials to help you prepare for college entrance exams.
8. Have a strong senior year and give explanations as to how/why your school record demonstrates improvement. This is often as important as maintaining good grades throughout your high school years. Honestly address the challenges faced and the failures that were overcome.

9. Admissions departments like to see trends in your record.
10. Prepare to give a strong interview that can also help balance out your record.
11. List action steps you can take to enhance your record this year.
12. Talk to people who have gone through this experience and can pass on some suggestions.

Is there anything else you want to add to the above list?

Another important decision to make is what type of school you would like to attend. What types of schools—four-year, two-year, public, and private—are you interested in applying to? (Brainstorm out loud.) Decide why you want to go to college. How does the institution you are considering fit with your career aspirations? How does it fit with your financial situation? How will you get information about each of these institutions?

Forty-one percent of people twenty-five or older in Minnesota have a college degree. What interpretations do you make from this statistic? How does this coincide with future work worlds and the growing global economy?

INSTRUCTIONAL IMPLEMENTATION

Large Group Activity: Viewing Mike Rose Video—*Lives on the Boundary*

Mike Rose has been working with people in the margins of society for over twenty-five years. In this video with Bill Moyers, Mike Rose talks about them and his ideas on education.

For this activity, give a brief background on Mike Rose and his book *Lives on the Boundary*. Show his video, and have students list two ideas they pulled out of his interview that particularly struck them. Here are some other possible discussion points:

1. What similarities or differences do you see with your present lives and experiences?
2. What is Mike Rose's view on education?
3. Who are people on the margins of society?
4. What does he mean by lives on the boundary?
5. How was the point of view constructed in this video?
6. Do you consider yourself as being "on the margin"?
7. What fears do you have about attending college?

Small Group Activity: Redefining the Future

Distribute the preface from Mike Rose's book *Lives on the Boundary* (fig. 4.11) and read it aloud to the class. Ask students, "Why do you think he has written this book?"

In small groups, discuss what Mike Rose has said and then list the top concerns that you have for college and your future career plans. Each student must list his or her concerns and what strategy he or she will put in place to address concerns. How do these concerns fit with your list of concerns? Each group will compile a master sheet for class reporting and post it on the walls and then have seven minutes to report their findings and get feedback from the rest of the class.

Large Group Activity: Influences on Traditions, Culture, and Other Decisions and Goals

Have students free write on the following questions:

1. What are the challenges you face in continuing your education after high school?
2. What concerns do you have about continuing your education?
3. Why do you think you belong, or do not belong, in college?
4. How does postsecondary education fit, or not fit, with your career plans?
5. How is your future being defined by other people?
6. What is your idea of a desirable future and what do you have to do to have such a future come about?
7. Does making decisions about postsecondary education go beyond or violate familial patterns and traditions and/or societal expectations of who you are and what your place is?

Engage students in a conversation on how/why a college education is or is not supported by their friends, family, and relatives. How will this influence you? What if the decision to attend postsecondary education is not supported by family, friends, and/or relatives? You may want to have the students brainstorm with each other about:

1. How to deal with not being supported
2. How to help their family understand so that they can support them (it is important to read the mood of the class, however; don't force the issue if the class discussion is not heading in that direction).

What types of careers have your family, relatives, and friends chosen? How does the media shape the type of careers you think you might want? Does your culture conflict with your ideas for career and college? What other barriers—both internal and external—exist for you as you make decisions about your future?

Small Group Activity: College and Career Activity

Students will work in groups of three. They must all complete as much of the College and Career Activity sheet (fig. 4.12) as they can. Then each will have a chance to discuss their ideas with the two other members of their group. Everyone needs to listen carefully, ask questions, and provide appropriate feedback.

Large Group Activity: Preparations and Procedures for Guest Speakers

Student leaders will take charge of organizing the discussion for guest speakers. Following are some preparations that need to be addressed:

1. Individual or small group writing of questions.
2. Who will set the stage and make introductions?
3. Who will facilitate the discussion?
4. Who will collect and list the questions that need to be asked?
5. Set parameters for guiding appropriate conversation and behavior.

Performance-Based Assessments

- Responses to College and Career Activity sheet
- Large group discussions and feedback
- Video review and discussion

CONCLUSION

This is the beginning preparation for making college decisions. Continue to ask specific questions regarding college admissions and how to network with others to develop support for your interests. Distribute the sheet with web sites regarding information on college resources and scholarships (fig. 4.13). For example, the web site www.tomjoyner.com has loads of information on black colleges around the nation.

If possible, set up a computer and an LCD projector to demonstrate access and content of these college web sites so all students have access to them, or collect hard-print materials and leave in the learning center in the classroom.

ASSIGNMENT

1. Bring in two or three questions you will ask the university panel members tomorrow. Please remember procedures for guest speakers.

Unit 2B

Postsecondary Preparation

LESSON TOPIC: PLANNING FOR THE COLLEGE YEARS

Teaching Note

Preparing for the guest panel of university professors is another unfamiliar activity for many of the students. Before the guests arrive, it is helpful to provide a list of the professors' names, how they want to be addressed, and their areas of interest, and go over them with the students. It is also helpful to generate a list of framework questions so that the guests will have an idea of what areas students are interested in before they arrive. Students are excited to have this time to work with the professors—it breaks through another "hidden and mysterious" experience that they are anticipating. As many of them stated, "This is the first time I have ever been so close to a professor—and it was all right. They are nice and they gave us lots of good information." This seminar has always proven to be successful—the students ask important questions and are engaged throughout the entire time. The panel session is also videotaped for future viewing. We also take photos of the entire class with the professors during this session. The professors receive copies of the photos and many have submitted them to their college newspapers for publication with a short summary describing the event and the program. Voyager students then each receive copies of the college newspapers. Through these activities a lot of good information is exchanged about young adults and their Voyager program. Also, another unexpected outcome of this seminar was that the professors volunteered to become mentors to some of the students. Through email and telephone conversations, students formed another type of mentorship relationship and were supported by another adult throughout their senior year. The panel discussions are lively, engaging, and filled with humor. Professors also enjoy the experience. They are inspired by the level of honest questions and concerns regarding college. They are reconnected to the high school climate and young adult thinking patterns. It is recommended that this panel be repeated with guests from other postsecondary training schools so that students receive multidimensional career information. Both days provide a plethora of good information as well as demonstrate to students that there is much overlap in what they must do no matter what path they choose.

Objective

To discuss the realities of college preparation, plans, expectations, and challenges with university faculty

Domains

Cognitive: Practice critical thinking skills
Affective: Value and appreciate individual interests for career and college
Skills: Identify college processes and plans

Academic Standard: Peoples and Cultures

Career Investigation
Readjust professional goal

Pre-Instructional

Bring master list of concerns and plans that students created in their small groups from the previous class for dialogue. They will have called or written to the guest speakers for autobiographical information that they need for making introductions.

Materials

Autobiography outline

Introductory Framework

Today we will have the entire session to dialogue with university faculty.

Motivation

Student leaders will introduce panel members. Each student then introduces him- or herself and states career aspirations and/or college choices and aspirations. A student leader will give background on the Voyager program to the panelists.

INSTRUCTIONAL IMPLEMENTATION

Large Group Activity: Panel Discussion—Life and Learning after High School

Guest panel consists of university/college faculty. Generate questions that fit your students. Some sample questions might be:

1. What was the hardest lesson you learned in college? How did you choose your college? How would you describe your experience?
2. How did you choose your career? Did you ever have another career other than being a professor?
3. Were you ever thinking of another career?
4. How did you make your decision to go to college? Did you think about alternative training?
5. What are some of the things you remember from being a freshman? What would you do differently? How did you make friends?
6. Did you ever feel lost and lonely during your first year of college?
7. How did you navigate making new connections—or just finding out about things when you were in college?
8. What are some of the things that are practical to learn about in order to make the college experience a success?
9. What is the worst thing you ever did as a college freshman?
10. What do we need to know about professors?
11. What do we need to know about succeeding in classes in college?
12. What would you do differently today if you were going to college?
13. What do you expect from your college students?
14. What is some advice you can give to us? (Each panel member was asked to respond to this question.)
15. How and when did you choose your major? Did you have more than one major?

Optional Plans

1. Have students invite Voyager alumni back for a panel to discuss their senior year experiences with college admission and their current experience in college.
2. Have students make videotapes interviewing Voyager alumni or other college freshmen on their college experiences.
3. Invite instructors/faculty from other postsecondary institutions for a panel discussion. Follow the same format as above.
4. Compose a panel of college admissions personnel to discuss admissions procedures and policies.

5. Arrange field trips to various college campuses, including public, private, two-year, and four-year schools. Most campuses have a set half-day program that orients prospective students in which they review all aspects of entering college, including financial needs and available scholarships; other colleges will send representatives to the high school classroom.

CONCLUSION

Student leaders thank guests for this informative session. We will have another session next semester.

ASSIGNMENT

1. Continue working on postsecondary admission materials.

Unit 2C

Postsecondary Preparation

LESSON TOPIC: WRITING THE COLLEGE AUTOBIOGRAPHY

Teaching Note

There are many intended outcomes in approaching college admissions through an examination and analysis of admissions forms and writing the autobiography. Filling out college admission forms is another component that looms ominously over the students, especially when they first begin to read the college application requests. Many commented on how many times they had to read the form before they actually understood what was being asked. During the large group discussions, many students disagreed with each other as they interpreted, quite differently many times, what the college form requested. Students agreed that once they started to work together on this activity it proved to be a good discussion and activity in critical analysis and in learning how to respond to application forms. They discussed what they thought were the "subtexts" in some of the questions and then they took the perspective of the college admissions officer to understand how decisions for admission are made. For many of the students, this was the only time they would receive direct help with the college admission process because many of their family members were unfamiliar with the procedures or were unable to read English. Some family members had been educated in other countries, where applying to college required different procedures. There were also some students who were able to get help from an older sibling who had just completed the process. Overall, this was a mutually enhancing experience and an exchange of information session that provoked many new questions and generated many new perspectives on postsecondary education.

Objective

To write a clear narrative essay for college admission

Domains

Cognitive: Clearly express ideas in an effective and organized writing style
Affective: Value and appreciate interests for career and college
Skills: Practice organizational skills for thinking and writing

Academic Standard: Write and Speak in the English Language

Materials

Preparing the College Essay handout (fig. 4.14)
Sample College Application Essay Questions (fig. 4.15)
Excerpts from selected autobiographies

Pre-Instructional

Autobiographical outline to be completed at home

Introductory Framework

Writing for college admissions provides another way, in addition to your grades and your test scores, for you to present yourself to the admissions board. Therefore, it is important to take the time to think about this part of the admissions process and decide how to present yourself most clearly and succinctly.

Motivation

What do you think when you hear the word *autobiographical*? Are there any autobiographical or biographical works (films, books, artwork) that you have

Figure 4.14. Preparing the College Essay

When applying to college there are various parts of the application to fill out. Carefully read what is being asked of you for each component, and then respond accordingly. List and make any helpful notes about events that influenced your life. When preparing the college essay or autobiography, list and make any helpful notes about people who influenced your life. List and note experiences that led you to your career choice.

Open topics—list issues that you are interested in, or note circumstances in your life that you want the committee to know about. Describe yourself. List work competencies. Know that it will take several drafts to get the essay you're proud to submit. If you are stuck, feel free to research other sample essays on the various college web sites.

Figure 4.15.   Sample College Application Essay Questions

> 1. Write an essay of no more than 500 words on any subject that interests you. For example, you may choose to write on an issue or an experience that has greatly influenced your life, or other circumstances that you would like the admissions staff to consider in reviewing your application. These are only suggestions, however; the choice of topic is yours.
> 2. The Admissions Committee would like to know more about you in your own words. Please submit a brief essay, either autobiographical or creative, which you feel best describes you. Please choose one of the essay topics below. Please attempt to limit your response to no more than 300 words.
>
> - What do you believe is most important for us to know about you?
> - When you reflect upon the past four years, what makes you most proud? How will the experience enhance your ability to succeed at our institution?
> - Write your own question and answer it.

enjoyed? Why did you enjoy these works? Why are people drawn to autobiographical, or biographical, works? Have students brainstorm and explain their reasons for enjoyment. What are the particular characteristics about these works that stand out for you? Autobiographies and biographies give us a firsthand glimpse of how people perceive their lives and how others perceive them. They give us a more in-depth look at who we are. Read excerpts from autobiographies such as *Malcolm X;* Nathan McCall, *Makes Me Want to Holler*; Maya Angelou, *I Know Why the Caged Bird Sings*; and excerpts from *O* magazine for good short pieces.

For the college essay, we have a similar chance to look at who we are, what we have accomplished, and what challenges we have overcome. Colleges are interested in finding out about students from multiple perspectives; they want information that goes beyond a student's GPA. In the admissions essay, we get to relate significant parts of our lives to others, what we think has been important in our lives, and how various people and events have influenced us. We also get a chance to relate why we are embarking on this new part of our life. After all, going to college is a new part of our lives, therefore, we want to put our best efforts forward.

INSTRUCTIONAL IMPLEMENTATION

Large Group Activity: Exploring the College Application and Sample College Essay

Distribute the sample essay portions from the Boston College, Georgetown University, and Marquette applications. Have students read over the applications together. Ask them to brainstorm the following question together: "What are some questions and concerns that you have when you read these college application essay forms?" List all responses on the board (overwhelming, unknown material, etc.). Becoming familiar with college applications and understanding what is being asked of you is important. Most colleges ask for similar information, but you still need to read each application carefully and respond to what is being asked of you. By beginning to write out the college essay, you are already addressing one of the challenges in this unknown process.

Individual Activity: Preparing for Writing the College Essay

1. Distribute the Preparing the College Essay handout (fig. 4.14).
2. Have students go through each category.
3. Ask them to think about areas in their own lives that fit these categories and then complete the handout the best they can.

Small Group Activity: Exploring Possibilities for Writing

Have students get into their small groups. Each member will take five minutes to tell his or her group members what he or she will include in his or her essay. After listening carefully, everyone gives the speaker feedback for five minutes. Follow the same appropriate guidelines that were established in previous feedback sessions.

Large Group Activity: Writing the First Draft

You will now take the ideas you wrote down and the feedback from your classmates and begin to write your first draft for the college essay. Write your first draft without thinking about spelling or grammar, but your final drafts must be carefully edited and proofed. Here are some effective writing ideas for the first draft. Ask students to interpret and comment on each of these:

1. Choose an area that you are interested in.
2. Remember that this is a chance for the college to get to know you in a different way.
3. Be clear, concise, and organized.
4. Read it out loud to hear errors, to change styles.
5. Have at least one other person read it and give you feedback.
6. Your group members will give you feedback on your first draft as well.

What other suggestions can we give each other?

Optional Plans

1. Create a part 2 to this lesson that has students peer editing and revising their essays; students are also encouraged to read their essays

aloud to others so that they can hear the actual words and ideas they have created.

2. Community guests can be invited to read and hear the students' essays and then to give feedback.

3. Have students audiotape their responses to each other's essays.

CONCLUSION

What happens if you get stuck writing this first draft? What are some suggestions we can give each other? Choose one or two people to read your essay before you bring it back to class.

ASSIGNMENT

1. Your college essay is due in two seminar meetings.

Unit 3A

The Résumé

LESSON TOPIC: TYPES AND FUNCTIONS OF RÉSUMÉS

Teaching Note

The authentic need and use for a résumé is ever present in students' lives this year. They see a real need to develop an effective written snapshot of themselves for prospective employers. The résumé becomes a tool to use in negotiating their entrance opportunities in the workplace. Through their discussions and examination of different types of résumés, they study succinct strategies to present information about themselves, they explore the standard endorsement of traditional résumé formats, and they can experiment with creating their own formats.

One of the key components of this lesson is for students to spin and spark with each other to help sketch the best possible portrait of themselves. The discussions help explore assumptions they have about themselves, how they perceive each other, and what other information they might consider including in their traditional or nontraditional résumé format. Students are expected to prepare both chronological and functional résumés. In this way, they compare the process of preparing both kinds and can critically analyze the role of résumés in job hunting. The students engage in thoughtful conversations as to what is an authentic representation and what is an unethical representation of their information. They explore why it is not worth it to embellish their qualities. What becomes equally important is the discussion and reflection regarding the "possession of skills." What does it really mean to possess skills in the workplace in today's information age and global economy? The skills people possess will be dependent on a variety of combinations, such as human capabilities, job requirements, and opportunities. Some of the unexpected outcomes of these lessons are the research students do for different careers and the ideas that they hear about from each other.

Objective

To begin preparing a successful résumé by considering experiences, qualifications, and career interests

Domains

Cognitive: Identify the components of an effective résumé
Affective: Appreciate this specific style of writing
Skills: Read and communicate effectively

Academic Standard: Write and Speak in the English Language

Interpersonal Communication Skills
Effective speaking and listening skills

Materials

Sample résumés
What a Résumé Is overhead (fig. 4.16)

Pre-Instructional

Have students bring in the first draft of their résumé.

Introductory Framework

This is an important time in your career, as you will be applying to colleges, to postsecondary training programs, and to prospective employers. You will need an effective representation of yourself, your attributes, and your characteristics. An effective résumé is an important tool for you to have. Let us build on the previous résumé draft you wrote.

Motivation

Résumé is an interesting word; it comes from the French word meaning *summary*. A résumé is defined as a summary of one's history and experience (fig. 4.16). In essence, it is an executive summary of who we are today. Our résumés change as we change. They never represent the total value of who we are, our capabilities, or all of our experiences. The résumé is usually accompanied by a job or college application. It is therefore quite important to write an accurate representation of your education and experiences as it presents your professional image. It is also a good jumping-off document that prospective employers will use during your job interview.

Figure 4.16. What a Résumé Is

- Presents a concise and logically organized statement which effectively and efficiently summarizes your EXPERIENCE, QUALIFICATIONS, and CAREER INTERESTS to employers or other professionals
- Allows perspective employers to ASSESS your ABILITIES and POTENTIAL with respect to a specific job
- Presents your PROFESSIONAL IMAGE

Sometimes referred to as a vita or a personal data sheet, the résumé is defined in a standard dictionary as a "brief account of one's educational and professional experience" or "a summing up." Preparing a résumé both assists you in a review of your personal assets and presents them in the most favorable way to a prospective employer. To accomplish both purposes you must know a great deal about yourself and the position. The well-prepared résumé should convince the employer that you are a "perfect match" for the position. Accomplishing this is difficult work; take time to thoroughly review your qualifications before beginning the preparation.

Figure 4.17.   Why Prepare a Résumé?

Is your placement file not enough? Will you not be duplicating the information that is already in the placement file or on an employer's application? The answer is yes, but in a résumé, you will represent yourself in the most advantageous and unique way. A well-prepared résumé serves several uses that can assist you in your job search:

1. It serves as an introduction to accompany your letter of inquiry or application.
2. It introduces you in chance meetings with potential employers, such as at a PTA meeting or family reunion. Use your résumé as a "calling card."
3. It details your background in a follow-up of an earlier contact.
4. It facilitates an interview. Take extra copies of your résumé with you to an interview; offer them to members of the interview committee who might not have had the chance to read your placement file. Always keep one copy for your reference as well. In this manner, you may call attention to items you consider important—items that may be overlooked in the limited time reserved for an interview.

INSTRUCTIONAL IMPLEMENTATION

In order to write an effective résumé you must be well acquainted with yourself and you must be able to understand the purposes résumés accomplish. In your résumé you want to bring out the best of what you have accomplished and your potential for the future. You do not want to put forth any untruths about yourself. What are some examples of information you should not put forth about yourself? The résumé is your passport to an interview. College admissions boards and prospective employers take the résumé seriously and will use it as a basis for your interview. There are different types of résumés with which you should become familiar.

Large Group Activity: What Does a Résumé Help Accomplish?

Discuss the following factors of the résumé before looking at samples:

1. What are the uses of the résumé? (fig. 4.17)
   - Accompanies letter of application
   - Introduces you
   - Facilitates an interview
   - Is a resource for the employer
   - Is a negotiating factor for salary
2. What are the types of résumés?
   - Chronological—this résumé format represents an organized overview of major factors in a person's work and work-related history.
   - Functional—this résumé format presents focused attention on particular kinds of work-related skills and illustrates their relevance for a particular job.

There is no one résumé for every job and you should be intentional about choosing the format and the information you include. As we look at these two different types, does one seem to present personal capabilities and related experience more successfully than the other? Which seems more difficult/easier to write? Why do you think one format is more effective than another? How can you effectively transform your résumé: alternative formats, new categories, overall résumé length, and the order in which categories are presented? It is necessary to keep your résumé on a disk and have different styles for the different job applications and college admissions.

Use overheads/PowerPoint for students to compare stylistic differences between the functional and chronological résumé. Have students discuss what they like about each sample. Which one works best for you and in your job search process? What do employers want to know about job applicants? Remember that employers will see both your résumé and your portfolio, so it is in your best interest to connect the two as you develop them.

Today, many job applicants include a variety of artifacts in their portfolios: videos of their work, copies of their own web site, a speech they gave, or a multimedia presentation. What do job applicants want employers to know about them? Does this change with different jobs for which you are applying? What type of information seems awkward, inappropriate, and at times embarrassing to supply? What information do you not want to supply? Who is disadvantaged by supplying certain kinds of information?

What are the first things that an employer looks at when he or she receives a résumé? (See fig. 4.18.) Style and appearance of the résumé are important—it should be neat and well organized. Have peers look over your work and give you feedback on all areas (content, style, grammar, spelling).

Figure 4.18.   Résumé Style, Appearance, Format

You have now selected the content of your résumé. Next, carefully phrase this information into brief statements in the telegraphic or outline writing style. Use a minimum of words to tell your story. Readability is enhanced by leaving ample open space on the page to emphasize the content. Résumés should be professionally produced. Check the Yellow Pages of your local telephone book for professional résumé services. You may want to use several fonts to add variety and emphasis to your résumé, which should then be saved on a computer disk to facilitate updating as frequently as necessary.

Many colors and several different varieties of résumé paper stock are generally available at local stationery stores. Although white paper is the most frequently used, your résumé may attract favorable attention on tan or beige paper. Use a good quality paper, perhaps with a textured surface.

Finally, review and revise. Share your résumé with others; check it out with the "pros." Go beyond the placement office to ask employing officials and administrators for opinions and advice.

The résumé is an essential tool in your introduction to career opportunities. Make it serve to your best advantage. It will not secure the job for you, but will help to obtain the interview and consideration for the position. Your résumé also serves as the basis for your constant review of your career plans and for your continued success in the future.

Small Group Activity: Assessing Résumés

Have students assess a sample résumé. Ask them what they learn about the "applicant" by looking at the résumé. Have students tell why they would or would not hire or interview the person, based on the résumé. Each group synthesizes their assessment and gives one three-minute report to the entire group.

Small Group Activity: Note Gathering for Filling in the Content of a Résumé

Begin working in your small groups. Take the sheet with the content of a résumé and begin to fill in information about yourself. After each individual member completes what he or she can, each member will then ask the group for help in an area he or she had trouble filling out, did not understand, or just wanted feedback on. Everyone must seek help and get feedback from his or her group members.

Activity: Selected Samples of Student Résumés

Coordinator uses student résumés volunteered by the group. The résumés that follow illustrate some of the varieties of approaches to résumé writing. An employer must select several of the most interesting applicants (i.e., those best fitting the specific job situation) in order to arrange for interviews.

1. How would you react to each of the following résumés?
2. What types of material do you consider irrelevant to your field, if any?

3. What materials do you think need expanding in your résumé to best present your qualifications?
4. Which résumé style seems most appropriate for your field?
5. In your opinion, which résumés appear most well organized, legible, and appealing to the eye of the employer sorting through them?
6. Do any of the résumés appear "too general"? Do any of the résumés appear to be especially well targeted to the type of job sought by the candidate? Why? Why not?

Optional Plans

1. Students invite business partners in to talk about what they want to see in a résumé and how they assess résumés that come to their offices.
2. Business partners assess students' actual résumés.
3. Students create alternative résumé formats that represent them more effectively: Vary types of categories, change order of presentation and résumé length, present information differently dependent on job position; they can explore more fully why a particular format is more effective for each Student.
4. Students use web-based resources for researching résumé software, résumé formats, and résumé tips.

Performance-Based Assessments

• Student discussions interpreting various résumé models

CONCLUSION

What are some new pieces of information you have about résumés? Do you have additional questions regarding résumés?

ASSIGNMENT

1. Complete all information on the Résumé Content sheet (fig. 4.19). Write a second draft of your résumé for the next seminar meeting. As you write the next draft of your résumé, think about how to best position it for each job or field you are interested in. What will you be able to change either in form or content to be a good fit for a specific job?
2. Students research different new books and ideas for writing the résumé. They can gather information online from different web sites (and they must assess these web sites for credibility) and visit libraries for new books on résumés and their role in securing the right jobs for the future.
3. Students can ask coworkers and colleagues at work for copies of their résumés for specific jobs. They will bring them to class for review— all names, titles, and companies will be removed before distribution.

Figure 4.19.   Résumé Content

Carefully choose the headings that work best for your résumé and prospective position:

Objective
Part-time and Summer Work Experience
Job Objective
Volunteer Activities
Career Objective
Related Activities
Professional Objective
Civic Activities
Position Desired
Professional and Community Activities
Community and Other Activities
Education
Educational Background
Activities and Distinctions
Educational Preparation
Special Honors
Academic Background
Honors and Distinctions
Academic Training
Honors/Awards
Special Training
Memberships, Affiliations, Organizations
Certificates
Affiliations
Endorsements
Organizations
Areas of Knowledge
Special Talents
Areas of Experience
Leisure Activities
Areas of Expertise
Special Skills
Educational Highlights
Interests
Background Highlights
Travel Abroad
Career Highlights
Travel
Professional Skills
Language Competencies
Military Service
Coaching Experience
Credentials
Experience Summary
Experience Highlights
References

(continued)

Figure 4.19. Résumé Content *(continued)*

Professional Background
Achievements
Career Achievements
Employment
Other Work
Additional Experience

Here are some suggested words to use in your résumé in sketching an overview of your work or training activities:

ACTION WORDS	**MODIFIERS**
accomplished	capable
acquired	consistent
arranged	effective
assisted	experienced
conducted	knowledgeable
coordinated	proficient
created	successful
designed	
developed	
directed	
established	
expanded	
implemented	
improved	
initiated	
instituted	
introduced	
maintained	
managed	
motivated	
organized	
originated	
participated	
planned	
prepared	
promoted	
revised	
scheduled	
strengthened	
supervised	
trained	
taught	

(continued)

Figure 4.19. Résumé Content *(continued)*

Listed below are some examples of important professional skills, many of which you probably use. Identify which of the following descriptors could become part of your résumé as part of the description of your work experience. You are very likely to use these skills in related employment or work in other areas:

Communicating
Communicating clearly what you expect in the way of performance
Directing and supervising staff assistants
Encouraging, motivating, generating enthusiasm
Selling yourself as a worthwhile individual
Planning daily, weekly, monthly goals/objectives
Communicating successfully with coworkers, managers, administrators, community members
Writing reports
Assessing performance
Writing goals and objectives for staff and projects
Solving human relations problems
Motivating for effective achievement and excellence in performance
Demonstrating skills and techniques
Initiating and developing job-training programs for staff assistants
Interviewing and counseling
Directing public relations programs using community resources
Writing instructions
Communicating answers to questions
Maintaining discipline and order
Selling yourself as a trustworthy person
Illustrating ideas and varying the instructional program by using multimedia materials
Solving problems of financial management
Creating innovations in your specialized field
Budgeting and ordering supplies
Relating instructions verbally
Communicating instructions to staff assistants
Creating atmosphere conducive to learning and working successfully
Selling yourself as a skills person in your field
Revising and updating materials, plans, and techniques
Researching and coordinating pilot programs

Unit 3B

The Résumé

LESSON TOPIC: RÉSUMÉ WORKSHOP

Teaching Note

This class is held totally in a workshop format. Students know they are in class to write and work to complete this project. Scheduling this workshop in the computer lab is helpful. Even with two or more students working together at a computer, they are able to brainstorm and make changes to their work immediately. Editing, interpreting work, providing verbal feedback, and demonstrating good listening skills are all vital components to this workshop lesson. Students learn to effectively change their own work after they practice reading and dialoguing with each other. The changes that take place in their abilities after they practice reading, assessing, and exchanging ideas become quite apparent. The challenge is to get them to speak directly to their peers' work and move beyond just giving compliments to their friends so that they do not hurt each other's feelings. It is a good day to also have extra room and tables for them to use as they talk about their work away from the computer stations. Additionally, having supplies such as magic markers, scotch tape, and scissors to cut and paste and help with the editing rounds was very helpful to the process as they worked together.

Objective

To practice ways of editing for success and assessing one's own abilities and
potential

Domains

Cognitive: Identify the components of an effective résumé
Affective: Appreciate this specific style of writing
Skills: Read and communicate effectively

Academic Standard: Write and Speak in the English Language
Interpersonal Communication Skills
Effective speaking and listening skills

Materials

Sample résumés
Overheads
Scissors
Blank paper
Colored paper
Markers

Pre-Instructional

Bring résumé drafts to class. Need multiple résumé formats that were discussed in class.

Introductory Framework

Today we will spend the bulk of our day proofing and rewriting our résumés. This takes a lot of time and careful planning. Good writing has a variety of steps and will generate a variety of drafts that are cyclical, not linear, in practice. For some writing, you may have to write four or five drafts, while for others only two drafts are necessary. Remember, good, effective writing involves thinking and practice in writing:

1. Brainstorming
2. Second draft
3. Revisions based on feedback
4. Third draft
5. Revisions

Writing several drafts ensures that you are organizing and presenting yourselves in the best possible image.

Motivation

What are some of the concerns or questions you have about this process before we begin? What is the difference between "selling yourself" through a positive presentation and an outright distortion of the truth? When do you "go too far" in a résumé? For example, if you have lots of experience with one type of word processing, can you claim a high knowledge of technology? If you babysit for your family, can you say you have experience with child development? If you have not completed high school or have gaps in your employment, can you omit this information? How would you handle being "let go" from your previous job because of work quality or attendance? What other questions can we raise for each other as we prepare to revise our résumés?

INSTRUCTIONAL IMPLEMENTATION

Résumé Workshop (Hand Out Checklist as Students Come in the Door)

We will work in our base groups. Each member of your group will receive a copy of your two résumés and give you feedback. Use the materials provided for you to cut and paste, write notes, and note all changes on your résumé. You have one hour to work in your groups. Remember that each person gets time to present and receive feedback from each group member. With any additional time left over, you can take your disks to the computer and start to rewrite your résumé with the final edits. The coordinator works with each group throughout the session listening and giving feedback. This is a hands-on workshop where all participants roll up their sleeves and help to put the best foot forward.

Optional Plans

1. Students will use job descriptions from the newspapers and create a résumé that they believe would respond to an ad.
2. Student groups work with creating alternative models of résumés.
3. Go to a local newspaper web site or other employment web site to enter both an employment-seeking profile and online résumé if this option is available. (For example, www.workavenue.com. Accessed June 2003.)

CONCLUSION

Reality check to see how the students are progressing. Do we need another workshop after school?

ASSIGNMENT

1. Bring back two completed résumés—one chronological and one functional—for the next seminar meeting.

Unit 4A

Interviewing

LESSON TOPIC: PREPARING FOR THE JOB INTERVIEW

Teacher Note

Interviews serve many purposes in addition to providing entrance to a real job. Most students have not experienced a formal interview before this time, only semiformal interviews for their part-time jobs. If any students have had formal interviews, invite them to share their experiences. It is interesting for students to record their thoughts on what an interview felt like, what they remember about it, and what they learned from it. This lesson explores looking at the job interview on a variety of levels. Although it is important to understand some of the "dos and don'ts" of interviews (effective interviewing skills are necessary to know), it is also important to see the event as an interaction where the student has the ability to be proactive. The students are impressed to find out they are not powerless during the dynamics of this experience and that they can prepare for a successful interview even if they do not get the job. It is also important for students to have information about the current job market and the average number of interviews a person completes before securing a job. After a few mock interviews and viewing themselves on tape, students are confident about their power to influence an interview. Again, the topic of an ethical interview is important; what students can accentuate about themselves and what constitutes false representations become important classroom discussions.

Learning about interviews as well as experiencing them becomes an empowering process. It is also important to remember that a single practice session does not accomplish substantial learning for any of the students. Students need to have as many occasions as possible to practice and experience this complex event. As one student told us, "I was actually asked the question we talked about in class, and I felt good about how I was able to answer it for this particular job." Through this preparation, students are also alerted to discriminatory practices during the interview process. Knowing what to do both legally and ethically during this process is important for all students. They need to have practical ideas and be able to think through the multiple situations they will encounter during their job hunt.

Objectives

To prepare for a job interview
To learn about the legal and ethical parameters in job interviews

Domains

Cognitive: Develop strategies and techniques for interviewing
Affective: Learn to respond appropriately
Skills: Apply effective communication skills

Academic Standard: Write and Speak in the English Language
Interpersonal Communication Skills
Effective speaking and writing skills

Materials

Typical Interview Questions handout (fig. 4.2a)
Video camera

Pre-Instructional

Write out questions you have about preparing for a job interview. For example, questions that deal with the "nuts and bolts" of an interview—do you want to know what types of clothes are appropriate to wear for an interview or if you can negotiate salary, and so on? What other types of questions do you have? What are your fears? Excitements? Worst-case scenarios?

Introductory Framework

The Voyager program offers possibilities for jobs through its internship program. Although many of you have had jobs before, it is important to prepare for interviews connected to both internships and your future job possibilities. Interviews are important because they offer both the employer and the job applicant some important information about each other. Many companies today have hired consultants who research how best to interview a candidate. They examine what questions to ask of an applicant, how an applicant's answers are to be analyzed, and how to determine if the applicant is a good fit for the position being sought. Many times companies will conduct a series of interviews for a position, beginning with telephone interviews and proceeding to face-to-face interviews with a variety of company representatives. It is as important for the company to find the right applicant as it is for the applicant to find the right job. Let's see what is involved in an effective job interview and how to prepare for it.

Motivation

What types of experiences have you had on interviews? How was the interview connected to "why you did/why you did not" get the job? Did you ever feel unfairly treated during the interview? Were you a good fit for the job? Why or why not? How did you decide to apply for a particular job? How much influence did your family and friends have in determining your application for a job? All of the student responses will be listed and categorized on poster paper for future reference and use.

What do we mean by a marketing strategy? (List some on the board.) Now take the time to describe one that has impressed you most. Turn to your partner and exchange your ideas on a marketing strategy. In what ways can you see an interview being a type of marketing strategy?

How is the interview a two-way form of communication? Turn to your partner and answer this question together. How can you make your role easier in this two-way communication process? One important way is to look at questions that are most frequently asked in an interview. It will be easier to answer questions comfortably in an interview if you have an idea of what is expected of you. What are questions you should ask of the employer? Why is this a way you can show research you have done on the company or fill in the knowledge gaps regarding the company?

INSTRUCTIONAL IMPLEMENTATION

Large Group Activity: Role-Play and Feedback

Ask two students to volunteer to demonstrate a fishbowl exercise for the class. Give students a copy of the sample questions before the exercise. As the coordinator you may want to invite someone in, another teacher or business partner, to model the interviewing activity. Make sure that the class sees that, many times, there are follow-up questions to each of the questions in this exercise, as most interviewers do not feel constrained by just asking one list of questions.

Here are some sample questions for them to ask:

1. Tell me about yourself.
2. Why did you take your current position? What other alternatives did you consider? Would you change your decisions if you were making them today?
3. What are your principle responsibilities in this position?
4. What do you like best about what you do? What do you like least?
5. What kind of training did you have for your current position? What additional training would you like to have and why?
6. How do you balance all of your responsibilities—family, home, job?
7. Where do you see yourself in five years?
8. What do you like to do in your spare time?

Ask the class to give feedback: First have them write out responses and then orally express what they saw, what they heard, and what their analysis was. Remember that all feedback should be helpful suggestions (e.g., what did they notice about eye contact, body language, clear pronunciation, correct grammar, direct responses to questions, lack of responses?). This segment is to be videotaped (students need to sign permission sheets for this taping) so that, after the initial feedback is given, students can review what they saw, assess, and then compare the tape with what they thought took place. Do they see anything differently in the playback? How do the students who are videotaped respond to viewing themselves? Are there differences in what they experienced during the role-play and when they observed themselves in the video? What suggestions can be made for improvement? What mannerisms have you been alerted to and will want to include or control during an interview?

Small Group Activity: Typical Interview Questions— Personal Qualifications and Background (Fig. 4.20)

Hand out the Personal Qualifications and Background sheet (fig. 4.20). Go over the use of an Interview Feedback Sheet (fig. 4.21). In small groups, practice some typical interview questions and responses found on the handout (fig. 4.22).

As two people are interviewing each other, the rest will comment and give feedback. Everyone must participate. Give all feedback sheets to the candidate at the end of the interview for her or him to review. Together develop a comment sheet for the large group. Small groups need to answer the question: Are these interview questions difficult or easy to answer?

Figure 4.20. Typical Interview Questions: Personal Qualifications and Background

Why do you want to work in this field?
What gives you the most satisfaction as an employee?
What can you contribute to our company/organization?
Tell me about your personal background.
What are your hobbies and interests?
What would you like to be doing professionally five years from now?
Why do you think you will be a successful (banker, markct analyst, nurse, lawyer, etc.)?
Why should I hire you instead of other applicants?
What additional duties would you be willing to assist with?
What are your strongest traits? Your weakest traits?
What personal goals have you set for yourself?
What do you look for in a job?
What do you look for in a company?

Activity: Typical Interview Questions—Interpersonal Relationships (Fig. 4.23)

Hand out the Interpersonal Relationships sheet (fig. 4.23). In small groups, practice the questions found in the section Interpersonal Relationships. As two people are interviewing each other, the rest of the group will watch in order to comment and give feedback.

Figure 4.21. Interview Feedback Sheet: How Am I Doing?

Some areas to observe are use of language, eye contact, body language, grammar, effective response to question(s), and overall use of two-way communication skills.

1. List three things you thought were done well by the applicant.
2. List three things you thought needed improvement by the applicant.
3. Rate the applicant in the following areas using a 1-5 scale, where 1 represents least and 5 represents most:

Appropriate use of language   COMMENTS
1   2   3   4   5

Appropriate body language   COMMENTS
1   2   3   4   5

Appropriate eye contact   COMMENTS
1   2   3   4   5

Use of correct grammar   COMMENTS
1   2   3   4   5

Effective responses to questions   COMMENTS
1   2   3   4   5

Figure 4.22.   Some Typical Interview Questions and Responses

The following is a list of some typical interview questions with suggestions for responding in a positive manner. Cite specific examples from past work experiences when you answer questions to provide the employer with a real idea of your capabilities. These suggestions are meant to be general guidelines. In fact, allow your personality to show—your smile and your unique qualities will be your most effective selling tools.

Using a separate sheet of paper, write out answers to each question and then compare your answers to the suggestions below.

Q: Tell me about yourself.
A: Tell the employer about your skills and interests, especially ones relating to the position for which you are applying. Indicate positive personality characteristics, such as being dependable, honest, and able to get along well with others. Most important, cite examples from your past to give weight to what you say. Limit the amount of personal things you say about yourself, and be certain that your answers are nothing for which you could be discriminated against such as age, marital status, or political or religious affiliations.

Q: Why do you want to work here?
A: Mention positive things you might have learned about the company, its products or services, and its personnel. ("I've read that you are a growing company . . .") This is an excellent time to show the interviewer you have done your homework about the company and the job, and that you are highly enthusiastic about working there. Be certain to let the interviewer know you can do the job and that you would fit in well.

Q: Why do you think I should hire you?
A: Clearly and specifically point out your related skills and experiences. Tell the employer about successes in past jobs and describe yourself as hardworking and dependable. State your interest in working for that employer and let the interviewer know that you are informed about the company and the position. Also mention education, training, and any hobbies or community activities that would be in any way related to the position or the skills necessary to do the work.

Q: Why did you leave your last job?
A: It is best to be truthful in most cases. Keep your answers brief and positive ("I need to be challenged" or "There was no room for growth"). Be certain not to blame others for your leaving. Remember, the interviewer is likely to identify more with your former employer than with you during the interview, so watch what you say about past employers, supervisors, and company policies.

Q: How would your past supervisor(s) describe you?
A: If it is true, talk about yourself as your best friend would. The interview is no time for modesty. State positive traits and give specific examples to back up what you say. ("I was very dependable. In my last job I missed only two days of work in three years. I was never late and was always willing to work overtime.")

(continued)

Figure 4.22.   Some Typical Interview Questions and Responses *(continued)*

Q: What is your biggest strength?

A: Be prepared to answer this one—it's a favorite! Don't be afraid to say good things about yourself. Describe positive past experiences as examples of things you say about being dependable, honest, hardworking, creative, or whatever else you claim. ("I learn new ways of doing things quickly. For example, I taught myself desktop publishing.") These examples will stand out in the interviewer's mind much beyond the general responses that most interviewees provide.

Q: What is your biggest weakness?

A: This one can be difficult. Employers don't really expect you to confess your true faults and weaknesses, though they will never stop you from doing so. The trick to this response is that you should state something that would actually be perceived by the employer as a strength. ("My weakness is probably that I am somewhat of a perfectionist in my work. I find that it is hard for me to stop working on a project until it is nearly perfect. However, I have learned that I cannot let perfection get in the way of getting the job done on schedule.")

Q: What would you like to be doing in five years?

A: The employer wants to know if you plan to stay with the company. The interviewer is also checking out your maturity and whether or not you are a person who likes to continue to grow and learn. Avoid mentioning that you would like to be the "manager" or "supervisor" unless you are positive that would be the career path the company would have you follow. Remember too, you are probably being interviewed by that supervisor and she or he may see you as a personal threat to her or his own job security. Be a bit more general in your approach, assuring the interviewer that you would like to be with that company in five years, growing professionally and contributing to the organization.

Q: Have you ever been fired or asked to leave a job?

A: If you have ever been fired or asked to leave a job and this information is likely to be uncovered during reference checks with former employers, be certain that it is you who tells the interviewer. Be as positive as possible and don't blame the former employer. ("Unfortunately, I did have a problem with my last supervisor. It did result in my leaving the job. However, I learned a lot from that experience about the importance of communication and I'm confident it won't happen again.") Employers appreciate honesty and a positive attitude. Do tell the truth, but don't dig back into insignificant and negative things from your past to "confess all."

Q: What are your salary expectations?

A: First of all, never introduce the topic of salary or benefits into the initial interview. Wait for the employer to bring up the issue unless you are offered the job and the salary has not yet been addressed. It is usually wise to approach the question of salary expectations by stating that you can be "flexible" or "negotiable." Then try asking the employer what she or he typically offers someone with your qualifications for that type of position. Hopefully, the employer will respond with an idea of the salary range the company has determined is fair. If not, say what you feel would be fair. Of course, this means that you should have done your homework

(continued)

Figure 4.22. Some Typical Interview Questions and Responses *(continued)*

ahead of time and learned as much as you could about the company's reputation salary-wise. Be sure to also take into consideration the monetary worth of the employer's benefit package (if there is one), which usually includes insurance, pension plan, and other items.

After you have been offered a position, and before you have accepted, you probably have the most negotiating power you are likely to have for quite some time. The employer has decided to hire you and will likely be more flexible and open to your point of view. Be careful, though—money is usually a sensitive topic. Being too pompous or lacking tact could have a long-term damaging effect on your reputation and get you started on the wrong foot.

Q: When would you be willing to start work?
A: In most cases, the sooner you can start, the better for the employer. If you are presently working and need to give a fair notice of resignation to your current employer, most employers can make arrangements to give you that time. However, if you are unemployed, it could make a negative impression to ask for too much time before you start work. Remember, you want to make a good initial impression with your new employer—one that shows you will be hardworking, motivated, and cooperative.

Q: Do you have any questions you would like to ask?
A: It is usually a good idea to ask one or two relevant questions of the interviewer. Asking, "What do you consider to be the most important aspect of this position?" or "Would I be working closely with other staff?" Or "What would a typical day on this job be like?" shows a real interest in the position. Avoid asking trivial questions just for the sake of saying something. Never, never put the interviewer on the spot by saying, "When do I start?" This type of question is usually seen as pushy and tactless and can be very uncomfortable for everyone involved. Rather, ask something like, "By when do you expect to make your hiring decision?" Incidentally, most interviewers say they prefer an applicant who asks five or six questions during the interview as a natural course of the conversation. Remember that an interview should be a dialogue—two people sharing thoughts and ideas—rather than an interrogation. The interviewer will want to hire someone with whom she or he feels comfortable—someone who will "fit in" with the staff and that someone can be you!

Figure 4.23. Typical Interview Questions: Interpersonal Relationships

What quality in other people is most important to you?
Would you enjoy working as a member of a team?
What do you believe your role and obligations to be toward other members of the company/organization?
How do coworkers react to your work?
What techniques do you use in developing rapport with coworkers?
What are the qualities of some of the best (bankers, market analysts, nurses, lawyers, etc.) you have worked with?
How do you feel you relate with diverse cultures in the workplace?
How would you work with coworkers who are differently abled in some way?

Develop a comment sheet to be shared with the entire class. One person will be selected to be videotaped for this group of questions as he or she is interviewed by an instructor or an administrator. The entire class will observe and give feedback.

Large Group Activity

Small groups give feedback report and list answers to the following questions on the board:

1. What are some commonalities shared by the group experiences and responses?
2. What are some surprises in the feedback, or in the actual interview process?
3. What seem to be key turning points in the interview?
4. When things are going poorly for the interviewee, what are some things he or she could do?
5. What interview strategies are being used?

Small Group Activity: Typical Interview Questions— Professional Qualifications and Experiences (Fig. 4.24)

In small groups, practice the questions found in the section Professional Qualifications and Experiences (fig. 4.24). Follow the same procedure as with the two previous interviewing activities. One volunteer for this group of questions will be videotaped as she or he is interviewed by an instructor or administrator with the class observing.

Individual Activity: Preparing for the Interview

This is an activity to help you think about and explain to an employer your qualifications as they RELATE to the job for which you are interviewing.

Figure 4.24. Typical Interview Questions: Professional Qualifications and Experiences

Why did you choose this field?
What kinds of past work experiences have you had in this field?
What have you learned from past work experiences in this field?
How do you remain current in regard to innovations in this field?
What would you do if . . . (hypothetical situations regarding coworkers, managers and administrators, workplace environment, business ethics, etc.)?
What did you do to prepare for this interview?
Tell me about one of the great successes you had in your last job?
What type of training will you need to remain current in this field?
What has been an outstanding innovation in this field that prompted you to enter it?

Consider the following and jot down your responses as you prepare for your mock interviews:

1. Past Work Experience
2. Education and/or Training
3. Aptitudes and Transportable Skills
4. Special Interests or Hobbies
5. Personal Qualities
6. Important! Be positive . . . but brief!
7. Handling problem questions
8. Why a problem happened
9. What was done to alleviate the problem
10. Why it won't happen again
11. How to turn a negative into a positive
12. How to turn a tough question to your advantage

Individual and Small Group Activity: Consider Which of These Are Your Personal Assets

Choose the qualities that pertain to you and make a personality concept map using Post-its on poster board. Each student in the class also has to make up a bag for the other three members of his or her group, writing each person's name on the outside. Then the students fill each bag with their list of descriptors for that person. After the bags are filled, they are distributed to the appropriate people in each group. In this way, each student gets feedback from his or her peers and learns something about how others see him or her.

Enthusiastic	Dedicated/Loyal
Dependable	Independent
Organized	Analytical
Honest	Calm
Responsible	Meticulous
Creative	Diligent
Reliable	Ambitious
Imaginative	Sensitive
Efficient	Flexible
Self-motivated	Punctual
Personable	Trouble-shooter
Confident	Adaptable
Congenial	Friendly
Persistent	Attentive
Constructive	Well-educated

Perceptive	Amiable
Self-educated	Independent
Physical stamina	Self-starter
Respected	Healthy
Helpful	Compassionate
Fast learner	Sense of humor
Patient	Assertive
Consistent	Accurate
Understanding	Thorough
Effective	Mature
Trustworthy	Energetic
Practical	Stable
Resourceful	Loyal
Resilient	Thoughtful

Optional Plans

1. Have students invite business partners to conduct mock interviews and to provide feedback.
2. Have students gather information regarding fair employment practices. They can bring in human rights codes from their jobs and present to class for review.
3. Bring in representatives from human rights agencies to discuss discriminatory practices and what they do to help workers involved in such cases.
4. Bring in actors to conduct "mock interviews from hell" that help students practice and deal with unethical and discriminatory practices and uncomfortable situations.
5. Have the class view professional videotapes of job interviews (there are a variety that can be purchased for classroom use) and then respond to the following sample questions. The theme is: Would you hire this person?

   - How were the first five minutes of this interview crucial?
   - What observations have you made regarding the following: body language, posture, interest and engagement, language use, ability to describe and use past experiences and history, effectiveness in answering difficult questions? List other strengths and weaknesses.
   - What role is the interviewer playing in this situation? What interview strategies are being used? How do you know the interviewer is pleased or displeased? Does the interviewer have a consistent approach with all interviewees? Were there any inappropriate questions?

- Was there a turning point in this interview? What suggestions would you make to the interviewee?
6. Have students research different interview formats—Panel or interview with a small group or team from a company; a demonstration or an audition interview where the candidate is expected to perform in some way; behavioral interview that is steeped in how you made decisions in your last job and what the results were. This activity provides good training and preparation for all types of interview formats, encounters, and challenges.

Performance-Based Assessments

- Observe and collect responses and appropriate feedback activities from large and small groups

CONCLUSION

What does a good interview accomplish? How would you describe the role of the interviewer and the interviewee? How will you approach an interview differently from now on? What has changed for you with what we have practiced today?

ASSIGNMENT

1. Complete the qualification sheet for preparing for the interview.
2. Write a journal entry response to, "As I read my feedback sheets, I was surprised to learn that . . ." "I was happy to read that . . ." Reflect upon your feedback sheets and write your reflections on today's observations and comments.
3. What new questions have come up for you regarding job interviews after today's lesson?

Unit 4B

Interviewing

LESSON TOPIC: INTERVIEW—EFFECTIVE COMMUNICATION

Teaching Note

The role-playing process, using different types of role-play, continues throughout the semester. Once nervous and tentative about interviewing, students become comfortable with the practice and process. It is beneficial to schedule mock interviews with business partners on corporate sites and at school. This is also a good opportunity to practice active listening skills and respectful feedback skills. Practicing with each other using audiotapes allows them to concentrate on hearing themselves—they have to self-interpret and decide on changes they would like to make, like being more adept at quick responses or more reflective in their answer as appropriate. It again reinforces that the interview process can be personally empowering and not just a test to pass. Through practicing the role of the interviewer, they can gain additional insights about how to present themselves by reflecting on the kinds of responses they wanted from the interviewee. Practicing the interview process makes interviewing a more tangible and real experience while also increasing each student's ability to have a greater sense of self and to be relaxed and poised in actual interview situations.

Objective

To prepare for an effective two-way communication interview

Domains

Cognitive: Develop strategies and techniques for interviewing
Affective: Learn to listen and to respond appropriately
Skills: Apply effective communication skills

Academic Standard: Write and Speak in the English Language

Interpersonal Communication Skills
Effective speaking and writing skills

Materials

Interview questions for practice
Tape recorders for each small group
Audiocassettes, one for each student

Pre-Instructional

Homework assignment: Write a journal entry about your reflections on the interview process and feedback from peers.

Introductory Framework

Last session you began developing effective interview skills. What we begin to see are a number of areas that need to be explored and developed. What are some areas for improvement that you listed in your journal entry? Was this assignment helpful for you to do? Today we will look at some other important areas.

Motivation

A two-way communication means that both parties are involved in the process in order to make the interview most effective. Yesterday we concentrated on the applicant's side. Today we will look at both sides for a deeper understanding.

Think about interviews you have had. Did you ever wonder what the interviewer is thinking throughout the interview? What cues were you picking up on and how did you interpret them? Many times when we leave the interview we relive the experience and try to determine if we will be seriously considered for the job and how we were rated. Dialogue about interviews students completed. What were your perceptions about how the interview went? Write all answers on the board.

Remember, as the interview proceeds, there are many questions the employer wants answered. It really is an information-gathering session. Assessments are being made throughout the interview—on both the interviewer's and the applicant's side. If we think about this more, we know that we get information from each other all day long—when we talk to colleagues, teachers, supervisors, clients, coworkers, and so on. The difference here is the connection to employment. Let's see what some of the questions and criteria might be and how we can communicate information without being asked directly.

INSTRUCTIONAL IMPLEMENTATION

Large Group Discussion

Here are some thoughts coming from the interviewer's perspective:

1. Does this person seem sincerely eager to succeed? What does this question mean to an interviewer? How is eagerness demonstrated? What are some ways you would identify eagerness to succeed in an applicant? (For example, through past successes in your professional life, future goals, knowledge about the company, etc.) What are some things you might mention about yourself? Although you might be eager, what are some things you might want to avoid during the interview? (For example, overflattering the company, exaggerating your abilities to work in the company, always smiling and agreeing with the interviewer, etc.)
2. Does this person have a clear idea of her or his value to this company/organization? Again, how do you translate this? What are ways you can demonstrate this during your interview? A manager will take this person around to meet other employees and watch the interaction. How will you interact? Ask the applicant to read information about the company and then ask for impressions, ideas, or questions.
3. Does she or he show evidence of being assertive? What does this mean? What is the difference between being assertive and being aggressive? How do we demonstrate being assertive? (For example, the manner in which we speak, confidence in our skills, knowledge of the field, questions you ask about the company, etc.)
4. Is this a person who can grow with the company? What does this mean? How can you demonstrate this in an interview? (For example, highlighting longevity and growth in a previous job, articulating this through statement of employment and career objectives.)

Partnered Activity: Review Your Qualifications

Practice interviews in pairs—student to student—with the use of audiotapes. Students will sit facing each other and practice asking each other about their qualifications from the sheets that they have prepared and practiced in the fishbowl exercise during the previous session. Many times what has been written down needs to be clarified and communicated in a succinct (define this word) manner. The person playing the role of the interviewee states the job she or he is applying for (relate this to job shadowing/internship). Some sample practice questions for the interviewer include:

1. Tell me about yourself and how you are a good fit for this job.
2. Why do you want this job?
3. Where would you like to see yourself in five years?
4. What type of education and/or training have you had that fits this position?
5. What do you do for fun?
6. What are three adjectives you would use to describe yourself? How would your friends describe you? How would your former supervisor describe you? How would former coworkers describe you?

Begin tape playback and take notes. You can add to the questions above by combining and adding different questions from the previous day's list.

Performance-Based Assessments

• Observe response and appropriate feedback activities in large and small groups

CONCLUSION

Recap major points. What important elements did you learn today that you would use in your interviews? What are any further ideas and/or questions that you have? What other opportunities for practicing interviewing can you set for yourself?

ASSIGNMENT

1. Complete/review your Personal and Professional Qualifications sheets for preparing for the interview.
2. Play your tape and listen to yourself. What did you hear? What are some things you would like to change? Have someone else listen to the tape and give you feedback. How will you do this? Practice answers to your questions by retaping yourself at home.

Unit 4C

LESSON TOPIC: EXPERIENCING THE INTERVIEW

Teaching Note

This culminating lesson allows a review of what has been studied and then provides time for actual videotaping of an interview by invited guests such as teachers, business partners, or other colleagues. The authentic experience of the interview process by an outside person provides another level of developing and practicing a two-way communication. Students receive feedback from multiple perspectives and are able to review the video, observing body language and communication styles. Good discussions ensue regarding interview expectations such as appropriate behaviors, competency levels, assessment procedures, and misunderstandings in communication. Interviews by business partners are also conducted on corporate visits during junior and senior years. The comfort level for the students increases with each of these sessions. One of the students remarked, "I was not that nervous when it came time for this last interview. I really felt that I was more relaxed and confident." Since students are audio- and videotaped a variety of times, the sessions can be used to examine specific areas that either have been learned or need additional improvement.

Objective

To participate in the interview

Domains

Cognitive: Develop strategies and techniques for interviewing
Affective: Learn to respond appropriately
Skills: Apply effective communication skills

Academic Standard: Write and Speak in the English Language

Interpersonal Communication Skills
Effective speaking and writing skills

Materials

Tips for interviewing successfully
Large poster paper
Video camera and tapes for taping interviews

Pre-Instructional

Students have practiced responses to typical interview questions and made changes to their Personal and Professional Qualifications sheets.

Introductory Framework

In the past few sessions, we have worked to put together a positive profile of ourselves and to develop strategies for succeeding during our interviews. Now it is time to review these strategies and prepare for the videotaped interviews with our business and community partners.

Motivation

What is your greatest fear about the interview? In what areas of the interview do you feel most confident? What do you want to gain from the interview? What can we do to anticipate problems and solutions? What is the worst thing that can happen to you either during or as a result of the interview? How is such a situation always a learning experience, no matter how it turns out? (See fig. 4.22 for some typical interview questions and responses.)

INSTRUCTIONAL IMPLEMENTATION

Large Group Discussion (Fig. 4.25)

Have figure 4.25 on an overhead or as a PowerPoint presentation. Ask students the following questions: How can we avoid making these kinds of errors? What types of prior preparation will help to avoid them? Are there ways to remind yourself of pitfalls during the interview?

Here are some considerations to make before the interview itself: How can we create positive impressions? What are impressions? Brainstorm in the large group the "interview preparation" that everyone can use for any interview situation.

Figure 4.25. Most Frequent Interviewer Complaints about Interviewees

1. Lack of personality, manners, poise, and confidence; appears arrogant, egotistical, or conceited.
2. Poor appearance, lack of neatness, careless dress, dressed more for evening out than for the office.
3. Shows no enthusiasm or interest; overall lack of drive with little evidence of initiative.
4. No real goals apparent; demonstrates poor planning; not motivated, does not know or articulate interests; indecisive.
5. Poor communication habits and use of speech.
6. Unrealistic in terms of salary for this level of job and skills.
7. No leadership potential.
8. No outside interests or activities—does not really know why either.
9. Not familiar with the company, did not do any research to prepare for the interview, does not ask good questions.
10. Lack of interest in security and benefits.

Small Group Activity: Interview Suggestions

In small groups, take the time to list the top five interview suggestions you will need to remember. Have students write their top five on poster sheets. When they are finished, have them put them up on the walls. Discuss if all are applicable; prioritize the tips with the group. What other ideas do you want to add to this list?

Large Group Activity: Videotaping Interviews by Invited Guests

Invited guests can include business and community partners or other teachers in the building; this can cover more than one seminar. Students observe as the invited interviewer conducts an actual interview. There is a succession of at least four interviews before observations are made and feedback is given. After all the interviews are completed, students watch the tapes together and give helpful feedback. If possible, it is helpful to have all the videotapes consolidated onto a CD or DVD for continuous viewing.

Optional Plans

1. Have students write tips in their notebooks for future reference.
2. Have students interview their friends: either an actual interview or interview them on what it was like getting their first job.
3. Have students write up characteristics of poor and active listening behaviors that will help them during the interview.
4. Have students bring in and distribute excerpts from current books that describe "how one gets the best job." After the excerpts have been read

out loud, discuss the merit of these suggestions and how they apply to the students. How will they use them? Are they just gimmicks?

Performance-Based Assessments

- Observe response and appropriate feedback activities in large and small groups

CONCLUSION

Recap major points. Which tips were most useful to you today? Now that you have practiced and experienced the interview process, how is an interview more than just asking questions? How will you prepare for the questions you want to ask?

ASSIGNMENT

1. Complete/review the Personal and Professional Qualifications sheets for preparing for the interview.
2. Complete the final rewrite of your résumé to bring to mock interviews at the corporate site with human resource representatives next week.

Unit 5A

Letter Writing

LESSON TOPIC: TYPES AND FUNCTIONS OF LETTERS

Teaching Note

Writing letters is an art. Many students will have experienced writing and receiving friendly letters at some time in their lives, but may not have had experience with writing a formal business letter or cover letter for an application. Some only know email as letter writing. This session provides time to tie in some historical and literary information about the nature of letter writing, its importance, and the value it has in illuminating one's history with substance and character.

Objective

To examine the different types, functions, and organization of effective letters (inquiry and application)

Domains

Cognitive: Identify the components of good letter writing
Affective: Appreciate this specific style of writing
Skills: Read and communicate effectively

Academic Standard: Write and Speak in the English Language

Interpersonal Communication Skills
Effective speaking and listening skills

Materials

Samples from historical and literary letters—epistles (biblical, Horace, and Cicero), love letters (Peter Abelard and Heloise; Ronald Reagan's letters to Nancy), books (*Pamela and Clarissa* by Richardson; *Griffin and Sabine: An Extraordinary Correspondence*, *Sabine's Notebook*, and *The Golden Mean* by Nick Bantock).
Sample business letters
Basic Principles of Letter Writing handout (fig. 4.26)
Some Basic Rules for Writing Readable Letters handout (fig. 4.27)
Letter of Inquiry handout (fig. 4.28)
Letter of Application handout (fig. 4.29)
Sample résumé cover letters
Letters to the editor

Figure 4.26.   Basic Principles of Letter Writing

1. Your letters must be:
   - Word processed.
   - In black ink on a machine with clean type and like-new ribbon, or on a word-processor/printer for rapid revision.
   - Correct as to name, title, and address of the person to whom you are writing.
   - Perfect in spelling, grammar, and punctuation.
   - Free of obvious corrections.
   - On standard size (8½" × 11") stationery.
   - On good quality paper (white or lightly tinted).
   - Folded not more than twice.
   - An acceptable business letter form with proper spacing and appropriate margins.
   - Mailed in a #10 envelope that matches the paper used for the letter. Paper stock should also match your résumé paper stock.
2. What's in a name? Letters are generally more effective if they're specifically addressed to an individual. Whenever possible, address letters directly to the specific personnel officer, manager, supervisor, and so on.

   Do not assume titles or gender. When writing to a specific individual, use that person's title only if you are sure of what it is. If you are not sure, it is best to omit the title and address the letter directly to that person (e.g., "Dear Dean Smith" instead of "Dear Vice President Smith"). The same is true if you are unsure of the individual's gender (e.g., "Dear Pat Jones" instead of "Dear Ms./Mr. Jones") or if only initials are given for the individual's name (e.g., "Dear C. A. Johnson").
3. Keep a record of when and to whom you wrote each letter. Be sure to track information such as when you applied for a position, when you received a response, and what the response was. Don't put off any letter writing—do each appropriate letter as soon as possible.

Figure 4.27. Some Basic Rules for Writing Readable Letters

- "Hook" the reader with your opening paragraph.
- Do not try to be fancy. Write in plain English—be yourself.
- Write positively. Your letter should give the impression of self-confidence.
- Use the active voice.
- Do not make all your sentences the same length.
- Do not bury your message in the verbiage. Put the idea(s) and word(s) you wish to stress at the beginning or end of the sentence.
- Keep your paragraphs short, with each one limited to a single idea.
- Tie your paragraphs together.
- Prefer short words to long words.
- Be exact in your use of words. If you have to look up the meaning of a word, perhaps you should not use it.
- Use adverbs and adjectives sparingly; avoid a "flowery" style.
- Be wary of compound or bookish prepositions and conjunctions.
- Do not use contractions or abbreviations.
- Avoid trite expressions and slang.
- Do not use unfamiliar words or other jargon.
- Do not repeat yourself.
- Keep your letter to one uncrowded page.
- Above All: Do not write as though you were applying for a position. Write as though you were applying for an opportunity to be of service, as a professional, to the potential employer addressed.

Pre-Instructional

Students are to bring in the names, addresses, and newspaper employment ads of three different companies. It is most helpful if they choose companies in which they are interested.

Introductory Framework

In our modern world, there are many different ways to communicate messages and ideas to each other. Certainly technology has provided opportunities for effective written communication—electronic mail. Yet this is a different type of writing than is needed in formal letters. The art of letter writing dates back to biblical times. In the early centuries, well before the advent of the printing press, letter writing was the one way most people communicated with each other There are different types of letters: romantic, historical, political, ultimatum (show samples). Discuss the place and importance of each type of letter example. Ask students to make interpretations for the different categories.

Motivation

When do you use letters in your personal life? Who do you write to? Who writes to you? Have you received formal letters? What type of paper do you write on? What is the content of your letters? What style of letter do you use most frequently? With what style do you need the greatest practice?

INSTRUCTIONAL IMPLEMENTATION

Writing formal letters has been equated to making a presentation or writing a research paper. The necessary skills are planning, organization, and good writing technique.

Figure 4.28. Letter of Inquiry

1. The purpose of the letter of inquiry is to introduce yourself to an employer and to inquire if a vacancy exists or is anticipated. You write a letter of inquiry if you are interested in the availability of jobs in a specific business or location, having done some preliminary research. It is not meant to be an application for a specific position.
2. The letter of inquiry should be a single page.
3. The opening paragraph generally states why you are writing and the type of position you are seeking. Some candidates also include a few sentences on why they want to live/work in the employer's area. Request application forms and promotional information about the employer and community if necessary.
4. The middle paragraph(s) should include information on your qualifications based on your understanding of what the employer's needs are, your education, and past employment experiences. You may want to mention when and where you received your degree. Sometimes relevant extracurricular interests are important to include. State your qualifications broadly. Mention that you are enclosing your résumé and limit your comments to highlighting particular skills and experience relevant to your perceived needs of the employer but do not restate your résumé.
5. The concluding paragraph includes information about how you can be contacted. This is also a good place to thank the potential employer for his or her consideration of your inquiry.

Following are some tips:

1. Go fishing—a letter of inquiry is not meant as a letter of application—it is a form of "fishing" for information about a specific business.
2. Do not write in such a manner that you appear to be sending out a mass mailing of indiscriminate "feelers" to any and all employers.
3. Give a plausible reason for writing to that particular employer (e.g., your family has relocated to the area; you enjoy the area for its particular professional, cultural, recreational offerings, etc.). Don't force it.
4. Be convincing, because this will personalize the letter.
5. Enclose your résumé.

(continued)

Figure 4.28. Letter of Inquiry *(continued)*

SAMPLE LETTER OF INQUIRY

3216 West 20th Avenue
Minneapolis, MN 55414

March 24, 1987

Ms. Louise Johnson
Assistant Director of Personnel
Memphis Textile Incorporated
1445 Ashland Avenue
Minneapolis, MN 55413

Dear Ms. Johnson:
I am writing to inquire if there will be a position at Memphis Textile Incorporated for which I might be considered. Currently, I am concentrating on business administration in my studies and have experience in business finance as well. If you anticipate any vacancies in either management positions or your finance department, I would appreciate receiving an application form and information regarding your interviewing procedures.

I have enclosed my résumé for your consideration. I am eager to contribute to the success of Memphis Textile Incorporated and hope to hear from you soon.

Sincerely,
Roberta Taylor
Enc.

(Adapted from Rebecca Anthony and Gerald Roe, 1982, *Contact to Contract,* Rhode Island: Carroll Press.)

Large Group Activity: Letters to the Editor

Ask students if they read letters to the editor. Distribute copies of letters to the editor and have students read some of them out loud. Discuss the students' observations: What topics are covered in these letters? What are some of the elements they all have in common? What interpretations can you make about the person who writes each letter?

Large Group Activity: Form and Function in Letters

What role do these formal letters play? Let us look at some basic principles of letter writing (fig. 4.26). Some people have described the art of letter writing as having certain commandments—let's see what that means (fig. 4.27). Look at other types of letters and discuss as a large group:

1. Letters of inquiry—purpose, contents (fig. 4.28)
2. Letters of application—apply for an actual position (fig. 4.29)

Small Group Activity: A Letter of Inquiry

1. Write a letter of inquiry.
2. Use a name from the businesses on your list of interests.
3. You can choose from one or two companies and write a letter as a group.
4. Write a second letter of inquiry to another company, again using the ideas from the lesson.

Figure 4.29.   Letter of Application

1. The purpose of a letter of application is to apply for an actual position.
2. You never get a second chance to make a good first impression. The letter of application may be your first communication with a potential employer, so it is your chance to present yourself in a way that attracts attention to your qualifications and encourages interest in your candidacy.
3. Format (single space preferred).
4. The opening paragraph should clearly indicate the purpose of the letter. State the exact title of the position for which you are applying and let the reader know how you heard about the position. A good first paragraph will orient and assist the reader in understanding the rest of the letter.
5. Use the body of this middle paragraph to expand upon or highlight your relevant experience and background in relation to the information you have about the position (i.e., administrative assistant).
6. Do not recopy your résumé—give a broad overview of your experience and qualifications and show how they relate to the qualifications needed for that specific position.
7. In the concluding paragraph, indicate your interest and availability to interview with the business. If the employer is out of state and you can plan to interview in that area, include this information in the letter, outlining when you could schedule an initial telephone interview and a subsequent in-person interview. Enclose your résumé if this letter is your first communication with the employer. Request information about any additional application procedures that may be required. If you have already received an application form, carefully complete it and enclose it with your letter and résumé.

Responses to a letter of application vary. You can expect an employer to:

- Acknowledge receipt of your materials
- Request additional information
- Send you an application form
- Arrange for an interview

However, some employers may not respond at all, especially if many candidates apply for the position. If this happens, phone or write a follow-up letter to verify that your letter/résumé was received and ask when you can expect to hear from the employer. Keep an up-to-date record of when and where you applied, and the response you received to your application. Keep photocopies of your completed application forms.

(continued)

Figure 4.29. Letter of Application *(continued)*

SAMPLE LETTER OF APPLICATION

3204 Harriet Avenue South
Minneapolis, MN 55408

May 23, 1987

Mr. Phil Smith
Director of Personnel
Hansen Limited
600 E. 16th Street
Minneapolis, MN 55420

Dear Mr. Smith:
I would like to apply for the position you have available for a Department Assistant at Hansen Limited. I learned of your vacancy through the May 15, 1987, issue of the *Minneapolis Star and Tribune*. I believe I possess a number of skills and qualities that make me an excellent candidate for this position.

As you can see from my enclosed résumé, I have experience in administrative assistance. In my current position as Program Assistant for Cobb & Gregg, I am responsible for assisting nine full-time program members and I am responsible for communicating effectively, in writing and orally, the most current information available on our program. I am also responsible for collecting and disseminating information collected at departmental meetings and for maintaining written records of correspondence with clients and other company members. In addition, I maintain a variety of databases, manage the program budget, and monitor program records for full compliance with our agency.

I have enclosed my résumé for your consideration. I am eager to contribute to the success of Hansen Limited and am available for an interview at your convenience.

I look forward to hearing from you.

Sincerely,
Roberta Taylor

Enc.

(Adapted from Rebecca Anthony and Gerald Roe, 1982, *Contact to Contract*, Rhode Island: Carroll Press.)

Optional Plans

1. Students can think about writing a class letter to the new, incoming Voyager group.
2. Begin a series of letter communications with junior year students.
3. Students can use letter writing as part of their Voyager project as they communicate with their business partners regarding ideas and issues to be explored and unpacked.

4. Begin letter writing communication with mentors.
5. Students can write letters to the editor regarding current issues or opinions they want to express.
6. Write a letter to an elected representative to convey a position on a community issue.

Performance-Based Assessments

- Letters created in response to job advertisements (inquiry and application) both in and out of class

CONCLUSION

What are the different styles to keep in mind when writing these different types of letters—letters of application, letters of inquiry, and letters to the editor? How will you use letter writing for college or postsecondary training program applications?

ASSIGNMENT

1. Write one letter of inquiry and one letter of application to a company that has caught your interest. These letters will actually be sent out to the company. Remember you must know and demonstrate the difference between each type of letter. Have one other person proofread your letter before it is sent out.

Unit 5B

LESSON TOPIC: HANDS-ON REAL LETTER WRITING

Teaching Note

Letter writing provides another hands-on component of real-world application in the program. As in the lessons for writing résumés and preparing for the interview, letter writing becomes a text in the seminar. Students discuss the need for and purposes of the cover letter and how the résumé and interview are all connected. Students have the opportunity to create and send a tailored communication to a prospective employer. This is the time when they learn to highlight what is specific about what they bring to the position and draw attention to their skills and information that may not be included in the résumé. It is great practice for students to customize their skills to a series of specific jobs, therefore enabling them to see how they possess skills and attributes that have a broader application than they might have initially envisioned. It also provides more opportunities for them to learn more about each other and to work in a community as they read and provide feedback to each other.

Objective

To understand and apply knowledge of different types, functions, and organization of effective letters (follow-up, acceptance, and thank-you letters)

Domains

Cognitive: Identify the components of good letter writing
Affective: Appreciate this specific style of writing
Skills: Read and communicate effectively

317

Academic Standard: Write and Speak in the English Language

Interpersonal Communication Skills
Effective speaking and listening skills

Materials

Types of Follow-Up Letters handout (fig. 4.30)
Letter Checklist handout (fig. 4.31)

Pre-Instructional

Letter of inquiry and letter of application in response to an ad.

Figure 4.30.   Types of Follow-Up Letters

There are many reasons to follow up on an initial contact with an employer. Letters are used to submit required materials, to follow up on an interview, and/or to accept or decline an employment offer. Never send or return any document to an employer without a brief cover letter. The cover letter will not only clarify the reason for submitting the materials, but officially document what you have sent and when.

1. **To Return an Application Form:** Include a brief cover letter indicating your compliance with a specific instruction (e.g., you are returning the form by a specific date). If you have picked up an application and have had no "formal" contact with the employer, include a typical letter of application and enclose your résumé.
2. **To Accept or Reject an Interview Offer:** After your interview (or in response to your letter of application), you may be invited to interview with other personnel or to tour the facilities where you'll be working. Even if the offer was made in a telephone call from the employer, it is appropriate to confirm the date and time of the interview in writing.
3. **Follow-Up to an Interview:** Always follow up an interview with a letter to the interviewing person, thanking her or him for the interview and either stating your continued interest or removing your name from consideration. A follow-up letter is a must. The letter can reemphasize particular aspects of your training or experience as it relates to the position. It can even introduce pertinent information that did not occur to you to discuss during your interview.
4. **Accept/Reject an Employment Offer:** Respond as soon as possible with an acceptance or refusal. If you do not wish to accept the offer, write a letter of refusal immediately! This will give the employer the opportunity to identify other candidates. You should, of course, express your appreciation for the offer and the reason for declining the position.

    If you are in doubt about accepting an offer but are definitely interested, you may request time to consider your decision. State a definite time period (it should be short, perhaps a week) and make your decision known by the end of that time. You may refuse or accept by phone, but for your own protection (and for that of the employer), an acceptance must also be in writing.

(continued)

Figure 4.30.   Types of Follow-Up Letters *(continued)*

SAMPLE FOLLOW-UP LETTER

2403 N. 57th Street
Minneapolis, MN 55414

April 4, 1992

Ms. Molly Gregg
Personnel Director
Parkway Bank
2115 Grand Avenue
Minneapolis, MN 55406

Dear Ms. Gregg:
I wish to thank you, once again, for the time you spent with me on Friday, April 1, discussing the marketing analyst position at Parkway Bank. I have reviewed the materials you gave me and my interest in the position remains high.

I feel that working at Parkway Bank would be a rewarding experience and I am confident that I could contribute to the continued success of the Marketing Department.

As you requested, I will arrange to have a list of references sent to your office. I look forward to hearing from you.

Sincerely,

Michael Kemmer
Enc.

(Adapted from Rebecca Anthony and Gerald Roe, 1982, *Contact to Contract,* Rhode Island: Carroll Press.)

Figure 4.31.   Letter Checklist

- Is my letter personalized (directed to a specific individual by correct name and title)?
- Does my letter begin with a strong first statement?
- Is the purpose of my letter clearly stated?
- Is my letter concise and free of unnecessary jargon?
- Does my letter reflect my personality as well as my qualifications?
- Have I overused the personal pronoun "I"?
- Have I checked for errors in grammar, spelling, and punctuation?
- Does my letter require enclosures?
- Do I have a copy for my records?

(Adapted from Anthony and Roe, 1982.)

Introductory Framework

We will look at two more types of letters. Letter writing is an important part of job seeking and success. It is equally important to keep a separate file on each of the companies you have written to, including all correspondence with them. In this way, you have an accurate record of what was written, to whom you wrote, and what responses you received. This is also true when writing for college admission information and applications. As we make more inquiries, it is difficult to keep all of the information only in our heads; therefore, having an organized record and files is an advantage. In each file you will also need to write down when and with whom you have had an interview, keep any materials you have gathered about the company, be sure to write comments on how you thought the interview or telephone conversations went, and list any future suggestions you have for yourself. Although this takes lots of time, it is worth it in the end as you will have a clear idea of what you have done with each of the organizations you have written to and interviewed with.

Motivation

What was most challenging for you when writing letters of inquiry and application? What tips from the sample letters and discussion in our last class were most helpful?

INSTRUCTIONAL IMPLEMENTATION

Large Group Activity

Using figure 4.30 as a guide, discuss follow-up letters—their format, purpose, and content. Then discuss thank-you letters. Why are these letters just as important as the inquiry and application letters? How many of you have written either one of these letters? What are some of the common points for each of the letters? It is also important to remember that the format and appropriateness of each of these letters is as important as your résumé. Mistakes in style and names, misspellings, and grammatical errors will immediately halt a company's or a school's consideration of you.

Small Group Activity

In small groups, have students read each other's letters. Reading the letters out loud helps to catch mistakes and also to highlight portions of the letter where tone needs to be changed or information clarified. Have students dialogue about what they heard versus what the writer intended. Use the Letter Checklist (fig. 4.31) included here.

CONCLUSION

Review basic rules for writing readable letters. How many of the rules are reflected in the letters you wrote and what rules do you need to pay more attention to? Did your letters convey the information you wanted known?

ASSIGNMENT

1. Write one letter of thank you to the work site you most recently visited.
2. Write a letter of thank you to one of the business partners.
3. Rewrite any of the letters using the guides provided.

Unit 6A

The Voyager Company

LESSON TOPIC: COMPANY REORGANIZATION

Teaching Note

Students continue their work in building and developing their Voyager Company. The Voyager Company is a signature piece of this program. In addition to providing students exposure to real learning opportunities and connections with the business and social communities, it allows them to leave their imprint of change and influence on the program. These sessions require:

1. attention to detail
2. an involved engagement with expanding ideas
3. continuing research
4. finding solutions

The Voyager Company includes authentic situations that are addressed through a variety of means and perspectives. Much of the work is done after class when students meet to problem solve and make decisions. We found that students willingly spent the extra time to work together as their projects were connected to actual people and events. At times they stayed so late that the coordinator had to end the session in order to meet a previous engagement. It is one of the most collaborative activities as the students continuously practice negotiating, attentive listening, and active engagement with each other.

Objectives

To review reports and activities of the Voyager Company from junior year
To organize the company for senior year

Domains

Cognitive: Understand organizational development
Affective: Become aware of the complex structures of organizations
Skills: Appreciate different aspects of company processes

Academic Standard: Decision Making

Career Investigation
Determine personal interests, aptitudes, and abilities
Investigate a career through research

Materials

Project Status Report outline
Meeting agenda and minutes forms
Guide to facilitating a meeting

Pre-Instructional

Students are to write a one-page summary of what they learned about their interests, aptitudes, and abilities in relation to a selected career based on their experiences from a summer internship or employment. Additionally, each student is to write two personal goals she or he wants to set in relation to the Voyager Company.

Introductory Framework

Your company is one year old and you have gained additional skills and abilities from your education and internship/employment experiences. Today you will hear reports from your fellow shareholders/workers about the increased assets (abilities and skills) they have learned and will be bringing into the company this year. You also need to reevaluate the composition of your work teams and create a plan for this year. We will break into work teams after the reports are presented. In the next session of this unit, we will hear from several presenters who will talk about the qualities, skills, and abilities of highly effective people. In the third session, you will create a marketing piece, conduct an analysis of your work in the Voyager Company, and assign tasks for creating a final report.

Motivation

Reviewing your additional skills and abilities and reflecting on internship and employment experiences will give you a base for adding more creative solutions or new ideas. Your work in the Voyager Company is an opportunity to build the kind of company that you would like to work in. There are no limits to dreaming and visioning how you want to run the company, the kind of work environment you want to have for yourself and your partners/shareholders, and the ethics you want to apply to the operations. Consider what you have learned about democratic workplaces and weaving socially responsible and just practice in to the operations of the company. As you listen to the reports, be sure to write down any ideas that come to you. You will also want to write down the skills and abilities that each person talks about in order to compile a complete resource list. Make as many Assets and Presentation Listening Guides (fig. 4.32) as you will need for students to write a response on each presentation.

INSTRUCTIONAL IMPLEMENTATION

Small Group Activity: Reflections and Internships

Each student will either read her or his report or make a summary presentation to the small group. Give the students the opportunity to give comments to one another after all the presentations are completed. They should take notes on each presentation. This is an important time to renegotiate and learn, from individual and group reflection, what is needed to move forward in the next year. Reflection sheets are available for each member of the group to also provide written feedback. In addition, each team must answer the questions: What went well for the Voyager Company last year? Were we satisfied with how we worked with our clients? Do we need different community projects? Can we recruit other business partners? Through team discussions, everyone will benefit from the multiple perspectives as you set a new course for this year's work in the company.

Figure 4.32.   Assets and Presentation Listening Guide

Presenter
Ideas:
1.
2.
3.

Skills and Abilities

Other Notes and Comments

**Figure 4.33.   New Directions and Other Recommendations: Voyager Company
Reflection Sheet**

Each team must fill out a reflection sheet.

1. What went well for the Voyager Company last year?
2. List some things that went well and how the team worked with clients.
3. What could the team improve about client relationships?
4. Do we need different community projects?
5. How can we recruit other business partners?
6. Additional suggestions?

Large Group Activity: New Directions and Other Recommendations (Fig. 4.33)

What went well last year for the Voyager Company? What recommendations is each team making? Many times this discussion requires a lot more time and then a lot more research. Students nominate certain projects, community groups, or business partners, then do research on each of these and bring them back to the entire group for a final discussion and decision.

Use the following questions to guide your discussion about teamwork:

1. To what extent are your team and teamwork cohesive? To what degree do all members of the team feel engaged, feel like integral members, and want to remain within their existing team?
2. Has your team made good decisions? Has there been a high rate of job satisfaction?
3. What conditions need to be present for you to work as a group?
4. Do you have shared and compatible goals for the company's direction and vision?
5. Is there any competition from outside groups or external threat to what you are doing?
6. How is the company encouraging creativity?
7. How are selection and evaluation of projects taking place?

Team Activity: Recomposing Teams

Now you will break into your work groups and accomplish the following:

1. Reassess the composition of your team and determine if you want to negotiate an exchange of team members with any of the other work groups. Your decisions should be based on personal preferences, on

skills needed in your group, and on maintaining enough diversity of personal attributes to spark creativity.

2. Also, everyone should have the opportunity to experience being team members of different parts of the company in order to gain experience and practice multiple skills.

3. Use the Project Status Report Outline (fig. 4.34) to review the past year and as a guide to developing your annual plan. Incorporate the personal goals each of you wrote as a part of your homework in the annual plan. Include a written business concept in your annual plan.

Write the following statement on the board for teams to use as a reference: A business concept is a summary of key technology, concepts, or strategies on which your business is based. Please use the meeting agenda and minutes (same figures as for junior year) forms in the same manner as you did last year.

Activity: Business Concepts

In the big group have each team write its business concept summary on the board and facilitate a discussion that leads to a consensus statement as to which of the concepts will be adopted.

Optional Plans

1. Have students establish contact and set up communications with a sampling of worker-run companies around the country in order to research democratic worker-run organizations. You can make contact through the web or a letter requesting information about the company. It is a good idea to include a brief description of the Voyager program and the Voyager Company. Ask for opportunities to interview owners, workers, and worker/owners. The vision of this type of work is that workers use their democratic participation in the firm to work for the commonwealth. Examples include:

   • Mondragon Group in the Basque Provinces of Northern Spain
   • Firms with Employee Stock Ownership Plans (ESOPs)
   • Food co-ops and organically grown produce
   • Springfield Remanufacturing in Missouri
   • The Rochdale Pioneers in England
   • The Antigonish Movement in Nova Scotia
   • The Worker's Council Movement in Algeria
   • Northeast Cooperatives—a Vermont-based wholesale food distributor

Figure 4.34.   Project Status Report Outline

Project Name
[Presenter Name]
Status Summary
   Is the project on track for delivery as expected?
   What is the final date for delivery?
   What are the final cost estimates?
   Status against any other high-level shipping goals
Manufacturing Rate
Delivery
Partners, etc.
Progress
   List achievements and progress since last status update was given
   Address schedule implications
   Highlight those things that made progress possible
Attention Areas
   List delays and problems since last status update was given
   List corrective actions being taken
   Address schedule implications
   Make sure you understand
      Issues that are causing delays or impeding progress
      Why problem was not anticipated
      If customer will want to discuss issue with upper management
Schedule
   List top high-level dates
   Keep it simple so audience does not get distracted with details
   Distribute more detailed schedule if appropriate
   Make sure you are familiar with details of schedule so you can answer questions
Deliveries
   List main critical deliverables
   Yours to client
   Yours to outside services
   Outside services to you
   Other departments to you
   Understand your confidence rating to each deliverable
   Indicate confidence level on slides if appropriate
Costs
   List new projections of costs
   Include original estimates
   Understand source of differences in these numbers—be ready for questions if there
   are cost overruns
   Summarize why
   List corrective or preventative action you've taken
   Set realistic expectations for future expenditures
Technology
   List technical problems that have been solved
   List outstanding technical issues that need to be solved
   Summarize their impact on the project
   List any dubious technological dependencies for project

(continued)

Figure 4.34.   Project Status Report Outline *(continued)*

Indicate source of doubt
Summarize action being taken or backup plan
Resources
   Summarize project resources
   Dedicated (full-time) resources
   Part-time resources
   If project is constrained by lack of resources, suggest alternatives
   Understand that customers may want to be assured that all possible resources are be-
   ing used, but in such a way that costs will be properly managed
Goals for Next Review
   Date of next status update
   List goals for next review
   Specific items that will be done
   Issues that will be resolved
   Make sure anyone involved in project understands action plan
References and Resources for the Company
   Team Builders Plus: http://www.imc.org.uk/services/coursewa/ada/ad3.htm#ses-
   sion1
   Center of the Study of Work Teams: http://www.workteams.unt.edu
   International Team Management Systems: http://www.tms.com.au/reference.html.
   University of Wisconsin - Eau Claire: http://www.uwec.edu/Academic/Curric/Sampsow/
   Sources/Group.html.

---

2. Look up and interview local and national labor leaders. What can we learn from labor and the history of negotiation and workers' rights?

3. Have students use one of their Voyager Company projects to critically examine the workplace of the project and to participate in a "constructive reconstruction of the workplace."

4. Research and present the concept of critical consciousness in the workplace. How does this transform the meaning of knowledge in the workplace? How does this have consequences for teaching and learning and how are all components in a democratic firm interdependent?

5. Discuss what changes students will suggest for the Voyager Company that are more in line with John Dewey and Paulo Freire, both philosophically and pragmatically.

6. What are the strategies for overcoming barriers in work education and workplaces for women and nontraditional workers? Students are encouraged to research companies that have been founded by women and nontraditional workers. How are these companies different? What concepts and practices do you want to incorporate into the operation of the Voyager Company, your work team, and your own participation? This might also be a good time to review segments of *Union Maids* (1977), *The Global Assembly Line* (1988), and *With Babies and Banners* (1978).

CONCLUSION

What new team combinations have you created? What further work needs to be accomplished in order to set a course for this year's work?

ASSIGNMENT

1. Make copies of every team's annual plan for each student. Each student is to compile the individual team plans and prioritize the tasks and activities in the order he or she believes is needed to accomplish goals. This assignment is to be completed and turned in by the end of Unit 7.

Unit 6B

The Voyager Company

LESSON TOPIC: HIGHLY EFFECTIVE PEOPLE

Teaching Note

For Voyager students, the experience of actually working with people who influence their community and city was crucial and significant. They were able to connect a name and a face with a person that they had read or heard about in the media. The session was informative and allowed them to practice dialogue skills that addressed hard questions. The speakers were both surprised and impressed by the range of questions and the level of interest generated by the students. This seminar was another activity connected to students' interests, lives, and concerns. In addition to having a variety of guests, there was also a trainer living in town who came in and taught a workshop on the seven habits of highly effective teens. Both types of guests are worth having as they present different perspectives to students who are struggling to discover who they are and where they would like to go. The panel of speakers from businesses and the community anchors students in the actual worlds they live in, and they see how change is being made by others; they also talk about what personal changes are necessary for future work success. The panelists provide wonderful stories that are powerful sources of hope and learning. They tell their own stories of success and struggle, which give all of the students ideas, suggestions, and options for the future. The feedback from the students included, "This is so much more fun and interesting than someone just telling you what to do. The stories told us things that were important in our lives as well." The workshop on effective teens and their habits focuses solely on them and how to create strategies for change. Students were highly focused on the habits and strategies in their lives and they completed exercises that they could use again in the future. One of them said, "This workshop is so fun. You get to talk and think about who you are. Even the questions are interesting—like making major attitude adjustments and listing the positive things about myself."

Objective

To learn about the characteristics, abilities, and skills of highly effective people from the information provided by guest speakers

Domains

Cognitive: Identify necessary skills for corporate functions
Affective: Appreciate the variety of skills and knowledge needed in each corporation
Skills: Apply successful skills for highly effective people

Academic Standard: Decision Making

Career Investigation
Determine personal interests, aptitudes, and abilities
Investigate a career through research

Materials

Speaker Response Sheet (fig. 4.35)
Guide to facilitating a meeting

Pre-Instructional

Contact and schedule guest speakers to talk about what it means to be a highly effective person in their sphere of influence. You may want to ask the students to suggest speakers and have them assist you in making contact; many times the students have met highly influential people who they would like more communication with through the Voyager program. The business partners and local entrepreneurs are pleased to be invited and very willing to participate. Have students keep a running list of speakers they would like to invite to the seminar throughout the program.

Introductory Framework

To remain competitive in a global economy, businesses must have highly effective workers at every level of the company. Today we are going to hear from several speakers who will talk about what makes people effective, how this success influences their personal mission, and what effect it has on a company's mission and success.

Motivation

As you listen to the presentations, think about areas of your own life where you would like to be more effective. Think about what it means to become an effective leader. Listen to strategies and practices that you can use to become more effective. How does hearing about habits as positives change your view of yourself, and how can you use this concept to support your success? Please take notes on the Speaker Response Sheet (fig. 4.35) so that we can discuss your findings at the next seminar meeting. Coordinator is encouraged to use a current personal example to begin the discussion.

INSTRUCTIONAL IMPLEMENTATION

Each of the guest panelists will present ways that they believe prepare people for success in their life. They combine and use strategies that they believe reflect success in both personal and professional life. The students have also been given copies and work from *The 7 Habits of Highly Effective Teens* by Sean Covey (1998). In order to prepare effectively for the session and the panelists, students complete a host of exercises as suggested by the panelists. Here are some examples from past panelists:

1. Map out ways for improving your personal effectiveness and your impact on others.
2. How and where do you spend most of your time?
3. Each student receives a copy of the seven habits and writes out how she or he uses them or will consider using them in her or his life.
4. Describe when you have been proactive or reactive in your life.

Figure 4.35. Speaker Response Sheet

Speaker's name:
Topic/Title:

1. Content: Notes on what is said.

2. Reflection: What does this have to do with me?

3. Questions/Changes I wish to make.

5. What crossroads do you feel you are experiencing in your life?
6. What contributions do you want to make to your community, to your profession, and to others?
7. Choose a quote or proverb that describes your life at this time.
8. What are some of your fears and what are some ways of facing them?
9. What do you do to balance and refresh yourself—how do you take *me* time?
10. What is synergy among people? How does it work in this program?

Here are some possible questions for Voyager students to pose to the guest panelists:

1. Did you ever encounter conflict with your family, that is, your ideas and their ideas of your future were not the same?
2. Have you always felt that you could be an effective person?
3. What event in your life changed how you felt about yourself?
4. Who were your role models?
5. What attitude adjustments did you have to make?
6. What is the best advice you ever received?
7. Do you believe in synergy in business—have you seen or experienced this? How does one develop this as a leader?
8. How would you describe time management and how does it work?
9. Talk about your understanding of management versus leadership.
10. What habits have you cultivated and how have they helped you?
11. What did you do with difficulty and failure that you experienced in your work world and your private life?
12. What is the single most important learning you want us to take away from today?

CONCLUSION

Thank guests for their time and willingness to come to Voyager. Students give their perception of what they experienced today and how they were impacted by the speakers and their presentations.

ASSIGNMENT

1. Write a one-page report summarizing what you learned from the presentation, including new strategies, habits, and practices you will use to become more effective.
2. Write one way in which you will live out each of the seven habits of highly effective teens.
3. Use the facilitation guide (fig. 4.36) and set the agenda items for the next Voyager meeting.

Figure 4.36. Facilitating a Meeting

Facilitation skills are utilized when presentations become interactive meetings. The facilitator sets the agenda, coaches participants, and guides the pacing.

Opening
Stimulate interest with:

- a noteworthy event
- a personal experience
- a testimonial
- a quotation

Bridge
Tie your opening directly to your key topic. Your energy and attitude set the tone and provide momentum for this meeting.

Key Topic

- Define the topic/problem/opportunity.
- State the reason for importance.
- Invite comments by audience.
- Encourage participation.
- Record and display key comments on key ideas.

Goals and Problems

- Define the goals.
- Define the problems.
- Encourage participants to focus on the issues and assign priorities.

Solutions and Opportunities

- Invite comments and ideas from the audience.
- Record and display their comments regarding action plans and solutions.
- Invite participants to prioritize options.

Action Plan

Describe the following (where additional information is needed assign responsibility to the logical person):

- Action steps
- Materials needed
- Training needed
- Schedules
- Costs

Close

- Ensure understanding.
- Describe first steps.
- Get commitment.

Unit 6C

The Voyager Company

LESSON TOPIC: COMPANY AGENDA

Teaching Note

This is another take-charge session by the students. They set their own company agendas, develop their own discussion formats, and decide how to achieve their goal by the end of the session. This session is also when they make decisions about how to pass on the company and its ideas to the upcoming Voyager students for further explorations and development.

Objective

To conduct a company meeting that results in an agenda for today's session. The agenda should include the presentation of homework reports and the development of marketing slogans and an advertising piece for the Voyager Company.

Domains

Cognitive: Identify the elements of a company meeting
Affective: Become aware of advertising and marketing skills and strategies
Skills: Make choices for company needs

Academic Standard: Decision Making

Career Investigation
Determine personal interests, aptitudes, and abilities
Investigate a career through research

Materials

Meeting facilitation guide
Sample of marketing and advertising materials

Pre-Instructional

Each student is to research, collect, and bring to class several examples of effective marketing brochures and advertisements.

Introductory Framework

The Voyager Company will run for this entire session. Students are in charge of the entire company and its various functions. The company must realign itself with the goals of this year. A specific format and plan is to be developed with marketing strategies and brochures.

ASSIGNMENT

1. Division leaders assign tasks.

Unit 7A

Intercultural Communication Skills

LESSON TOPIC: DIVERSE CULTURES AND WORKPLACE ISSUES

Teaching Note

Intercultural communication skills within a multicultural world are necessary for success in students' professional and personal lives. Students have learned throughout these two years that they need to engage with people locally and globally, crossing boundaries for the purposes of creating a social world that supports everyone. A primary goal of Voyager is to help students develop an understanding of cultural customs, practices, beliefs, and styles different from their own. This can be accomplished by:

1. Learning to work with people from different backgrounds whether in a diverse workplace or in jobs that require travel
2. Communicating with international contacts
3. Learning with class members from diverse and co-cultures
4. Interacting with colleagues and clients who are differently abled

Living, working, and effectively communicating daily allows students to form new habits. In their own words, "we had to engage—otherwise we would not survive." The students did not accept a facile decision of "since we co-exist, and must find ways to get along, I will tolerate you." It was important for them to choose an ethical posture of mutual respect and a racial and cultural solidarity. What does engagement look like in this context? How are the tensions, frustrations, and fears addressed in class—these are important questions without any simple solutions. There are bursts of success during these times that then lead us to other bursts of success—and soon there is an engaged community of learners. Sometimes there are bursts of resistance, with students digging their heels in deep and not wanting to make any shifts. Other times, there are individuals who want to speak for the group, but the group does not want them to speak for the whole. There are those who want to make peace at any cost and those who need to get angry. Each attitude appears during the various developmental stages of the group. All phases are necessary for Voyagers' successful development. We find that none of them could be skipped along the way. We also learned to ask: What happens when students and teachers attempt to engage with issues of power, culture, and difference or what happens when students and teachers don't attempt to engage in these questions? These are significant questions to ask throughout the program and arenas that need to be grappled with in order to secure a strong foundation of trust and bring these kinds of interactions into daily life.

Objective

To identify diversity issues in society and workplaces in order to develop effective communication strategies

Domains

Cognitive: Analyze the challenges of living in an intercultural world
Affective: Value differences in culture and communication styles
Skills: Listen and communicate effectively

Academic Standard: Write and Speak in the English Language

Interpersonal Communication Skills
Effective speaking and listening skills

Materials

Handbook on intercultural communication
Overheads
Videos on diversity issues in the workplace

Pre-Instructional

Bring in examples of conversations involving intercultural communication from work. Students were asked to observe conversations among various people at work and then write down a brief description of what they heard/saw and draw some conclusions as to what was actually going on. The conversations could be among any number of people, in various positions/jobs, both in formal and informal settings.

Introductory Framework

The twenty-first century clearly speaks to change in society, education, and the workplace. The need to recognize change and the markers for change are upon us. Learning to be an effective communicator in an intercultural society poses many challenges. As leaders and workers, we must look at the needs of our workforce both domestically and internationally. It is time for us to realize the profound changes in our society—how can we accommodate these changes and how can we still all stay connected to valued cultural roots? Additionally, how can we connect ideas of principled behavior and effectiveness—what do we mean by ethical communication?

Motivation

"Immigration is the acid test for a society's character; people do not immigrate to lands where they are less free, less able to realize their dreams. By this measure, modern America is a startling success. The success has come at a price. America is a more messy Babel of a place than it was in the 1950s. My children have friends whose parents were born in India, Turkey, Thailand, Guatemala, Ireland, France and many other countries. This delights me. In the next century, everywhere is going to be multiethnic and America has gone there first. My kids are learning what it means to grow up in an ethnic mosaic with shared values" (Elliot, July 10, 1995, p. 30).

"The United States was built by adventurous immigrants from all over the world who forged a remarkable new society. Rather than seeing more immigrants as a liability and a threat, they are people of value, some stepping in the footprints of those who preceded them. We need new, imaginative and forward thinking that finds innovative and creative solutions to modern, global problems" (Alcock, August 13, 2000).

What are these writers saying? What resonates for you in these quotes? What impact do their words have on all of us? What are some of the disagreements regarding this current issue? What are the challenges and opportunities for you in a multicultural world? What are the challenges for you to live in a multicultural world?

INSTRUCTIONAL IMPLEMENTATION

Group Activity: Being American

The United States is a multifaceted and complex society. Over the years, the profile of what it means to be "American" has changed to include the many ethnic and racial components of who we are. Learning to live and work with each other becomes a formidable task for everyone. If we look at various school districts around the nation, we observe many changes in the cultures of our students—even in states and cities that we did not think would change. How is the face of the new Minnesotan, New Yorker, Californian, Nebraskan, Georgian continuously changing? All over we see veiled women draped in long skirts on their way to work or taking their children to school, young Latino/Chicano men playing ball, a Russian couple strolling around the lakes, and a Hmong family buying groceries. These are small examples of the second wave of immigrants and refugees whose populations have increased all over the United States. These newest immigrants have come for opportunity and refuge and are experiencing many stress factors as they go through their readjustment period. They also bring the ethics of work and cultural richness with them. Many of our cities, large and small, across the nation are experiencing change because of their influence and entrepreneurship. They are certainly part of the workforce helping bridge labor shortages and support expansion of the economy. Read the following Garrison Keillor essay out loud:

> Heroes, all of them—at least they're my heroes, especially the new immigrants, especially the refugees. Everyone makes fun of New York cabdrivers who can't speak English: they're heroes. To give up your country is the hardest thing a person can do; to leave the old familiar place and ship out over the edge of the world to America and learn everything over again different than you learned as a child, learn the new language that will never be so smart or funny as in your own true language. It takes years to start to feel semi-normal. And yet people still come—from Russia, Vietnam and Cambodia and Laos, Ethiopia, Iran, Haiti, Korea, Cuba, Chile, and they come on behalf of their children, and they come for freedom. Not for our land (Russia is beautiful), not for our culture (they have their own, thank you), not for our system of government (they do not even know about it, may not even agree with it), but for freedom. They are heroes who make an adventure on our behalf, showing by their struggle how precious beyond words freedom is, and if we knew their stories, we could not keep back the tears. (Keillor, July 4, 1988)

What do you think about when you hear his words? How many of you have made time to listen to the stories of new immigrants? Why/why not? How do you think they would feel if all of us made different gestures and offers to know more about them? Students are invited to talk about their immigration and/or relocation experiences.

Large Group Activity: Diversity in Action and in Conflict

With all of the changes going on in our cities and communities, conflict and misunderstandings will result. Let's look at some of the diversity issues in society and in the workplace. Here are some areas of current thinking that cause conflict:

- Incorrect information about other cultures that leads to false assumptions
- Expectations that others will conform to American standards
- Different assumptions about what American standards are
- Biases against the unfamiliar and the changing habits, customs, and traditions
- Undeveloped understanding of intercultural competence
- Collision of cultures and values

What other areas would you add to this list? Discuss each and give examples as to how these issues play out in the world already and in your lives. What are the basic, and unique, features of communication? Show the overhead with model of communication identities. How does culture frame communication patterns? How are cultures reflected in communication patterns?

Model of Communication Identities

Sender	Message ———————▶ Information that has been encoded	Receiver

Encode   Decode

Attitudes   Attitudes
Knowledge   Knowledge
Perceptions   Perceptions
Experiences   Experiences
Skills   Skills
Style   Style
Culture   Culture
Age   Age
Geographic region   Geographic region
Gender   Gender
Religion   Religion
Class   Class

Feedback

Small Group Activity: Influences in Your Life

Discuss the answers to the following questions. Make sure your answers include the following: peers, family, politics, community, country of origin, physical environment, religion, and media.

1. What influences caused you to think about yourselves and your environment in certain ways?
2. Who are the people who influenced you and how did they influence you both positively and negatively?

After discussing these questions in your groups, be prepared to discuss responses with the entire class.

Large Group Activity

How are population, racial, ethnic, and gender changes influencing the workplace? Table 4.1 shows some statistical changes that are taking place. This table shows for the United States the difference between the population by race in 1990 and the population by race in 2000. Because individuals could report only one race in 1990 and could report more than one race in 2000, and because of other changes in the census questionnaire, the race data for 1990 and 2000 are not directly comparable. Thus the difference in population by race between 1990 and 2000 is due both to these changes in the census questionnaire and to real change in the population.

The difference in population for a race between 1990 and 2000 using race alone in 2000 (column 5) and the difference in population between 1990 and 2000 using race alone or in combination in 2000 (column 7) provide a "minimum-maximum" range for the change in population of that race between 1990 and 2000.

There will be more and more people entering our country to work and to live. Is there an overriding culture in the United States of America? Is it demographically supported or is it financially supported? How do dollars equal power?

How might the diversity of the workplace change interactions at work? Show three segments from the video *Diverse Communications—Employee Workshop* and have the class analyze what is going on in each of these interactions. What knowledge and information do each of us need to gain in order to make communication more effective? What do we need to do to acquire this knowledge and information?

Large Group Activity: Stereotypes, Bias, and Prejudice

Discuss each of the following:

1. What are stereotypes and why do people hold them?
2. What is one stereotype you have or had?
3. Where do stereotypes come from and what are their effects?
4. Prejudice—what does this look like? Have you ever been on the receiving end of prejudice and bias—what did it feel like? What is the difference between prejudice and bias?
5. What new pathways can we create for intercultural learning and communication?
6. Why does it bother us when people are different? How do differences in body language, tone of voice, accent, facial expressions, hand gestures, and so on all contribute to our stereotyping, bias, and prejudice?
7. What do you know about your own comfort zone with differences? How can you begin to extend your comfort zone?

Optional Plans

1. Have students research companies across the nation and their policies for hiring individuals from diverse backgrounds; diversity is used here to go beyond race, class, and gender and to include age, abilities, orientation, economics, and so on.
2. Have students develop a set of interview questions for local businesses and set up times to meet or email executives to gather information about their practices.
3. Research multinational businesses to see what is necessary to work in such companies; look at various sites on the web, such as the following, for additional information: http://www.businessweek.com/careers/content/oct2000/ca20001025_485.htm. (Accessed June 2003.)
4. Have students compare and contrast the policies and practices in hiring for diversity of local, national, and multinational businesses. What differences exist and why?
5. What are the resources available to provide training for the development of cultural competence in workplaces? Have students develop a resource list for such available trainings.
6. Reflect and write about the following: Think about a time or situation when you were stereotyped. What factors contributed to that stereotype? How did it make you feel? How did it affect the outcome of the situation you were involved in when the stereotyping took place? Now think of a

Table 4.1. Difference in Population by Race and Hispanic or Latino Origin, for the United States: 1990 to 2000

	1990 Census		Census 2000		Difference between 1990 and 2000			
					Using race alone for Census 2000		Using race alone or in combination for Census 2000	
Subject	Number	Percent of total population	Race alone¹	Race alone or in combination	Numerical difference (2000 minus 1990)	Percent difference (based on 1990)	Numerical difference (2000 minus 1990)	Percent difference (based on 1990)
	(1)	(2)	(3)	(4)	(5)	(6)	(7)	(8)
RACE								
Total population	248,709,873	100.0	281,421,906	281,421,906	32,712,033	13.2	32,712,033	13.2
White	199,686,070	80.3	211,460,626	216,930,975	11,774,556	5.9	17,244,905	8.6
Black or African American	29,986,060	12.1	34,658,190	36,419,434	4,672,130	15.6	6,433,374	21.5
American Indian and Alaska Native	1,959,234	0.8	2,475,956	4,119,301	516,722	26.4	2,160,067	110.3
Asian	6,908,638	2.8	10,242,998	11,898,828	3,334,360	48.3	4,990,190	72.2
Native Hawaiian and Other Pacific Islander	365,024	0.1	398,835	874,414	33,811	9.3	509,390	139.5
Some other race	9,804,847	3.9	15,359,073	18,521,486	5,554,226	56.6	8,716,639	88.9

HISPANIC OR LATINO AND RACE

Total population	248,709,873	100.0	281,421,906	281,421,906	32,712,033	13.2	32,712,033	13.2
Hispanic or Latino (of any race)	22,354,059	9.0	35,305,818	35,305,818	12,951,759	57.9	12,951,759	57.9
Not Hispanic or Latino[3]	226,355,814	91.0	246,116,088	246,116,088	19,760,274	8.7	19,760,274	8.7
White	188,128,296	75.6	198,177,900	194,552,774	6,424,478	3.4	10,049,604	5.3
Black or African American	29,216,293	11.7	35,383,751	33,947,837	4,731,544	16.2	6,167,458	21.1
American Indian and Alaska Native	1,793,773	0.7	3,444,700	2,068,883	275,110	15.3	1,650,927	92.0
Asian	6,642,481	2.7	11,579,494	10,123,169	3,480,688	52.4	4,937,013	74.3
Native Hawaiian and Other Pacific Islander	325,878	0.1	748,149	353,509	27,631	8.5	422,271	129.6
Some other race	249,093	0.1	1,770,645	467,770	218,677	87.8	1,521,552	610.8

Source: U.S. Census Bureau. Internet Release date: April 2, 2001.
NOTE: Data not adjusted based on the Accuracy and Coverage Evaluation. For information on confidentiality protection, sampling error, nonsampling error, and definitions, see http://factfinder.census.gov/home/en/datanotes/expplu.html.
—Represents zero or rounds to 0.0.
Numbers for the six race groups may add to more than the total population, and the percentages may add to more than 100 percent because individuals may indicate more than one race.
The differences between 1990 and 2000 for the total population, the Hispanic or Latino population, and the Not Hispanic or Latino population are not affected by whether data on race are for race alone or for race alone or in combination. The Hispanic or Latino population may be of any race.

time when you stereotyped someone else. What factors contributed to that stereotype? How did it make you feel? What would you do differently?

CONCLUSION

What are the challenges to intercultural communication? What steps are you willing to take at this time?

ASSIGNMENT

Write up any interesting interaction you have or observe during the next couple of weeks and bring it to the next class. Some examples would be people from different cultures helping each other, disagreements due to cultural misunderstandings, biases during any interactions, and the like. Be ready to present the situation and your thoughts about it. Go back to our discussion regarding attitudes and behaviors that block or promote intercultural relations and apply these to your interaction.

Unit 7B

Intercultural Communication Skills

LESSON TOPIC: THEATRE OF THE OPPRESSED AND OTHER STRATEGIES FOR CHANGE

Teaching Note

Directly engaging and confronting classroom and workplace discrimination issues requires courage and trust. Students are filled with stories regarding their firsthand experiences with prejudice—racial, ethnic, gender, physical. The videos on intercultural communication in the workplace are helpful in demonstrating the challenges in working with diverse cultures. The collision of cultures is clearly identified as the conflicts that result from misunderstandings and lack of knowledge. Many times the students laughed out loud as they observed interactions between two people. When asked why they responded this way to the video, they stated that the behaviors were so bizarre (e.g., when working with a receptionist who was American Indian, the other person started speaking louder and slower, using hand signals), it was hard for them to believe people still acted in this manner. As the counterpart to this activity, students are introduced to the work of Augusto Boal, where they create their own scenarios shedding light on the inequities of certain behaviors and language use.

Objective

To develop strategies in order to deal directly with diversity issues and disagreements

Domains

Cognitive: Analyze the challenges of living and working in an intercultural world

Affective: Value differences in communication and work styles
Skills: Listen and communicate effectively

Academic Standard: Write and Speak in the English Language

Interpersonal Communication Skills
Effective speaking and listening skills

Materials

Nine Trends Revolutionizing the American Workforce handout (fig. 4.37)
Definitions handout (fig. 4.38)
Action Plan Sheets in handbook
Case studies for discussion (fig. 4.39)
Personal Influences Sheet (fig. 4.40)

Pre-Instructional

Students need to bring a written description of an observed conversation. Students have been asked to observe a conversation among people—at work, in a restaurant, at school, in a community meeting, and so on. They are to observe how the people interact—if possible, to write out and describe the scenario as close to the real situation as it happened. They are then to analyze what was going on in the conversation and then make suggestions as to how this conversation/situation could have been handled differently.

Introductory Framework

During last week's lesson we observed ways in which we interact with each other. These observations illuminated workplace issues, as outlined in the Nine Trends Revolutionizing the American Workforce handout (fig. 4.37),

Figure 4.37.   Nine Trends Revolutionizing the American Workforce

1. Worker numbers are falling.
2. Average age of workers is rising.
3. More women are visible on the job.
4. The culturally diverse make up 1/3 of new workers.
5. More newcomers from all over the world are in the workforce.
6. Workforce and companies are in action 24/7.
7. Service and information jobs are increasing.
8. Higher skill levels are required.
9. Technology increases the volume of work accomplished and requires different levels of workers' adeptness.

Figure 4.38. Working Definitions

Stereotype. A belief or fixed idea about a person or group that is held and sustained by generalizations that make assertions about all people in a category. Stereotypes come from incomplete, distorted information and limited personal experience or outside sources such as others' interpretations of cultural behavior. Stereotypes are destructive because they are unfair, do not allow for individuality, ignore differences, and interfere with communication.

Prejudice. A preconceived idea or negative attitude, formed before the facts are known and sustained by overgeneralizations. A bias without reason, resisting all evidence. Prejudice implies inferiority, leads to suspicion, and is detrimental to communication and interpersonal relations.

Bias. A mental leaning or bent that supports stereotyping and prejudice.

that need to be examined and handled in ways that take cultural differences into consideration.

Motivation

Your assignment was to observe, describe, and present your thoughts about one episode between any two or more people that showed miscommunication, cultural conflicts, stereotyping, or prejudices. What did you hear and see? What were your responses? Student leaders will list all the ideas on the board.

INSTRUCTIONAL IMPLEMENTATION

Large Group Activity: *Diversity in the Workplace* Video

Revisit the *Diversity in the Workplace* video, which focuses on employer and employee relationships and inequities in the workplace. From what we studied last time, what ideas and practices are being demonstrated through these episodes? How would you respond differently in these situations? What stereotypes, biases, or prejudices (see fig. 4.38 for definitions of these words) did you see evidenced?

Small Group Activity: Case Studies for Discussion (Fig. 4.39; Adapted from Hart, 1994)

Read through Case Studies 1–7. What is going on and what would you do? Each small group will have ten minutes to read and discuss a case study. Each group will choose a recorder and a speaker to report on their discussion and observations to the entire class.

Figure 4.39. Case Studies for Discussion (Adapted from Hart, 1994)

Case 1: Cultural Joke
In one of your weekly meetings there's usually a general feeling of camaraderie, with many jokes and laughter going on all before the manager comes in. It becomes clear to you that a cultural joke has just been told by one of your colleagues and as you look up, you see the face of the person whose group has been discredited and slandered. You immediately see how she's been hurt. There is an awkward silence for a moment and then general sports banter takes over and the subject is changed.

1. What should you do?
2. How do you feel and how should you handle the situation?

Case 2: A New Colleague
Your team is told that new colleagues are coming on board and that each of you is getting a new officemate. You are all given their names and backgrounds. Howard, a white coworker, is informed that his new officemate is a black man from Georgia. Before Howard has ever met his new officemate, he's heard grumbling and groaning about all the trouble he's going to have and how he doesn't have time to offer the new man all the help he knows he will need. You are standing nearby when he describes his feelings.

1. Why was the white employee so concerned?
2. What was going on here?
3. What could you do to help the situation?

Case 3: English or Nothing
You are eating in the employee cafeteria and talking passionately about your oldest daughter's letter of acceptance to a good college with a coworker. All of a sudden, a small group of workers walks in, speaking a language you do not understand. You look around and, sure enough, within earshot you realize there is another group of coworkers already seated and speaking yet another different language. You become anxious and storm out of the cafeteria.

1. How do you feel?
2. How should you handle the situation?
3. Would your action be different if you had overheard your name in the middle of one of the conversations?

Case 4: Hiding or Embarrassed?
Carole Anderson, the supervisor, calls in Vou, the Laotian employee, for a semiannual evaluation. After the supervisor offers some positive aspects of the evaluation, she begins to discuss areas for improvement. Because the Laotian employee looks down at the floor during the entire feedback session, the supervisor concludes that the employee is hiding something and feels she needs to address this issue. When the supervisor tries to draw it out of him, the employee begins to giggle.

1. How might this behavior be explained?
2. What do you think is taking place?
3. How should you address this situation? What procedure should you set up?

(continued)

Case 5: Getting Things Done

Sally, an American-born manager, is extremely pleased with the work done by one of her employees, Tuey. She has repeatedly shown her desire to get things done and willingness to do them well. Tuey is from Cambodia and has been in the United States about seven years. Because there is some physical labor involved in Tuey's job (moving packages of new products), Sally decides to help out the employee. Together they work to get all of the packages moved and finish the job. The manager feels good about the situation, yet when Tuey goes home that night she feels bad about how things went with her manager and tells her family.

1. What happened here?
2. What should be done?

Case 6: The "Those People" Comment

You have just overheard one of your coworkers say to another, "I'm sick and tired of dealing with those people; with some of them, you can't understand a word they say, and I'm not even sure you can trust them. Why don't they go back where they came from? I'm ready to transfer out of this department."

1. What is the significance of these comments?
2. What is really going on here and is there anything you should do?
3. How would you handle the situation?

Case 7: Nobody Listens to Me

Harry is a successful marketing manager with a reputation for being hard working, ethical, and fair. In his regular Monday morning buyers' meeting, the participants are Harry, Charlie, Jim, Ben, and Christene. Ben gets along with all of the participants.

After the latest meeting, Ben is surprised when Christene approaches him almost in tears and complains, "Ben, first thing in today's meeting, I suggested we consolidate the commodity purchasing into one section. Before I was halfway through, you cut in to let Jim speak. By the end of the meeting, you agreed with my idea, but gave Jim all the credit." Christene has thought to herself, "Nobody listens to me; is there something wrong with me?"

Ben doesn't know what to think, and besides, he can't even remember Christene bringing up the idea in the first place. "Is something wrong with Christene today?" he wonders. "Why is she making a federal case out of this?" He makes a joke to minimize the situation.

1. What's happening here?
2. If you were Ben, would you have been able to understand what was going on and avoid it?
3. If you put yourself in Christene's shoes, how would you handle the situation?

Large Group Activity

What are communication breakdowns and how do they originate? Introduce strategies that may help resolve communication breakdowns across cultures—stress that these ideas should be used as a beginning guide and that all participants are encouraged to develop their own personal style. Here are some possible strategies:

1. Define clearly what behavior is being demonstrated and therefore under discussion. Be as specific as possible.
2. State your feelings clearly about the situation. ("I am confused." "I am upset." "I am frustrated.") Always start with "I."
3. What new behavior do you prefer? What alternative approaches are you proposing? Give examples. Describe the new outcome and expected results from this new behavior.

The following is a sample response: "Today, when I was giving my report to the Leadership Council, I observed you closed your eyes for a while and then when you opened them you started writing in your notebook. I did not know if my report was understandable to you—I understand if you are demonstrating your attention in a different way. I would appreciate any feedback you could give me. I really enjoy working with you." Analyze this response.

Each small group reporter will summarize their case study and the findings. The class will offer feedback to the group's findings and then will discuss alternative ways to handle the situation. How do we build new pathways that create intercultural learning and communication?

Small Group Activity: Personal Influences

Students should take a minute to read and discuss with one another responses to the questions in figure 4.40.

Students will develop a roadmap to cultural competence. Indicate the direction of your path and actions you will take to reach competence (for example, listening carefully, raising awareness, taking action, etc.). Additionally, consider

Figure 4.40. Personal Influences

Take a minute to reflect on some of the factors that influenced you when you were growing up, and then answer the questions below.

1. Where did you live, and how did that influence who you are now?
2. As a child, what adult had a major influence in your life?
3. What do you remember most about your favorite holiday and tradition?
4. What factors influenced the educational decisions in your life?
5. What was your first memory of an encounter with someone from another culture?

the significant people and events that have influenced your way of thinking. List them below and describe the positive and negative messages that you may have received from each:

1. Significant people involved
2. Significant events
3. Negative messages that I received
4. Positive messages that I received

Large Group Activity: Augusto Boal—Theatre of the Oppressed

What is theatre of the oppressed and who is Augusto Boal? Give a mini-introduction with connection to its purpose and rationale (see resource list for background information).

There are two options for this activity, both of which employ the performance methods of Augusto Boal. One is to have the students use the above case studies and role-play their interpretations. The second is to use the case studies as guides/models to write original scenarios that they would then perform for the rest of the class. The students can choose to act out incidents that they have encountered in their homes and community as well. As a result of the diverse backgrounds in Voyager, many of the students wrote scenarios describing how one or both of their parents were made fun of at work for their accents, ways in which bank representatives tried to trick them into signing certain contracts, hospital experiences that had conflict because the family was talked down to, school experiences where personnel would shout at families, authentic discussions regarding the experiences of being in two cultures at the same time, their experience of the dominant culture pressuring them to assimilate, and how many of them had parents who could not find work as professionals even though they were physicians or professors in their native country. The students get to write and act out the "right" and "wrong" way of handling behavior.

Following the methods of Augusto Boal's (1979) concept of the Theatre of the Oppressed, there are some exciting techniques that can be taught so that students write and act out their versions of social change scenarios.

Augusto Boal's (1979) groundbreaking work is a highly provocative and engaging way of prompting students to uncover and examine troubling assumptions and truths that they hold about the world. Boal (1992) has developed imaginative exercises and games to stimulate debate and encourage performers and audiences to explore untapped parts of themselves. The process begins when participants act out on stage an unresolved problem in their lives and the audience is invited to suggest and enact solutions. The problem involves a protagonist confronted by an oppressor. The initial scene or vignette (known as the model) is acted out; then it is repeated. During this second performance, any member of the audience can shout, "Stop!" and replace any of the characters at any time, thereby changing the outcomes of the scene. A "joker" presides over the action and ensures the process runs smoothly by teaching the audience the rules of intervention. The rules can change, however, as different spectators intervene, and the scene can be done an unlimited number of times. The result of these exercises is a pooling of knowledge held by the participating spectators as they go up on stage to change the dialogue and alter the outcome.

This activity stimulates debate, shows alternatives, and illuminates our habits of mind, rituals, and everyday assumptions. Through this theatrical process, people participate in observing and changing entrenched rituals and ways of interacting. It is great fun to watch normally shy individuals jump up enthusiastically and stop the action in order to effect change and find alternatives. The laughter of recognition is often heard as the familiar patterns, phrases, and intonations of interaction are portrayed and as participants search for possible alternatives.

Optional Plans

1. Students will videotape a series of speeches given by a variety of people on television. The subject matter of these speeches is not important nor is the type of television show they are taken from. Without any volume on, observe and note the speaker's effects of dress, behavior, posture, body language, facial expressions, eye contact, hand use, stance, and so on. Discuss what these components of a communication delivery suggest about the speaker's competence, status, engagement, sincerity, and enthusiasm.

2. Students will tape a series of situational comedies from television that include a range of cultural families and organizations. What are some of the components of communication that are different even when the subject matter is the same? How does the difference in communication influence communication strategies? How do the differences influence how you relate to each of the families or people? What are some of your challenges?

3. Students will watch a television show or film in a different language. They need to record what factors and clues helped them to understand what was going on. List any other observations made during this activity.

4. In small groups, watch some intercultural films. Some examples are *The Circle* (Iranian), *Cry the Beloved Country* (South African), *Kundun*

(Tibetan), and *A Walk in the Clouds* (Latino). Have students record their responses to the characters, portrayals, and cultural settings of each film. What stereotypes were "busted open" for them? What new information did they learn?

5. Have students research online resources such as Web of Culture at http://www.worldculture.com, and The World Factbook athttp://www. odci.gov/cis/publications/factbook/index.html.

Performance-Based Assessments

- Case study examinations and feedback
- Boal Performance of case studies or scenarios

CONCLUSION

What are the challenges to intercultural communication? What are some ways we can engage in mutual respect and trust in this class? How can we create our own pathways to intercultural communication?

ASSIGNMENT

1. Using the Action Plan in your handbook (fig. 4.41), set up an action plan for future interactions and situations such as the ones we have discussed. Begin to write your own action plan for intercultural communication.

Figure 4.41. Action Plan

Based on the intercultural skills covered in this workshop, what can I now do differently?

Issue/Concern:
Objective:
Action Steps:
Time Frame:
Measure(s):

To address this issue/concern, what objective will I set?
To achieve this objective, what action steps and time frame will I take?
What measure(s) will I use to monitor my progress?

Unit 8A

Leadership and Ethics

LESSON TOPIC: WHAT IS EFFECTIVE LEADERSHIP?

Teaching Note

There is a myriad of research on the concept of leadership. Certainly there are challenges facing people who are in positions of leadership and power today. There are also multiple ways of looking at and understanding leadership today, whether from a positional or nonpositional perspective. The goal of this unit is to examine traditional concepts of leadership, power, and change. Students are asked to identify attributes of effective leadership, examine how models of leadership have become associated with specific attributes (assertiveness, independence, competitiveness), critically examine accepted business practices, and redefine leadership in terms of ethical, political, and social activity. The challenge is also to examine nontraditional concepts of leadership and how leadership has been transformed from a one-dimensional style of leadership—the effect of a multinational and global society and its needs for leadership. Going beyond traditional notions of leadership can be a challenging concept. For many, the concept of leadership is one of a powerful person who tells people what to do. Yet as the discussions continue, all of the students are quite enthusiastic to engage in brainstorming models of leadership that go beyond the traditional to identify notions of leadership and multiple models of leadership. They began to see others in their lives who they referred to as leaders and many were excited to see that in developing new models, they too could be included in ideas of leadership. Leadership soon became the idea that leading means going beyond what is. They began looking at the idea of power as power with others rather than power over others and at leadership that includes diverse backgrounds and genders. There are lots of good debates surrounding this concept and what becomes important is to discover that the leaders they have observed may be ineffective because of the new demands of the workplace, work, and the emerging workforce.

Objective

To analyze and describe the attributes of effective leadership

Domains

Cognitive: Learn to develop leadership skills
Affective: Work in teams to meet goals
Skills: Develop brainstorming skills

Academic Standard: Decision Making

Career Investigation
Identify leadership skills
Develop and understand business ethics

Materials

Perspectives on Leadership handout (fig. 4.42)
Leadership ideas and pictures/overheads
Small group handouts
Traditional headers and attributes handout (fig. 4.43)

Figure 4.42. Perspectives on Leadership

Gender
Age
Degree/education
Occupation

1. What does power mean to you?
2. What does the concept of leadership mean to you?
3. How are you similar to and/or different from your male/female colleagues in their leadership styles?
4. What do you most like about your position?
5. What do you like least about your position?
6. What aspects of your position do you find most stressful? How do you cope with these stresses?
7. Are the secrets to leadership different for women and men? How?
8. What role models in leadership most influenced you and your vision of leadership?

Pre-Instructional

Students are to write out any questions they have about leadership. Students also write what they see as successful leadership characteristics and styles, describe situations that they feel demonstrate leadership, and ways in which they see themselves as leaders in their journals. Students are encouraged to watch the news or scan the newspaper for stories on leaders and to bring these in to class. Students are to have read "What Is a Leader?" (no. 90309) from the *Harvard Business Review*. Excerpts from other books or articles are fine as the idea is to get students to read about leadership from a variety of perspectives.

Introductory Framework

Many times in today's world, leadership is an elusive, unknown, and intangible concept. Yet when we speak to CEOs and upper-level managers, we often hear of their dire need to develop effective leaders. What are the characteristics and competencies of effective leaders for the twenty-first century? How can we become effective leaders in both our personal and professional lives?

Motivation

Most of us have our own ideas of and experiences with the concept of leadership. Let's take the time to write out our answers to the following questions on the sheet Perspectives on Leadership (fig. 4.42) What does the word *perspective* mean? List responses on the board. Everyone may have his or her view/ideas of what leadership means. Today we will look closely at our personal views, discuss and compare them with other views in class, and then decide what new information we have learned that has changed our views.

INSTRUCTIONAL IMPLEMENTATION

Large Group Activity: So These Are World Leaders (Fig. 4.43)

Brainstorm about leaders and characteristics of leadership. Look at the photo of World War Two leaders Churchill, Roosevelt, and Stalin. Why were these men considered leaders? Look at the photo of Mt. Rushmore. Who are the men depicted here (Washington, Jefferson, Lincoln, and Teddy Roosevelt)? What qualities do they represent for people? What is meant by traditional leaders? If the class is not familiar with the above men, give some background information and explain or have students research online why they have been considered world leaders. In contrast look at other historical leaders (e.g., Imelda Marcos, Cleopatra, Margaret Thatcher, Golda Meir, Dalai Lama, Mahatma Gandhi, Anwar Sadat, Lao-tzu, Mao Tse-tung, Aung San

Figure 4.43. Traditional Leaders and Attributes

1. Traditional leaders and their qualities:

   - white, male
   - logical, rational, unemotional
   - strong and charismatic
   - strategic, good decision maker
   - competitive, in control, and powerful

2. Write out your response to these traditional attributes.
3. How would you change "tradition"? List all the qualities you can that are important for today's leaders.

Suu Kyi, etc.). What qualities do they have that are different from or similar to the above group of leaders?

What do you think about these qualities? Are there other qualities that you think are important for leaders to have? Let's divide up and brainstorm in our groups. Place all answers from each of the groups on the board for later reference.

Small Group Activity: Best and Not-Best Leaders You Know

Divide class into base groups. Have students make a list of the Best and Not-Best Leaders. Give the groups twenty minutes to choose people they consider to be best and worst leaders and to decide what characteristics those people demonstrate. Each group must come to consensus and list their top five and bottom five leaders with characteristics and present the list to the rest of the class.

Small Group Activity: Ethics and Leadership

What are ethics? Define in your own words and give examples. How are ethics involved with effective leadership? How are values and beliefs related to effective leadership? Do you think ethics and leadership must go together? Why? Does the end justify the means? List student answers on the board or flipchart for the entire class to see.

Large Group Activity: Leadership in the Twenty-first Century

What does leadership need to look like in the twenty-first century? How are organizations being impacted and how will this influence effective leadership strategies? Why do so many corporate leaders state that new times demand new kinds of leaders?

What do the following terms signify and how do they impact the work-place of the twenty-first century?

1. Global marketplace and political turmoil
2. Economic instability
3. Emerging nations
4. Natural disasters
5. Worldwide technological innovations
6. Global village accountability and leadership
7. Changing workforce
8. Multinational companies, organizations, and business treaties
9. Technology

Leadership will be impacted by a variety of important issues that will require effective leaders to look at their positions and their companies differently. They will need to be leaders who lead "for the future." What are some of the characteristics new leaders will need to possess and to develop?

Looking at companies differently is also the beginning of another one of our topics connected to leadership—the changing structure and culture of organizations. All of these concepts are interconnected and need to be ad-dressed in relation to one another. We will continue to investigate these ideas at a later time.

Large Group Activity: Panel—"Radical Transformation of the World of Work"

What do we mean by the radical transformation of the world of work? This is a good time to link the perspectives of leadership and the rapidly chang-ing world of work with local community and business leaders. Have students and guest speakers address how work and the workplace are being trans-formed. How do new words/phrases such as "manage continuous white-water change," "high-performance work organizations," "responsibility for key business processes from beginning to end," "noncore work will be out-sourced," "cluster organizations or ad-hoc-racies," and "develop core com-petencies" describe the work and structures of the future? What new roles and expectations do you think there will be for workers? Ask each represen-tative to present what is radical transformation in her or his workplace.

Optional Plans

1. Students will begin writing responses to the leadership questions that they brought with them.
2. Students will have peers at work fill out Other Perspectives on Leader-ship survey (fig. 4.42) and bring data to class for synthesis and analysis.

Figure 4.44. Other Perspectives on Leadership

Gender
Age
Degree/education
Occupation

What are the top five traits of leadership that you admire in leaders you work with?
What are the top five traits of the worst leadership you and others have experienced?
What is an effective leader?
How do you connect power and leadership?
Describe one incident in your workplace which demonstrated effective leadership.
Who were your childhood models for leadership?
Relate a time in your life when you were very effective leading others.
What skills, behaviors, and traits does a leader for the twenty-first century in a global society need to have?

3. Students will interview their work peers on who they feel have been the best or not-best leaders they have known and what impact that has had on companies they have worked in. Your group is to list the top four people they agree upon as being the best leaders they have known. Next to each name/person, list the qualities that you feel this person models. Then make a list of people you feel exhibited the worst kind of leadership you have known. Leaders do not need to be famous—they can be community leaders or local businesspeople.

4. Bring in a team of community leaders to talk about leadership and the need for transformative leadership in community projects.

5. Have students research generational differences and discuss how innovative leaders need to see these differences as critical factors for motivating workers (i.e., generation X born between 1964 and 1975, baby boomers born between 1946 and 1963, and traditionalists born between 1925 and 1945).

6. What is an information technology leader? Invite Internet/intranet managers, web masters, vice presidents or chief information officers, and other corporate communication managers to discuss the explosion of knowledge leaders and work in organizations.

7. Research what are other new types of work and work titles in organizations today that are needed and will be pivotal in steering organizations through global work and workforce changes.

8. Research and present the profile of the workplace or workscape of the future. You may want to bring in guest speakers or interview them via telephone. A range of workplaces need to be included: factory, corporate, cooperatives, manufacturing, and so on.

9. What is the virtual workplace and how/why is that connected to new leadership?
10. Interview leaders of various companies and ask them for advice for future twenty-first-century leaders.
11. Consider leadership as both a positional and nonpositional concept. How can people be leaders who are not in a traditional position? Who are the leaders at school? How do the students see themselves as leaders and what skills do they want to develop as leaders? What are the benefits and disadvantages of each type?
12. Have students research and present the impact and influence of women and people of different cultures attaining leadership roles.

Performance-Based Assessments

- Response and appropriate feedback activities in large and small groups
- Leadership debates: the best and worst leaders you know and why you think they are the best and worst

CONCLUSION

Recap major points on leadership:

1. Traditional and emerging concepts of leadership
2. Leadership for the twenty-first century
3. Models of leadership
4. Changing organizations and cultures

ASSIGNMENT

1. Write in your journal a response to each of the following questions: How have my views changed about leadership after today's discussions? How will I apply what I learned today about leadership to my own life? What kind of leader might I be and why? Be specific and write clearly what you will do.

Unit 8B

Leadership and Ethics

LESSON TOPIC: HOW ARE LEADERSHIP AND CHILDHOOD ROLE MODELS CONNECTED?

Teaching Note

In the last three decades, research regarding leaders has produced an impressive body of new knowledge and has contributed to new conceptions of leadership, leadership styles, the nature of collective leadership, and the need to redefine leadership beyond positions held by both men and women. A new vision of leadership immersed in a profound sense of social justice informs us that we can choose to make our institutions more democratic. Examining leadership in terms of vision, personal commitment, and empowerment, and acknowledging that leadership involves a diversity of effective styles, strategies, risks, and initiatives begins to write a new narrative about this concept. Good leadership is not reduced to just "good tips for leaders." Research has also demonstrated that it is important for students to connect their leadership abilities with past experiences in their lives. How have they demonstrated leadership abilities from a very young age? It is also important for students to acknowledge and connect how their cultural backgrounds affect their leadership style. The students begin to discard familiar notions of leadership as they connect leaders with changes in world organizations and in the workforce. One of the students commented after interviewing some local business leaders, "There really is no time to waste if you want to be a leader. There is so much to do. I am impressed as to how busy they are all of the time."

Objective

To connect leadership and mentoring through childhood and adolescent role
   models

Domains

Cognitive: Learn to understand childhood influences on concepts of leadership
Affective: Work in partnership with a classmate
Skills: Communicate ideas and develop a position about a role model

Academic Standard: Decision Making

Career Investigation
Identify leadership skills
Develop and understand business ethics

Materials

Flipcharts
Markers

Pre-Instructional

Refer to last session's homework assignment (journaling on leadership).

Introductory Framework

We come to conclusions regarding certain ideas and concepts of leadership
as a result of our past experiences. After the last lesson, were there any ideas
that changed for you? Read over your journal entry and share what ideas
changed for you. List student ideas on the board or flipchart and refer back
to the list at a later time.

Motivation

Many successful leaders had role models that they emulated from their childhood or their adolescence. These role models influenced them in many
ways—both positively and negatively—especially in the future attitudes, beliefs, values, and behaviors they subsequently adopted and used. The seminar coordinator may give her or his role models.

INSTRUCTIONAL IMPLEMENTATION

Partner Activity: Role Models in Childhood

Place chairs in pairs facing one another. Each person is to identify for his or
her partner role models he or she had a child. Students will have five min-

utes to tell their partner everything they can about any adults in their childhood and how they modeled leadership for them. Keep in mind that role models may be parents, relatives, friends, schoolteachers, religious people, or neighbors.

Poll the group for a sample of ideas learned from this first set of people. Create a chart of role models with their attributes.

Small Group Activity: Heroes and Heroines

Have each pair join another pair and arrange seats to face each other. Each group member is to reflect upon the heroines and heroes they had in their childhood and to share their recollections. Heroes and heroines can be actual people or fictional characters. Students need to focus on why they admired these people and what they learned from them. Each group will have fifteen minutes to do this. What attributes from these heroes/heroines would you like to develop?

Large Group Activity: A Spectrum of Heroes and Role Models

Poll the small groups for ideas learned from childhood. Groups can place their ideas on separate flipcharts. After all groups have reported, discuss the following as a large group:

- Did any men have female heroes?
- Did any women have male heroes?
- Did anyone have heroes from cultures other than their own?
- What are superheroes and why do we create them?

Have the group summarize their findings and draw some conclusions.

For many women and people of color, there is a barrier to leadership because of the fixed beliefs of who leaders are. We will look at this barrier in subsequent discussions on leadership.

Small Group Activity: A Person I Would Like to Know

In your small groups, first write down the answers to the following questions and then share them with your group: Who are the people you admire most now? Who would you like to meet because you admire them? How have you changed your ideas about adults and heroines/heroes as a result of our class discussions? Compare your responses with earlier responses to questions in the previous lesson. What has changed for you?

Create your dream dinner. Who would you invite? Your guests can be people from now or from history. Why would you invite them? What do they have to offer? What type of dinner conversation and topics would you like to have with them? What questions would you ask to provoke these conversations?

Optional Plans

1. Read an excerpt from a leader's biography. Describe what you learn and present your impressions of this leader. Please be sure to include the successes and failures.
2. Review biographies on television or on video. Bring snippets to class and analyze what makes the people being profiled leaders.
3. Write a biographical sketch of a leader you admire. Exchange your sketches within your small groups.
4. Poll coworkers and ask them to identify the differences between a manager and a leader. Look at John Kotter's book *A Force for Change* and compare his research findings with your interviews and analysis. Then each person in the group will self-assess what leadership characteristics he or she has.

Performance-Based Assessments

- Response and appropriate feedback activities in large and small groups
- Childhood role models

CONCLUSION

Summarize and poll major points made by groups regarding lessons on leadership.

ASSIGNMENT

1. Have students write responses to the following question: How have my values, beliefs, and behaviors been influenced by my role models, heroes, and heroines? Be specific after today's discussions.

Unit 8C

Leadership and Ethics

LESSON TOPIC: EXPLORE AND IDENTIFY OUR VALUES AND BELIEFS AND SEE HOW THEY ARE CONNECTED TO OUR LEADERSHIP QUALITIES

Teaching Note

Connecting leadership and ethics and illuminating the risks and problems in the workplace today that are placing extraordinary demands on corporate executives for ethical leadership is foremost for any discussion on leadership. In today's business environment with a focus on ethical beliefs and the implications for business leaders, it is important to look at both the need for and the breakdown of ethical discipline in business. Students are first asked to examine and unpack their own sense of moral development. What are the core beliefs that they have grown up with, how do they connect with them today, how do these beliefs translate into their personal, professional, and social lives? What becomes apparent in the class discussions is that not only are individual behavior and integrity matters of importance, but how does a leader also create and maintain a workplace environment that upholds ethics in its day-to-day operations? What are the required elements for an ethical climate to build and prosper within a participatory climate versus an authoritarian structure?

Objective

To connect concepts of leadership, values, and beliefs that support ethical conduct

Domains

Cognitive: Identify core beliefs and values
Affective: Develop listening skills
Skills: Connect values to effective leadership

Academic Standards: Decision Making

Career Investigation
Investigate career choices and matching personal goals and values

Materials

Flipcharts
Markers
Overheads
Handouts

Pre-Instructional

Assignment on how beliefs and values have been influenced and changed. Bring in reflection feedback sheet Core Values and Beliefs in Everyday Life (fig. 4.45).

Introductory Framework

Effective leaders clarify their values and beliefs very consciously. They spend time reflecting on which values and beliefs drive them. For the most

Figure 4.45.   Core Values and Beliefs in Everyday Life

Values are those beliefs we hold so strongly that they guide our words and behaviors, that we would fight for them, and that we are comfortable sharing with those around us. Researchers have found that we form our first core values at the ages of seven through ten. Our first core values are usually the values our parents, teachers, or other adults in our lives have passed on to us. We challenge these values as we grow through adolescence.

What is one value you hold for each of the following categories?

- Money
- Politics
- Friends
- Family
- Health
- Work
- Time
- Education

effective leaders, their behavior is consistent with their values and beliefs. Their followers describe them as reliable and predictable. Very clearly, they walk their talk.

Motivation

1. How would you explain the expression "walk the talk"? Research on leadership shows that effective leaders are clear about their beliefs and values and articulate them to their followers, colleagues, bosses, and customers. Brainstorm about what the word *belief* means to you. List all responses on the board or on a flipchart.
2. Write out this definition: A belief is anything you accept as the truth for you. Beliefs are those tenets, creeds, or doctrines that you have accepted as real and true for your life. Take out your journals and write down some of your core beliefs and connect them to your personal ethics.

INSTRUCTIONAL IMPLEMENTATION

Partner Activity: Core Beliefs

In pairs with chairs facing each other, everyone is asked to reflect upon his or her core beliefs with a partner. As one is discussing her or his core beliefs, the other is listening, taking notes, asking clarifying questions when necessary, and paraphrasing.

As you reflect, use the Belief Reflections Feedback Sheet (fig. 4.46) to respond to the following questions: What do I believe in strongly? When have I acted on my strong beliefs? Did my beliefs come into conflict with the beliefs of others in my life? Was this ever resolved? What did I do to resolve these conflicts? Are my public and private beliefs congruent?

Each of you should take about ten minutes to talk. (Notes are to be placed in the respective partners' portfolios for future reference.) Poll the large group for their beliefs. What are the similarities and discrepancies in the group? Are there any surprises?

Figure 4.46.   Belief Reflections Feedback Sheet

Areas to observe: Use of language, eye contact, body language, grammar, effective response to question(s), overall use of two-way communication skills.

1. What do I believe in strongly?
2. When have I acted on my strong beliefs?
3. Have my beliefs ever come into conflict with the beliefs of others in my life? Was this ever resolved? What did I do? Would I do something differently next time?
4. Do my beliefs and behavior coincide? How? (Give a concrete example.)

Large Group Activity: Effective Leaders and Their Beliefs

Should effective leaders possess certain beliefs? Why? Give specific examples. Why and how should effective leaders communicate their beliefs to others?

Small Group Activity: Challenging Our Assumptions

Values are those beliefs we hold so strongly that they guide our words and behaviors; we are comfortable telling those around us what we believe in; we would fight for them. Researchers have found out that we form our first core values between age seven and ten. Our first core values are usually the values our parents (or teachers or other adults in our life) have passed on to us. We challenged these values as we grew through adolescence.

Individually, first look at the following areas of your life and reflect how you feel about them. One way to hone in on our beliefs is to think about these questions: What are you passionate about? What pushes your buttons and gets you angry? Using the Core Values and Beliefs in Everyday Life sheet (fig. 4.45), record one value you hold for each of these categories. Example: I will work very hard to provide my family all the things I had to do without while I was growing up (money, health, friends, time, family, work, politics, education, etc.). Students will then share ideas in small groups. Small groups will then share their ideas and write some examples on the board for the entire class to discuss.

Small Group Activity: Actual Events Scenario

Students will create a scenario that demonstrates either a leader describing a tough situation she or he faced and how she or he met the challenge of holding to her or his beliefs and values, or a conflict in values between a leader and her or his followers. Each group will then role-play their scenario in front of the class. Audience will respond to the scenario regarding the leader and how the challenge was met or not met.

Optional Plans

1. Students will use the above activity but take the opposite views in each scenario.
2. Have students create a self-assessment scale on how they and others perceive themselves. They are to make a list of personal traits and then use a scale of 1-5 with 5 being the highest and indicating that you display this trait all of the time. Some examples: positive self-image, confidence, integrity, consistency, ethical, passion for living, highly

motivated, responsible, disciplined, reliable. Then have students compare their self-ratings with the ratings from others. Each must share findings with her or his small group.

3. Each small group is responsible for researching leadership theories and models (e.g., James Kouzes and Barry Posner, *The Leadership Challenge*, 1987; Walter Bennis, *Why Leaders Can't Lead*, 1990; Joe Batten, *Tough-Minded Leadership*, 1991; Steven Covey, *Principle-Centered Leadership*, 1989; Tom Peters, *Thriving on Chaos*, 1988; Louellen Essex and Mitch Kusy, *Fast-forward Leadership*, 1999). Each group presents their research findings to the class and also identifies ways in which they will apply what they have learned to their own lives.

4. Develop concept maps on leadership models. The concept maps can either illustrate the model of a company or a series of research models and theories.

5. Learning from risks. Create a Risk Chart and Plan of Action that lists risks that they took either at work or personally and future plans.

   - List the risk.
   - Describe how you felt during this time.
   - What did you learn and/or gain?
   - What did you lose?
   - What options did you choose from?
   - What plans will you put into action for the next time?

6. Students will raise and list some ethical issues that they will research and debate in their small groups. These ideas can be based on documentaries, media coverage, television dramas, a work of fiction, a film, or issues they themselves have experienced in the workplace or in their personal lives. Students need to clearly identify the conflicts that make their issue an ethical dilemma as opposed to a logistical, interpersonal, or technical problem. Debate teams will present their issues to the class and then hold an open question and answer session.

7. Students will collect the readings from Randy Cohen's column, "The Ethicist," in the Sunday *New York Times Magazine* each week and take a stand on whether they agree/disagree with the stand he takes. Make sure there is a wide representation of his writings (students can get past columns online) so that everyone will have good practice in discerning the ethics and the stands taken.

8. Have students research their relevant professional code of ethics and ask them to connect specific principles from the code that apply to the current issues they are facing. They might want to consider how the specific principles are congruent/not congruent with their personal code of ethics.

9. Ethics and decision making: Have students process a personal ethical dilemma and use the following questions as guides (adapted from Nash, 2002):

- Can I rationally defend my decision and can I live with myself after I make my decision?
- Could my professional community support me after I make my decision and take action?
- How would I act if my decision received heavy media coverage?
- Could I explain my decision to those whom I clearly hold close and love—family, children, confidantes, closest friends?
- Could I defend my decision legally in court?
- Could I defend my decision in front of my professional community and its ethics committee?
- Would I feel good if a friend, family member, or colleague made the same decision?

10. How have terrorism and new political doctrines changed what we view as ethical behavior in the global arena?

Performance-Based Assessments

- Response and appropriate feedback activities in large and small groups

CONCLUSION

What is the connection between leadership and beliefs? How do you see this struggle (between leadership responsibilities and responsibilities to one's own values/beliefs) after our discussion today? What are two ideas that have changed for you today?

ASSIGNMENT

1. Write down one belief or value that you feel you must communicate more clearly to those around you.

Unit 8D

Leadership and Ethics

LESSON TOPIC: WOMEN AND LEADERSHIP

Teaching Note

Women have taken a leadership role in redefining many aspects of our lives—work, home, equality, and justice. They have also influenced the way we define reality, conceive of knowledge, and model leadership. In this lesson, concepts of leadership are taken into consideration that reflect a more complex and thoughtful exploration of diverse styles of leadership, and ways in which women's efforts have modeled leadership through empowering others and enabling all groups to take action are considered. Students become quite interested to discover the differences in male and female styles, how their personal styles fit into each of the models, and then how their own experiences have contributed to their leadership style thus far. It is also a grand opportunity to discuss gender differences, gender bias, and gender equity in the different parts of the students' lives. There were many rousing discussions when the young women came forth with stories of discrimination both in their country of origin and here in the United States. The lesson also provides great ideas for how both men and women schedule their days, manage their time, and respond to personal and professional responsibilities.

Objectives

To identify female leadership models
To recognize the different styles of leadership and decide which works for
each individual

Domains

Cognitive: Identify gender bias
Affective: Value different styles of leadership
Skills: Connect personal values and leadership qualities

Academic Standard: Decision Making

Career Investigation
Identify leadership skills
Develop and understand business ethics

Materials

Overhead
Leadership Development Plan
Exercise Activity

Pre-Instructional

List three outstanding women leaders and the reasons why you believe they are outstanding.

Introductory Framework

We are going to look at effective leaders and, this time, focus on effective women leaders. Today, in this changing and unknown world, we must develop a clear understanding of our present and future selves. Once we are able to do this, we begin the initial steps to a pathway that we can begin to follow in our lives, especially as we confront the different dilemmas and myriad choices along the way.

Motivation

What do we mean by the "glass ceiling"? Show pictures from the media that illustrate an individual fighting the glass ceiling. Do you believe such a thing exists? Why/why not?

INSTRUCTIONAL IMPLEMENTATION

We will be studying gender differences and their implications. Here are some examples:

1. How are men and women different? Different does not mean deficient—just different!

2. Do women lead differently than men? How? Why? How does the idea of gender stereotypes work here? Leadership is not an either/or choice between masculine- and feminine-based traits. It is an "AND" formula requiring both sides of our brains and all of our strengths, energies, and talents. Who are some women leaders you admire? Why do you admire them? Have you ever been called on to be a leader in your life? Give some examples.

Many people, especially young girls, do not realize how many times they act in a leadership capacity without being given a title. We need to recognize that people lead differently because they have different styles and models. For many years, only one leadership model was acceptable and considered successful. Today, with changes in corporate culture, organizations, and a developing global marketplace, we encounter people with different communication and leadership styles. Let's look at the influences of different leadership styles on organizations.

Individual Activity: Checking Your Personal Leadership Style

Look at the following models and styles of leadership. Pick and choose from the aspects listed that describe your leadership model best. Explain why you feel these aspects are a good match for you. Describe how you exemplify them.

1. Operating Style: competitive, cooperative
2. Organizational Structure: hierarchy, team
3. Basic Objective: winning, quality output
4. Problem Solving: rational, intuitive/rational
5. Key Characteristics: high control, lower control, strategic, collaborative, unemotional, empathetic, analytical, high performance standards

After you have completed selecting the concepts that describe you, go down the list again and place an M (male) or F (female) in terms of what you perceive as different leadership styles.

Small Group Activity: Profiles of Leadership

After completing both parts, students then meet in their small groups to exchange their ideas. The recorder will list a series of profiles for each student. Then the small groups will report their analysis to the entire class.

Small Group Activity: Different Leadership Styles

Have students arrange themselves in groups of four. Explain or hand out a copy of the following scenario to them. Your company just decided to pilot test its products internationally. You have been asked to organize a group of employees to plan and implement this project. Decisions that need to be made include which products to pilot, which countries to target, implementation strategies, and pilot evaluation criteria and methods.

Now have the students discuss the following:

- How will decisions get made?
- Who will participate and who will do what?
- How will progress be tracked?

After each person describes how she or he will address the above issues, the groups will examine and list differences and similarities in how the problem was addressed. What are the different leadership styles presented by your group members?

Small Group Activity: Women Leaders

Have students read excerpts regarding women leaders. Some examples are: *Conversations with Uncommon Women* (Wymard, 1999), *The Female Advantage* (Helgesen, 1990), *Talking Leadership* (Hartman, 1999). Each member of the group will give feedback on what made this woman successful, which characteristics they admire, which characteristics they want to emulate and develop. Each group will compile a larger list to present to the entire class.

Individual and Partner Activity: My Leadership Skills

Have students complete the My Leadership Skills sheet (fig. 4.47) and then work with their partners to come up with a list of their personal leadership skills and attributes.

Individual and Small Group Activity: My Leadership Development Plan (Fig. 4.48)

After students complete the previous activity, they need to reflect on what they would like to develop more fully in terms of their leadership abilities. Have students complete individual leadership plans. In small groups of three,

Figure 4.47. My Leadership Skills

Think of two situations (work related or personal) when you played a leadership role. Describe them to your partner. Together, brainstorm and list below the leadership skills you demonstrated in those situations.

Figure 4.48. My Leadership Development Plan

1. Create a concept map for your leadership development plan.
2. After you define your development goal, ask yourself why you want to achieve it and what benefits you hope to gain.
3. Getting from where you are today to your goals requires lots of steps along the way. List the various action steps you will take to develop your plan.
4. Decide on a timeline and completion date.

each person in the group will discuss her or his plan. Others will listen and ask probing questions (e.g., "Why is that a goal?" "How is that a goal?" "Do you think your completion date is real and achievable?" "What other action steps can you take?").

Optional Plans

1. Invite women leaders from different local companies to come in and talk about their leadership style and their professional successes. What barriers did they face as they advanced in their company structure?
2. Read and excerpt the many books on women in leadership to synthesize the research and materials. What do we know about women and leadership today?
3. Create and implement a study of gender styles; for example, one class looked at female and male responses in class discussions. They examined who spoke more, who the teachers called on more frequently in a week; another group of students observed after-school playgrounds where boys and girls play together.
4. Study the sexual harassment laws and bring in experts to discuss how they are used in their corporation.
5. Study the language of leaders—do men and women talk differently? How do they demonstrate their differences in language use? What effect does their language have on the workplace?
6. Read excerpts from Tony Buzan's book *The Mind Map* to explore the concept of mind mapping. Then individually create a mind map of discovering your own defining values, talents, desires, dreams, and visions. This is a creative and stimulating activity that is then shared in your small group.
7. Have students research male and female pay equity. Are there differences in pay for the same jobs or roles?
8. Generally, girls do not act out in class or attract as much attention as boys. As a result, their unique needs are sometimes overlooked.

Because of this differential treatment, they are sometimes lost in the cracks. On the other hand, there are also pressures on girls via advertising, media, fashion, and entertainment to become "the perfect girl." Have students respond to the above as well as survey girls in their school. What have been the consequences of the girls' experiences at school and at work, and how have these consequences shaped them? How have their family beliefs also affected them? Plan a teleconference with women leaders around the state or nation. Send them a list of questions beforehand, such as: What is your definition of success? What obstacles do women face as they climb the ladder of success? Who helped mentor and support your professional success? What advice do you have for future women leaders?

9. Research information on what careers women have historically had and what new career paths are open for them today.

Performance-Based Assessments

- Response and appropriate feedback activities in large and small groups
- Small group sheets

CONCLUSION

What are some leadership development strategies we can all remember and use successfully (networking, education, skill development, volunteer, on-the-job activities)? After our discussion, do you think there are secrets to leadership that are different for women and men? What are the attributes of female leadership that you want to incorporate and emulate?

ASSIGNMENT

1. Interview a woman you admire as a leader and ask about her secrets to leadership. Be sure to take into consideration those hidden leaders (women not known publicly) as well as those obvious leaders. How has she achieved her goals? What advice would she give to you?

Unit 9A

Reflection, Assessment, and Future Work

LESSON TOPIC: PORTFOLIO REVIEW

Teaching Note

The final two seminars in the senior year are filled with excited voices and multiple questions. The accomplishments of two years are finally ready for review. Students willingly help and support each other during this final preparation process. The portfolio process is meaningful as it provides time for students to reflect individually and as a community on their work and development over the course of the program. During this seminar, developing a process for the final review and assessment and creating closure to their two years of study together are completed. All of the components of cooperative learning and learning to learn are put into motion. Students prepare themselves for the final assessment by outside reviewers and by their peers. They are in charge of their destiny at this point. They must ask out loud, reflect, and then answer the following: How do I want to represent myself? What does it mean to put my best foot forward? They make the final decisions for their portfolios and their presentations.

Objective

To continue to develop and apply the process of self-assessment for portfolio review

Domains

Cognitive: Comprehend and apply self-assessment and outside assessment
Affective: Value individual empowerment
Skills: Make critical choices for self-presentation

Graduation Standard: Decision Making

Career Investigation
Identify short- and long-term career choice
Finalize ideas for college or postsecondary course of study

Materials

Student portfolios
Outside Review Sheet for Portfolio (fig. 4.49)
Peer Review Sheet for Portfolio (fig. 4.50)
Self-Assessment Inventory Sheet (fig. 4.51)
Student-Teacher Conference Inventory sheet (fig. 4.52)
Suggested Rubric for Organizing Portfolios (fig. 4.53)

Pre-Instructional

Bring in portfolios, journals, Portfolio Review sheets (outside review and peer review), Self-Assessment Inventory sheets, and Student-Teacher Conference sheets.

Introductory Framework

This is the last unit in our program where we will have the chance to reflect upon and make decisions about our academic growth and future plans. As we review these last two years, portfolios allow us to reflect on and analyze our work differently than through standard measurements. Remember we have

Figure 4.49.   Outside Review Sheet for Portfolio

Date:
Name of Student:
Name of Outside Reviewer:
Position of Outside Reviewer:

1. Browse the portfolio.
2. Choose three entries and identify the best or the unique features of each entry.
3. Explain how these features enhance the student's work.
4. Make general comments about the portfolio and how the assessment guide is set up.

Entry 1
Entry 2
Entry 3

General Comments and Suggestions

Figure 4.50.   Peer Review Sheet for Portfolio

Date:
Name of Student:
Name of Peer Reviewer:

1. Browse the portfolio.
2. Choose three entries and identify the best or the unique features of each entry.
3. Explain how these features enhance the student's work.
4. Make general comments about the portfolio and how the assessment guide is set up.

Entry 1
Entry 2
Entry 3

General Comments and Suggestions

Figure 4.51.   Self-Assessment Inventory Sheet

From the list of Voyager program themes below, choose two items to focus on for your self-assessment using the prompts below:

Voyager Program Themes (choose two):
Work-site success (internships, mentorships, job shadowing)
Academic success—work that is related to the program in other areas (if connected and aligned with Voyager)
Outside activities and work (relevant to the program and course of study)
Personal and professional growth plans
Reflective writing
Journal completions
In-class assignments and activities
Career investigation standard
Other

On the next page, write the themes you chose to focus on for your self-assessment in the space provided ("Choice 1" and "Choice 2"). Then answer the questions below each theme you list.

Choice 1:
Why I chose this particular theme:
What I learned:
What my strengths are in this area:
What my future goals and needs are in this area:

Choice 2:
Why I chose this particular theme:
What I learned:
What my strengths are in this area:
What my future goals and needs are in this area:

Figure 4.52.   Student-Teacher Conference Inventory

Portfolio conferences are created so that students and teachers can have an authentic conversation regarding student achievement, future goals, and further teaching instruction. The goals are to benefit both parties.

1. Student
Present and select pieces that you would like to talk about.
Why did you choose these pieces? What have you learned?

2. Teacher
Ask about the student's strengths and future needs.
Make notes about the uniqueness of each portfolio.

defined reflection as a dialogue with oneself, a private inner dialogue—one where we recall the details of the experience and continue by considering the question: What meaning does this experience hold for me?

Motivation

Considering your two years of work, reflect upon and define success for you personally and professionally. Brainstorm all ideas on the board.

Figure 4.53.   Suggested Rubric for Organizing Portfolios

The categories for rating the Portfolios are: Outstanding, Very Good, Good, Needs Work.

1. Organization
   • presentation and order of work

2. Focus and Framework
   • Voyager themes and competencies clearly illustrated
   • aligned with graduation standards
   • demonstrates successful completion of all projects
   • journal entries submitted

3. Design
   • professional in appearance
   • table of contents
   • easy to navigate and to find materials
   • easy to understand and to follow
   • presentational software is user friendly

4. Mechanics
   • correct usage, grammar, and spelling

INSTRUCTIONAL IMPLEMENTATION

Cooperative assessment invites peers, community, and business people to be part of the process. When you review each other's work, make sure that you pay careful attention to the differing aspects within each portfolio. Your feedback is important and is taken seriously. The final assessment completed by the assessment teams will follow the same procedures.

As we approach the end of our work together, we need to prepare for the:

1. Panel Review Board
2. Completion of all in-house assessments
3. Final presentation to the junior class
4. Celebration and closure
5. Follow-up alumni and reunion meetings

Small Group Activity

Review assessment procedures (see fig. 4.54). What are the ways you have fulfilled and demonstrated each of the categories?

Small Group Activity: Peer Review of Portfolios

Students begin peer process review of portfolios. Each group needs Self-Assessment Inventory Sheets for each member, reading time, and response time. Students will present two areas from their portfolios in preparation for the final panel review, using the Self-Assessment Inventory Sheet as a guide for their notes and discussion. As students work and evaluate their portfolios in groups, student-teacher conferences will take place simultaneously.

Whole Class Activity

There will be closure rituals so the students can say good-bye to each other. Each class has created their own set of rituals. Some of the Voyager students

Figure 4.54. Portfolio Checklist for Student-Teacher Conferencing

1. How is assessment based on your inventory of artifacts?
2. What are the frameworks for the overall portfolio and what are your unique features?
3. How are you demonstrating completion in the overall program (themes and Minnesota graduation standards)?
4. How are you demonstrating ownership of your work?
5. How does your portfolio demonstrate diverse abilities, strengths, other work, interests, and versatility, and trace your development of achievements?
6. How does the assessment clearly delineate the Career Investigation standard?

will continue on in the program, others are moving away to attend college, and some are just interested in completing the two-year program. This is an emotional session as this is the completion of an intense program together as well as graduation from high school.

Performance-Based Assessments

- All activity sheets

ASSIGNMENT

1. Continue working on individual self-assessment inventories. Complete feedback for peers' folders. Collect any other outside review sheets and suggestions for organizing the portfolio (see fig. 4.55).

Figure 4.55.   Suggestions for Organizing the Portfolio

1. A one-page reflective opening piece introducing the portfolio
2. Table of Contents
3. The student's personal philosophy of education and work
4. A personal reflection of the Voyager experience
5. A professional résumé
6. Artifacts that demonstrate student's best ideas (as determined by the student) and work from:
   - class work
   - the business experience
7. The student's professional development career plans and goals
8. The student's personal development goals
9. The student's best (as determined by the student) junior/senior projects
10. A complete set of journal reflections
11. A one-page final reflection stating the student's future goals, dreams, and aspirations

Unit 9B

Reflection, Assessment, and Future Work

LESSON TOPIC: ASSESSMENT AND CAREER INVESTIGATION

Teaching Note

These are the final preparations before students meet with their assessment teams. They are concerned that they have the "correct" materials and that they will say the "right thing." What became important to observe is that they were prepared for this day and actually participated fully, enjoying their achievements. It is also a time for closure. This is a time for self-reflection and evaluation as well as looking back on the program of study as a whole and making insightful observations. The students take time to critically examine their growth, who they are today and where they want to be next year. Many will continue in the Level 2, Postsecondary Program; others will leave and attend out-of-town schools or they will assume full-time working positions. Whatever their decisions, it is important for them to create their closing ritual as they complete an important plateau in their lives.

Objective

To continue to develop and apply the process of self-assessment for portfolio review and finalize all work for graduation and certification

Domains

Cognitive: Comprehend and apply self-assessment and outside assessment
Affective: Value individual empowerment and achievements
Skills: Make choices

Graduation Standard : Decision Making

Career Investigation
Identify short- and long-term career choice
Finalize ideas for college or postsecondary course of study

Materials

Student portfolios
Self-Assessment Inventory sheets
Portfolio Outside Review sheets
Portfolio Peer Review sheets
Student-Teacher Conference sheets
Program Evaluation sheets

Pre-Instructional

Bring in portfolios, journals, Portfolio Review sheets (outside review and peer review), Self-Assessment Inventory sheets, and Student-Teacher Conference sheets.

Introductory Framework

As we approach the end of our work together, we need to finalize our plans for the following:

1. Panel Review Board
2. Completion of all in-house assessments
3. Celebration
4. Final presentation to the junior class

Motivation

Do you feel differently during this assessment process than you have previously? Explain. Write all remarks on the board.

Are there any suggestions you have for all of us as we proceed along with the final components of our work? List on the board.

INSTRUCTIONAL IMPLEMENTATION

Small Group Activity: Peer/Critical Friend Review of Portfolios

Students continue the peer process review of portfolios. Each group needs Self-Assessment Inventory sheets for each member, reading time, and response time. Students will present two areas from their portfolios in preparation for the final panel review, using the Self-Assessment Inventory sheet as a guide for their notes and discussion. Student-teacher conferences are taking place simultaneously.

Students construct the rest of the lesson in order to work on their final ideas for junior year presentation, celebration activities, and final changes to their portfolios.

Large Group Activity and Closure

Each student takes times to say good-bye to the group. All of the groups have chosen different ways. Some have had their private celebration in school with foods from many countries; others have met in a restaurant for final good-byes; others created a critical friends circle and wrote to each other; others presented each other with books, artifacts, or other tokens of friendship and community. They read *Through the Cracks* (Sollman, Emmons, and Paolini, 1994) and talked about the changes they had made in their homes, school, and communities. They also read Dr. Seuss' *Oh the Places You'll Go!*

Closing Celebration and Voyager Certification

There will be a commemorative dinner and celebration to honor Voyager candidates and to thank all community stakeholders. Students who have successfully achieved all of the required competencies and standards are awarded Voyager certificates for completing Level 1 of the program.

Performance-Based Assessments

- Peer, parent, and community review sheets

CONCLUSION

Provide an environmental check for how close everyone is to completion for final review. What are some closing words you want to say to each other after spending these two years together?

ASSIGNMENT

1. Continue working on individual self-assessment inventories. Complete feedback for peers' folders. Collect any other outside review sheets. Return final pieces to the instructor in one week. Students will name panel reviewers so their work can be sent directly to these members. Remember, all panel members need your work prior to the review and celebration day.

Voyager Program Evaluation

See figure 4.56 to complete the Voyager Program Evaluation.

Figure 4.56. Voyager Program Evaluation

At the end of your Voyager program, you will be asked to supply feedback regarding various factors in the program. Below are some points for you to consider. Please go through each point and tell us what you think we need to know to keep Voyager dynamic and meeting the needs of students. We appreciate and value your feedback.

1. What were your ideas about this program and career work-site seminar when you first began? What did you think it was going to be about?
2. Now that you have successfully completed Level I of the program, how would you describe it to future Voyager students?
3. The program has been described as an authentic learning and school-to-career program, preparing students to be highly skilled workers in the new global millennium. Do you agree with this statement or should something be added to it? If you do agree, explain what this means to students who are just starting the program.
4. What did you enjoy most throughout the program?
5. What did you enjoy the least?
6. Write any suggestions or comments that you feel would be useful to the instructor and to future Voyager students.

Epilogue

WHAT SCHOOLS AND BUSINESS CAN DO: CRITICAL PEDAGOGY AND THE NEW WORK ORDER

As I look back over the topography of the two-year secondary program, I am heartened by the memories of all the voices that took part in the process and made the experience of designing and growing the program challenging, exciting, and rewarding. I want to take this time to extend some of the thoughts and concepts in the book.

The need to develop a skilled workforce and educate critical learners is at the core of the Voyager program. It is a program that supports, celebrates, and engenders learning, living, and working in the twenty-first century for twenty-first-century students and workers. Understanding that both policy and practice must change is essential to the school-to-career paradigm shift. Classroom practices need to reflect learning that is authentically linked to real-world experience, and policy must guide the development and account-ability of authentic change. We must intentionally grapple with philosophies that keep students in alternative programs and connected to discriminatory practices that truncate their futures and abilities to become full and active cit-izens in the world. When we all work differently to articulate a broader ar-ray of student talent and success in the context of revised beliefs and expec-tations, true reform will take root.

Voyager's history emphatically documents the journey and success of a school-to-career program that motivates young adults to learn and to further pursue their education and training. They take the time to think about and to craft who they want to become. In our view, schools are not training grounds for fulfilling the imperatives of the business world nor are they sites where education is commodified and quantified to calculate excellence, economic success, or student deficiency. Schools are sites for developing a dynamic democratic citizenry that has the ability to think and act critically and that sees the concept of democracy as a way of life that is defined and redefined with each generation. By participating in this form of dynamic democracy and critical discussion, Voyager students become empowered, self-reliant citizens who look at education and work as collaborative sites where they can create possibilities for themselves and a new society. But they cannot just learn to criticize; they must go beyond social commentary and learn to take action for change. This is critical empowerment both at school and at work.

It is also our view that businesses are not enemies who want to take over and implement a dumb-downed curriculum in order to meet their current short-term work needs or treat school-to-career programs as charity components of their organizations. The businesses became partners in change, were pleased to see the array of contributions our students brought to their organizations, and readily acknowledged the benefits of participating in Voyager. Many of the students were employed by the same company throughout the entire program. Their imprint on business and community leaders and organizations was unmistakable and remains evidenced by the continuing involvement and support from business for the Voyager program.

Critical pedagogy is woven into this school-to-career program through a broad range of radical educational perspectives. Critical pedagogy is an educational philosophy of praxis, one that is not shy about asking all stakeholders to critique the type of education that students receive, to examine how teachers and businesspeople teach in this context, and to make policy changes. Voyager asks how curricula and the chief subject areas of work education study have changed in content, not just in titles or in the recombining of status quo elements, since the turn of the twentieth century. Critical work education insists that curriculum and pedagogy enhance student achievement and strengthen their commitment to lifelong learning by creating spaces where all students are treated with dignity and care. Through the presentation of pluralized curricula, these multicultural materials and practices nurture favorable attitudes and values as they highlight students from nondominant groups. All students are given shared representation and see that they have a place of value in society.

In this post–September 11 era, it is imperative that we courageously question the apparent and all-too-evident inequities in our schools and workplaces and then forge alternative paths to social change. How exciting to see and hear a group of eager students who engage in critical talk, build a democratic learning community, collaborate on social change projects, and take on "what is yet possible" in education and in the workplace. Learning is a complex process that includes many components to which we must pay attention. A critical and empowering learning environment exists when staff and students consistently interact, develop meaningful relationships with each other, and engage in a personal examination of identities and experiences to transform their own practices. To become Freirean, one must engage in rigorous scholarship, maintain a commitment to social justice, and stir in a huge helping of radical love. Teaching is a political act, an act of love with vision.

Schools and business are invited to create new learning and sites where powerful and compelling change takes place: where creativity and genius are unleashed, where they share visions of what can be, where difference is appealing and attractive, and where all constituents are invited into the controversies of future school-to-career programs to collectively reflect on and take action for change.

There are many wonderful and engaging topics that have not been addressed in this book. Rather, these seminars and lessons are springboards from which all constituents working with school-to-career programs can create. We need to keep asking questions: What are the responsibilities of educators and businesspeople to our future workers? What can schools and businesses do together? How do we develop rigorous, inclusive, democratic classrooms? What we have learned over the years is that every Voyager program will produce new theories for teaching, learning, and workplace practices.

All schools differ from each other, and therefore any single blueprint for success is inappropriate. Each group will reenvision and reinvent the topics, structure, and curriculum of Voyager to fit the particular context in which they are taught—an exciting process for all participants. Foundational to all of our work is the belief and optimism we hold for all of our Voyager students. They know how worthy and capable of learning we believe them to be, and this makes a dramatic difference in the outcomes for all. The first step for all interested parties is to discuss the existing assumptions, generalizations, or images that influence how students, teachers, learning, and working are perceived. Beliefs and assumptions left unexamined are powerful obstacles to change. On the other hand, when beliefs are openly discussed and examined, a supportive alignment among all components and parties occurs, and a positive cycle of achievement is nurtured. We must all be willing to reinvent our thoughts and actions so that the ultimate aim is to transform learning to learn and learning to work in the new millennium.

I hope that these writings will stimulate thought about these issues and encourage further readings and new practices. I also hope that readers will discuss what they have learned with all of the stakeholders in the Voyager community — parents, colleagues, business and community leaders, and students. It would be great to hear your thoughts about this program and curriculum. My email address is e9roulis@stthomas.edu. I invite you to pass on your thoughts and extend the knowledge. Thank you.

Bibliography

Abt, Vicki, and Mel Seesholtz. (1994). The Shameless World of Phil, Sally, and Oprah: Television Talk Shows and the Deconstructing of Society. *Journal of Popular Culture* 28, no. 1: 171–192.

Adams, Maurianne, Lee Anne Bell, and Pat Griffin, eds. (1997). *Teaching for Diversity and Social Justice*. New York: Routledge.

Adams, Maurianne, Warren Blumenfeld, Rosie Castanada, Heather Hackman, Madeleine Peters, and Ximena Zuniga. (2000). *Reading for Diversity and Social Justice*. New York: Routledge.

Addressing the Problem of Juvenile Bullying. Fact Sheet. (June 2001). Washington, D.C.: U.S. Department of Justice, Office of Justice Programs, Office of Juvenile Justice and Delinquency Prevention.

Adler, Ronald, and Jeanne Marquardt Elmhorst. (2002). *Communicating at Work. Principles and Practices for Business and the Professions*. 7th ed. Boston: McGraw-Hill.

Advanced Tracking Source. Human resource training videos such as *Tearing Down Walls*; Stephen Covey video that shows ways to dismantle barriers between individuals and in organizations; *Who Moved My Cheese?*; The Diversity Series. Available at: www.atsmedia.com/docs/cat.

Affluenza: Consumerism in America. (1998). Videos. Berkeley: Media Resource Center, Moffitt Library, University of California-Berkeley.

Alcock, Barbara J. (2000). *Immigration and the Value to Our Society*. St. Paul, Minn.: Minnesota Human Rights Commission.

Alvesson, M., and H. Willmott. (1992). On the Idea of Emancipation in Management and Organization Studies. *Academy of Management Review* 17, no. 3: 432–464.

Alvesson, Mats, and Yvonne Due Billing. (1997). *Understanding Gender and Organizations*. London: Sage.

American Management Association: www.amanet.org. Accessed September 28, 2003.

Anderson, Sarah. (1990). *Some of My Best Friends Are Polka-Dot Pigs*. Seattle, Wash.: Sarah Anderson Publications.

Anthony, Rebecca, and Gerald Roe. (1982). *Contact to Contract*. Carroll Press.

Anzaldua, Gloria. (1999). *La frontera/Borderlands: The New Mestiza*. St. Paul, Minn.: Consortium Book Sales & Distribution.

Apple, M. W., and J. A. Beane, eds. (1995). *Democratic Schools*. Alexandria, Va.: ASCD.

Arnot, Madeleine, and Jo-Ann Dillabough, eds. (2000). *Challenging Democracy. International Perspectives on Gender, Education, and Citizenship*. London: Routledge.

Aronowitz, Stanley, and William DiFazio. (1994). *The Jobless Future: Sci Tech and the Dogma of Work*. Minneapolis: University of Minnesota Press.

Aronson, Eliot. (1978). *The Jigsaw Classroom*. Beverly Hills, Calif.: Sage.

Arrendondo, Lani. (2000). *Communicating Effectively*. San Francisco: McGraw-Hill.

Asante, K., and W. B. Gudykunst. (1989). *Handbook of Intercultural Communication*. Newbury Park, Calif.: Sage.

Asher, Donald. (1999). *From College to Career: Entry Level Resumes for Any Major from Accounting to Zoology*. San Francisco: Wet Feet Press.

AskERIC Lesson Plans. This site provides lesson plans that help make the Internet an accessible classroom tool. Available at: ericr.syr.edu/Virtual/Lessons/. Accessed June 11, 2003.

Astin, Helen, and Carol Leland. (1992). *Women of Influence, Women of Vision*. San Francisco: Jossey-Bass.

Auerbach, Elsa R., and Nina Wallerstein. (1987). *English for the Workplace: Problem-Posing at Work*. Reading, Mass.: Addison-Wesley Publishing Company.

Bailey, T. (1991). Jobs of the Future and the Education They Will Require: Evidence from Occupational Forecasts. *Educational Researcher* 20, no. 2: 11–20.

Barlow, M. L. (1967). *History of Industrial Education in the United States*. Peoria, Ill.: Charles Bennett Co.

Batten, Joe D. (1989). *Tough-Minded Leadership*. New York: AMACOM.

Beamer, Linda, and Iris Varner. (2001). *Intercultural Communication in the Global Workplace*. New York: McGraw-Hill.

Bellanca, J., and R. Fogarty. (1991). *Blueprints for Thinking in the Cooperative Classroom*. Palatine, Ill.: Skylight Publishing, Inc.

Benjamin, S. (1989). An Ideascape for Education: What Futurists Recommend. *Educational Leadership* 7, no. 1: 8–14.

Bennis, Warren G. (1989). *Why Leaders Can't Lead: The Unconscious Conspiracy Continues*. San Francisco: Jossey-Bass.

Beyer, Landon, ed. (1996). *Creating Democratic Classrooms*. New York: Teachers College Press.

Bickmore, K. (1984). *Alternatives to Violence: A Manual for Teaching Peacemaking Alternatives to Youth and Adults*. Akron, Ohio: Peace Grows.

Bigelow, Bill, Linda Christenson, Stan Karp, Barbara Miner, and Bob Peterson. (2000). *Rethinking Schools—Teaching Equity and Justice*. Vols. 1 and 2. Milwaukee, Wisc.: Rethinking Schools Ltd.

Bigelow, William, and Norman Diamond. (1988). *The Power in Our Hands*. New York: Monthly Review Press.

Bill Cosby on Prejudice. (1990). Video. Los Angeles: Budget Films.

Bluestein, J. (1988). *21st Century Discipline: Teaching Students Responsibility and Self-Control*. Jefferson City, Mo.: Scholastic.

Bly, Carol. (1996). *Changing the Bully Who Rules the World*. Minneapolis, Minn.: Milkweed Editions.

Boal, Augusto. (1979). *Theatre of the Oppressed*. London: Routledge.

Boal, Augusto. (1985). *Theatre of the Oppressed*. Translated by A. & Maria-Odilia Leal McBride. New York: The Communications Group.

Boal, Augusto. (1992). *Games for Actors and Non-Actors*. London: Routledge.

Boal, Augusto. (1995). *The Rainbow of Desire—The Boal Method of Theatre and Therapy*. London: Routledge.

Bogue, G. (1994). *Leadership by Design*. San Francisco: Jossey-Bass.

Boje, D. M., and R. F. Dennehy. (1993). *Managing in a Postmodern World: America's Revolution against Exploitation*. Dubuque, Ia.: Kendall/Hunt Publishing.

Bolles, Richard. (1999). *Job-hunting on the Internet*. 2nd ed. Berkley, Calif.: Ten Speed Press.

Bolles, Richard Nelson. Job Hunters Bible is a megasite offering links to job-hunting tasks. Available at: www.jobhuntersbible.com. Accessed June 10, 2003.

Bolman, Lee, and Terrence Deal. (1991). *Reframing Organizations.* San Francisco: Jossey-Bass.

Booher, Dianna. (1992). *The Complete Letterwriter's Almanac: A Handbook of Model Letters for Business, Social, and Personal Occasions.* Upper Saddle River, N.J.: Prentice Hall.

Boone, L. E., D. L. Kurtz, and J. Block. (1997). Effective Employment Interviewing. In *Contemporary Business Communication*, 555–592. Englewood Cliffs, N.J.: Prentice Hall.

Borman, K. M. (1991). *The First Real Job: A Study of Young Workers.* Albany: State University of New York Press.

Bowers, C. A., and D. J. Flinder. (1990). *Responsive Teaching: An Ecological Approach to Classroom Patterns of Language, Culture, Thought.* New York: Teachers College Press.

Boyer, Ernest. (1995). *The Basic School: A Community for Learning.* Princeton, N.J.: The Carnegie Foundation for the Advancement of Teaching.

Bradford, L. J., and C. Raines. (1992). *Twentysomething: Managing and Motivating Today's New Workforce.* New York: MasterMedia.

Bridges, W. (1994). *JobShift: How to Prosper in a Workplace without Jobs.* Reading, Mass.: Addison-Wesley Publishing Company.

Brody, Ed, Jay Goldspinner, Katie Green, Rona Leventhal, and John Porcino. (2002). *Spinning Tales Weaving Hope: Stories, Storytelling and Activities for Peace, Justice and the Environment.* Gabriola Island, Canada: New Society Publishers.

Brookfield, Stephen. (1995). *Becoming a Critically Reflective Teacher.* San Francisco: Jossey-Bass.

Brown, Cherie. (1998). *Healing into Action: A Leadership Guide for Creating Diverse Communities.* Washington, D.C.: National Coalition Building Institute.

Bruner, Jerome. (1996). *The Culture of Education.* Cambridge, Mass.: Harvard University Press.

Building United Judgment: A Handbook for Consensus Decision-Making. (1985). Philadelphia: New Society Publishers, Center for Conflict Resolution.

Cantor, Dorothy, and Toni Bernay. (1992). *Women in Power: The Secrets of Leadership.* Boston: Houghton Mifflin Press.

Careerlab. This site helps people with their careers. Available at: www.careerlab.com/. Accessed June 10, 2003.

Career Magazine. Register and review job postings. Available at: www.careermag.com/. Accessed June 10, 2003.

Carroll, R. (1988). *Cultural Misunderstandings: The French American Experience.* Chicago: Chicago University Press.

Center for the Social Organization of Schools, Johns Hopkins University. www.csos.jhu.edu. Accessed September 28, 2003. [Offers material about the team planning approach of Robert Slavin.]

Cheney, George. (1999). *Values at Work.* Ithaca: Cornell University Press.

Child Development Project. (1994). *At Home in Our Schools: A Guide to Schoolwide Activities That Build Community.* Oakland, Calif.: Developmental Studies Center.

Child Development Project. (1996). *Ways We Want Our Class to Be: Class Meetings That Build Commitment to Kindness and Learning.* Oakland, Calif.: Development Studies Center.

Chinese Cultural Connection. (1987). Chinese Values and the Search for Culture-Free Dimensions of Culture. *Journal of Cross-Cultural Psychology* 18: 143–164.

Choices for the 21st Century Education Project. (1996). Providence, R.I.: Brown University.

Christensen, L. (1994). Building Community from Chaos. *Rethinking Schools* 1: 14–17.

Circles of learning. (1983). Minneapolis: Cooperative Learning Center—University of Minnesota. Film on cooperatively structured learning.

Clark, C. L. (1996). *A Student's Guide to the Internet.* Upper Saddle River, N.J.: Prentice Hall.

Clemons, J., L. Laase, D. Cooper, N. Aregado, and M. Dill. (1993). *Portfolios in the Classroom: A Teachers' Sourcebook.* New York: Scholastic.

Cleveland, H. (1993). *Authentic Leadership*. San Francisco: Jossey-Bass.

Cliff, F. (1998). Winning the War for Talent. *Harvard Business Review* 76, no. 5: 18–19.

Cohen, Richard. (1996). *Students Resolving Conflict*. Glenview, Ill.: Scott Foresman.

Cohen, S., G. E. Ledford Jr., and G. M. Spreitzer. (1996). A Predictive Model of Self-Managing Work Team Effectiveness. *Human Relations* 490, no. 5: 643–676.

Controlling Interest. (1978). San Francisco: California Newsreel. Documentary about the power and influence of the multinational corporations in international politics and trade.

Copeland, L. (1988a). Making the Most of Cultural Differences at the Workplace. *Personnel* (June): 53.

Copeland, L. (1988b). Valuing Workplace Diversity. *Personnel Administrator* 11: 38–39.

Covey, Stephen R. (1991). *Principle-Centered Leadership*. New York: Summit Books.

Create Your High School Portfolio: An Interactive Career and Life Planning Workbook. (1998). JIST Works, Inc. Available at jistworks@aol.com.

Dadzie, Stella. (1999). *Took-Kit for Tackling Racism in School*. Stoke on Trent, United Kingdom: Trentham Books, Ltd.

Daloz, Laurent Parks, Cheryl Keen, James Keen, and Sharon Daloz Park. (1996). *Common Fire: Lives of Commitment in a Complex World*. Boston: Beacon Press.

Danielson, Charlotte, and L. Abrutyn. (1997). *An Introduction to Using Portfolios in the Classroom*. Alexandria, Va.: ASCD.

Darder, Antonia. (1991). *Culture and Power in the Classroom*. New York: Bergin and Garvey.

Deal, T. E., and A. A. Kennedy. (1982). *Corporate Cultures*. Reading, Mass.: Addison-Wesley.

Deemer, Candy, and Nancy Fredericks. (2003). *Dancing on the Glass Ceiling*. New York: Contemporary Books.

Deutsch, M. (1973). *The Resolution of Conflict*. New Haven, Conn.: Yale University Press.

Deutsch, Morton. (1945). An Experimental Study on the Effects of Cooperation and Competition on Group Process. *Human Relations* 2: 199–231.

DeVries, Mary. (1998). *The Business Writer's Book of Lists*. New York: Berkley Books.

Dewey, John. (1916). *Democracy and Education*. New York: Macmillan.

Dillon, J. T., ed. (1994). *Deliberation in Education and Society*. Norwood, N.J.: Ablex.

Diverse Communications—Employ Workshop (video). BNA Communications Inc. Rockville, MD RT 21 minutes (www.bna.com/bnac). Accessed 10/31/03.

Dodd, Carley. (1998). *Dynamics of Intercultural Communication*. New York: McGraw-Hill.

Dumain, B. (1994). Creating a New Company Culture. *Fortune*, December 26, 127–131.

Dunlap, D. M., and P. A. Schmuck, eds. (1995). *Women Leading in Education*. New York: State University of New York Press.

Duster, Troy. (1991). Understanding Self-Segregation on the Campus. *The Chronicle of Higher Education* (September 25): B2.

Edson, C. H. (1979). Sociocultural Perspectives on Work and Schooling in Urban America. *The Urban Review* 2, no. 3: 127–148.

Educators for Social Responsibility. Available at: www.esrnational.org/homenoflash.htm. Accessed September 28, 2003.

Elliot, Michael. 1995."Here to Stay: An Adopted Son Embraces the Land of 'More'" *Newsweek*, July 10, 37.

Embry, Dennis D. (1995). *Peacebuilders Curriculum*. Tucson, Ariz.: Heartsprings.

E-portfolios for the classroom. Available at: www.efoliomn.com.

Epstein, E. M. (1987). The Corporate Social Policy Process: Beyond Business Ethics, Corporate Social Responsibility, and Corporate Social Responsiveness. *California Management Review* 28: 126–141.

Essex, Louellen and Mitchell Kusy. (1999). *Fast-Forward Leadership: How to Exchange Outmoded Practices Quickly for Forward-Looking Leadership Today*. London: Financial Times Prentice Hall.

Eye of the Storm. (1985). Storrs: University of Connecticut Film Library. Classic blue eye/brown eye story and the effects of difference and power.

Fennimore, T. F., and M. B. Tinzmann. (1990). *Restructuring to Promote Learning in America's Schools: Video Conference 2: The Thinking Curriculum.* Elmhurst, Ill.: North Central Regional Educational Laboratory.

Filipczak, B. (1997). Innovation Drivers. *Training* (May): 36–40.

Fishman, Stephen M., and Lucille McCarthy. (1998). *John Dewey and the Challenge of Classroom Practice.* New York: Teachers College Press.

Fitzgerald, F. Scott. (1936). The Crack Up. *Esquire* (February).

Flipdog.com. Offers extensive job listings. Available at: www.flipodog.com/. Accessed June 10, 2003.

Flores, Lisa, Judith Martin, and Thomas Nakayma. (2002). *Reading in Intercultural Communication: Experiences and Contexts.* New York: McGraw-Hill.

Foster, Douglas. (1994). Today's Teens: Dissed, Mythed and Totally Pissed: A Generation and a Nation at Risk. *Utne Reader* 64: 50–67.

Freeman, R., and D. Gilbert. (1992). Business, Ethics, and Society: A Critical Agenda. *Business and Society* 31, no. 1 (Spring): 9–17.

Freire, Paulo. (1992). *Cultural Action for Freedom.* Cambridge, Mass.: Harvard Educational Review.

Freire, Paulo. (1970). *Pedagogy of the Oppressed.* New York: Seabury Press.

Freire, Paulo. (1972). Education: Domestication or Liberation. *Prospects* 2: 173–181.

Freire, Paulo. (1973). *Pedagogy for Critical Consciousness.* New York: Seabury Press.

Freire, Paulo. (1985). *The Politics of Education: Culture, Power, and Liberation.* Translated by Donaldo Macedo. Westport, Conn.: Bergin & Garvey.

Freire, Paulo. (1997). *Mentoring the Mentor. A Critical Dialogue with Paulo Freire.* New York: Peter Lang Publishers.

Freire, Paulo. (1998). *Teachers as Cultural Workers. Letters to Those Who Dare to Teach.* Translated by Donaldo Macedo, Dale Koike, and Alexandre Oliveira. Boulder, Colo.: Westview Press.

Frost, P. J., V. Mitchell, and W. R. Nord, eds. (1997). *Organizational Reality: Reports from the Firing Line.* New York: HarperCollins.

Fullen, Michael. (1999). *Change Forces. The Sequel.* Philadelphia, Pa.: Falmer Press, Taylor & Francis, Inc.

Gagliardi, P., ed. (1990). *Symbols and Artifacts: Views of the Corporate Landscape.* New York: de Gruyter.

Gallo, Donald, ed. (1990). *Visions: Short Stories by Outstanding Writers for Young Adults.* New York: Dell Publishing.

Gandhi, Mahatma K. (1848). *Nonviolence in Peace and War.* Ahmedabad, India: Garland.

Gardner, Howard. (1985). *Leading Minds.* New York: Basic Books.

Gardner, Howard. (1995). *Leading Minds: An Anatomy of Leadership.* New York: Basic Books.

Gathercoal, Paul, and Virginia Nimmo. (2002). Judicious Discipline: Democracy in Education. *Journal of Thought* (Summer): 73–86.

Gay, Lesbian, Straight Education Network. For resources addressing the needs of gay and lesbian youth. Available at: www.glsen.org. Accessed June 2003.

GE: Just Your Average Everyday $60 Billion Family Grocery Store. (1994). *Industry Week* (May): 13–18.

Geertz, Clifford. (1973). *The Interpretation of Cultures.* New York: Basic Books.

Gerzon, M. (1992). *A Choice of Heroes.* Boston: Houghton-Mifflin.

Gibbs, Jeanne. (2001). *Tribes: A New Way of Learning and Being Together.* Windsor, Calif.: CenterSource Systems, LLC.

Girard, Kathryn, and Susan J. Koch. (1996). *Conflict Resolutions in the Schools—A Manual for Educators.* San Francisco: Jossey-Bass.

Giroux, Henry A. (1988a). *Schooling and the Struggle for Public Life: Critical Pedagogy in the Modern Age*. Minneapolis: University of Minnesota.

Giroux, Henry. (1988b). *Teachers as Intellectuals: Toward a Critical Pedagogy of Learning*. New York: Bergin & Garvey.

Giroux, Henry. (1993). *Disturbing Pleasures: Learning Popular Culture*. New York: Routledge.

Global SchoolNet Foundation. Find contacts for international keypals and cooperative Internet projects. Available at: www.gsn.org.

GLSEN. Available at: www.glsen.org/templates/index.html.

Gods of Metal. (1982). Wilmington, Ohio: Wilmington College of Peace Resource Center. Documentary about people who have taken risks and collective action to challenge the arms race.

Goleman, Daniel. (1998). *Working with Emotional Intelligence*. New York: Bantam Books.

Goodman, J. (1992). *Elementary Schooling for Critical Democracy*. Albany: State University of New York Press.

Graves, Ted, and Nancy Graves. (1985). *Broken Circles, Broken Squares.* Santa Cruz, Calif.: Graves, 136 Liberty Street, Santa Cruz 95060.

Gray, Mattie. (1988). *Images: A Workbook for Enhancing Self-Esteem and Promoting Career Preparation, Especially for Black Girls.* Sacramento: California Department of Education.

Green, Timothy, and Abbey Brown. (2002). *Multimedia Projects in the Classroom*. Thousand Oaks, Calif.: Corwin Press.

Grunbaum, J. A., L. Kann, S. A. Kinchen, B. Williams, J. G. Ross, R. Lowry, and L. Kolbe. (2002). Youth Risk Behavior Surveillance—United States, 2001. *MMWR,* no. SS-4 (June 28): 51.

Gudykunst, William B. (1991). *Bridging Differences—Effective Inter Group Communication.* Thousand Oaks, Calif.: Sage.

Gudykunst, William, and Yun Kim Young. (2003). *Communicating with Strangers: An Approach to Intercultural Communication*. New York: McGraw-Hill.

Guffey, Mary. (1990). *Business English*. Mason, Ohio: South-Western Publishing.

Gurian, Michael. (2001). *The Wonder of Boys.* New York: Atria Books.

Gurian, Michael. (2002). *The Wonder of Girls.* New York: Atria Books.

Gutmann, Amy. (1987). *A Democratic Education*. Princeton, N.J.: Princeton University Press.

Hagberg, Janet. (1994). *Real Power: Strategies for Personal Power in Organizations*. Salem, Wisc.: Sheffield Publishing Co.

Haizlip, Shirley T. (1994). *The Sweeter the Juice: A Family Memoir in Black and White*. New York: Simon & Schuster.

Halberstam, James. (1994). *Everyday Ethics: Inspired Solutions to Real-Life Dilemmas*. New York: Penguin.

Hansen, Katherine. (2000). *A Foot in the Door: Networking Your Way into the Hidden Job Market*. Berkeley, Calif.: Ten Speed Press.

Hansen, Katharine, and Randall Hansen. (1995). *Dynamic Cover Letters*. Berkeley, Calif.: Ten Speed Press.

Hart, Lois. *Multicultural Strategies*. (1994). Amherst, Mass.: HRD Press.

Hartman, Mary. (1999). *Talking Leadership. Powerful Conversations with Women*. New Brunswick, N.J.: Rutgers University Press.

Harvard Business Review on Leadership. (1998). Boston, Mass.: Harvard Business School of Publishing.

Hecht, M., S. Ribeau, and M. Sedano. (1989). An Afro-American Perspective on Interethnic Communication. *Communication Monograph* 56: 385–410.

Hecht, M., S. Ribeau, and M. Sedano. (1990). A Mexican Perspective on Interethnic Communication. *International Journal of Intercultural Relations*, 14: 31–55.

Helgesen, Sally. (1990). *The Female Advantage. Women's Ways of Leadership*. New York: Double Day Publishing Group.

Herman, Joan, Pamela Aschbacher, and Lynn Winters. (1992). *A Practical Guide to Alternative Assessment*. Alexandria, Va.: Association for Supervision and Curriculum Development.

Higgenbotham, Elizabeth, and Mary Romero. (1997). *Women and Work. Exploring Race, Ethnicity, and Class*. Thousand Oaks, Calif.: Sage.

Hoffman, C., and J. Ness. (1998). *Putting Sense into Consensus: Solving the Puzzle of Making Team Decisions*. Alexandria, Va.: Association for Supervision and Curriculum Development.

Home Economics. (1990). Harriman, New York: New Day Films. A documentary of suburbia, directed by Jenny Cool.

hooks, bell. (1994). *Teaching to Transgress: Education as the Practice of Freedom*. New York: Routledge.

hooks, bell. (1998). *Cultural Critique and Transformation*. Videos. Berkeley: Media Resource Center, Moffit Library, University of California–Berkeley.

http:// www.onr.com/schoolhouse. The Internet School House—a web site that provides a Virtual School promoting and supporting global friendship and twenty-first-century learning for teachers and students.

http://careershop.resumesshotgun.com/resume/. Accessed June 2003.

http://collegegradjobs.about.com/careers/collegegradjobs/msubresume.htm. Accessed June 2003.

http://ericcass.uncg.edu/virtuallib/bullying/bullyingbook/html. Lots of good books, articles, and links. Accessed September 28, 2003.

http://falcon.jmu.edu/~ramseyil/index.htm. Internet School Literacy Media Center: For multicultural resources and books.

http://guides/library.fullerton.edu/sph/videos.htm. Videos on speech communication. Accessed June 2003.

http://historymatters.gmu.edu/mse/letters/whatkind.html. How letters and diaries are sources of history. Accessed June 2003.

http://hometown.aol.com/Resume1st/index.html. Accessed June 2003.

http://jobstar.org/internet/res-main.htm. A site to find information on résumé banks. Accessed June 2003.

http://library.ucf.edu/media/mediagdv.htm. Hundreds of videos with case studies on diversity, culture, and curriculum in the workplace. Accessed June 2003.

http://www.bls.gov/oco. Accessed September 28, 2003. This site allows you to use the occupational handbook and other career resources online for lists of keywords and ideas for specific careers.

http://www.aaeo.ucsf.edu/video.htm. Videos on affirmative action, diversity in the workplace, racism, and communication skills. Accessed June 2003.

http://www.americas.org. The Resource Center of the Americas. Offers information on migrant and immigrant experiences in the United States.

http://www.census.gov/ipc/www/world.html. World census figures. Accessed July 2003.

http://www.census.gov/prod/2001pubs/c2kbr01-2.pdf. U.S. census figures showing population changes. Accessed July 2003.

http://www.census.gov/prod/2002pubs/01statab/pop.pdg. U.S. census figures showing population trends and data. Accessed July 2003.

http://www.chemistrycoach.com/lbe6.htm#Speaking. A site that offers links to speech anxiety sites and related topics. Accessed June 10, 2003.

http://www.edc.org. The Women's Educational Equity Act Equity Resource Center. Offers information and resources to promote gender equity.

http://www.eresumes.com/tut_eresume.html. Helps you choose a format for an electronic résumé. Accessed June 2003.

http://www.filmo.com/ve_workplace_skills.htm. Includes fifty videos on workplace skills, résumés, careers. Accessed June 2003.
http://www.geocities.com. Build your own web site. Accessed June 9, 2003.
http://www.gsh.org. Global School House is designed to help teachers connect with the education community at large.
http://www.jobmakerplus.com/. Accessed June 2003.
http://www.vpc.org/. Good updated stats on violence and conditions in schools.
http://www.religioustolerance.org/var_rel.htm. Accessed September 28, 2003 Census figures
related to world religions. (Accessed July 2003.)
http://www.shareware.about.com/compute/shareware/library/homeandoffice/blecvxpressre-
sumes.htm. Accessed June 2003.
http://www.splcenter.org. Southern Poverty Law Center. The Southern Poverty Law Center is
a nonprofit organization that combats hate, intolerance, and discrimination through education and litigation.
http://www.uttyler.edu/meidenmuller/speechbank.htm. A site with mega links to speeches,
texts, audio, and video versions of debates and lectures.
Hudson Institute. (1987). *Workforce 2000*. Washington, D.C.: United States Department of Labor.
Huffman, H. (1994). *Developing a Character Education Program: One School District's Experience*. Alexandria, Va.: Association for Supervision and Curriculum Development.
Hunter, Brenda. (1994). *In the Company of Women*. Sisters, Ore.: Multnomah Books.
Intercom Journal. For educators on worldwide interdependence and preparation to live in a
global village.
Jackson, Thomas, and Ellen Jackson. (1996). *The New Perfect Résumé*. New York: Main
Street Books.
JobOptions: http://www.joboptions.com/. Provides opportunities for networking, posting ré-
sumés, and helping you develop your ideas to connect with a job. Accessed June 10, 2003.
Johnson, D. W., R. T. Johnson, and E. J. Holubec. (1991). *Cooperation in the Classroom*. Ed-
ina, Minn.: Interaction Book Company.
Johnson, David, and Frank Johnson. (1991). *Joining Together: Group Theory and Group
Skills*. 4th Ed. Boston: Allyn and Bacon.
Johnson, David W., and F. P. Johnson. (2000). *Joining Together: Group Theory and Group
Skills*. 7th ed. Boston: Allyn & Bacon.
Johnson, David W., and Roger T. Johnson. (1995). *Reducing School Violence through Conflict
Resolution*. Alexandria, Va.: Association for Supervision and Curriculum Development.
Jones, B. F., and T. F. Fennimore. (1990). *The New Definition of Learning: The First Step to
School Reform*. Chicago: North Central Regional Educational Laboratory.
Jones, J. Hamilton. (1991). *Business Letters That Get Results!* Avon, Mass.: Adams Media.
Kafrissen, Binnie Shusman, Fran Shusman, and Joanna Smith Bers. (2000). *Winning Roles for
Career-Minded Women: Understanding the Roles We Learned As Girls and How to Change
Them for Success at Work*. Palo Alto, Calif.: Davies-Black Publishing.
Keillor, Garrison. (1988). *The New Immigrants*. St. Paul, Minn.: Minnesota Human Rights
Commission.
Kerr, M. E. (1981). *Dinky Hocker Shoots Smack*. New York: Dell Publishing.
Khospropour, Shirin (Austin Community College), and James Walsh (University of Texas,
Austin). That's Not Teasing—That's Bullying: A Study of Fifth Graders' Conceptualization
of Bullying and Teasing. Paper presented at the American Educational Research Associa-
tion, April 2001, New Orleans.
Kincheloe, Joe L. (1999). *How Do We Tell the Workers*. Boulder, Colo.: Westview Press.
Kingore, B. (1993). *Portfolios*. Des Moines, Ia.: Leadership Publishers.
Kingsolver, Barbara. (1996). *High Tide in Tucson*. New York: Harper Perennial.
Kirk, Gwyn, and Margo Okazawa-Rey. (2001). *Women's Lives—Multicultural Perspectives*.
2nd ed. London: Mayfield Press.
Klein, E. (1990). Tomorrow's Work Force. *D & B Reports* (January-February): 30–35.

Kliebard, Herbert. (1990). Vocational Education as Symbolic Action: Connecting School with the Workplace. *American Educational Research Journal* 27, no. 2 (Spring): 9–26.

Knowles, Malcolm S. (1986). Using Learning Contacts. San Francsico: Jossey-Bass.

Kofman, F., and P. M. Senge. (1993). Communities of Commitment: The Heart of the Learning Organizations. *Organizational Dynamics* (Autumn): 5–23.

Kohl, Herb. (1994). *I Won't Learn from You and Other Thoughts on Creative Maladjustment.* New York: New Press.

Kohn, Alfie. (1996). *Beyond Discipline: From Compliance to Community.* Alexandria, Va.: Association for Supervision and Curriculum Development.

Kotter, J. P., and J. L. Hesekett. (1992). *Corporate Culture and Performance.* New York: Free Press.

Kouzes, James, and Barry Posner. (1987). *The Leadership Challenge.* San Francisco: Jossey-Bass.

Lakes, Richard. (1985). John Dewey's Theory of Occupations: Vocational Education Envisioned. *Journal of Vocational and Technical Education* 2, no. 1 (Fall): 41–47.

Levine, David. (1994). The School to Work Opportunities Act of 1994: A Flawed Prescription for Education Reform. *Educational Foundations* 8, no. 3: 33–51.

Levine, J. B. (1993). For IBM Europe, This Is the Year of Truth. *Business Week* (April): 45.

Lewin, Kurt. (1948). *Resolving Social Conflict.* New York: Harper.

Lickona, Thomas. (1991). *Educating for Character: How Our Schools Can Teach Respect and Responsibility.* New York: Bantam Books.

Lieberman, A. (1989). *Building a Professional Culture in Schools.* New York: Teachers College Press.

Lindsell-Roberts, S. (1995). *Business Letter Writing.* Lawrenceville, N.J.: Arco Publishers.

Locke, D. (1992). *Increasing Multicultural Understanding: A Comprehensive Model.* Newbury Park, Calif.: Sage.

Loden, Marilyn. (1985). *Feminine Leadership: Or How to Succeed in Business without Being One of the Boys.* New York: Times Books.

Lustig, Myron W., and Jolene Koester. (1999). *Intercultural Communication: Interpersonal Communication across Cultures.* 3rd ed. New York: Addison-Wesley.

Luvmour, Josette, Ba Luvmour, and Kara Albee. (2002). *Win-Win Games for All Ages: Cooperative Activities for Building Social Skills.* Gabriola Island, Canada: New Society Publishers.

Macbeth, Fiona, and Nic Fine. (1995). *Playing with Fire: Creative Conflict Resolution for Young Adults.* Gabriola Island, Canada: New Society Publishers.

MacInnus, Carole, and John Portelli. (2002). Dialogue as Research. *Journal of Thought* (Summer): 33–44.

Marin, Peter. 1975. "The new narcissism." New York: *Harpers Magazine*, October.

Mayo, Peter. (1993). When Does It Work? Freire's Pedagogy in Context. *Studies in the Education of Adults* 25, no. 1: 11–30.

McCarthy, Cameron, and Warren Crichlow, eds. (1993). *Race Identity and Representation in Education.* London: Routledge.

McGraw, Phillip C. (2001). *Self Matters. Creating Your Life from the Inside Out.* New York: Free Press.

Mckay, Harvey. (1997). *Dig Your Well before You're Thirsty.* New York: Currency/Doubleday.

McKinney, Anne, ed. (2000). *Real Resumes for Teachers.* Fayetteville, N.C.: PREP Publishing.

McLaren, Peter L., and Colin Lankshear, eds. (1994). *Politics of Liberation: Paths from Freire.* London: Routledge.

McQuillan, Patrick James. (1998). *Educational Opportunity in an Urban High School. A Cultural Analysis.* Albany: State University of New York Press.

Miller, Ron. (2000). *Creating Learning Communities—Models, Resources, and New Ways of Thinking about Teaching and Learning.* Brandon, Vt.: The Foundation for Educational Renewal.

Minnesota Center for Conflict Resolution, 9149 Vincent Avenue South, Bloomington MN 55431: 952.884.1128. http://www.mincava.umn.edu. Accessed September 28, 2003.

Minnesota Department of Education. Graduation standards. http://mecr.state.mn.us/statirubrics.htm. Accessed June 14, 2003.

Monster.com. http://www.monster.com/. For job search and career advice. Accessed June 10, 2003.

Muller, Lauren. (1995). *June Jordan's Poetry for the People: A Revolutionary Blueprint*. New York: Routledge.

Mumby, D. (1988). *Communication and Power in Organizations: Discourse, Ideology, and Domination*. Norwood, N.J.: Ablex.

Nadar, Ralph, and Lori Wallach. (1996). GATT, NAFTA and the Subversion of the Democratic Process. In *The Case against the Global Economy*, edited by Jerry Mander and Edward Goldsmith, Chapter 8, pp. 85–97. San Francisco: Sierra Club.

Nansel, Tonja R., Mary Overpeck, Ramani S. Pilla, W. June Ruan, Bruce Simons-Morton, and Peter Scheidt. (2001). Bullying Behaviors Among US Youth: Prevalence and Association with Psychosocial Adjustment. *JAMA* 285: 2094-2100.

Nash, Robert J. (2002). *Real World Ethics: Frameworks for Educators and Human Service Professionals*. 2nd ed. New York: Teachers College Press.

National Issues Forum. http://www.nifi.org. Web site featuring booklets on a range of issues connected to Voyager topics, published by Kendall Hunt.

National Resource Center for Youth Services. http://www.nrcys.ou.edu. Accessed June 2003.

Neal, J. E. (1996). *Effective Résumé Writing: A Guide to Successful Employment*. Perrysburg, Ohio: Neal Publications.

Nelson, L., and S. Kagan. *Psychology Today* 9, no. 72: 53–56, 90–91.

Net-temps. http://www.net-temps.com/. Recruiting and job postings. Accessed June 10, 2003.

The New Beer. Adapted from Velasquez, Manuel G. (1998). *Business Ethics: Concepts and Cases*. 4th ed. Upper Saddle River, N.J.: Prentice Hall.

New Society. http://www.newsociety.com. Web site that focuses on books that contribute in fundamental ways to building an ecologically sustainable and just society.

Nieto, Sonia. (2003). *What Keeps Teachers Going?* New York: Teachers College Press.

Noonan, Sarah J. (2003). *The Elements of Leadership: What You Should Know.* Lanham, Md.: Scarecrow Press.

O'Malley, Susan, Robert C. Rosen, and Leonard Vogt, eds. (1990). *Politics of Education. Essays from Radical Teacher.* Albany: State University of New York Press.

O'Reilly, B. (1997). The Secrets of America's Most Admired Corporations: New Ideas, New Products. *Fortune* (May 3): 60–64.

O'Reilly, Patrick, Elizabeth Penn, and Kathleen deMarrais, eds. (2001). *Educating Young Adolescent Girls*. Mahwah, N.J.: Lawrence Erlbaum Associates.

O'Toole, James. (1995). *Leading Change*. San Francisco: Jossey-Bass.

Oakes, Jeannie, and K. H. Quartz, eds. (1995). *Creating New Educational Communities (Ninety-Fourth Yearbook of the National Society for the Study of Education)*. Chicago: University of Chicago Press.

OJPCR: The Online Journal of Peace and Conflict Resolution. This journal is intended as a resource for students, teachers, and practitioners in fields relating to the reduction and elimination of destructive conflict. It is a free, yet valuable, source of information to aid anyone trying to work toward a less violent and more cooperative world.

Orlick, Terry. (1982). *The Second Cooperative Sports and Games Book*. New York: Random House.

Osbourne, K. (1995). *In Defence of History: Teaching the Past and the Meaning of Democratic Citizenship*. Toronto, Ontario: Our Schools Our Selves/Lorimer.

Pajak, Edward. (2003). *Honoring Diverse Teaching Styles*. Alexandria, Va.: ASCD.

Paley, Vivian Gussin. (1992). *You Can't Say You Can't Play*. Cambridge, Mass.: Harvard University Press.

Paley, Vivian Gussin. (1995). *Kwanzaa and Me*. Cambridge: Harvard University Press.

Parker, W. C., ed. (1996). *Educating the Democratic Mind*. Albany: State University of New York Press.

Parker, Yana. (1996). *The Damn Good Résumé Guide: A Crash Course in Résumé Writing*. Berkeley, Calif.: Ten Speed Press.

Pasternak, Ceel, and Linda Thornburg. (1999). *Cool Careers for Girls Series*. Manassas Park, Va.: Impact Publications.

Peters, Thomas J. (1987). *Thriving on Chaos: Handbook for a Management Revolution*. New York: Knopf.

Peterson, Ralph. (1992). *Life in a Crowded Place. Making a Learning Community.* Portsmouth, N.H.: Heinemann.

Powell, G. (1993). *Women and Men in Management.* 2nd ed. Newbury Park, Calif.: Sage.

Powell, Gary N. (1999). *Women and Men in Management*. London: Sage.

Provenzano, Steven. (1995). *The Guide to Basic Cover Letter Writing*. Columbus, Ohio; Lincolnwood, Ill.: VGM Career Horizons.

Regan, Helen, and Gwen Brooks. (1995). *Out of Women's Experience: Creating Relational Leadership*. Thousand Oaks, Calif.: Corwin Press.

Rehm, Marsha. (1989). Emancipatory Vocational Education: Pedagogy for the Work of Individuals and Society. *Journal of Education* 171, no. 3: 109–123.

Resnick, L. B., and Klopfer, L. E. eds. (1989). Toward the Thinking Curriculum: An Overview. In *Toward the Thinking Curriculum: Current Cognitive Research (1989 Yearbook of the Association for Supervision and Curriculum Development)*, NA. Alexandria, Va.: ASCD.

Résumé Maker. (1989). San Francisco: Individual Software Inc. A software program that assists users in preparing a chronological résumé.

Rich, Dorothy. (1992). *Megaskills*. New York: Houghton Mifflin.

Roditi, H. F. (1992). High Schools for Docile Workers. *The Nation* 254, no. 10: 340–343.

Rose, Mike. (1996). *Possible Lives: The Promise of Public Education in America*. New York: Penguin Books.

Rosenberg, Arthur, and David V. Hizer. (1996). *The Resume Handbook: How to Write Outstanding Resumes and Cover Letters for Every Situation.* 3rd ed. Avon, Mass.: Adams Media Corp.

Rosenholtz, S.J., and S. H. Rosenholtz (1997). Classroom organization and student stratification. *Elementary School Journal* 85:21-37.

Roulis, Eleni. (2003a). Transforming Learning for the Workplace of the New Millennium: Students and Workers as Critical Learners—Book 4: Community Handbook Set. Lanham, Md.: Scarecrow Education.

Roulis, Eleni. (2003b). Transforming Learning for the Workplace of the New Millennium: Students and Workers as Critical Learners—Book 3: Postsecondary Curriculum. Lanham, Md.: Scarecrow Education.

Sadalla, Gail, et al. (1987). Conflict Resolution: A Secondary School Program. San Francisco: The Community Board Program.

Safety Issues Serious in Nation's Schools: Principals Taking Action. (1997). Reston, Va.: National Association of Secondary School Principals.

Samovar, Larry A., and Richard E. Porter. (2000). *Intercultural Communication: A Reader*. Belmont, Calif.: Wadsworth Publishing Company.

Schniedwind, N., and E. Davidson. (1987). *Cooperative Learning, Cooperative Lives*. Iowa City, Iowa: Wm. C. Brown Company Publishers.

Schon, Donald. (1983). *The Reflective Practitioner*. New York: Basic Books.

School-Associated Violent Deaths in the United States, 1992–1994. (1996). *Journal of the American Medical Association* 275, no. 22: 1729–1733.

Schulman, Cory. (1997). *Résumés for Higher Paying Positions: A Complete Guide to Résumé Writing for a More Rewarding Career.* Best Seller Publications, Inc.

Schwartz, Stuart, and Craig Conley. (1999). *Writing a Résumé*. Mankato, Minn.: Capstone High/Low Books.

Sealin, Jeffrey. (1996). *The AMA Handbook of Business Letters*. New York: AMACOM.

Senge, Peter M. (1990). *The Fifth Discipline: The Art and Practice of the Learning Community*. New York: Doubleday Currency.

Seuss, Dr. (1990). *Oh the Places You'll Go!* New York: Random House.

Shein, E. H. (1985). *Organizational Culture and Leadership*. San Francisco: Jossey-Bass.

Shor, Ira. (1980). *Critical Teaching and Everyday Life*. Boston: South End Press.

Shor, Ira. (1988). Working Hands and Critical Minds: A Paulo Freire Model for Job Training. *Journal of Education* 170, no. 2: 103–121.

Shor, Ira. (1989). Developing Student Autonomy in the Classroom. *Equity and Excellence* 23, no. 3: 35–37.

Shor, Ira. (1992). *Empowering Education: Critical Teaching for Social Change*. Chicago: The University of Chicago Press.

Shor, Ira. (1996). *When Students Have Power. Negotiating Authority in a Critical Pedagogy*. Chicago: University of Chicago Press.

Shorris, E. (1984). *Scenes from a Corporate Life: The Politics of Middle Management*. New York: Penguin Books.

Simon, Sidney B., Leland W. Howe, and Howard Kirschenbaum. (1972). *Values Clarification*. New York: Hart Publishing Company.

Skewl Sites Online. http://www.skewlsites.com. Featuring the best in educational web sites. Accessed June 11, 2003.

Sleeter, Christene. (2002). *Cultural Difference and Power*. Multimedia CD-ROM. New York: Teachers College.

Smith, P., and M. Peterson. (1988). *Leadership, Organizations and Culture*. London: Sage.

Sodor, R., ed. (1996). *Democracy, Education, and Schools*. San Francisco: Jossey-Bass.

Sollman, Carolyn, Barbara Emmons, and Judith Paolini. (1994). *Through the Cracks*. Worcester, Mass.: Davis Publications.

Soloman, Muriel. (1990). *Working with Difficult People*. Englewood Cliffs, N.J.: Prentice Hall.

Starratt, Robert. (1993). *The Drama of Leadership*. Great Britain: Burgess Science Press.

Stewart, Charles, and William Cash. (2000). *Interviewing: Principles and Practices*. 9th ed. New York: McGraw-Hill.

Stewart, John. (2002). Interpersonal Communication. In *Bridges Not Walls,* 8th ed., edited by J. Stewart, Chapter 2, pp. 31–45. New York: McGraw-Hill.

Stewart, T. A. (1997). *Intellectual Capital: The New Wealth of Organizations*. New York: Doubleday Currency.

Strunk, William Jr., E. B. White, and Roger Angell. (2000). *The Elements of Style*. 4th ed. Boston: Allyn & Bacon.

Stuckey, Marty. (1992). *Basics of Business Writing (Worksmart Series)*. New York: American Management Association.

Takaki, Ronald. (1993). *A Different Mirror: A History of Multicultural America*. Boston: Little, Brown.

Tannen, Deborah. (1979). Ethnicity as Conversational Style. *Sociolinguistics* no. 55. Austin, Tex.: Southwest Educational Development Laboratory.

Tannen, Deborah. (1986). *That's Not What I Meant*. New York: Ballantine Books.

Tannen, Deborah. (1990). *You Just Don't Understand*. New York: William Morrow Books.

Tannen, Deborah. (1999). *Nine to Five: Women and Talking at Work*. New York: William Morrow.

Tanner, Laurel N. (1997). *Dewey's Laboratory School: Lessons for Today*. New York: Teachers College Press.

Team Building Simulations. Developed by AVIAT. Ann Arbor, Mich.

The 28th Annual Phi Delta Kappa/Gallup Poll of the Public's Attitudes toward the Public Schools. (1996). *Phi Delta Kappan*.

The Global Assembly Line. (1988). Directed by Lorraine Gray. Harriman, New York: New Day Films.

The Unofficial Guide to Writing Your Résumé and Cover Letter. (1999). Lawrenceville, N.J.: Arco Publishers.

Thornberg, David. (2002). *The New Basics: Education and the Future of Work in the Telematic Age*. Alexandria, Va.: ASCD Press

Thomas, Kenneth W., and Ralph H. Thomas-Kilmann. (1974). *Conflict Mode Instrument*. Tuxedo, N.Y.: Kilmann Xicom Publishing.

Tierney, R., M. Carter, and L. Desai. (1991). *Portfolio Assessment in the Reading-Writing Classroom*. Norwood, Mass.: Christopher-Gordon Publishers.

Tierney, W. G. (1989). Advancing Democracy: A Critical Interpretation of Leadership. *Peabody Journal of Education* 66, no. 30: 157–175.

Tinsdale, R. S., ed. (1997). *Applications of Theory and Research on Groups to Social Issues*. New York: Plenum.

Trifonas, Peter Pericles, ed. (2003). *Pedagogies of Difference. Rethinking Education for Social Change*. London: Routledge.

Troop, W. P., and S. R. Asher. (1991). Teaching Peer Relationship Competence in Schools. In *Teaching in American Schools*, edited by Robert J. Stevens, Chapter 8, pp. 184–209. Upper Saddle River, N.J.: Prentice Hall.

Tsujimoto, Joseph. (1988). *Teaching Poetry to Adolescents*. Urbana, Ill.: NCTE.

Union Maids. (1977). Harriman, N.Y.: New Day Films. Documentary combining interviews with three women who were active in labor organizing, with footage from those collective efforts from the 1930s and 1940s.

Ury, W., J. Brett, and S. Goldberg. (1988). *Getting Disputes Resolved*. San Francisco: Jossey-Bass.

Vaill, Peter B. (1989). *Managing as a Performing Art: New Ideas for a World of Chaotic Change*. San Francisco: Jossey-Bass.

Vale, Peter. (1996). *Learning as a Way of Being*. San Francisco: Jossey-Bass.

Venolia, Jan. (1995). *Better Letters: A Handbook of Business and Personal Correspondence*. Berkeley, Calif.: Ten Speed Press.

Vocational Training News. (1992). Voc. Ed. Shortchanges Girls. *Vocational Training News* 20, no. 8 (February): 1, 3.

Wald, Penelope, and Michael Castlerberry, eds. (2000). *Educators as Learners: Creating a Professional Learning Community in Your School*. Alexandria, Va.: Association for Supervision and Curriculum Development.

Wallerstein, Nina, and Elsa R. Auerbach. (1987). ESL for Action. Reading, Mass.: Addison-Wesley.

Web66 School Directory. The oldest and most complete list of K–12 web servers. It provides direction to a compendium of great projects and resources.

Weiler, Kathryn. (1988). *Women Teaching for Change: Gender, Class, and Power*. Westport, Conn.: Bergin & Garvey.

Whaley, Liz, and Liz Dodge. (1993). *Weaving in the Women: Transforming the High School English Curriculum*. Portsmouth, N.H.: Heinemann.

Willis, Gary. (1994). *Certain Trumpets: The Nature of Leadership*. New York: Simon & Schuster.

Willliams, Arlene. (2002). *Tales from the Dragon's Cave*. 2nd ed. New York: Waking Light Press.

Wirth, A. G. (1992). *Education and Work for the Year 2000*. San Francisco, Calif.: Jossey-Bass.

With Babies and Banners. (1978). Directed by Lorraine Gray. Harriman, N.Y.: New Day Films.

Woods, George. (1986). *The Democratic Classroom*. Video. Toledo, Ohio: The University of Toledo.

Workman, Brooke. (1992). *Teaching the Sixties: An In-Depth, Interactive, Interdisciplinary Approach*. Urbana, Ill.: National Council of Teachers of English.

www.curry.edschool.virginia.edu. Multimedia case studies in instructional technology and design.

www. questia.com. World's largest online library. Accessed June 12, 2003.

www.acresolution.org. Provides innovative ideas, strategies, and articles for conflict resolution and alerts educators as to what is happening in the field.

www.ceoforum.org. CEO forum that gives information on the best of education and technology.

www.cew.wisc.edu. Center on education and work learning.

www.eericcass.uncg.edu/virtuallib/bullying/bullyingbook.html. What's new in school-based bully prevention programs for children. Accessed September 28, 2003.

www.employeeuniversity.com. Diversity workplace issues for case study.

www.flipdog.com. Review résumés, get help with a job search, learn about compensation, and navigate salary negotiations; employers will review your résumés.

www.joboptions.com. Helps candidates and companies find the right matches.

www.jobweb.com. Career development and job search help for graduates; help with résumés, interviews, and career fairs, and interesting career articles.

www.monster.com. Supplies the same information in multiple areas, including global jobs; learn your market value; information in multiple languages.

www.marastar.com/toonup. The company has a series of cartoon videos that deal with workplace diversity issues for high school students.

www.wallbuilders.com/resources/search/historicalwritings.php. Historical letters documenting American history and famous people. Accessed June 2003.

www.womenwriters.net. Letters and women's activism in the nineteenth century. Accessed June 2003.

www.writeexpress.com. Help with letter writing. Accessed June 2003.

Wymard, Ellie. (1999). *Conversations with Uncommon Women. Insights from Women Who Have Risen above Life's Challenges to Achieve Extraordinary Success.* New York: American Management Association.

Yarrow, Peter. (1999). Don't Laugh at Me Project. www.don'tlaugh.org.

Yuen, C. Y. (1983). Internal barriers for women entering nontraditional occupations. A review of the literature. *Occupational Education Forum* 12, no. 2: 1–14.

Zindel, Paul. (1972). *The Pigman.* New York: Bantam Books.

About the Author

Eleni Roulis, Ph.D.

Voyager curriculum writer Eleni Roulis taught language arts, reading, and French in grades 5–12 in New York City public schools for over fourteen years. She taught students from all cultures, backgrounds, and abilities—students who have left an indelible impression on her life. Her teaching career in NYC inspired her to seek out deeper meanings and ways to create democratic classrooms. Dr. Roulis received her B.A. in English from St. John's University in New York, an M.A. in English Literature from New York University, New York, and a Ph.D. in Education/Curriculum & Instruction from the University of Minnesota, Minneapolis.

Since transplanting to Minnesota in 1984, Roulis has taught in higher education. She has taught courses in effective writing and teacher education preparation at the undergraduate and graduate levels at the University of Minnesota and Augsburg College and was an education specialist for the Minnesota Department of Education. She has written numerous articles, chapters, and book reviews and presented her research at national and international conferences on gender issues in communication, equity, curriculum development and assessment, multicultural workplace opportunities, and leadership for women. Dr. Roulis's expertise in program development and training in leadership and diversity has resulted in regional and national consulting for schools, districts, businesses, and corporations.

Dr. Roulis is currently the Chair of Advanced Studies in Curriculum & Instruction in the School of Education at the University of St. Thomas in Minneapolis, Minn. Roulis is also the Director of the Ed.D. in Critical Pedagogy, the first of its kind doctoral program nationally and internationally which is committed to developing a critical education that links concepts of critical pedagogy, democracy, and empowerment for personal growth and social change. Her work at St. Thomas is keenly focused on developing innovative programs on the master's and post-master's levels that build caring classroom communities and uphold the ethics of social justice. The programs are developed nationally and internationally and are always built in partnership with school districts and teachers so that all voices are brought to the table. When her schedule permits, she also teaches electives in Language, Culture and Education, in Curriculum Development, and in Gender, Feminism, and Sexuality.

In Voyager Roulis saw the opportunity to apply the concepts of critical pedagogy, democracy, and personal empowerment within a social change oriented program supported by both the business and educational communities. Says Roulis of Voyager: "It is an example of the kind of educational success we can achieve when we embrace a common set of goals, follow democratic principles, and focus on the use of pragmatic, practical strategies. Voyager recognizes that preparing students to be both work ready and career bound is the hallmark of successful twenty-first-century school-to-career programs. It has been exciting to work with a program that builds partnerships between businesses, students, schools, families, and colleges and universities."